VICTORY RODE THE RAILS

"The Yankees Can Build Bridges Quicker Than the Rebs Can Burn Them Down."

Victory Rode the Rails

The Strategic Place of the Railroads
in the Civil War

by

George Edgar Turner

Maps by George Richard Turner

GREENWOOD PRESS, PUBLISHERS
WESTPORT, CONNECTICUT

Library of Congress Cataloging in Publication Data

Turner, George Edgar.
   Victory rode the rails.

   Includes bibliographical references.
   1. United States--History--Civil War--Transportation.
2. Railroads--United States--History. 3. Railroads--
Confederate States of America. I. Title.
[E491.T95 1972]   973.78   73-184842
ISBN 0-8371-6331-5

Originally published in 1953
by The Bobbs-Merrill Company, Inc., Indianapolis

Reprinted with the permission
of The Bobbs-Merrill Company, Inc.

Reprinted by Greenwood Press,
a division of Williamhouse-Regency Inc.

First Greenwood Reprinting 1972
Second Greenwood Reprinting 1975

Library of Congress Catalog Card Number 73-184842

ISBN 0-8371-6331-5

Printed in the United States of America

To Leona

ACKNOWLEDGMENTS

Without the gracious assistance of a host of friends who were interested in seeing the project completed this book never would have come to publication. It is my pleasure to acknowledge the help given by each of them.

To Robert S. Henry—vice-president, Association of American Railroads, distinguished author and authority on Civil War history, grand gentleman and fine friend—I am deeply grateful for wise counsel, tireless help in solving difficult problems and critical reading of manuscript. Without his continuous encouragement the writing of this book would not have been undertaken and once started would have been abandoned in its early stages.

Various railroad companies have willingly searched their old records for me, and special acknowledgment is made to Mrs. Virginia T. Reilly, Librarian of the Baltimore and Ohio, for her help in connection with material relating to that road.

The members of the Civil War Round Table of Chicago have been uniformly gracious in response to all calls made upon them for assistance. To the Union League Civic and Arts Foundation of Chicago I am deeply indebted for help in extending my research. For their patient aid, acknowledgment is made to the librarians and their assistants in each of the many libraries where I have worked.

With gratitude I acknowledge assistance rendered by Messrs. George I. Haight, Paul Angle, Monroe Cockrell, Ralph Newman, Joseph Matter and Edward M. Martin, all of Chicago. Special acknowledgment is made also to Mrs. Harry S. Pringey of Palatine, Illinois, for her help in research and in preparation of manuscript.

The author wishes also to express his gratitude for permission to quote or adapt material from the following works:

Festus P. Summers, *The Baltimore and Ohio in the Civil War*, G. P. Putnam's Sons, 1939.

Edward Hungerford, *The Story of the Baltimore and Ohio Railroad*, G. P. Putnam's Sons, 1928.

Charles W. Turner, "The Richmond, Fredericksburg and Potomac Railroad at War, 1861-1865," in the *Historian*, 1946.

Standard & Poor's Corporation, *Poor's Manual of Railroads for 1890*.

Charles W. Turner, "The Virginia Central Railroad at War," in the *Journal of Southern History*, 1946.

U. B. Philips, *A History of Transportation in the Eastern Cotton Belt to 1860*, Columbia University Press, 1908.

Samuel R. Kamm, *The Civil War Career of Thomas A. Scott*, 1940.

Lloyd Lewis, *Sherman, Fighting Prophet*, Harcourt, Brace and Company, 1932.

E. P. Alexander, *Military Memoirs of a Confederate*, Charles Scribner's Sons, 1907.

Home Letters of General Sherman, Charles Scribner's Sons, 1909.

Life and Letters of George Meade, Charles Scribner's Sons, 1913.

Douglas Southall Freeman, *R. E. Lee* (4 vols.), Charles Scribner's Sons, 1934.

Douglas Southall Freeman, *Lee's Lieutenants* (3 vols.), Charles Scribner's Sons, 1942.

Charles W. Ramsdell, "The Confederate Government and the Railroads," in the *American Historical Review*, American Historical Association, 1917.

R. S. Cotterill, "The L. & N. Railroad, 1861-1865," in the *American Historical Review*, American Historical Association, 1924.

James Ford Rhodes, *A History of the Civil War*, The Macmillan Company, 1917.

David H. Bates, *Lincoln in the Telegraph Office*, The Century Company, 1907.

Robert M. Sutton, *Illinois Central Railroad in Peace and War, 1858-1868*, 1948.

Dwight Agnew, "Jefferson Davis and the Rock Island Bridge," in the *Iowa Journal of History*, State Historical Society of Iowa, 1949.

PREFACE

There is little evidence that at the outbreak of the Civil War either North or South had given serious consideration to the railroads as a factor in the impending struggle. General interest in rail transportation as a possible element of importance in military affairs first was aroused by its service in army mobilization. However, it was not until the common confidence in quick success had been dispelled that both sides began to realize they were confronted by an entirely new problem in logistics. The recent development of the railroads had changed the entire aspect of the war as originally contemplated.

Soon after the first great battle failed to end the struggle, it began to appear that important railroad junction points were to become major military objectives, and, as time passed, many of the bloodiest battles of the war were fought in defense of them. Now famous campaigns were planned and conducted for the primary purpose of capturing or destroying railroad lines of particular value to the enemy. As each successive year ended, it became increasingly apparent that the side which controlled the railroads held a tremendous advantage, and in the end it was the Confederate loss of two railroads which led to the surrender at Appomattox.

The reader will not find this book an attempt to tell in brief the whole story of the Civil War. Many operations, both military and naval, are not mentioned because they had little or no direct relation to the subject at hand. This is the story of the part played by the railroads in the deadly conflict, the story of their first great military test and how they met it.

It must not be assumed that only those roads named in the text were considered important. All were important, but it is impossible to tell in a single volume what each contributed to the cause it supported. Neither is it possible to recount here all minor military operations in which railroads were involved. If enough of the story is told to bring the reader an appreciation of how vitally the conduct and final outcome of the war was influenced by the railroads, the writer will be content.

GEORGE E. TURNER

CONTENTS

LIST OF ILLUSTRATIONS

MAPS

CHAPTER 1

THE RAILROADS DRAW THE BOUNDARIES

I

At sunrise on April 18, 1861, only six days after Fort Sumter was fired on, those citizens of Manassas Junction, Virginia, who were already awake had the opportunity of seeing something that had never happened before: the tactical use of railroads in war, a new way to solve problems in logistics. At this early hour three light Confederate troop trains, northbound over the Orange & Alexandria Railroad, clattered into the small yard at Manassas Junction. Aboard were the extravagantly uniformed Albemarle Rifles, the resplendent Monticello Guards and other colorful units of Virginia militia. The unusual racket made by trains and troops probably brought a crowd of villagers down to the track to stare in wonder at all the soldiers riding on the cars. They had only a few minutes to enjoy the spectacle, for shortly after arrival the trains were shunted over the Y to the track of the Manassas Gap line and in close order hurried away westward toward Strasburg in the Shenandoah. The early-morning spectators were probably more interested in the uniforms than in the novel fact that troops were being moved by rail directly to anticipated action against the enemy.

In command of the leading train was young Captain John D. Imboden of the Staunton Artillery. For two nights he had slept scarcely at all. It was past midnight before Governor Letcher finally approved the audacious scheme to use the cars in a swift expedition against the Federal arsenal at Harper's Ferry. Still later in the night Presidents Edmund Fontaine of the Virginia Central and John S. Barbour, Jr., of the Orange & Alexandria and the Manassas Gap railroads joined Imboden and his fellow planners for a secret conference in a room in the Exchange Hotel in Richmond. Daylight found the weary group still struggling with arrangements for special trains to carry the expedition over the three railroads involved.

At noon Imboden finished telegraphing instructions to the commanders of the militia companies the special trains were to pick up en route. That done, there remained the matter of requisitions and the loading of arms and supplies from the Richmond arsenal. At sunset the first train got under way. All night long they were picking up companies from Charlottesville, Gordonsville, Staunton, Culpeper and other way stations. There had been no time for sleep and now, at Manassas, it was morning of the second day.

Scarcely five miles beyond Manassas the lead train slowed to a crawl. Imboden was irritated by the delay. The success of the venture on which he had set his heart depended on speed, and precious time was being lost. On a slightly ascending grade the train came to a complete stop. Infuriated, he climbed down from the cars and made his way forward to find the engineer lolling at the window of his cab. On the opposite seat the fireman dozed in the morning sun while the steam gauge on the boiler fell lower and lower. Sizzling words passed between the engineer and Imboden as the latter mounted the cab and promptly ended an argument as to whether a "Union man" would haul "rebel soldiers." Covered by the captain's navy revolver, the frightened fireman kicked open the firebox door, heaved in good dry wood and quickly reversed the action of the falling steam gauge. With Imboden riding the cab, cocked gun in hand, the train made a good forty miles an hour the rest of the way to Strasburg.[1]

The Manassas Junction villagers were not aware that on this April morning they were witnessing the tactical use of a machine which was to work a greater change in warfare and its methods than had been wrought by any other instrument since the invention of gunpowder. They had heard how Beauregard's guns had reduced Fort Sumter, but all the world knew how in other wars other forts had been bombarded and other walls had crumbled under shellfire. About that, there was nothing new except that in the old manner a new war was beginning.

Now that war was certain, no prophetic vision was required to anticipate the clash of foot soldiers, the wildly galloping horse or the blast of the blazing gun on wheels. For more than a century these had been the things with which war was waged. What no man foresaw was how the use of these familiar devices was to be revolutionized by the introduction of an implement utterly new to warfare, the locomotive. Nothing strange attaches to this lack of foresight. Practical railroading on any considerable scale was new —so new, in fact, that when Robert E. Lee was graduated from West Point no railroad in the world had attained a length of one hundred miles. Fifteen years old at the time of Lee's graduation, Grant was to receive his military training and serve seven years in the Army before the first railroad crossed the Allegheny Mountains. Less than ten years before he became president of the Confederate States of America, Jefferson Davis, then Secretary of War, was opposing the building of the first railroad bridge across the Mississippi.[2]

In the cabinets of both Lincoln and Davis were men who had been active in railroad promotion, but their planning had been for commerce and not for war. In both Union and Confederate armies able leaders had left important railroad posts to take up the sword, but their brief railroad experience was related only to the ways of peace and trade. Perhaps some of them may have known that in Europe studies were being made of the railroad as a potential factor in national defense and that in 1859 France had made some use of her railroads in connection with the Austro-Sardinian War.[3] If so, they gave no evidence of having taken those European experiments seriously or of regarding the American railroads as of importance to anything save commerce and convenience.

With few exceptions the railroads were much younger than the men who were to direct the affairs of the Union and Confederate governments as well as those who were to

lead their battalions in the field. April 1861 marked the
date from which men began to learn the practical relation
of the railroad to waging war. Many commanders failed to
grasp its significance until long after the battle lines were
drawn. However, to John Imboden and his associates the
potential value of the railroad appeared quickly and clearly.
Seldom has the reward for military foresight come more
swiftly. When the Union commander at Harper's Ferry
learned of the rail expedition bearing down on him he set
fire to the arsenal and fled without a struggle.

As spring turned to summer, the April-morning scene at
Manassas Junction was repeated there with such frequency
and ever-increasing magnitude that the villagers no longer
looked up from their work to see whether the trains were
loaded with soldiers or with more of the supplies which were
accumulating by hundreds of tons beside the tracks. Their
little railroad yard grew far beyond April proportions, and
day and night engines whistled and cars bumped and banged
together in ceaseless racket. Bull Run was in the making.

From the time of Imboden's adventure until after
Appomattox, leisure was lacking for evaluation of the wartime
feats of the railroads or for comparison of them with previous
achievements. When the war was over, however, students
came to realize that the railroads' greatest contribution to the
final outcome was made not during the war at all but in the
decade before secession. Those were the years in which railroad builders extending their trackage in pursuit of trade and
commerce unwittingly turned Atlanta, Chattanooga, Corinth
and other places into objectives of major strategic importance;
the years in which the North was crisscrossed with tracks
over which later rolled the vast supply of men and matériel
that finally brought death to the Confederacy. Even more
significant than all of this was the railroads' influence on the
alignment of the combatant states.

2

Much blood was spilled before the political boundary between the United States and the Confederate States of

America was established. Separated by no definite geographical frontiers, North was North and South was South only as individual states declared their allegiance to one side or the other and thus created an artificial frontier between the belligerents. Territorial legality of slavery was not sufficient to establish that line. After more than a year of fighting, its location was still uncertain. Richmond continued to cherish the hope Maryland would secede and move the frontier up from the Potomac to the southern boundary of Pennsylvania. Meanwhile the Unionists of northwestern Virginia set up a new state and thus drove a salient of the artificial border deep into the area which was to become the greatest of the battle zones.

Slave-holding Kentucky ultimately cast her lot with the Union and thus pushed the line down from the Ohio to the northern boundary of Tennessee. After months of bitter fighting between the loyal and Secessionist citizens of Missouri the cause of secession was defeated there and the line west of the Mississippi became the northern border of Arkansas rather than the southern line of Iowa. Of the states which fought for the Union these were not the only ones where the question of allegiance was seriously involved. The Confederate government did not give up the efforts to break Illinois, Indiana and Ohio away from the Union until late in 1864.

To speculate on what might have been the end result had these or any other of the states withdrawn their support of the Union armies is fare for a "historian's holiday." Even more engaging, perhaps, would be speculation as to what the alignment might have been had the war started ten years earlier. However, consideration of what might have happened in different circumstances is left for those who find pleasure in such mental exercises. To recount the facts of railroad development which had a direct bearing on the alignment of people and states in the struggle is sufficient for this narrative.

Twenty years before the war, sectionalism was weakening the ties of a Union seemingly overgrown from its small beginnings along the Eastern seaboard. Within the highly industrialized Northeast, with its vast merchandising and

ocean-shipping interests, the integration of a social and
economic unit had been accomplished. All essential elements
of a separate and independent nation were contained. It is
not at all surprising that this area should arrogate a certain
superiority and claim title to political preference in national
administrative affairs. But all such claims were hotly disputed
by the lower belt of states which stretched west from salt
water and composed the section known as the South. This
section also had matured its own economy and social structure
but along totally different lines from those of the Northeast.
The institution of slavery had driven a wedge between the
two sections and the confidence of the South in its self-
sufficiency ultimately found expression in secession.

The less mature and wholly different Northwest presented
still another problem in national unity. Cramped by no social
traditions and debtor to no industrial order, it stood firmly
on a spirit of political independence, devotion to the rich
soil wrested from the forest, and a disposition to make what
it would of the area in which freedom from economic
restrictions had been found. It would have none of either
slavery or the inferior place assigned it by the two older
sections. Under such conditions, major political stresses
were inevitable. In the fierce struggle to build its own
agricultural economy the Northwest suffered forbidding
natural handicaps. Since it was practically shut off from the
Northeast by the great granite barrier of the Alleghenies,
with no markets in the Far West and no means to employ
the great fresh-water lake area, the only profitable outlet for
its products lay through the Mississippi River system. Thus,
although hundreds of tedious miles to the southward, New
Orleans came to be the port of the prairies. With travel to
the Northeast difficult and expensive and the transport of
merchandise slow, uncertain and costly, the political and
economic stresses ran counter to the establishment of closer
relations between Northwest and Northeast. Meanwhile it
became increasingly apparent that the Mississippi formed a
controlling tie between the Northwest and the South.

These alignments and antagonisms were established almost as soon as the Northwest was settled. In the 1820s, advances in transportation twice disturbed the balance but could not deeply alter it. In 1825 the Erie Canal linked Lake Erie with the Hudson River at Albany. At last a waterway was open from the Great Lakes to the Eastern seaboard. Tireless energy and millions of Eastern capital had accomplished cheap and more rapid transport between the older industrial unit with its ocean ports and the growing inland empire. As the cost of freighting dropped, the price of farm products rose in the Northwest. Land values leaped to new heights. As prices went up, more money was available for the development of industry. It is understandable that the builders of the canal should have regarded the capture of the Northwest markets finally accomplished.

Had not steam come to the rivers as the canal came to the lakes they might have been right. While the last miles of the canal were being completed, steam engines were being mounted on the river boats and used to turn great paddle wheels astern. No sooner had the heavily laden canalboats come to crowd one another from Buffalo to Albany than the baying whistles of the river steamboats announced a competitive bid for transport of the farmers' grain and livestock. The Ohio and the Mississippi were no longer one-way traffic lines. The Northwest had always been able to float its products down the river and sell them. Now it could exchange them for the goods it needed, driven upriver by steam against the current.

Without the river steamers there could be little doubt of the influence of the Erie Canal on the unification of the Northeast and the Northwest in both politics and economy. Without the canal the coming of the river steamboat scarcely could have failed to tie the Northwest closer to the South. As it was, each worked a standoff against the other.

During the years between 1840 and 1850 the attention of the entire country was turned to a great new promise for future transportation. Onto the scene of sectional controversy rolled a steam power plant on wheels. Much experimentation with the locomotive had at last convinced Americans that this seemingly incredible machine was a practical thing. Skeptics said it would never replace the canalboat, but while they talked, men of means and vision set about putting it to work. Railroad construction began in earnest.

However, it was not the amount of construction accomplished before 1850 that mattered so much as what was learned during those years about construction and operation. The South was early in the field, but there the primary purpose of building was to provide transportation for cotton from the back-country fields to its port cities. These early Southern roads formed no new links with other sections of the country and served not at all to reduce the feeling of sectionalism. The South remained a unit apart, even more closely integrated by its new railroads.

By 1850 no more than 1,400 miles of track had been laid in the Northwest. This was only a beginning and its significance lay in the promise it held for the solution of the harassing problem of internal transport within the area. Precisely as in the South, the early effect was more in the direction of confirming sectionalism than of destroying it.

On the other hand, in the Northeast the greater mileage built and operating during this period accomplished much more than a further integration within the region. In the seaboard cities of Boston, New York, Philadelphia and Baltimore, the great merchandising and ocean-shipping interests eyed the railroads of the forties and foresaw the vast significance of coming rail transportation in American trade and commerce. Before the end of the decade they were prepared to finance attempts to drive the railroads through, over or around the mountain barrier to reach the markets of the rapidly developing Northwest. Their purpose was purely commercial and took no account of political and military considerations. They showed no realization of the important effect their successes would have on the political unity of the two sections; no conception of how quickly such unity was to become vital to the preservation of the Union.

3

During the ten-year period immediately preceding the war, events moving with incredible swiftness stabilized the relations between the Northwest and the Northeast and thus made certain the ultimate miracle of union which is America. Although the coming of the early railroads had accelerated the trend toward sectionalism in the Northwest, shortly thereafter an astounding railroad accomplishment wrought a sudden and totally unexpected reversal of that trend.

From the days of first substantial development in the Northwest, some of its people doubted that a union of all the states under a single government was practical. The vast distances involved and the hardships imposed by the intervening mountains seemed to them naturally to imply the ultimate necessity of a separate government for the vast Northwest. Foreseeing the future development of a still greater area as far west of the Ohio Valley as that valley is west of New England, they asked how a single government ever could comprehend it all. These men knew that political questions peculiar to each of the widely separated regions had risen and would continue to rise in greater number and perplexity. For illustration they had only to point to the issue of slavery in the South. They did not want slavery extended to the Northwest; but if, in Washington, New England abolitionists could harass the cotton states, there was nothing to prevent the ocean shipping interests of the seaboard states from harassing the food producers of the prairies. With such wide divergence of interests, they reasoned it might be better for each of these great geographical districts to govern itself.

Many of these men saw little or no hope for common economic interests between the sections. With transportation presenting a problem of such gigantic proportions, they argued, the only solution was for the valley states of the Northwest to set up their own mills, factories and fabrication plants. That such a policy might necessitate a separate republic, they accepted as part and parcel of the burden geography had laid on them.

Then the locomotive moved on the scene to capture the
attention of all who would travel or ship merchandise to
market. The concept of railroad lines between the Lakes and
the Ohio and from the Alleghenies to the Mississippi was
thrilling. The thought of railroads crisscrossing the deep
interior and fertile prairies beyond the reach of rivers or
canals challenged imagination. Geography no longer necessarily controlled either the direction of traffic or its terminals.
There was nothing to prevent the ultimate extension of rail
transportation to the Gulf ports. The locomotive was fast—
incredibly fast. The fascination of the picture was shared by
farmer, merchant and manufacturer alike.

At first a new sense of independence and self-sufficiency
pervaded the Northwest. Railroads over the Allegheny hump
were no part of this fresh and inspiring picture of things to
come. Definitely now the future of the Northwest seemed
to lie within its own natural boundaries. If its political and
economic interests were to be tied up with any other section,
it would be with the more accessible South.

By 1852 some 2,000 miles of railroad were in operation
there. Lines either were built or were building through the
heart of Ohio, Indiana and Illinois to the Ohio River and the
Mississippi, to the Great Lakes and on beyond Chicago to
Wisconsin and the upper lake ports. More hundreds of
miles of rails were being spiked into place as fast as roadbeds
could be prepared for them. If all of this meant separate
government, the people generally were ready for it. There
was little to recommend sending their congressmen on
journeys of long weeks to Washington just to enact laws to
govern them. And all the legislation they sought was subject
to approval by other members of the Congress, many of
whom had no conception of the country west of the
mountains and north of the cotton fields.

The country was too big. Washington was much too far
from Illinois to make for efficient government. There was too
much natural difference of opinion on matters of governmental policy. It was too far to the Eastern markets. The
coming of the railroads had emphasized the slowness of the

Erie Canal. Besides, the canal went only to New York. Cargo assigned to or from Boston, Philadelphia or Baltimore had to be reloaded.

Such was the mind of the Northwest in 1852. However, except for a comparatively few rabid sectional and professional politicians seeking personal gain, there was no open and militant advocacy of terminating political union. The trend in that direction arose not so much from desire as from inability to see any other answer to the local problems. The potential danger lay in the lack of positive motivations toward maintenance of the Union rather than in the influence of rabid and vociferous sectionalists. Fortunately, no untoward event occurred at this time to supply the Northwest with a positive reason for attempting to move out. That disaster might well have followed such an event is evidenced by the fact that Kentucky and Missouri were to be split wide open on the issue of war to maintain the Union, and as late as 1864 the secret organization which opposed pushing the war to victory over secession claimed many thousands of members in Ohio, Indiana and Illinois alone.

At this stage of political and economic thought in the Northwest, the merchants and capitalists on the Eastern seaboard decided to make relentless attacks on the Allegheny barrier, flank and center, with determination to conquer it with railroad iron.

4

Four railroad companies, armed only with pick and shovel, crowbar and black powder, began their assaults on the stubborn mountains. They had no power shovels to gnaw single bites of forty-five cubic yards from the hills, no dynamite to split the rocky cliffs of mountain spurs, no giant bulldozers to shove thousands of tons of earth from hillock into depression. With the tools and equipment then available, these undertakings would by present-day calculations be judged endless and well-nigh impossible.

From its western terminus opposite Harper's Ferry, the

Baltimore & Ohio bridged the Potomac River and drove its roadway into the rugged hills beyond. Tortuously, month after month, it shelved the cliffsides, clawed its way deeper and deeper into the mountain forests, bridged streams and trestled ravines. Following the course of the upper Potomac, it climbed up and up and over into the wild country soon to become West Virginia. Having reached the crest of the ridge, it patiently continued the slow process of conquering curve and gradient until at last in December 1853 it reached the Ohio River at Wheeling.[4]

With envious eyes Pennsylvania watched this Maryland project creep forward along her southern border. Already her citizens had spent millions of dollars attempting to reach the Ohio through a complicated system of canals which involved pulling canalboats up a series of inclined planes to a height of some 3,000 feet above sea level. This audacious venture was voraciously eating into their capital with most discouraging results, and the interested Philadelphia businessmen were forced to recognize that it could not meet the challenge of the railroad their Baltimore competitors were battering through to the Northwest.

From the fantastic canal project their attention shifted to building a railroad to compete with the Baltimore & Ohio. From the western terminus of the Pennsylvania Central they struck at the breast of the ridge and pounded relentlessly until a continuous line of rails connected the cities of Philadelphia and Pittsburgh. Taking advantage of the slash cut in the foothills by the Juniata River, they approached the greater height at a point where the ranges were narrower than on the route selected by their competitor and thus reached the confluence of the Monongahela and Ohio rivers before the Baltimore & Ohio reached Wheeling. Through service between Philadelphia and Pittsburgh opened in 1852.[5]

At an earlier date the Erie had struck out from Piermont on the Hudson. Following a more northerly course and headed for a terminal on the Great Lakes, its builders tackled the mountains in New York State. Without benefit of modern engineering tools and skills, the task was one of gigantic proportions. In spite of recurring financial problems, the road moved with incredible courage and energy from one natural barrier to another until on April 22, 1851, it reached Dunkirk on Lake Erie.[6]

Meanwhile a number of short lines, ultimately to form the New York Central System, were being welded into a continuous line which would flank the more difficult mountain terrain. Already the Hudson River Railroad extended from Albany to New York City. As early as 1841 the Boston & Albany had conquered the Berkshires and given Boston direct rail connections with the valley of the Hudson. From Albany westward, the route of the combined interests followed the less tortuous Mohawk Valley. Passing around the northern end of the Catskills, this route of easier grades reached Buffalo in 1853, and thus a second line connected Lake Erie with the Eastern seaboard.

These four feats of railroad construction were accomplished as the result of intense commercial rivalry. Boston, New York, Philadelphia and Baltimore strove mightily to be the first to reach the Northwest. For all practical purposes the race ended in a dead heat. Since all succeeded within a period of three years, the matter of which was first is of no importance to this story. That all succeeded before secession began is a thing for which all Americans may remain forever grateful.

Though the fact was quite unknown to the builders of these railroads, time was rapidly running out. While they hacked at forests and hammered at the rocks, deadline for the Union was just ahead. Theirs was a race for trade, run without knowledge of the tremendous political and military consequences which were to attend the outcome.

Perhaps no commercial event in American history has had effects comparable in national significance to the completion of the trans-Allegheny railroads. In the nick of time they brought an awakening of national interest, an awareness that the states were in fact united, and an abrupt end of the potential danger of sectionalism in the Northwest. During the short time yet remaining before the war, men traveled back and forth between the prairies and the Eastern seacoast. The seat of government was now accessible. Goods were shipped both ways with dispatch and assurance. Over the hills the cars brought thousands of families from the less fertile and more crowded farmlands of the older regions to settle on the lush prairies of the valley states. These people experienced no such feeling of remoteness and isolation as had possessed the pioneers. They had no cause to think of their new home as a country apart from the one they had previously known.

In the remainder of the decade before the war, the Northwest developed at a remarkable rate. Railroads were laid down as rapidly as workmen could be hired from the farms and imported from the Eastern cities. Little was left to nurture the thought that perhaps this country was too big for government as a single nation. Sentiment for separation, widely felt in 1852, slowly withered away. The attempt during the war to revive it through the Copperhead movement and the Northwest Conspiracy came too late and failed. The Northwest would fight for the Union.

CHAPTER II

ROADS NORTH AND SOUTH

I

About 1830 business in the old port city of Charleston was in the doldrums. Cotton, the money crop of South Carolina, was slipping down the Savannah River to the rival port in Georgia. Against such low-cost transportation Charleston could not compete; not since road tolls on a four-horse-wagon trip from Columbia and return had risen to nine dollars. Hope for revival came with the locomotive. On first proof that the iron horse was a practical machine, men of affairs in Charleston set about building a railroad to tap the cotton fields of the Piedmont. By 1833 the line was open to Hamburg on the upper Savannah, 136 miles inland, and from the back country cotton began rolling over rails to revive the fortunes of Charleston. It was the first railroad in all the world to attain such length.[1]

Locally financed, it was far less a railroad enterprise than a port developer, but it set a pattern in Southern railroad construction for the years immediately following. From cotton-shipping ports all the way from Savannah to Norfolk similar undertakings fingered out along the fertile valleys of the streams which led down from the mountains to the sea. Like the Charleston & Hamburg they were locally financed, built for local convenience and with no relation one to another. Like the rivers of the area they went nowhere except from the fields to the sea. They did not constitute parts of a rail system. As they were built in the interest of rival port cities, connections with other roads were carefully avoided

rather than sought. Anchored in the seaboard cities, they had
loose ends that frayed out over Georgia, the Carolinas and
southern Virginia like a starched fringe. Cotton was king,
and the king located the early Southern railroads to suit the
king's convenience.

Although this remained the basic pattern of rail transportation in the seaboard states of the South, later on new
aims in building and financing began to tie the loose ends
together and provide a modicum of facilities for relatively
long-distance north-south transportation. By 1861 something
of a railroad system had been created, or at least patched
together, but north-south traffic was neither rapid nor direct.
By a long series of transfers passengers or freight could follow
a route from Thomasville, Georgia, to Richmond and northern
Virginia. It was made up of a series of deep arcs, swinging
in and out of the coastal cities in such tedious fashion as to
make it of little use for through traffic. Also, by means of a
number of connecting short lines, two or three other routes
were open from Virginia to various parts of the Carolinas.

In the Mississippi Valley, north-south traffic was much
more adequately developed. Nearest the river the newly completed Mississippi Central ran directly north from New
Orleans to Grenada, and from there the Mississippi & Tennessee continued to Memphis. Roughly paralleling it and
about 100 miles eastward, the Mobile & Ohio provided a direct
route between Mobile and Columbus, Kentucky. Greatly
contributing to the co-ordination of these two main lines, and
of tremendous importance during the war years, was the
continuation of the Mississippi Central, which ran diagonally
northeast from Grenada to Jackson, Tennessee, on the Mobile
& Ohio. Another line ran diagonally northeast from Memphis, crossing the Memphis & Ohio at Humboldt and connecting with the Louisville & Nashville at Bowling Green,
Kentucky, thus giving both main lines a connection with
Louisville. Across middle Kentucky and Tennessee, the
Louisville & Nashville connected the two cities from which it
took its name and linked with the Nashville & Chattanooga
which ran south to Stevenson, Alabama, before turning east

YARDS ON OUTSKIRTS OF ALEXANDRIA, VIRGINIA
Probably in the Summer of 1863.

WRECKED YARD AT MANASSAS JUNCTION LEFT BEHIND
BY GENERAL JOSEPH E. JOHNSTON IN MARCH 1862

MODELS OF PENNSYLVANIA RAILROAD ROLLING STOCK
AT THE TIME OF THE CIVIL WAR
(Top to bottom) Boxcar, Livestock Car and Gondola.

to its terminus. From Chattanooga the Western & Atlantic reached southward to Atlanta. Thus, in the western part of the Confederacy the dominant railroad lines ran north and south rather than east and west to permit easy contact with the states east of the mountains.

In fact, at the first impact of war, the eastern states of the Confederacy were connected with those of the west by a single line of railroad, much of which was new, lightly constructed and poorly equipped for the enormous load it was called on to carry. Moreover, it was not one road, such as the Pennsylvania or the B.&O. Instead, it was composed of a number of separate roads, tied together shortly before the war to form the only continuous line of track between the Mississippi and the east coast, but it constituted the most important prewar railroad development in the South.[2] From Memphis this line, known as the Memphis & Charleston, extended east to Chattanooga, from which point its connections followed the valley in a northeasterly direction to emerge from the Blue Ridge Mountains through a pass west of Lynchburg, Virginia, thence east through Burkeville to Petersburg and on to the coast. Since it was the only east-west trunk line, its junctions with lines running north and south were of utmost commercial and military importance. East of Memphis, the first of these was at Grand Junction where it crossed the Mississippi Central, midway between its start at Memphis and the crossing of the Mobile & Ohio at Corinth, Mississippi. At Stevenson, Alabama, it intercepted the Nashville & Chattanooga and ran over its tracks to Chattanooga, the northern terminus of the Western & Atlantic, which later was to form part of Sherman's long supply line from Louisville in the Atlanta campaign.

Once beyond the mountains it touched the southern terminus of the Orange & Alexandria at Lynchburg. This line, though of a different gauge, made a tolerable connection north to Manassas, the scene of the first great battle of the war. The main line continued east to Burkeville, where it crossed the Richmond & Danville line, and on to Petersburg, where it crossed a second line to Richmond.

The nearest approach to a supplementary line from the Mississippi to the east coast was over a long, roundabout route which bore south all the way to Mobile and required ferriage across Mobile Bay. Starting from Vicksburg, the Southern of Mississippi was surveyed straight east to Montgomery, Alabama. Construction was completed through Jackson, where it crossed the Mississippi Central, but only to Meridian at a junction with the Mobile & Ohio. Traffic had to detour south to Mobile. At Mobile the water transfer was slow and difficult. The next leg of the journey led northeast to Montgomery, where reasonably direct connections could be made to Savannah. But travel from Vicksburg to Virginia was much more difficult. From Montgomery cars had to be routed through Atlanta all the way to Chattanooga for connection with the Memphis & Charleston, or find their way eastward from Columbus, Georgia, or Atlanta to the coast and thence northward through the maze of connections which formed the wholly inadequate north-south lines of the seaboard states.

Large areas of the Confederacy were far removed from rail transportation. In all of Texas, Arkansas and Louisiana only 700 miles of track were in operation.[3] Much of the interior of Alabama and Mississippi was entirely without rail service, and from Lynchburg to Chattanooga not a single line crossed the east-west trunk. In all the mountain area of North Carolina, east Tennessee and southwestern Virginia the only rail facilities other than the trunk line were three short spurs, the longest of which did not exceed twenty miles. Of the 30,000 miles of railroad in operation in America at the outbreak of the war, only about 9,000 miles lay within the Confederacy.[4] A far greater disadvantage to the South than this disparity in mileage was the loosely knit pattern of its rail lines. As the war would quickly prove, the military inadequacy arose largely from the lack of connections to provide alternate routes between the eastern and western regions.

Another vital weakness lay in the lack of north-south connections in the eastern and seaboard districts to tie the loose ends of the short lines of the Deep South to Virginia. Moreover, the railroads of the South were not supplemented by either natural or artificial waterways. For the Confederacy, her rivers ran in the wrong directions.

2

In the North the railroads presented an entirely different pattern. In sharp contrast with the cotton economy of the South, widely diversified industrial and agricultural interests had dictated the placement of rails to accommodate the flow of traffic in all directions. As in the South, the very early building had been locally financed and for local convenience. But the early short lines of the North had been designed to connect one city with another and with inland waterways as well as with ocean ports. Much earlier than in the South, capital turned to railroading as a business in itself rather than as an incidental scheme for the benefit of other enterprises in which the investors were interested.

As a result, individual roads were pushed to greater and greater length. Rival roads competed briskly for useful connections while Southern lines were still avoiding them. The Northern investor foresaw that the future prosperity of his railroad depended on reaching out to as many mines, mills, farms and towns as possible. So when war came, not one but four trunk lines tied together the industrial East and the vast agricultural areas of the Great Lakes and the Mississippi. Each of them touched salt water at one end and navigable fresh waters at the other.

The New England short lines had access to the Northwest by an east-west line from Boston through connections at Albany. Another line through Massachusetts and Connecticut gave them an outlet to New York City. The numerous shorter lines of New Jersey, eastern Pennsylvania and upper New York tapped the trunk lines as well as navigable waters and canals.

West of the mountains, the newer roads formed a gridiron so complete that few spots in Ohio, Illinois, Indiana and lower

Michigan were more than twenty-five miles from rail transportation. Through central Ohio ran the lines which connected Lake Erie with the Ohio River at several points from Cincinnati to Pittsburgh. From the foot of Lake Michigan another road traversed central Indiana to the Ohio at Louisville. A little farther west lay the newly completed Illinois Central which, with its main line and diverging branch, provided direct service from Chicago and Galena to Cairo at the southernmost tip of Illinois and the confluence of the Ohio and Mississippi rivers.

Between Freeport and Cairo, the main line of the Illinois Central was crossed by eight east-west and diagonal lines, all of which reached the Mississippi, four of which ran directly to Chicago, and four of which crossed the width of Illinois and continued east into Indiana and Ohio.

At the center of Indiana, Indianapolis formed a railroad hub from which radiated lines touching the Ohio at Cincinnati, Madison and Louisville on the south and reaching Michigan City on the north, Terre Haute and Peoria on the west, and Columbus, Ohio, on the east. All of them crossed or connected with lines running oppositely through the state. In Ohio a network of roads covered the state in all directions. Scarcely an Ohio town of consequence lacked railroad connections with Lake Erie and the river, with Chicago and the Mississippi. From the west bank of the Mississippi, short lines were reaching westward through Iowa and Missouri, forerunners of the iron trails to the Far West.

Integrated by the trans-Allegheny trunk lines, this rail network of the Northwest and the short lines of New England and the East formed an effective system of rail transportation in Union territory. Both the civil and the military effectiveness of this system was greatly enhanced through its coordination with lake and river transport and with the canals.

Between the North and the South, not a single all-rail connection existed when the war began. No railroad of the Northwest had a terminal south of the Ohio, and no Eastern line had its terminal south of the Potomac. The two rivers were not bridged where Northern and Southern lines approached each other. As vice-president of the Illinois Central, young George B. McClellan had worked out the closest approximation of an all-rail route between the Northwest and the Deep South. Between Cairo, Illinois, and Columbus, Kentucky, twenty miles of river intervened. With their Southern correspondents, McClellan and his associates devised a working agreement whereby, with its own river boats, the Illinois Central established a river transfer for freight and passengers between the terminals at Columbus and Cairo. The arrangement, however, did not become effective until late 1860 and lasted only until April 1861, though for a short time the Illinois Central advertised the sale of through passenger tickets between Chicago and New Orleans.

Meanwhile another scheme for rail connection between the North and the South was in the mind of John W. Garrett, president of the Baltimore & Ohio. His plan contemplated the extension of his Washington branch across the Potomac to link with the northern terminus of the Orange & Alexandria. The coming of the war put an end to this plan as well as to McClellan's.

No specification of railroad facilities available to either North or South at the outset of the war would be complete without special reference to the peculiar position occupied by the Baltimore & Ohio. To both sides it represented political and strategic relations of incalculable importance. For a distance of eight miles south of Baltimore it was double-tracked to a point known as Relay House. From there the main line turned west, while a single-track branch continued southward to Washington and provided the only railroad approach to that city.

Located entirely within slave territory, it was one of the most solidly built, adequately equipped and efficiently managed roads in the country. Except for its location it was in all particulars more akin to the North than to the South. It was built like a Northern road, its principal competition on the main line was with the Pennsylvania, and in the prewar decade it had spent large sums of money in developing Northern connections beyond the Ohio. At Benwood, six

miles below Wheeling, a ferry service was established to Bellaire directly across the river, and through financial assistance
and traffic inducements, two Ohio roads terminating at Bellaire
provided the B.&O. valuable connections with Cincinnati and
Columbus. Thus an outlet to the entire western network was
accomplished. Meanwhile, by its financial aid the Northwestern Virginia Railroad had been completed from Grafton
on the main stem of the B.&O. to Parkersburg on the Ohio,
some seventy miles below Benwood. Leased to and operated
by the B.&O., this road was commonly referred to as the
Parkersburg branch. Through another ferriage it provided a
second and more direct connection with Cincinnati.

From end to end the main line ran through that twilight
zone which in 1861 was neither North nor South. Though its
western mileage was on Virginia soil, the counties through
which it passed were violently opposed to secession and were
more in sympathy with their neighbors across the Ohio than
with Virginians who lived east of the mountains. The balance
of its track lay in Maryland. Its main shops, locomotive works
and general offices were located in Baltimore, where sentiment
was more secessionist than Union. Whether the B.&O. was
to be at the disposal of the Union or the Confederate side in
the early days of the war depended on the decision of Maryland as to secession and the action of the northwestern
counties of Virginia as to sustaining the mother state. The
great military value of the railroad made both these political
decisions vastly important at the outset of the war.

Strategically the B.&O. was vital to the South, for, in the
possession of the North, it threatened a dangerous line of
approach for an invading army from the Northwest and
provided an invaluable supply line for any army which might
penetrate Virginia. When hostilities opened, no other road
occupied a like or remotely comparable relation to the
conflict.

Washington, situated as it was within gunshot range of
the Confederacy, was soon to realize its dependence on this
railroad for survival. While one bank of the Potomac, which
provided the water route from Chesapeake Bay, was under

control of the enemy, the single-track branch of the B.&O.
was the sole means of reaching the city by steam travel.

In addition to the doubtful adequacy of thirty miles of
single track from Relay House to Washington, a vulnerable
bottleneck in Baltimore constantly threatened to interrupt
or break Washington's communications with the rest of the
North. No locomotive way ran through the city of Baltimore. Cars moved between the terminal of the B.&O. and the
Northern Central or the Philadelphia, Wilmington & Baltimore, were transferred by horsepower over light tracks laid
through the city streets. On this slow and easily interrupted
transfer depended Washington's rail connections with the
states on which Lincoln called for troops to suppress rebellion
in the South. Within the week after the fall of Sumter, the
tragic weakness was to appear. Communications between
the North and its capital were tenuous indeed!

It is well to note here that when Richmond became the
Confederate capital it suffered no such handicap of communication with its people. Situated beside the navigable
James River, it enjoyed the most extensive railroad service
of any city in the South. Directly east, the York River Railroad joined Richmond with the navigable stream from which
the railroad took its name. To the southward the Richmond
& Petersburg opened the way to the Carolinas. To the southwest the Richmond & Danville reached almost to the Carolina
border. Both the Petersburg and Danville roads gave it access
to the trunk line to the Mississippi. From the upper Shenandoah came the Virginia Central which connected at Gordonsville with the Orange & Alexandria and thus gave Richmond a
tolerably direct route to northern Virginia. A second road
to the north was the Richmond, Fredericksburg & Potomac
which came to the Potomac at Aquia Creek, some forty miles
below Washington.

In sharp contrast to Washington's dependence on a single
track, Richmond was the terminus of five railroads. These
facilities made it easy to move passengers and freight to but
not through the city. Richmond suffered the severe handicap
common to most Southern cities, large and small. Munici-

palities had invested heavily in early railroad building. A city which had invested in a railroad's securities expected the road to serve its interests. Since it received no profit or other benefit from passengers and freight merely passing through, it was strongly opposed to direct track connections between lines meeting within it. Through trains or through cars carried the fat profits to be derived from transferring passengers and local freight handling elsewhere and city investors wanted these profits kept at home.

For some years before the war, railroad management, seeing the fallacy of such reasoning, had sought to establish direct track connections between lines and common terminals in Richmond, as well as in other Southern cities. Strong elements in municipal politics opposed the step. Hotels did a thriving business with travelers who arrived on one railroad and were obliged to stay over while waiting for a departing train on another line. Draymen reaped a harvest hauling freight from one depot to another; the farther apart the stations could be kept the better the carters liked it. Warehousemen found big profits in the continued separation of the various lines. Restaurants swelled their business by feeding waiting passengers, and liquor dealers fought any change which might shorten the time travelers had to wait between trains. These interests, using the still-surviving arguments of the earlier investor motive, had little difficulty in defeating the attempts of the railroads to win authority to connect their lines. The opposition never realized how effectively they were contributing to the ultimate defeat of the Confederacy.

Such, North and South, was the general pattern of railroads laid down at the dictates of trade and commerce before the guns were summoned to decide the fate of the Union.

CHAPTER III

ROLLING STOCK

Since the name of the engine Captain Imboden rode to Strasburg that April morning in 1861 is not known, its exact specifications cannot be traced. It seems safe to assume, however, that it was of the type in general use. If so, it might well have been resplendent in polished brass fittings and decorations of gold and crimson paint reflecting the gay youth of the locomotive age.[1] Of a certainty it was a woodburner and therefore carried the necessary funnel-shaped smokestack of huge proportions. Mounted on a bracket directly in front of the stack was a large, boxlike headlight containing a kerosene lamp. Far ahead of the pilot truck protruded a grotesque cowcatcher made of wood in such proportions as to suggest the use of the whole machine as a steam ram.

It was an eight-wheeler. Though a few ten-wheel engines were then in use, the Baltimore & Ohio was the southernmost road on which one might be found. If near an average, the eight-wheeler weighed about 55,000 pounds, and its four drive wheels each would measure about sixty inches tall. The engine would be equipped with a link motion reversing gear, but no braking mechanism other than the conventional hand brake operated by the fireman from the front of the tender.[2]

Probably the people of Manassas Junction who saw those first troop trains had never seen a coal-burning locomotive. The Pennsylvania, the Baltimore & Ohio and perhaps some other roads had experimented a bit with coal as locomotive fuel, but because of inappropriate firebox and boiler design coal accomplished little more than to promise a new fuel

for the future. Coal-burners did not come into general use
until after the war.

In the Manassas yard that morning there might well have
been an engine which presented a very different appearance
from the others. Some years before the war, Ross Winans,
chief engineer for the Baltimore & Ohio, had designed and
built a strange-looking machine which set off quite a controversy among locomotive manufacturers. Dispensing with
the pilot truck, he moved the driving wheels forward from
their conventional position, added another pair and balanced
the entire weight of the engine on the drivers. For this
arrangement Winans claimed much more traction and pulling
power. Enginemen who drove it readily admitted it to be a
powerful performer on steep grades, but most of them hated
it because of its tendency to leave the rails and upset when it
encountered even minor track irregularities or obstructions.
An elongated cab was built astride the boiler at its middle,
and from the strange appearance thus produced, railroaders
dubbed the type the "Camelback" or "Camel."[3] Throughout
the war a few of these machines were operated in the South,
but the "Camel" seems to have earned its chief distinction
through its peculiarly shrill and high-powered whistle, which
hungry soldiers came to recognize as a signal that rations
were coming.

Speed of the wartime locomotives was limited more by
track conditions than by engine capacity. Over a good track
they could pull a light train at sixty miles an hour. Forty
miles was not an unusual speed for a passenger train such as
that on which Lincoln and his party traveled from Springfield
to Washington. Twenty loaded freight cars did not overtax
the pulling capacity of the average locomotive of 1861.

Except for certain disparities in freight-car design, rolling
stock other than power units had attained a marked similarity
to that in use until luxury, capacity requirements and the
special demands of modern commerce dictated the radical
changes of recent years. Passenger coaches were entered
from platforms at the ends precisely as today except that the
platforms were open and not enclosed as vestibules. Plush-

upholstered seats for two in sufficient number to accommodate fifty to sixty passengers ranged the length of the car on both sides of a center aisle. Kerosene lamps, hung over the aisles, provided light, and a stove at each end furnished heat. Cuspidors were standard equipment. Except for refinements in heating, lighting and water supply, the wartime passenger coach was little less comfortable than that in service at the turn of the century.

In a Civil War freight train one might see a boxcar so similar in appearance to the modern one as to pass unnoticed except for its smaller size. It was mounted on four-wheeled trucks at each end. It might be loaded with ammunition, rations, forage or soldiers. It was the all-purpose car of the wartime railroad. Coupled with it might be a car with slatted sides but without a roof. If a hinged gate swung outward from each side at the center, probably this car would be loaded with horses, mules or cattle; it was the stock car of the period. If there were no gates, if the ends were open and if the train was running through the Deep South, it would be listed as a rack car, principally used to haul slash.

If a flatcar were in the train, its resemblance to those in use until recently would be so close, except for smaller size, as to require little description. Another familiar car had much the appearance of an ordinary flat on which strong sides and ends had been built up to a height of three or four feet. Though it was designed to carry coal or gravel, its war cargo might be anything from artillery to bridge timbers. On such roads as the Pennsylvania and the B.&O., where coal constituted a major part of the freight haul, a short wooden gondola with hopper bottom had become general. A coal car of greater capacity was built of two or three circular metal bins mounted on an iron platform.

In the South a few diminutive four-wheelers of 1840 design were still in operation, but for the most part this mounting had been superseded by two four-wheeled trucks. On all types of cars braking was limited to the wheel, spindle and chain device operated by hand. Couplings were slack and accomplished by link and pin through light buffers. Light construction, principally of wood, made the rolling stock of 1861 easy for an enemy to burn and destroy.

Less than adequate at the beginning, the supply of rolling stock available in the South dwindled rapidly as the war wore on. Capture and overwork without timely repairs took a heavy toll of the ever-scarce Confederate engines and cars. In the whole Confederacy there was not a single plant in which a locomotive could be built—at least not under wartime conditions. One must search far for better proof that the war potential of the railroads received small consideration from the promoters of secession. They might well have paused if they had conceived even in moderate measure the power to make war latent in the locomotive.

In contrast with the South's total lack of facilities to build engines, the North had no less than a dozen established locomotive manufacturers as well as numerous railroad and other shops in which construction was possible.[4] Not only did the North have virtual control of all locomotive building but it had a near monopoly of mechanics skilled in the business.

Little less complete was its control of car construction. While the Confederate roads desperately drove their rolling stock to ruin, most roads in the North maintained or increased their supply. Between 1863 and 1865, the Illinois Central increased the number of its locomotives from 112 to 148, while over the same period the number of its freight cars of all types grew from 2,312 to 3,337.[5]

As early as 1860 President Garrett of the Baltimore & Ohio reported his road in possession of some 4,000 engines and cars, and despite heavy losses in the early months of conflict its shops in Baltimore continued to turn out new equipment to supplement the large purchases made from other manufacturers. A few of the shorter roads of the North, without building facilities of their own, were not so fortunate, but none of them suffered the losses through overwork, capture and destruction common to all roads of the South.

While the trackage in 1861 was much more adequate than the supply of rolling stock, it was far less efficiently developed.

Much of the construction was so new that roadbeds were unsettled and tracks distressingly rough. Flimsy bridges trembled and swayed under the impact of running trains. Particularly in the Northwest much of sturdiness and stability had been sacrificed to speedy construction in order to set wheels rolling and announce competitive schedules. All too frequently sound engineering principles had succumbed to the demands of expediency.

On the whole, however, the roads of the North, being more adequately financed, were of heavier construction than those in the South. As a result they were able to sustain heavier traffic at higher speeds for a longer period of time when war suddenly switched the emphasis from new construction to maximum operation. Few of the older roads in the South had replaced the original U-type rail with the newer and more durable T iron. Roads of such vital importance to the Confederacy as the Virginia Central and the Nashville & Chattanooga entered the war laid with U-type. Some U rail was still found in the North but by 1861 it was no longer a factor in operation or construction.

Even the best T rail was light, made of malleable iron and subject to rapid wear. At the end of the war, only a few miles of experimental track were laid with steel. The process of rolling steel rails was so new and the product so expensive it did not become common until after the war.

Modern methods of tie treatment had not been developed and the older tracks, particularly in certain sections of the South, were beginning to suffer rapid deterioration from rotting timbers.

While the more substantial roads in the North had recognized the need for adequate sidetrack facilities and greatly increased them, the rush of new construction, hampered as it was by shortage of labor supply, forced a sacrifice of sidetrackage to main-line extension. Bad as this situation was in the North, it was much worse in the South. The distance between sidings and the lightness of their construction proved a veritable curse on Confederate operations. In the North the situation was largely corrected during the war years, but for lack of iron the South continued to suffer under the handicap imposed by earlier neglect.

Next to the lack of terminal connections in the South, perhaps no single factor worked a greater hardship on wartime railroading there than the divergence of track gauges. The fault was common to both North and South, but with its otherwise less adequate rail facilities the effect was more serious to the South. On both sides the loading and unloading of freight went on interminably. Precious time was consumed and much-needed man power diverted while hard-pressed soldiers waited for the transfer of rations and ammunition from cars built to a gauge of four feet eight and one-half inches to other cars which would run over a track of five feet, and then again to cars of still another gauge. So distressing did this become that while fighting was at its height many miles of track were converted from one gauge to another. The lesson was effectively driven home. The guns were scarcely silenced when the American railroads set about establishing the standard gauge of four feet eight and one-half inches which now prevails.

Without modern facilities of dispatching, one can only wonder at the success and speed with which thousands of wartime trains were operated over single-track roads in single and multiple units under all sorts of adverse conditions. To some extent the telegraph was employed for train dispatching, but train operation was mainly based on schedules which became progressively less effective as fighting areas were neared. In the war zones hundreds of trains moved with no orders except those dictated by caution, courage and necessity.

This was the physical equipment with which the railroads went to war, with which they faced tasks beyond precedent, met failures with new hardihood, and accomplished amazing feats of military and civilian transport for which they have received little credit.

CHAPTER IV

THE ITCHING PALM OF SIMON CAMERON

In proportion to the business available in 1861, perhaps the railroads in the North had been overbuilt. This opinion was quite freely expressed and there was credible evidence to support it. Many of the roads had been distressed by the depression of 1857, from which the country was only beginning to recover. Competing lines were in a wild scramble to procure such freight and passenger business as could be found. Especially acute was the competition between the trunk lines extending from the seaboard to the Northwest. Through rate cutting and all sorts of special inducements they battled one another ruthlessly and hoped for better days to come.

Though keenly aware of the national crisis provoked by secession and the grave possibility of war, railroad management continued to focus its attention on getting business. Therein lay hope for survival. Management reasoned that if war should come, railroad business would be only the harder to get and survival the more doubtful. No precedent existed from which to reason otherwise; nothing by which they might anticipate the use to which the roads were to be put. Railroads had never been called on to transport hundreds of thousands of troops over great distances and follow them with numberless tons of food, munitions and supplies. Military strategy based on long supply lines serviced by rail was yet to be devised. The co-ordination of railroad facilities necessary to forage thousands of army horses and mules far from the grainfields was undreamed of.

As the competitive struggle between the Northern roads was reaching its climax, President Lincoln proclaimed that a state of rebellion existed in the land and called on the various states to provide troops with which to put it down. Suddenly, on April 15, 1861, the railroads were snatched from rivalry for cargo and passenger traffic into the greatest adventure in American railroad history. The scene of rebellion was a long way from Maine and Minnesota, from Cleveland and Chicago. Tragic years were to pass before the magnitude of the transportation problem involved was fully measured.

Whether it was sound military judgment to begin the task of suppressing the rebellion by concentrating an army on Washington is not an appropriate question for these pages. Obviously the decision had been made before Lincoln's proclamation was issued, for on that same day Secretary of War Simon Cameron dispatched a historic telegram to Governor Andrew of Massachusetts. "Send your companies here by railroad,"[1] Cameron wired. With that message and similar messages to other governors began a new era in warfare as well as in railroading.

Whatever military virtue lay in the idea of bringing an army to Washington, it is difficult to conceive a better preliminary exercise in wartime railroading behind the lines. The experience gained from this maneuver was later to pay off handsomely. What consideration, if any, was given to problems of railroad relations does not appear from the records, but no sooner was the plan put in operation than they began to assume large proportions. To evaluate them and visualize the movement of that April army on wheels, it is necessary to look again at the pattern of Northern railroads in relation to Washington.

This was a great funnel narrowing at Baltimore to the neck represented by the single-track Washington branch of the Baltimore & Ohio. A hundred miles northeast of Baltimore lay Philadelphia, eastern terminus of the Pennsylvania Railroad and junction point with lines covering all of New York, New Jersey and New England. Between it and Baltimore, the Philadelphia, Wilmington & Baltimore provided a direct rail route.

Seventy-five miles northwest of Baltimore, and a little

over 100 miles west of Philadelphia, lay Harrisburg. The Northern Central, running from Baltimore to a junction with the Pennsylvania Railroad at Harrisburg, gave Baltimore a reasonably direct route through Harrisburg to Pittsburgh and the lines fanning from that point to the Northwest. Westward from Baltimore ran the main line of the B.&O. all the way to the Ohio River. Thus, when Lincoln called for volunteers and the War Department ordered a concentration on Washington, Baltimore immediately became the key military point in the Northern railroad system.

By virtue of his position as Secretary of War, Simon Cameron had full authority in matters pertaining to rail transportation of troops and of the heavy tonnage required to maintain them in camp and field. From this unfortunate circumstance arose complications which were to plague the North far into the conflict.

Success in exercising this vast authority could have come to him only at the price of forgetting his deep-seated animosities and subordinating his personal railroad interests to the public welfare. Such a price Cameron seemed unwilling or unable to pay. Despite the railroads' eagerness to serve the Union cause without reserve, Cameron's handling of military transportation provoked controversies which rocked the North during 1861, posed a serious political problem for President Lincoln, embittered railroad executives whose co-operation was of immense importance and allowed the facilities of one great trunk line to be lost with scarcely a struggle to preserve them. Unfitted by temperament for the task which came to him, he quickly got into difficulties because of personal business relations previously established.

The Cameron family owned a controlling interest in the stock of the Northern Central. Simon had a heavy investment in it, and his son was vice-president of the line. It was known as Cameron's road. By means of its tracks from Baltimore to Harrisburg the Pennsylvania Railroad was able to compete with the B.&O. for traffic between Baltimore and the Northwest, and thus developed for Cameron's road a large proportion of its total revenue.

As war drew near, this Pennsylvania-Northern Central combination was fighting the B.&O. tooth and claw for business bound to and from Chesapeake waters.

Once troops were ordered to Washington it became immensely important to keep traffic flowing freely over both the B.&O. and the Pennsylvania. The national safety depended on it. The public cared nothing about the bitter rivalry between them. The people's interest was in winning the war, and they soon discovered that the Pennsylvania Railroad alone could not provide sufficient carrying capacity. Cameron seemed to be actuated by other motives. The rumor was that he was more concerned with helping the Pennsylvania Railroad beat down the competition of the B.&O. than he was with speeding the war effort. Fact, rather ugly, appears to substantiate the rumor. Before mobilization of the first 75,000 troops was completed, through traffic over the main line of the B.&O. was stopped.

To determine the extent, if any, to which Cameron used the authority of his office to promote his own fortunes and to accommodate his friends of the Pennsylvania at the expense of the early war effort calls for most careful reading of the record. At any rate, it is certainly true that his conduct of military shipping provides the basis for the larger part of the railroad story of the North through 1861.

His first important move was to call J. Edgar Thomson, able president of the Pennsylvania, to act as his personal representative in co-ordinating rail transportation of troops and supplies to Washington. As Thomson's assistant he designated Samuel M. Felton, president of the Philadelphia, Wilmington & Baltimore. To avoid congestion at Harrisburg and speed up the transfer of Pennsylvania-borne shipping to Baltimore via the Northern Central, he stationed another personal representative at Harrisburg—Thomas A. Scott, vice-president of the Pennsylvania. These three were as able as any railroad men in America, but Cameron's critics soon noted that two of them were high-ranking officials of the Pennsylvania, while the third operated a coast-line railroad with no direct relation to Northwest trunk-line shipping.

Lincoln's proclamation of April 15 was scarcely off the wires when Cameron telegraphed the governors of the several states, specifying a quota of men to be supplied by each of them and designating one or more points within each state where its men should assemble.[2] For Iowa he designated Keokuk. At the request of Governor Kirkwood this was promptly changed to Davenport, because Keokuk had no direct rail or telegraph line to the East.[3] With this one change, every rendezvous in the Northern states had a rail outlet over which to send its men to points of larger concentration and thence to Washington. If it was true that for commercial purposes railroad building in the North had been over-extended, Lincoln's call for troops quickly set all criticism on that score at rest.

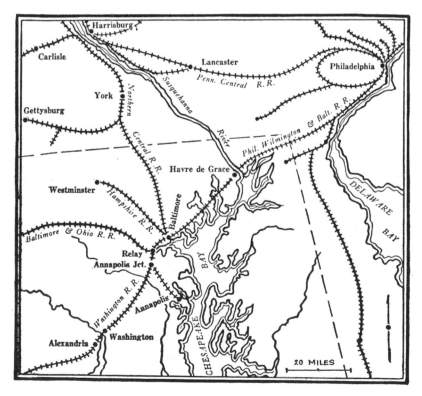

THE BALTIMORE BOTTLENECK

As the troop trains began to steam away from the various assembly points, Scott was at his post to supervise the Baltimore-bound movement of the regiments from western Pennsylvania and those coming from the Northwest. Felton was in Philadelphia to facilitate transport over his own road for the New England, New York and Eastern seaboard contingents. Things started moving smoothly and at a speed which, but a few years earlier, would have seemed incredible. The world was witnessing something new and startling in the business of concentrating an army. Nothing remotely like it had ever been seen before.

Only one thing threatened the swift and successful concentration of troops in Washington. No matter with what dispatch or in what numbers they were rushed to Baltimore, at that point they would be nearly forty miles from their destination and dependent on a single track to complete their journey. Unless they could be funneled through Baltimore and carried away by the Washington branch of the B.&O., they might as well have been left in Harrisburg or Philadelphia. Practical railroad men that they were, both Thomson and Felton foresaw the potential difficulty. In fact, as early as December 1860 Felton had warned General Winfield Scott of the danger inherent in the Baltimore situation if war should come.[4] The War Department gave no heed to this warning and to the obvious risk. Troop trains were approaching the city before any step was taken to prevent the complete closing of the Baltimore bottleneck.

Despite the vital importance of the B.&O. and particularly of its Washington branch, Cameron had not included its president, the redoubtable John W. Garrett, in his little circle of railroad advisers and assistants, nor consulted him at all. Possibly some justification for this may be found in the fact that on the eve of war unsavory rumors were afloat about the loyalty of B.&O. management and the safety of goods consigned over its lines. On the other hand Garrett had publicly charged representatives of the Pennsylvania with responsibility for originating and circulating these rumors, which he branded as insidious and false.[5] Whether or not Garrett's charges were true, the widespread publicity given them placed Cameron and Thomson in a difficult position, now that war was on them and Garrett's Washington branch was their sole reliance for rail transportation to the capital. Aside from all this, perhaps it was too much to expect for Cameron to take into his confidence this archenemy of the Pennsylvania-Northern Central combination which had so much at stake.

Whatever the reason for postponing any contact with Garrett, it was not until late afternoon of April 17 that Thomson first called on Garrett at the latter's office in Camden Station in Baltimore.[6] With what cordiality these two rivals in business discussed the military situation is not known. Two days before, Cameron and Thomson had been warned from hostile sources that, regardless of what the B.&O. management decided, the road would not be permitted to keep its lines open.[7] The War Department had taken no steps to protect them. The outcome of the conference was a frank admission by Garrett that, since Southern sympathizers stood ready to destroy his unguarded tracks and bridges, he could not move Union troops from the West over the main stem. But he was prepared to forward to Washington all troops brought into Baltimore from Harrisburg and Philadelphia.[8]

Since Confederate sympathizers' threats to destroy B.&O. property if the road undertook to aid the Union army must have indicated the gravity of the situation, it seems surprising that Thomson should have relied on Garrett's promise alone, with no other precautions to insure the movement of troops and supplies. Scores of such threats and warnings were pouring in on Garrett at the very time of his conference, yet at its conclusion Thomson left without making any arrangement to provide military protection for the railroad or even for the short Washington branch. It is true that Garrett had great influence in Baltimore and may have felt that he could get along more smoothly with the hot Maryland Secessionists alone than in the inflaming presence of military guards in Federal uniform. Secretary Cameron did nothing except warn

Governor Hicks that any interference with the passage of government troops would be deplorable.[9]

In sharp contrast with Cameron's inactivity in respect to the B.&C. was his quick action to protect his own line. At the first threat against the B.&O. he became so concerned over the safety of the Northern Central that he ordered Pennsylvania militiamen mustered into the Federal service and had them set on guard along the Central tracks.

The crisis came quickly. During the following afternoon, April 18, troops began to arrive in Baltimore. A small contingent of regulars and some Pennsylvania volunteers detrained from the Northern Central and started to march through the streets to cars waiting on the tracks of the B.&O. An angry and rapidly growing crowd followed and harassed them. Hoots, jeers and stone-throwing disclosed the temper of the citizens at the sight of Union soldiers on Maryland soil. They particularly resented the presence of the Pennsylvania volunteers. Fortunately this first demonstration resulted in more noise than damage.[10]

No sooner had the trains pulled out for Washington than all sorts of imprecations were heaped on Garrett for having lent aid to these troop movements. Confederate sympathizers let him know that if he permitted the B.&O. to be used again for troop movements, the line would be seriously damaged in reprisal.[11] No matter which way he turned, disaster was certain to follow. He was committed to Thomson and the War Department; he was helpless to protect the far-flung properties of the road if he undertook to fulfill his promise. What he would have done had circumstances not changed quickly can only be surmised.

The tragic events of the following day relieved him of making a decision. On detraining from the Philadelphia, Wilmington & Baltimore, the Sixth Massachusetts regiment began the transfer across town to the Camden Station. How these men were set upon by an enraged mob, clubbed and stoned and many of them disabled before finally reaching their waiting cars is the familiar story of the Baltimore riot of April 19. Not so well known is the fact that while the

Sixth Massachusetts was being mobbed in the streets, other troops arrived and stood at the President Street Station of the Northern Central, waiting orders to move through the city. While they waited, Baltimore officials, sitting in hurried conference with Governor Hicks, voted to close the streets to all troops.[12]

Since Garrett had assumed responsibility for taking the waiting men on to Washington, he was immediately notified of this and of their further resolution that "the troops now here be sent back to the borders of Maryland." Garrett communicated the facts to Felton, adding, "In this state of things we cannot undertake to carry any more Northern troops over any part of our road." Felton halted his trains en route to Baltimore and sent back toward Philadelphia those already arrived. Likewise men coming into town from the west over the Northern Central were returned to Pennsylvania soil.

So critical seemed the portents that Baltimore authorities, acting with Governor Hicks's approval, ordered the lines of the Northern Central and the Philadelphia, Wilmington & Baltimore cut outside the city limits.[13] There was no lack of willing hands and, as might have been anticipated, the destruction of track and bridges was carried far beyond all necessity. Not only was the P.W.&B. track broken but most of its many bridges between Baltimore and the Susquehanna River were burned.[14] Telegraph lines were wrecked, too.

So it came about that on the morning of April 20, when Lincoln's proclamation was but five days old, Washington woke to find its communications with the North completely cut off. At one stroke a Baltimore mob had severed the neck of the great railway funnel that should have been pouring Union troops into Washington. The flow had stopped.[15]

During the afternoon of the nineteenth, Thomson and Felton were in Philadelphia. As soon as they heard of the rioting in Baltimore, they wired Cameron that Governor Hicks had said no more troops could be passed through his biggest city. "We will wait for instructions," said they.[16] They had not long to wait. Cameron answered immediately:

"Governor Hicks had neither right nor authority to stop troops coming to Washington. Send them on prepared to fight their way through if necessary."[17]

Cameron was furious over the day's events. Fortunately, however, cooler heads were at work. On the twentieth, Lincoln asked Governor Hicks and Mayor Brown of Baltimore to come to Washington.[18] Obviously the President was not of a mind to permit Cameron's impetuous message to Felton to destroy the chance of holding Maryland within the Union. After a series of conferences the War Department policy was reversed and the next day, April 21, Cameron notified the officer in command to remove the troops from the vicinity of Baltimore.[19]

Meanwhile, in Philadelphia Thomson and Felton had not been idle. The Philadelphia, Wilmington & Baltimore was open to Perryville at the mouth of the Susquehanna. Tugs and ferryboats could be used on the Chesapeake from Perryville to Annapolis. From Annapolis the little Annapolis & Elk Ridge Railroad ran inland for eighteen miles to meet the Washington Branch of the B.&O. at Annapolis Junction. Thomson and Felton set about establishing this as a substitute route to the capital and received approval from the War Department, despite Cameron's obsession of forcing the way through Baltimore.

Scott, then in Harrisburg, disliked the plan and gave full support to Cameron's belligerent program for using the Baltimore route. He faced a problem of considerable proportions. Troop trains heavily laden with soldiers from the Northwest were already rolling toward Pittsburgh. In another day or two these men would be in Harrisburg and Scott's job was to get them to Washington. He had no enthusiasm for the substitute rail-water route which meant sending the arriving troops on to Philadelphia instead of directly south by the Northern Central. He seems to have been the first to appreciate the problem of providing Washington with adequate food and supplies even though the substitute route should prove sufficient for the troops. This he urged as another and sufficient reason to drive the way through Baltimore.

Cameron was pleased with Scott's persistence and continued at extraordinary lengths to support his position. Among other things he promptly extended the command of General Patterson to include the whole of Pennsylvania and ordered him to provide military protection for the railroads in the Harrisburg vicinity. In their effort to force open the Northern Central route, Cameron and Scott had the support of Senator David Wilmot of Pennsylvania.[20] Regardless of political or other repercussions, Cameron was determined to keep Northern Central trains running. He ordered Scott to take over operation.

But his hotheaded course was meeting formidable opposition. Lincoln and Governor Curtin of Pennsylvania were against it for political reasons. On military grounds General Patterson disapproved. Thomson thought it unwise, and Felton would have no part of it. Then came an unexpected turn of events which left Cameron quite alone and unsupported. By the time his message reached Scott in Harrisburg on April 22, Scott had realized the futility of Cameron's resolve to open the way through Baltimore by main strength.[21] Converted to the plan of Thomson and Felton to use the Annapolis route, he sent a courier to Cameron: "Secure the road between Annapolis and Washington. I will come and manage it for you if so directed."[22] Cameron promptly accepted his proposal, and on April 26 Scott arrived in Washington and was immediately assigned the job for which he had volunteered.

But the opening of the Annapolis route was not accomplished without resistance. In command of a Massachusetts infantry contingent, General Benjamin F. Butler had left Philadelphia on April 20 for Washington via Annapolis. On completing the water leg of the journey, Butler discovered that Southern sentiment in Maryland was not confined to the city of Baltimore. For several miles west of Annapolis the tracks of the Annapolis & Elk Ridge had been torn up. True to Butler form, he waited neither authority nor orders but immediately took military possession of the road and set his soldiers to reconstructing the track. At the same time the War Department took possession of that portion of the Baltimore & Ohio between Washington and Annapolis Junction. There the United States Military Railroad System was born.

By April 29 rail communication between Washington and Annapolis was restored.[23] Although the track and rolling stock south of Annapolis Junction belonged to the Baltimore & Ohio, no officer of that road was called on to operate it for the War Department. Instead, Simon Cameron placed an officer of the rival Pennsylvania in charge of this all-important Baltimore & Ohio property. Even if he had no purpose other than to serve best the Union cause, it is hard to understand why he preferred Tom Scott to some Baltimore & Ohio man familiar with the line.

As might have been expected, Scott soon ran headlong into trouble. The Baltimore & Ohio withdrew its rolling stock from the Annapolis & Elk Ridge and left him with only such engines and cars as Cameron had trapped south of Annapolis Junction. Scott's appeal to Thomson and Felton to ship in rolling stock brought only small-scale results. His next move was to schedule regular passenger service between Washington and Annapolis and time it to connect with Felton's trains on the Philadelphia, Wilmington & Baltimore. One can speculate whether the Pennsylvania group had in mind to use the emergency as a means to establish a future route to Philadelphia and New York which would by-pass Garrett. In any event, General Patterson put a quick stop to it through an order forbidding the sale of passenger tickets by the military line.[24] Two days later Cameron again took up the cudgel for Scott and ordered Patterson to remove the restriction on passenger traffic.[25]

With some regularity troops and supplies were now flowing into Washington over the Annapolis route, but it remained at best a makeshift arrangement—slow, tedious and wholly inadequate. With military guards posted over its entire length, Cameron decided on May 1 the route was reasonably secure and again turned his attention to the Northern Central and the Baltimore situation. Here he needed Scott's help. In order to relieve him of the burden of the Annapolis line, Cameron called F. Harrison Du Puy, another Pennsylvania executive, and assigned him the task of keeping it going. Arrangements were made to rebuild the Northern Central bridges and tracks north of Baltimore, and Scott's authority in the Cameron program was correspondingly increased.

Undoubtedly the Secretary of War was justified in wishing to reopen the Baltimore route. To assemble and maintain a sizable army in Washington, a line of communication more direct and substantial and with more capacity than the Annapolis line was vital. It was his personal interest in the Northern Central, his neglect of the B.&O. and the vindictiveness of the way he did things that drew a storm of criticism upon him. From the outset his determination to punish Baltimore and all concerned in the rail blockade had been apparent. Defeated in his first attempt, he brought the same spirit to his second effort.

Nowhere did his attitude stand out more clearly than in his relations with Garrett. Handicapped by shortage of rolling stock, yet scheduling passenger service on the Annapolis line, Scott had appealed to Garrett for enough Baltimore & Ohio engines and cars to meet the government requirements. Garrett promptly replied that the government could have all it needed.[26] Particularly in view of the treatment he had been accorded, this has the ring of Union loyalty in it. Garrett, regarding Scott's request as a friendly gesture, sent his master of transportation to see Cameron and Scott and request permission to reopen the Washington branch from Baltimore on a schedule that would not interfere with government use of the road. From Cameron's answer one can draw no other conclusion than that he purposed to humble Garrett as well as Baltimore. On May 2 he curtly notified Garrett

that his request would be approved only when free and uninterrupted transportation of troops, arms, ammunition and
supplies through Baltimore was assured.[27]

Not only did this show ingratitude for Garrett's generous
loan of rolling stock, but it is difficult to see how the government could be served by it. An open road to Baltimore was
essential to break the traffic bottleneck and was part of his
own program. Exactly what influence Thomson was exerting
is left to surmise from the record. As early as April 27 he
expressed to Cameron his trust that Baltimore would soon be
reduced to her allegiance.[28] Later he was to recommend
specific action against the Baltimore & Ohio.

Not content with his rebuff to Garrett, Cameron ordered
General Butler to occupy Relay House and allow no trains to
leave Baltimore. This extended military control of the
Washington branch from Annapolis Junction to the environs
of Baltimore, and operating responsibility was vested in
Scott.[29] Meanwhile repairs on the Northern Central and the
Philadelphia, Wilmington & Baltimore south of the Susquehanna were being rushed to completion. Next, General
Butler moved into Baltimore. Scott went along and established
his office inside the city. On May 13, Northern Central
trains began coming in. At last Cameron had won his fight.
Baltimore was under control of the military with Ben Butler
in command. Garrett's railroad to Washington was in government hands and operated by an officer of the Pennsylvania,
while Virginia soldiers stood unmolested astride the main stem
of the B.&O. at Harper's Ferry. Such was the reward of the
Baltimore & Ohio officers who had risked their lives to carry
Cameron's troops through Baltimore on April 18 and 19.

Into the railroad and telegraph service of the War Department Thomson and Scott had by this time introduced a large
number of their Pennsylvania officers and employees. They
may have been the most able and efficient men available, but
that does not alter the fact that Pennsylvania Railroad men
were riding high in the War Department. Apparently the
acidity of railroad competition was etching a pattern on
preparations to suppress the rebellion. The vital importance

of the B.&O. to the Union cause was receiving scant consideration from these men. Whole regiments of troops were detailed to guard the Pennsylvania, the Northern Central and the P.,W.&B., but nothing was being done to help Garrett recover and maintain control over his main line.

From the beginning the South had seen the significance of the B.&O., and it was fear of its falling into Union hands that had prompted the threats against Garrett and a letter of warning from Governor Letcher of Virginia.[30] General Lee was giving serious consideration to plans for saving it for the South, at the same time admitting they probably couldn't be executed. Even as this went on, Thomson was writing Cameron that "the War Department should at once destroy, if it has not already done so, the bridges on the main stem of the Baltimore and Ohio Railroad as high up as Harper's Ferry."[31] Cameron and Scott had been anxious to fight the way of the Northern Central and the P.,W.&B. through Baltimore, but not a hand was lifted to protect the shortest rail route from Washington to the Ohio Valley and the Northwest. If it was consideration of military safety which prompted the suggestion to destroy the road lest the enemy use it as an approach against the flank and rear of the Union Army, how explain Scott's next move?

It will be remembered that during the previous year Garrett was planning an extension of his Washington branch across the Potomac to join the Orange & Alexandria and form an all-rail line between the North and the South. The imminence of war halted this and left it for Scott to accomplish at government expense and to his own credit. On the theory that the army at Washington would ultimately invade Virginia, Scott procured authority to build a military railroad from the Baltimore & Ohio terminal in Washington across the Potomac to the Alexandria, Loudoun & Hampshire, which, with the connecting Orange & Alexandria, would at the proper time be taken and used as an invasion route. To this no objection was raised, though of course the enemy might reverse the procedure and use Scott's railroad to attack Washington.

Following Butler's occupation of Relay House on May 5 and the investment of Baltimore a week later, the Baltimore & Ohio was permitted to operate a limited and strictly supervised schedule on both the Washington branch and main line. It may well have been true that the attitude of Baltimore businessmen had much to do with relaxing the government restrictions on Garrett. Business in Baltimore had suffered intensely from the rail blockade. Much more grief had come to industry through the destruction of the rail connections under city orders than from Cameron's punitive policy. The businessmen took the lead in restoring rail traffic into and out of the city. Perhaps Butler and Scott thought it wise to make some concessions to Garrett in return for support in opening the other lines. It would clearly not be good policy to be too tough on him as long as the Virginia troops were, at least for the moment, letting his long trains of steam coal for the United States Navy pass Harper's Ferry unmolested.[32] The Navy would need that coal.

During the early summer and until the Bull Run offensive was mounted, the Northern railroad system continued, with ever-increasing efficiency, to play the role assigned it in the mobilization of a great army. Whatever that first army suffered from lack of food, munitions and supplies was in no way attributable to the railroads. With commendable promptness they hauled men and munitions, food and forage to whatever destination they were consigned, whenever called on. If the army went into the Bull Run campaign inadequately equipped, the fault could not be traced to lack of transportation.[33] Except for the amateurish bungling of the Baltimore scene, the première of the great drama of railroads at war was a performance worthy of sustained applause.

While the move for the defense of the capital held the center of the stage, not all locomotives had their headlights turned toward the east or beamed on the points of assembly and training. Some were pulling troop and supply trains across the Illinois prairies toward St. Louis where General Lyon's army was preparing to hold Missouri against Secessionist militia. In that railroad activity there was nothing remarkable except the speed and facility with which it was accomplished. Ten years earlier the move would have entailed weeks of slogging through spring mud and the dragging of long wagon trains over bottomless roads.

One bit of railroad action in the Northwest during this period deserves specific notice. Cairo, Illinois, situated at the confluence of the Ohio and Mississippi rivers, was the southern terminus of the comparatively new Illinois Central. Southernmost point reached by any Northern railroad, Cairo was to become a vital point in army operations in the West. Southwestern Illinois had its sympathizers with the South who were as full of venom as any mob in the streets of Baltimore. Warning came to Governor Yates that these partisans of rebellion were preparing to destroy the Illinois Central bridge across Big Muddy Creek in the southern part of the state. The railroad promptly took the initiative and organized a swift movement to prevent destruction of its property, keep its lines open and protect Cairo.

About midnight of April 21, the day on which Butler took control of the Annapolis & Elk Ridge, a special train with a pilot engine running ahead pulled out of Chicago. By arrangement with Governor Yates, the special had aboard 595 Illinois militiamen under command of Brigadier General R. K. Swift, forty-six artillery horses and four six-pound guns. It was a heavy train for that period. Many stops were made to post patrols at important bridges. With their horses and guns, the men not assigned to bridge patrols went on to Cairo. Despite the delays, the run was completed in approximately twenty-four hours, having covered more than 360 miles. These troops, forerunners of the thousands who would follow to form Grant's army of invasion, were the first to occupy the strategic point at the mouth of the Ohio.[34]

CHAPTER V

CONCENTRATION IN VIRGINIA

In the South there was no such grand première of the military railroad drama as in the North. No counterpart of Thomson, Felton or Scott was called to the Confederate service. No regiment of state troops engaged in a wild race with other regiments to be first on the scene of army concentration. The business of preparation and mobilization of troops was totally different. In his *Story of the Confederacy*, Robert S. Henry describes the early military scene in the South:

While in the North there were regimental camps, the South was dotted at first with the encampments of little companies. The courthouses, the schoolhouses, the scattered crossroads villages became recruiting centers. Every county had its company, many more than one. There were the old social-military organizations, brilliant companies with their bright and shining uniforms—tail coats, braided trousers, cross-belts shakos and busbies and fancy head-gear, buttons of gilt, white gloves on drill and duty; there were the new organizations commanded by young lawyers and planters and merchants, with no uniforms, no guns, nothing but martial ardor.[1]

Except in a few such cases as the Harper's Ferry and Norfolk occupations, no long lines of cars waited to rush these companies, old or new, to great concentration centers; no Simon Cameron ordered them to assemble by states. No precious railroad iron was worn out hauling unprepared troops; no irreplaceable locomotives were racked to pieces dragging tonnage hundreds of miles to feed and equip thousands of idle and unarmed soldiers.

Not all of this advantage may be credited to wisdom or

foresight. The Confederacy was new, and the government at Montgomery had not yet developed in its member states the spirit of confidence and obedient loyalty enjoyed by the United States Government at Washington. State sovereignty was as rampant in military affairs as in politics, and the states were reluctant to transfer the control of their troops to the Confederacy. Although his state had not yet officially joined, Governor Harris of Tennessee effectively expressed this attitude when, on May 1, he agreed to send three regiments to rendezvous at Lynchburg, Virginia, provided they were armed and provisioned there and remained the troops of Tennessee subject to his recall if and when needed at home.[2] Willing though the leaders were to support the newly formed Confederacy, each state approached the conflict determined to use its own men primarily to protect its own borders against invasion by "Lincoln soldiers." So it happened that the early military demands on the railroads of the South were largely for local and short-haul service, the sort of thing for which they were best prepared.

Gradually the Confederate leaders came to recognize that the first major stand in defense of the whole South must be made in Virginia. Since April 23, 1861, Robert E. Lee had been in command of all Virginia troops, and such was his reputation as man and soldier that the Confederate government wisely assigned to him all Confederate troops sent into the state. It follows therefore that Lee's preparations for the defense of Virginia largely set the pattern for military use of the railroads in the days before Bull Run.[3]

At least two wars ahead of his time, Lee refused to mobilize troops more rapidly than they could be prepared for the field or in greater numbers than the immediate defense problems required. Otherwise he left the militia in small units to be trained and equipped in their own camps near their homes.

Perhaps he remembered with what speed and facility the Baltimore & Ohio Railroad had carried him and his detachment of United States Marines to the scene of John Brown's raid on Harper's Ferry in 1859. At any rate, he seemed quickly to grasp the relation of the railroads to the task of defense.

More deeply concerned over the vulnerability of Virginia to attack from the United States Navy than over the danger of immediate invasion by a Union army, he first set about completing Governor Letcher's program of using the heavy guns captured at Norfolk to set up batteries on the Rappahannock, York and James. Initiated by Letcher immediately on the abandonment of the Norfolk Navy Yard by its Union garrison, this project was under way when Lee took command. Instantly he was plagued by one of the great weaknesses of the railroads of the South. At Petersburg no track connected the road from Norfolk with the road to Richmond. In Richmond no track linked the road from Petersburg to the road to Fredericksburg on the Rappahannock or to the York River line. Although time seemed the crucial element of the maneuver, at Petersburg soldiers, guns, ammunition and equipment had to be unloaded, moved from line to line and reloaded, and at Richmond the process repeated. Later Lee would remind the Virginia Convention of the precious time lost.

Because of its strategic value, its dry dock and the machinery at the Navy Yard, he decided to hold Norfolk if possible. Twenty-two miles to the southwest, the Norfolk & Petersburg Railroad crossed the Nansemond River at Suffolk. To that point the Nansemond was navigable for light craft which could enter its mouth at will from Hampton Roads. Lee foresaw with what ease the Union gunboats might ascend the river, take Suffolk, put a landing force ashore, cut the railroad and take Norfolk in reverse. Such an operation would also cut the Seaboard & Roanoke, which ran through Suffolk from Norfolk to Weldon, North Carolina. With both roads cut, not only would Norfolk be isolated, but North Carolina would lie wide open to invasion along the line of the Seaboard & Roanoke. To guard against such a possibility, he sent troops to protect the railroads at Suffolk until batteries could be planted on the banks of the Nansemond.

This done, a question arose—what should be done at Harper's Ferry? Strategically it was for the Union a gateway to the Shenandoah; for the South a bastion on the Potomac. The Union attempt to destroy the arsenal there had been none too successful and much valuable machinery remained set up and intact. Nothing was more needed by the South than machinery and shops with which to arm her soldiers. The machinery should be moved deeper into Virginia, to Richmond perhaps, but that would be hampered by another railroad weakness and it would take a lot of time. South to Winchester there was only the feeble little Winchester & Potomac, rough, lightly constructed and possessing only two engines. This line ended at Winchester. The Manassas Gap line approached it only as far as Strasburg. Between Winchester and Strasburg lay a stretch of eighteen miles with no railroad at all. Moving the machinery would be a slow business. Obviously much could be gained by operating the machinery where it stood as long as Harper's Ferry could be held. In addition to all this, maintaining a foothold on the Potomac there gave the Virginia troops a measure of control over train operation on the main line of the coveted B.&O. Impossible though it might be to defend Harper's Ferry against troops moving on it from Pennsylvania through Hagerstown and Cumberland, Lee decided to reinforce the original militia companies Captain Imboden had led up the Manassas Gap road that morning of April 18, hang on and make guns with all possible speed. Unless Harper's Ferry were surprised, the machinery could be moved at a more convenient time. This difficult and vexatious assignment he gave to Colonel Thomas J. Jackson, a little-known professor at Virginia Military Institute, who was to become a military immortal as "Stonewall."

Lee immediately perceived that as soon as Union troops crossed the Potomac, the Manassas Gap Railroad from Manassas to Strasburg would provide an easy approach to the rear of Jackson's command and a means of cutting him off from reinforcements and supplies. Lee could not believe his former commander, General Winfield Scott, would long neglect to avail himself of such an opportunity. Accordingly he called up another group of militia units and sent them to guard the railroad junction at Manassas. This was the beginning of the famed Manassas Line, a concentration of military manpower and matériel which was to grow in depth and importance until it included the whole of Beauregard's army of Bull Run.

His speedy action with respect to Suffolk and Manassas was by no means the only evidence of Lee's early appreciation of the railroads in the defense of Virginia. As a military instrument they might be new but Marse Robert was rapidly catching on. On April 24 he instructed General Ruggles, commander of militia on the Potomac below Mount Vernon, to station his troops at suitable points to command the Richmond, Fredericksburg & Potomac, a direct line from the Potomac to the Rappahannock and thence to Richmond.[4] On the same day he asked General Cocke, in command at Alexandria, to select points on or near the railroads leading to Alexandria where reinforcements assigned to him should be sent.[5]

With the men and matériel available, Lee had done his best to prepare against attack from the Union Navy via the Virginia rivers. What he could do to prevent invasion through the Shenandoah via Harper's Ferry was done. He reasoned that by the time General Scott could mount a frontal attack toward the Rappahannock, his troops in training would be ready. No one knew better than Robert E. Lee how long and wearisome would be the task of making a fieldworthy army of the unorganized thousands of militia and raw recruits the railroads were pouring into Washington.

But his task was far from done. Far away toward the Ohio hung a cloud which he did not know how to dissipate. No matter how effectively Virginia was defended against the approach of the Union Navy, and no matter how well prepared to meet the Union Army of the East, none of this would be enough should another army pour in on him from the Northwest over the Baltimore & Ohio Railroad. To guard against such a contingency seemed an almost hopeless task because of Union sentiment in northwestern Virginia through which the road passed. Although recruiting of local companies was moving rapidly ahead in the four military districts into which the state was divided, not enough troops were as yet properly armed and equipped to seize and hold the railroad from Martinsburg to Grafton. Even if the troops could have been made available without dangerously weakening the forces at Manassas and Harper's Ferry, the political situation would have made the undertaking perilous. Precisely as Lincoln sought to appease Maryland and save it for the Union, Virginia sought to appease the disaffected counties, lest they draw away and form a new Union state.

At the end of April conditions had not improved but in Richmond hope survived. To an increasing number of influential persons the importance of the B.&O. in the defense of the South became clear, and the pressure on Lee to do something to save it increased.

J. M. Mason, Virginia's Commissioner to Maryland, wrote:

The preservation of this road, I should presume, will be all-important to the Federal power and of correlative importance to us to have it in our power—if unable to hold it, to break it up at points where it will be impracticable to repair or restore it in any convenient time. The numerous tunnels through the mountains, the numerous bridges across the river, and especially the expensive and complicated viaduct along the Cheat River in the Alleghaney Mountains, furnish abundant places for such irremediable damage, provided we are in advance of the invaders. Nor would any large force be required, provided it was well distributed and under competent commanders.[6]

Still fearful, however, of the political effect of sending men from the eastern counties into the disaffected section, Lee saw nothing to do except appeal to stanch Southerners there to recruit their own force to protect the railroad. This was the policy adopted, but how ineffectual it proved and how quickly it led to battle and Virginia's first serious military defeat will soon appear.

Anticipating the movement of the Union Army into

Virginia, Lee began early in May to take account of the railroad situation should Alexandria have to be evacuated. From
Alexandria northwest for some forty miles to Leesburg, the
Alexandria, Loudoun & Hampshire paralleled the Potomac
and lay exposed to the first shock of any Union crossing
below Harper's Ferry. Colonel Terrett, commanding at
Alexandria, was instructed to make the rolling stock secure.
Again the problem of connecting track rose to vex the
defense. It was Lee's suggestion that Terrett work out a plan
by which a temporary track could be laid to connect with
the Orange & Alexandria and thus permit the rolling stock to
be run out at night.[7] Whether this was accomplished does not
appear, but on May 24, the day Alexandria was invested by
the Federals, Lee ordered Colonel Hutton at Leesburg to
destroy all bridges on the A.,L.&H. as far toward Alexandria
as possible.[8] As early as May 2, General Cocke had been
instructed to co-operate with the officers of the railroads
entering Alexandria with a view to securing the rolling stock
and effectually breaking up the roads themselves in event the
Virginians should be driven out.[9] Thus began the policy,
later employed by both sides, of using the railroads as long
as tenable, then destroying them to prevent their use by the
enemy.

On May 6 Jackson was instructed to destroy the B.&O.
bridge at Harper's Ferry in the event he became certain of
the approach of Union troops.[10] On the same date Ruggles
at Fredericksburg was notified that measures must be taken
effectually to destroy the railroad approach to the R.,F.&P.
wharf at Aquia Creek should he be driven from that point.[11]
If a retreat should become necessary, Lee meant to leave no
railroad intact over which the enemy could pursue.

Meanwhile recruiting went rapidly ahead in the several
Southern states. Governors, acting independently each of the
other and of the Confederate government, continued to dispatch contingents of their own state troops to guard their own
coastal cities. At the same time and from as far away as
Louisiana, company and regimental units began to move

toward Richmond and the Virginia defense areas Lee had marked out.

With this movement the military inadequacy of the South's rail facilities began to reveal itself distinctly. Roads which had their terminations at such important points as Lynchbur̴g, Savannah, Augusta, Charlotte, Raleigh and Petersburg had no track connecting with other roads terminating in the same cities. Troops, supplies and equipment had to be unloaded, carted across town and reloaded in order to continue their journeys. It was inevitable that congestion should result. Often it was aggravated by the difference in track gauges—for example, at Lynchburg.[12] No sooner had the larger units begun to move and this congestion develop than the shortage of rolling stock, particularly of engines, became apparent. Tracks began to suffer from traffic heavier than they were built to carry. This was especially true of the all-important but new line up the Tennessee Valley from Chattanooga to Lynchburg. As part of the South's only east-west trunk line, it could not be spared. The burden of heavy military traffic began to take early toll of its lightly constructed and still unsettled track.[13] Fortunately for the Confederacy, gradual mobilization and concentration offered time and opportunity in which to make such adjustments as were feasible.

Annoyed by the delay due to lack of linkage track between railroads, Lee wrote the Convention of Virginia urging that ". . . proper and easy connections of the several railroads passing through or terminating in Richmond or Petersburg should be made as promptly as possible."[14] In support he called attention to the delay in transport of guns and ammunition from Norfolk and reminded the Convention that in future situations the loss of time might be infinitely more serious. Already he had approved a plan to build a connecting link between Keysville on the Richmond & Danville line and Clarksville on the Roanoke route. With prophetic vision he said of this proposal: "It would afford not only an additional means of communications between Richmond and the South, but, in the event of the obstruction of one road, the other might be kept open for travel and transportation. Contingencies might occur to render this a matter of highest importance."[15]

Responsibility for the trouble Lee was trying to correct cannot be laid at the door of the Southern railroad management. Before 1861, as has been explained, the difficulty lay in the cities' refusal to let connecting tracks be laid within their limits. Once the war was on, the problem became more complicated. In response to the letter General Lee addressed to the Virginia Convention, P. V. Daniel, Jr., president of the Richmond, Fredericksburg & Potomac, wrote to Jefferson Davis. He explained that the railroads were well aware of the need, but even though the state should now require the cities to permit the construction of the tracks, the railroads were no longer financially prepared to meet the cost of the extensions. He pointed out that the Union had confiscated the Potomac River boats of his own line and this, with the blockade of the river, had seriously impaired both assets and earning power of the R.,F.&P.[16]

To Daniel's credit, it must be said that two months before he wrote this letter he had furnished Lee the copy for a proposed circular to be printed and sent to the president of each railroad in the South. In the preparation of the circular and his letter of transmittal he displayed much wisdom and foresight. He stated that the military authorities were running engines and trains over his road from Fredericksburg to the Potomac with unnecessary frequency, thus ". . . wearing out our engines which should, especially now, when others cannot be procured, be carefully husbanded." He added, "The hourly danger of collision and a consequent disabling of the engines and road require the cessation of this practice." In the circular he proposed seven rules to be promulgated. They covered directions for keeping rolling stock, not in necessary transit, removed from points likely to be attacked; keeping spare engines at all times under steam at proper emergency points; guarding of tracks and bridges with men instructed in the art of demolition in case of reverses; crippling of engines about to be captured; increasing both the number and strength of box and flatcars; and rules for safety in train operation.[17] Lee immediately indorsed the circular. Daniel may not have been the first to comprehend the emergency but he was the first to do something about it.

On the whole the railroad executives of the South were quite as alert and responsive to the duties imposed on them by the war as those of the North. In the first burst of enthusiasm most of the roads offered their services to the Confederate government free of charge, thus disclosing their total failure to conceive the nature and extent of the burdens war would lay on them.[18] Very quickly, however, they learned how completely they were to be engaged in military service and that they could not maintain that service without revenue from the government. Late in April the presidents of the roads met in Montgomery and agreed on a rate of two cents per mile for hauling a soldier, and half the regular tariff schedules for the transport of government freight. Then they made a mistake which was to cost them and the Confederate cause dearly. Perhaps there was no other way. They agreed to accept government bonds in payment for services.[19]

There is credible evidence that President Davis came rather early to appreciate the military potential of the railroads, but with equal clarity it seems that during the period of mobilization and training he did little to guarantee either the development or the continuity of their performance. One can only assume that his confidence in early victory blinded him for the time to the weaknesses of the railroad facilities of the South. Later he was to exert himself vigorously toward making such extensions and improvements in track and service as conditions would permit.

Meantime, from mid-April to early July, the process moved steadily forward of building an army of the South to defend at arms the right of the confederated states to secede from the Union and create a new nation on their own soil. Slowly, deliberately and with caution the great gray commander in Virginia disposed that growing army to meet the challenge offered by the vast assembly of Union troops at Washington. Virginia's own troops were supplemented by militia companies which came up from the Carolinas over the Seaboard & Roanoke to defend Norfolk; by small units coming over the Petersburg line to serve wherever Lee chose to place them. Units from Louisiana and Mississippi rode the long rails to Lynchburg and waited there. Later, regiments from Alabama, Georgia and Tennessee came in over the frail track which followed the valley from Chattanooga to where the Roanoke River breaks through the Blue Ridge. Gradually this process went on until thousands of soldiers camped on Virginia ground and waited orders from Richmond, to which city the capital had been moved from Montgomery.

At last McDowell moved out to face the Manassas Line. Confederate soldiers about Richmond entrained on the cars of the R.,F.&P. and moved up on the right of the defensive position. Others boarded Virginia Central trains and came to Manassas via Gordonsville. Those concentrated about Lynchburg and Charlottesville were hastily picked up by the Orange & Alexandria and carried to Beauregard's command. On that line more than 20,000 awaited McDowell's attack. Immediately in their rear lay Manassas Junction where the railroad yards contained a large depot of supplies. To it Manassas Gap trains brought abundant food from the fertile Shenandoah Valley. Back and forth between the ever-swelling depot and Gordonsville, Orange & Alexandria cars were shuttled, constantly bearing rations, munitions and supplies. Up from Richmond came the R.,F.&P. trains unloading their army freight at Aquia Creek, where Holmes commanded on the Potomac.

Three railroads brought food in great plenty. Such arms, ammunition and supplies as were available, they brought from Richmond and the Deep South and laid down within easy reach of the first great army of the Gray. Well fed but impatient, the soldiers waited until the morning of July 21 when the scream of a Parrott shell from across Bull Run and a cloud of dust rising from the Sudley Spring road told them the time had come.

CHAPTER VI

RAILROADS IN THE WESTERN VIRGINIA CAMPAIGN

An early clash at arms for control of the main line of the Baltimore & Ohio Railroad was inevitable. From Wheeling to Harper's Ferry it remained for a time the military deadline between North and South. In May 1861 the tide of sentiment in Maryland and northwestern Virginia was running strongly against the Confederacy. Well understanding the political advantage which would fall to the North if the South struck the first blow to control the road by force, the Union command could afford to wait. But Richmond dared not wait too long. So great an asset to her cause could not be allowed to slip from her grasp without a fight.

From the time he took command at Harper's Ferry, Jackson had respected the wish of Virginia to maintain a policy of liberality toward the B.&O. and its management. Until the middle of May long trains of coal continued unmolested to thunder down the hill and across the long bridge on their way to the Chesapeake. Never an appeaser and always fully conscious of the danger that Union troops might seize control of the unguarded road, Jackson chafed under the restraint of the liberal policy. He was a field commander and well understood the prerogatives and breadth of discretion attached to his station. In due time and without provoking a fight he exercised his freedom of action in ingenious fashion to accomplish a remarkable feat.

Toward the middle of the month he quietly extended his domination of the road to include some fifty miles. From Point of Rocks, thirteen miles east of the river, to Cherry Run, thirty-two miles west of the bridge, the line was double-tracked. It was this vital section which the sly hand of

73

Jackson soon began to finger a bit imperiously. His first interference with operation seemed more the act of a peevish martinet than of a shrewd military tactician. He notified Garrett that the incessant noise of his coal trains rolling down the hill at night, and his snorting engines dragging long strings of empties back toward Cumberland over the westbound track, interfered with the sleep and rest of his soldiers. Hereafter, said Jackson testily, the disturbing movement of freight trains must be confined to daylight hours.

Afraid to disobey the exasperating order lest something worse be visited on them by this V.M.I. professor, the railroad officials yielded to it and handled the resulting congestion as best they could. Little did Mr. Garrett suspect the nature of the cleverly concealed trap toward which he was being led! No sooner was this daylight schedule in effect than the grasp of Jackson's hand suddenly tightened. A second order was dispatched to Garrett. The racket set up by the daylong movement of clattering freight trains interfered with the training routine of Jackson's men and would have to be stopped at once. In the future all freight trains must pass Harper's Ferry between the hours of 11:00 A.M. and 1:00 P.M. With this peremptory and upsetting order, too, the railroad officials attempted to comply. As long as Jackson bestrode the bridge, nothing remained except to do his bidding. Spaced at the shortest intervals possible, one loaded train followed another across the bridge while strings of empties steamed west on the opposite track.

On May 23 Garrett discovered the real purpose of Jackson's seemingly eccentric orders governing the movement of trains. Festus P. Summers tells the story briefly and well:

Then suddenly Jackson posted his actors for the climax. On May 22, 1861, he directed Captain John D. Imboden to cross the Potomac next day and occupy Point of Rocks, the eastern end of the double track. Imboden was to permit all westbound trains to pass while none were to proceed east. At precisely twelve o'clock, noon, he was to close the line. Imboden followed instructions to the letter.

The crafty Jackson dispatched a like order to Colonel Kenton Harper who, now in Confederate service, commanded the Fifth Virginia Infantry at Martinsburg. From 11 to 12 o'clock on May 23, 1861, a long stream of coal and freight cars entered the eastbound track at Cherry Run but none passed west. Then, at noon, sharp, Harper closed the road and the scoop was complete. In the single hour the Virginians had bottled fifty-six locomotives and more than three hundred cars. Within the limits of their operations also were the railroad shops at Martinsburg with costly equipment. All were now held for the Confederacy.[1]

Sooner or later all of Lee's generals came to understand the handicap laid on their cause by inability to manufacture locomotives in the South, but from the beginning its seriousness was obvious to Jackson. Political repercussions in Maryland and western Virginia were not his major concern. He was a soldier and his army would need engines—many more engines than the South possessed. Mr. Garrett's railroad had plenty and they were of the best. Let others fret about politics! Fifty-six locomotives might not again be had for the taking.

Now that the game was bagged, how to get it home? Other than the little Winchester & Potomac, no line to the south tapped the B.&O. within the limits of Confederate occupation. Too light to handle the heavier engines Jackson held captive, the Winchester road could contribute little. Besides, there was that eighteen-mile gap between Winchester and the next railhead. Quickly Jackson selected four small engines at Harper's Ferry, shifted them to the adjoining bridge spans across the mouth of the Shenandoah River and ran them off to Winchester. A number of good cars were taken by the same route, while most of the heavy engines and the remaining cars were concentrated about the yards in Martinsburg to wait developments.

About that time Patterson's army began to stir. The high command at Richmond decided the time had come to evacuate Harper's Ferry. Jackson was ordered to destroy all property at the Ferry and retire to Martinsburg. On the night

of June 14, fire and gunpowder sent the great B.&O. bridge
sprawling into the Potomac. With it went the spans across
the Shenandoah, and from the ruins one of the biggest engines
taken in the scoop plunged to the river bed. The liberal
policy was at an end, superseded by a policy of destruction.
Henceforth control of the Baltimore & Ohio was to be determined with sword and gun.

Not long after his retirement to Martinsburg, Jackson
was ordered to destroy all railroad property there and withdraw toward Winchester. Reluctant but with soldierly
obedience, he assembled the precious rolling stock taken by
his brilliant coup, and to it and the great shops he applied the
torch.[2] With what sadness and disappointment he watched
the flames take from his hands the rich gift he had prepared
for the Confederacy, any student of Stonewall Jackson's
career will fully appreciate. In a letter to his wife he said:
"It was a sad work, but I had my orders and my duty was to
obey."[3] The account of a newspaper reporter who visited the
scene two weeks later discloses how thoroughly Jackson
obeyed.

For the *National Intelligencer* he wrote:

All along the railroad were scattered coal cars in long lines,
with the coal still burning, having been set on fire by the
"noble and chivalric." They had kindled huge fires around
them, burning all the wood work and a great deal of the iron.
They were all fine iron cars, holding about twenty tons each.
Here and there the road led above them, and, looking down
we could see the inside—a mass of red hot coals. Some small
bridges had been burnt with the cars on them, and giving way,
the cars were left piled one on another in the small streams
below, all battered and bent. We counted the line of locomotives that had been burnt (forty-one or forty-two in all)
red and blistered with heat. The destruction is fearful to con-
template.[4]

Jackson's distress did not arise from any qualms about the
destruction of B.&O. property. What bothered him was the
failure to get those fine engines and cars rolling on Con-

federate tracks before they had to be burned to prevent their falling into Federal hands.

At the same time events of great consequence were taking place on the western end of the B.&O. main line. Lee's policy of recruiting men from the northwestern counties in sufficient numbers to hold the railroad was put into effect. To Major Alonzo Loring he allotted the task of recruiting in the Wheeling area to protect the Ohio River terminus. In his letter to Loring under date of April 29, his liberal policy with respect to the railroad is made clear. "It is desirable," writes Lee, "that the business operations of the company and peaceful travel shall not be interrupted, but afforded protection."[5]

The next day he ordered Major Francis M. Boykin, Jr., of Weston, to enlist a force to cover the railroad junction at Grafton. He, too, was cautioned not to interfere with train operation but to make clear to the public his purpose of protecting the road for the benefit of Virginia and Maryland.[6]

Loring and Boykin found their assignments both unpopular and fruitless. The people of these river and hill counties wanted no part of the Confederacy. Their hearts were with their neighbors across the river and only a few could be persuaded to enlist. On the contrary, they urged Ohio troops to cross the river and take possession of their only railroad.

Until May 4, Lee waited and hoped in vain for results. Then he ordered Colonel George A. Porterfield of Jackson's command to cross the mountains and take charge in the Grafton area. His instructions called for posting a regiment at Moundsville, a short distance below Wheeling. He was to send a second regiment to guard the terminal of the Parkersburg branch at the river. Three more regiments he was to hold near Grafton Junction, both to guard the line there and to serve as a reserve if either of the other two regiments ran into trouble.[7] His orders had been based on the supposition that a considerable force, at least five regiments, had been recruited in the area. When he arrived at Grafton he was disgusted to find not a single soldier in sight. A few small companies were scattered about the country, but he could discover no unit as big as a battalion, let alone even one regiment. A little experiment convinced him the men could not be recruited in the neighborhood. He wired back to the capital for some soldiers.

Across the river young George B. McClellan, in command of the Ohio troops, was studying developments in the Virginia border counties and along the railroad. Governor Dennison had overestimated the progress Porterfield's subordinates were making in collecting recruits and he had misinterpreted Lee's purpose and objective. He was afraid the Virginians were planning to cross the river and make a sudden foray against the Ohio river counties. To forestall them he urged McClellan to take the initiative and cross to the Virginia side. At the same time messages came to McClellan from Wheeling and other communities near by that he and his men would be warmly welcomed if they would cross over. The young railroad executive turned major general was not sure. He worried about the genuineness of the invitations and, like Lee, feared that the presence of troops from another region might turn local sentiment away from them. He kept postponing going over and taking possession of the railroad before it was firmly in the hands of the enemy.

Lee was at last convinced that Union sentiment in the western part of the state was quite as rampant as reported, and recruiting there all but hopeless. He decided to reinforce Porterfield with troops from the Shenandoah. He had waited too long—no longer than McClellan, of course, but with an even start all the advantage lay with the man from Ohio. From the beginning McClellan had been enamored of a plan to march an army into the heart of Virginia by way of the Great Kanawha Valley. In preparation he concentrated his troops at points along the river opposite Wheeling, Parkersburg and the mouth of the Great Kanawha. Porterfield mistakenly foresaw in this movement an advance on his position, and, knowing the little force at his command could not possibly protect either branch of the railroad beyond Grafton, he acted without waiting for reinforcements to reach him.

At about the time Jackson was trapping rolling stock on the eastern end of the line, Porterfield dispatched squads to destroy bridges on the main stem near Wheeling and near Parkersburg on the branch.[8] Since he could not furnish these tracks the protection he was sent out to give them, he would delay as far as possible their being used to drive Jackson from Harper's Ferry. Irate Union men in the area where Porterfield was operating immediately informed McClellan. He put off his plans for the Kanawha campaign. The enemy was destroying a vital railroad which the North could not afford to lose and he must be driven from its line at once. Colonel B. F. Kelley, at Wheeling with a regiment of Unionists recruited from the vicinity, was nearest the scene. In the evening of May 26 McClellan wired him to move his command along the railroad line, drop guards at the bridges most likely to be attacked and repair those already damaged.[9] At the same time he ordered Colonel Steedman to cross the Ohio, occupy Parkersburg, then advance by rail toward Grafton, leaving adequate guards at Parkersburg and at bridges along the route.[10] Kelley got out swiftly, repaired the bridges on the main line and reached Grafton at 2:30 P.M., May 30. Steedman moved more slowly. Delayed in repairing the damaged bridges on the Parkersburg branch, he did not reach Grafton until Kelley had gone on in pursuit of Porterfield, who had retired to Philippi, some thirty miles south of the railroad.[11]

With the junction at Grafton and both lines of track west of it in his possession, McClellan set out to capture or destroy the Confederate forces in western Virginia. To that end both branches of the railroad were employed to concentrate a substantial body of Ohio and Indiana troops in the neighborhood of Grafton. Meanwhile Lee sent General Robert S. Garnett to supersede Porterfield, and hurried reinforcements over the Staunton Turnpike toward Beverly, south of Philippi, to which point Porterfield had again retired to take up a defensive position. From an affair of bridge-burning by the one side and repair and protection by the other, a full-sized military campaign was developing.

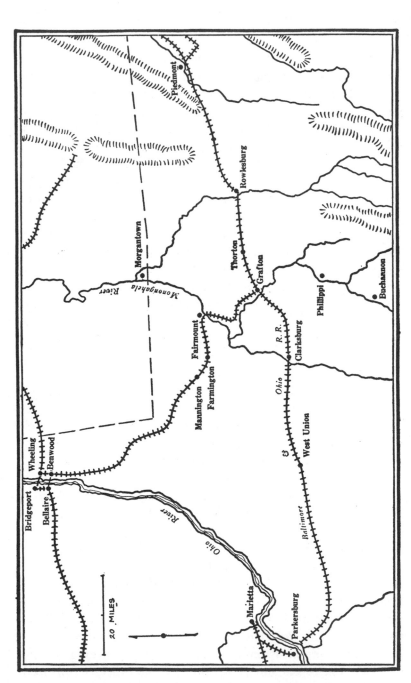

THE WHEELING-PARKERSBURG CUT-OFF ON THE B. & O.

The speedy concentration of McClellan's regiments at Grafton had been accomplished through the use of the railroads. As long as they remained upon those tracks, his troops could be easily fed and supplied. But to strike out through the rugged country south of the railroad to engage Garnett involved quite a different problem in logistics. Not only would McClellan be as dependent on the rails as ever, but he would have to supplement rail transportation by an ever-lengthening wagon haul. Besides, to move his army away from the railroad would expose the track to sabotage by hostile elements in the community as well as by raiding parties from Garnett's force, which lay forty miles to the south. To guard against such contingencies, he distributed detachments at vulnerable points on both lines between Grafton and the Ohio. East of the junction the guard was extended as far as Rowlesburg where the complicated Cheat River viaduct presented the most inviting spot for disabling sabotage west of Harper's Ferry.[12]

So concerned was McClellan with protection of the railroad that forty-eight companies were detached for the duty with Brigadier General Charles W. Hill in command.[13] To Hill he wrote:

The Commanding General . . . has intrusted to you the most important duty next to his own in this territory, viz; that of securing the base of his operations and line of retreat. At any cost—that of your last man—you will preserve the Cheat River line, Grafton, and the line thence to Wheeling. On this depends the entire success of the plan of operations.[14]

Thus, in the first offensive of the war, railroads took their place at the top of the list of essential factors in campaign planning. To McClellan a high evaluation of the railroad seemed to come instinctively and without effort. Strange, indeed, that in the months ahead he should be obliged to learn anew the lesson he recited so perfectly as an obscure commander when the war was new!

How, during the month of June, McClellan and Garnett

fought some lively skirmishes and minor battles in the rough terrain about Beverly, Laurel Hill and Rich Mountain can be read in any comprehensive history. All the action took place thirty miles or more south of the railroad and the details form no part of a railroad record. Except for the uninterrupted transport of supplies to McClellan's base, railroad operations did not again become significant until after Garnett's defeat.

In his high rating of the importance of the Baltimore & Ohio to this campaign, McClellan was not alone. In Richmond another commander, now on the defensive in fact as well as in policy, quickly appraised the new situation arising from Union possession of the western end of the great trunk line. From the outset Lee was disturbed by the possibility of an army from the Northwest coming east over the B.&O. to attack the Shenandoah in co-operation with the forces concentrated at Washington. In McClellan's campaign he saw this danger increase. As long as the railroad remained under Union control west of Jackson's command, there would be little to prevent McClellan from sending a strong force to join Patterson's army which lay at Chambersburg.

Hope of retaining the western part of the road for the Confederacy was gone. Nothing remained but to destroy it if possible, and chances even for doing that were slipping away. During the latter part of June, Garnett was reporting at great length the difficulties confronting him in his attempts to reach it at any point where a break would result in any serious delay.[15] He, too, had selected the Cheat River bridge as his most important objective if only he could discover a way to get to it. Not only was Richmond resigned to the demolition of the road, but it urged Garnett to strike if possible where repairs would be most difficult and require the most time. On July 1, Lee wrote him a letter as pregnant with railroad awareness as were McClellan's instructions to General Hill. "The rupture of the railroad at Cheat River would be worth to us an army," said Lee.[16]

Great as was his concern about the Baltimore & Ohio, the safety of another railroad was much in Lee's mind as McClellan pressed Garnett. He did not share Garnett's view that the Federal forces would not attempt to move farther into Virginia. On the contrary, he thought it McClellan's purpose to defeat the little force gathered about Beverly, then push on as far as Staunton.[17] Garnett was warned to make every effort to halt the drive, for, should he fail, there would be little to prevent McClellan reaching the Shenandoah, cutting the vital Virginia Central and thus early in the day working a major disaster on the South. Unknown to Lee, General Scott had averted this risk by ordering McClellan not to advance too far and outrun his communications.[18]

On July 11, Garnett's troops were swept from their stronghold on Rich Mountain and his defeat became conclusive. To avoid capture or annihilation of his army he started a hasty retreat over the Staunton Turnpike. Erroneously informed that McClellan had occupied Beverly and thus cut off that way of escape, he reversed his column and struck for the only other open route out of the valley. Some fifty miles northeast of Beverly the impassable mountain range which lay between him and safety dropped off abruptly. If he could turn the nose of that mountain spur while the route was still open, he could reach the cover of the Shenandoah forces. To succeed he must travel a road which for a short distance lay less than fifteen miles south of the B.&O. track east of Oakland, Maryland. Whether he grasped the significance of that fact remains unknown for he did not live to make a report.

Quickly divining Garnett's plan of escape, McClellan became the first field commander to attempt the use of a railroad in combat maneuver. He sent a dispatch to General Hill, ordering him to pick up his railroad guards by special trains and hurry them forward to intercept the fleeing column before it could pass the mountain and turn eastward.[19] In telegraphed orders to his regimental commanders, Hill designated Oakland as the point of assembly. The distance from Grafton to Oakland, forty-seven miles, was no greater than that which Garnett's men had to march. The situation presented an opportunity over which McClellan with good reason grew enthusiastic. Had it come later in the war, a brilliant success might have been achieved, but in July 1861 neither the railroad nor the military was prepared to make the most of it.

McClellan's order to Hill went out on the afternoon of July 12, but because of poorly maintained telegraph connections it did not reach him until eleven o'clock the next morning. Because no general depot of supplies had been established, the commanders of the separate units always had to rely on their own effort to procure wagons, horses, rations and supplies sufficient for any movement away from the railroad, no matter how short. This time, by reason of their scrambling for these things, they were unable to take full advantage of such rail transportation as was available. Cut off from headquarters at Baltimore, local railroad officials stumbled over one another in their attempts to provide the necessary cars to load the men and their equipment. Trains running on single track without centralized dispatching soon fell into complete confusion, and the trainmen, conscious of the danger of collision, grew more and more unwilling to cooperate or obey orders, finally threatening to abandon their posts.

Late in the afternoon of July 13, Hill succeeded in starting two light trains out of Grafton. Aboard one of them he reached Oakland about ten o'clock at night with approximately six hundred men inadequately equipped for the field. At nine o'clock next morning he was still waiting in Oakland for other trains supposed to be on the way with troops, horses for the three guns he had brought with him the previous day, and wagons to supply the little expedition. Evening of July 14 came to Oakland ahead of most of the troops McClellan had planned to throw across the Confederate line of escape. Despite the fact that Garnett had fallen in a rear-guard skirmish at about the time Hill left Grafton, the column he had set in motion moved swiftly toward its objective, and by the time Hill was prepared to execute his orders the Confederates had turned the mountain spur and held a safe lead on the eastern side of the range.[20]

In this fashion a well-conceived plan resulted only in a comedy of errors. Sharp criticisms have been offered and attempts made to place the blame for the failure. Too easily it has been forgotten that never before had a railroad been called on to perform a similar task; never before had a military commander sought to make infantry function as swift-moving cavalry through use of the locomotive. With no previous preparation, no briefing and no experience, McClellan's officers were summoned to execute a movement never before undertaken in military history. Soldiers had not yet learned that the first requirement for rapid railroad transport is the orderly and co-ordinated dispatch of trains. Railroaders had not yet learned to handle soldiers. Both branches of the railroad were open from Wheeling and Parkersburg to Grafton, and the main line was open from Grafton to Oakland. Within the region were plenty of engines and cars, and the run from Grafton to Oakland need have required no more than two hours. Experience was the only essential element to success which was lacking.

Doubtless this episode convinced some military experts that the railroad was not to become a great factor in the conduct of the war. If so, they would have found in McClellan no sympathy for their thesis. Less than a month later he was saying to President Lincoln:

It can not be ignored that the construction of railroads has introduced a new and very important element into war by the great facilities thus given for concentrating at particular positions large masses of troops from remote sections and by creating new strategic points and lines of operations.[21]

On August 4 he was also advising Lincoln that a move should be made through Kentucky against the railroad running east from Memphis; that the main line of the Baltimore & Ohio should be opened throughout and protected. "We must endeavor to seize places in the rear of the enemy's points of concentration."[22]

CHAPTER VII

FIRST BULL RUN

People and newspapers in the North fretted and complained. Three months had passed and the rebellion had not been put down. Many more than twice 75,000 men had volunteered for the three months' service Lincoln had specified in his first call, and what had come of it? Nothing at all; nothing except that a young man named McClellan had chased the enemy through the hills of western Virginia and that had been done with surplus troops from Ohio and Indiana. What ailed Lincoln and old General Scott? They had a big army idling on the banks of the Potomac and cavorting about Washington with the rebel army almost in sight, yet not a thing had been done to destroy it. The farmers allowed the war should have been over and the soldiers back in the fields in time for wheat harvest. With labor scarce, prices rising and the railroads clogged with government business, the people let it be known that they expected an end put to this rebellion without further dillydallying.

On July 21 they got the action for which they had been clamoring: a great, bloody battle on the field of Bull Run,[1] from which they learned that crushing the South was not the simple matter they had thought it to be. Over their new railroad system they had sped a great army to Washington, but throwing a mass of unseasoned soldiers against Beauregard's army had settled nothing except that the North had greatly underestimated the magnitude and complexity of its task. A successful operation to occupy Manassas Junction with its railroads would have cleared the whole of northern Virginia more effectually than a defeat of the enemy in the field, but explaining this to the people would have been futile. They wanted the whole business settled with one smashing blow, a blow which would immediately re-establish Federal authority in the seceded states. The crushing defeat of Bull Run was the price they paid to learn the war could not be ended that way.

Not the least important of the lessons they were obliged to learn through bitter experience was that the locomotive had stuck its long, ungainly nose into their affair with the rebellious South. They had seen it carry their soldiers off to camp; now they were to see it fight—and it was not always to be on their side of the controversy. Even as McDowell marched out through Centerville to deliver the blow demanded by the people of the North, Orange & Alexandria trains were delivering reinforcements to Beauregard's defense. Later, when the battle was at its height and fortune seemed at last to favor McDowell's weary men, a fresh and unexpected enemy force appeared in the woods before the Union right and delivered fire so heavy that the Federal line was broken and fell immediately into disorder. What seemed at three o'clock a likely victory became at four a fearsome rout.[2]

The Union plan for the battle contemplated that Patterson would keep the army of General Joseph E. Johnston so engaged about Winchester as to prevent its coming down from the Shenandoah to join Beauregard in the major action.[3] But while Patterson lay at Charlestown attempting the double duty of holding Johnston and guarding against a flank attack on Washington, Johnston slipped away from in front of Winchester and marched to Piedmont Station on the Manassas Gap Railroad where trains waited to carry his command to the scene of the impending battle. These were the troops, fresh from their trains, which assailed McDowell's right and demoralized his army.[4] Thus, in the first great battle of the war, victory for the South rode in on the rails.

Galled by the magnitude and suddenness of its defeat, the Union army reoccupied the positions from which the disastrous campaign had been launched. McClellan, the object of popular acclaim because of his victory over Garnett, was called to Washington to replace the unfortunate McDowell and prepare for the next move. The victorious Confederates, now under Johnston's command, reoccupied Centerville, where they had spent the months of May and June, re-established their outposts on the hills overlooking the Potomac, and set up batteries to blockade the river below Washington. Months of inaction followed. In October Jackson led the troops Johnston had brought down from Winchester back to the Shenandoah. Johnston and McClellan, facing each other where the two armies had been in the spring, went into winter quarters. From complaining because the war had not been ended in ninety days, the people of the North turned their attention to getting ready for a second year of the struggle.

When Johnston slipped away via the Manassas Gap Rail-road to help Beauregard at Bull Run, he had not taken all the men who were then in the valley, and those left behind did not wait idly for Jackson's return. As the Federals fell back into Maryland, those Confederates who had not gone to Bull Run followed and repossessed 100 miles of Baltimore & Ohio track west of Harper's Ferry. Much of the damage they had inflicted on the road before retiring to Winchester had been repaired during the Federal occupation. Now, from Harper's Ferry to North Branch bridge, small detachments attacked those expensive repairs, demolished additional bridges and culverts, and tore up miles of track.[5] "Baltimore and Ohio officials could only call off their workmen and wait for a turn of military operations."[6]

At Martinsburg the Confederates surveyed the ruins of the great fire Jackson had set little more than a month before their return. There, red with rust, lay the fine engines he had trapped for the South but had been unable to move before Patterson forced him to abandon them. Army mechanics said many of them could be repaired. After all, not much about a locomotive would burn! Unfortunately, however, there was no track upon which to roll them away to a place where they could be reconditioned. Doubtless soldiers were about who had seen Jackson haul four lighter engines and many good cars over the highway from Winchester to Strasburg in the previous May. Perhaps larger engines could be handled in the same way! From Martinsburg to Strasburg was thirty-eight miles, more than twice the distance from Winchester, but the road was good, and these engines either must be taken over the highway or left there to be eaten away with rust. The thing seemed worth trying. As a test a big engine was selected, its tender uncoupled and drawn away, all heavy removable parts were stripped off and loaded on strong wagons, leaving only the rear pair of flanged drive wheels in place. A heavy wooden truck was devised and placed under the front where the pivoted pony truck had been. When the crippled monster was fully prepared, many horses were brought in from the valley farms and hitched in multiple teams of four. Carefully the enormous load was pulled out upon the highway and the thirty-eight-mile journey was begun. Three days later the engine's wheels were replaced at Strasburg, and over the Manassas Gap line the prize was towed away toward the repair shops in Richmond.

So successful was the experiment that time after time the process was repeated until fourteen engines were rescued from the Martinsburg ruin and sent on their way to the shops.[7] One, a big Ross Winans camelback, was still at Strasburg at the time of the Second Battle of Bull Run, when destruction of the track stopped all traffic on the Manassas Gap line except for the thirty miles of track between Strasburg and the end of the road at Mount Jackson. Beyond that point was one of the many trackless stretches between railroads that so greatly reduced the military efficiency of the Southern lines. Between Mount Jackson and Staunton, the nearest point on the Virginia Central, lay seventy miles without a railroad. Already the camelback had been dragged thirty-eight miles without a track to carry her, and she was too valuable to be discarded without an effort to take her over those remaining seventy miles of highway. Days of struggle finally brought her in triumph to Staunton, and over the Virginia Central she rode to the Richmond shops to rejoin those which had made the journey via Manassas Junction.[8]

Later, all these engines were moved to the shops of the
Raleigh & Gaston Railroad at Raleigh, North Carolina, for
completion of the repairs.[9] One of the finest, a passenger
engine, was fitted with a walnut cab, ornately decorated and
named the "Lady Davis" in honor of the wife of the President
of the Confederacy.[10] All served the South for the remainder
of the war. Far from all the rolling stock scooped by Jackson
reached Southern rails, but such of it as did proved invaluable
to the cause which lacked facilities for building an engine.

Although for 100 miles west of Harper's Ferry the Baltimore & Ohio main line was weakly held by the Confederates
who daily wrought vengeance on the railroad they now considered dangerous to their cause, strong Union forces at
Hagerstown and Frederick made no effort to recover its
possession. Again the people of the Northwest demanded
action—not the sort of grand, decisive action they had called
for in the spring. A smaller move could be very important to
them. By early autumn the Northwest was beginning to feel
the serious effects of traffic congestion on the trunk lines
to the east due to their extensive use by the War Department.
Not only had freight rates risen sharply, but business was
suffering from a shortage of shipping capacity. With winter
coming on and water transport about to be closed, the prospect
was for still less capacity and still further rate increases. The
first significant dislocation of business and civil affairs arising
from the government's near monopoly of shipping space on
the trunk lines was hitting shippers. The *Cincinnati Gazette*
summed things up:

> The Mississippi River being closed, the produce of the
> entire West is driven from that channel to the Eastern rail-
> roads. In addition to this the Baltimore and Ohio Railroad is
> closed, and the Pennsylvania Central is largely occupied with
> Government business. Thus, railroad facilities as compared
> with last winter, have been reduced nearly one half, while
> business has largely increased; and if managers have put prices
> up fifty percent, while the canals and lakes are navigable,
> without being able to move all the property that is offered,
> what may be expected when the water lines shall be closed?

It is probable that the freight on flour to New York will advance to two dollars per barrel by the first of January, and on other articles in proportion.[11]

When the opening of the Baltimore & Ohio changed from a military issue to one of national civilian concern, Secretary Cameron found himself in an embarrassing difficulty. Newspapers, merchants, manufacturers and farmers of the Northwest stood together in demanding that something be done to restore service over the idle and ravaged railroad. Eighty years later Summers described this situation when he wrote: "Waiving only important military considerations, its reclamation became second only to the opening of the Mississippi."[12] Furthermore, the complaints of the Northwest were spreading to the East. A Baltimore newspaper was pointing out that as a war measure the government itself badly needed the railroad for the transportation of high-grade steam coal from the mines of western Maryland for the Navy; that the possession of the road by the enemy ". . . cripples the arm of the General Government, adding millions to its expenses in forwarding troops, provisions, etc. and causing ruinous delays in the concentration of its troops. . . ."[13] The *Cincinnati Gazette* publicized the fact that in the midst of the transportation shortage the Baltimore & Ohio had 2,000 freight cars and 200 locomotives standing idle.[14]

Despite increasing pressure, the War Department did nothing. Garrett, now an open Union partisan, said that the railroad itself would bear the expense of reconstruction if the Army would provide the necessary military protection. Still no action came from the administration. Union commanders in Maryland were well aware of the opportunity presented but dared not move without orders from Washington. Search for the cause of the incongruous attitude of the War Department started among the irked and disgruntled citizens who suffered from the inaction. Suspicion soon centered on Simon Cameron. Obscured by the early excitement and enthusiasms of the war, the fact that the Pennsylvania and the Northern Central had a virtual monopoly of business originating west of Harrisburg and destined for Baltimore, now became obvious. Equally apparent was the fact that Cameron and his Pennsylvania associates in the War Department could control the routing of the vast military business of the government.

Accusations from aroused citizens buzzed in Cameron's ears. They said he had raised rates beyond reasonable justification, and the Pennsylvania and the Northern Central had profited immensely by allowing the rival Baltimore & Ohio to remain in the hands of the enemy. They also accused Cameron of discriminating against the Philadelphia, Wilmington & Baltimore by fixing rates on government shipments originating in Philadelphia to favor the longer route through Harrisburg via the Northern Central. When the earnings of the "Cameron Road" and the Pennsylvania were published little doubt remained in the public mind why appeals to the War Department for the opening of the Baltimore & Ohio had produced no results. In April the people had not bothered to ask why the B.&O. tracks were not protected in the same fashion as the Pennsylvania and the Northern Central. In the autumn they had found what they thought a sufficient answer to the question they had previously failed to ask.[15]

Whether because of the pressure exerted on Cameron or for other reasons, the War Department in October took its first faltering step to satisfy the public demand. Though thousands of idle soldiers were at its disposal, no vigorous expedition to regain the railroad was ordered. Instead, General Frederick W. Lander was given military jurisdiction over a territory which embraced the Baltimore & Ohio line from Harper's Ferry to Cumberland. His command consisted of a few hundred recruits, his authority embraced the raising of additional forces, and his orders were to distribute his force "along the railroad where civilian working parties would need protection."[16] What results the Secretary anticipated from this short step remain undisclosed. The known facts are that Lander was immediately disabled by a wound in a skirmish and the command devolved on Brigadier General Benjamin F. Kelley whose scattered detachments lay from Cumberland west to the Cheat River bridge. These he assembled at New Creek and prepared for action. Kelley knew what was needed and he had a plan. The way to protect working parties on the railroad was to drive the Confederates back on Winchester, and the first move in that direction was to force them out of Romney. This he accomplished on October 26. At once Mr. Garrett's repair crews set to work replacing bridges on the long segment of track now made safe. By the middle of November the road was open from the Ohio to Green Springs, sixteen miles east of Cumberland.

Much more remained to be done before through traffic could be resumed, but Garrett's appeals for protection so that the eastern end of the damaged section could be restored remained unheeded in Washington. At last, Brigadier General William S. Rosecrans, who had succeeded McClellan in West Virginia, came to Washington with a proposal so closely integrated with the war in Virginia it could not well have been ignored had not untoward circumstances suddenly interfered.

Rosecrans proposed to concentrate his troops behind Romney under cover of Kelley's forces, send a flanking column eastward along the railroad to clear it of marauders while the main force would strike directly at Winchester. He contended that the occupation of Winchester would make it impossible for the Confederates to operate in the lower Shenandoah and thus stop their raids on the Baltimore & Ohio west of Harper's Ferry. No matter how little this part of the idea might have interested Cameron, he could not escape the argument that with Rosecrans in Winchester, strong Union forces would be on Johnston's left flank. The threat of their presence there might induce him to retire from his threatening position before Washington.

The strategy was good but while the proposal was still being considered in the War Department Jackson beat Rosecrans to the draw. News came that the wily Confederate had left Winchester and was marching on Cumberland. Rosecrans left immediately for his headquarters at Wheeling.

Jackson, too, had a plan, and while Rosecrans argued with

Cameron he started putting it into effect. It was the precise
reverse of Rosecrans'. He retook Romney and sent Kelley
flying back on the main army to the west. Detachments
hurried north to the railroad and again demolished the newly
repaired track. From Romney Jackson meant to push on
toward Grafton, flank Rosecrans out of the Kanawha Valley
and recapture the territory Garnett had lost to McClellan in
the spring. Stormy weather at the approach of winter halted
the westward drive at Romney. The mountains ahead
presented forbidding terrain for winter campaigning, but
Jackson had time left to take apart the railroad east of
Cumberland. Of the work of destruction to which Jackson
then turned his attention Summers says:

By December 1, 1861, the Confederates had removed
practically all of the double track between Harper's Ferry and
Martinsburg and seven and one-half miles of one of the tracks
west of the latter point. Their work was thorough and
systematic. The rails, all of which were the high English
grade, they transported to Harper's Ferry and Martinsburg,
there to await the call of Southern railroads; they stacked
and burned the crossties on the right of way. Early in
December, Jackson set men to work on the remaining track
west of Martinsburg. Although his force labored only
intermittently, by the opening of the new year it had removed
all tracks west to Back Creek and with them the telegraph
lines.[17]

So from the first day of the war until the last day of 1861,
the Baltimore & Ohio Railroad remained an object of major
concern for both Federal and Confederate commands. It was
a political issue in the appeasement of Maryland Secessionists
and West Virginia Unionists, the objective in numerous skirmishes and one sustained campaign, and victim of countless
demolitions. Costly bridges had been burned, rebuilt and
burned again, rails and rolling stock carried into the South.
The South had been unable to save the road for its own use,
but when winter came, 100 miles of ruined track lay useless

to the Union, and the fight had only begun. The Confederate policy of destruction had completely stopped the use of the road by the Federals as a through line from the Ohio to the Chesapeake. Many in the North charged this loss to Simon Cameron and his associates in the railroad business who held high places in the War Department and who stood to profit by the continued misfortunes of the B.&O.

CHAPTER VIII

No Compromise in Missouri

I

At no time or place during the course of the war was the difference between campaigning in a country with and a country without railroads better demonstrated than by the struggle in Missouri during 1861. In all Missouri there were but five railroads, not one of which crossed the state from north to south. Paralleling the northern boundary, the Hannibal & St. Joseph crossed from east to west and linked the Mississippi and Missouri rivers. Some sixty miles west of Hannibal and the Mississippi, at Macon, the Northern Missouri Railroad tapped this line and provided a connection with St. Louis. Between Macon and St. Louis there was not a junction or crossing on this road.

Almost directly west from St. Louis a third line, the Pacific Railroad, followed the general course of the Missouri River as far as Jefferson City, then pushed on another sixty miles to end without a connection at Sedalia. The Southwestern Railroad branched off from this line at Franklin, less than forty miles west of St. Louis, and ran about sixty-five miles southwest to the little town of Rolla. The fifth road was the Iron Mountain, less than one hundred miles long, running south from St. Louis to Ironton.

Except at Macon and Franklin there was not a railroad junction in the state outside St. Louis. All the vast southern and southwestern area was without rail facilities of any kind.

When in June Brigadier General Nathaniel Lyon set out from St. Louis to subdue the Secessionist state government

ORANGE & ALEXANDRIA NEAR UNION MILLS

REPAIRING THE O. & A. NEAR CATLETT'S STATION
OCTOBER 1863

Union Cavalry Guarding a Bridge on the O. & A. in 1864

and its militia under command of General Sterling Price, he had railroad transportation for his troops and equipment as far as Jefferson City. But before he arrived there Governor Jackson and General Price with their militiamen had abandoned the capital and retired into country where the sound of locomotive whistles had not yet been heard.[1] Neither the railroads from the East nor any benefits from them had reached the people of this part of Missouri. The railroads had crossed the mountains but they had not conquered the Mississippi. To these Missourians the river with its mouth at the warm Gulf meant more than cold rails stretching away to the east and a people with whom they had little in common. Geographically they were neighbors of the North but the breath of the South was still in them. As Price slowly retired through their country, they flocked by thousands to his army. Deeper and deeper Price moved into the southwest, gathering strength from time and retreat. Farther and farther Lyon was drawn into hostile territory where transportation was limited to poorly maintained wagon roads and his forces lost strength as steadily as Price's gained.

About the middle of July Lyon reached Springfield, but it was another hundred miles to Cowskin Prairie near which the decisive struggle for Missouri was to take place. At Springfield the weary pursuing column halted. Shoes had worn out; clothes were in tatters and food was scarce and poor. It was a long way back to Rolla, the nearest railhead and source of supplies.[2] Few more than 5,000 men remained with Lyon after the weeks of marching through blistering heat and the torment of repeated skirmishing. Price, too, had paused, but with every pause his army grew in numbers and lived on the products of a friendly country. With more than 10,000 men he waited on the west bank of Wilson's Creek for Lyon to take up the pursuit. The Union column moved out on August 9, but Price stood his ground and next day, after a long, shifting battle, killed Lyon and routed his exhausted army.[3]

Thus ended the first campaign of the Civil War in which a Union commander dared march an army into hostile territory

100 miles from a railroad. Such rail facilities as the state contained were in Lyon's control, but they were not sufficient to overcome the enemy advantage of retirement into a friendly country where the locomotive could not pursue. The outcome may give one cause to wonder when, if ever, the Federal government would have crushed the Confederacy if the war had come before the railroads had had time to push thousands of miles of track through North and South east of the Mississippi.

Not all of Missouri was Secessionist in sympathy. About St. Louis and in the northern tier of counties along the line of the Hannibal & St. Joseph Railroad lived thousands of citizens who remained loyal to the Union. As Franz Sigel led the remnant of Lyon's army back toward Rolla, Price retraced the route of his long retreat and struck out for the section served by the Hannibal & St. Joseph. He wanted desperately to reach that portion of the state from which the Federals were drawing a good measure of support. Across his path a force of about 4,000 commanded by Colonel James A. Mulligan was intrenched in Lexington on the Missouri River. For the second time the lack of railroad communications in Missouri was to work the undoing of a Federal command. On the morning of September 12, Price, who on his long marches through the back country had accumulated 18,000 men, laid siege to the Lexington Federals. Mulligan dispatched a courier to Jefferson City to explain his desperate situation and ask for immediate help. Day after day, while reinforcements pressed forward on foot, Price tightened the noose he had thrown about Mulligan. On the morning of September 20 the Federal force was obliged to surrender.[4] It was the sort of thing common to warfare in the days before the locomotive.

Despite the fact no railroad came near the major combat areas, the railroads played an important though indirect part in saving Missouri for the Union. Across the river from St. Louis, railroad train after railroad train delivered regiments from the Northwest states, the force which ultimately overcame Price and his supporters. With a population divided in allegiance, St. Louis was kept well fed with products brought in over her own railroads, all of which were under Union control. By way of the Northern Missouri and its connection with the Hannibal & St. Joseph, both of which roads were constantly guarded against marauding bands of Secessionists, communications and close relations were maintained with the loyal citizens of the northern counties and towns. In the autumn General Frémont greatly increased the military effectiveness of the roads by establishing a common terminal in St. Louis and laying track to join the three lines which entered the city. Fortunately their tracks were of the same gauge.[5]

For Lyon the rails ran neither far enough nor in the right direction; they could haul his troops and supplies no farther than Rolla. But while he marched and fought to his death in the southwest they helped mightily to consolidate and maintain a powerful Union bloc in northeast Missouri where Union military operations were based. In addition, the roads which lay east of the Mississippi made possible the ready mobilization and supply of the larger army which was to accomplish at Pea Ridge what Lyon had failed to do at Wilson's Creek.

2

During the late summer and early autumn, while the struggle for possession of the Baltimore & Ohio went on in the East, and in the West armies marched mile on mile through almost railroadless Missouri, war was on its way to Kentucky and Tennessee. The attempt to maintain neutrality in Kentucky had failed. Both Union and Confederate armies were on Kentucky soil. Though the population was sharply divided in allegiance, the state government had at last taken its stand for the Union.

Before frost came to the Kentucky hills a Confederate line was drawn across the southern part of the state all the way from Cumberland Gap to the Mississippi. This was the defense line hastily created by General Albert Sidney Johnston, determined more by the limitations of the force at his command than by strategic considerations. The Federals were massing south of the Ohio. Johnston could see that they might choose among four major avenues of approach, and he had scarcely enough troops adequately to defend even one of them. He set about creating the semblance of a line more than 300 miles long in the desperate hope that his bluff would hold until men and arms could be obtained to make it effective from end to end.

Into the rugged country at the southeast corner of the state he sent a little army under command of General Felix K. Zollicoffer, whose assignment was to watch the Union troops assembling at Camp Dick Robinson, near Danville, and create the illusion that the highway through the Gap into Unionist east Tennessee was closed.[6] This was the country through which Lincoln early had urged, without success, that a railroad be built to unite the loyal portions of Tennessee and Kentucky. There was not a mile of railroad within the area of Zollicoffer's command.

Crossing the center of the defense line almost at a right angle ran the Louisville & Nashville Railroad with the capital of all-important Tennessee at one terminus and Sherman's army at the other. To discourage any early Federal approach over it, Johnston sent 4,000 men under Simon Bolivar Buckner to occupy Bowling Green where the railroad crossed the Big Barren River.[7] This bold mask of the weak center was to prove particularly effective, for when a small detachment of Buckner's scouts quickly pushed north to the Rolling Fork of Salt River, only thirty miles south of Louisville, and burned the L.&N. bridge across the stream, they created consternation out of proportion to any threat inherent in Buckner's little army.

To the left of Johnston's center the Tennessee and Cumberland rivers, navigable ordinarily, paralleled each other and ran directly to the Ohio. Immediately below the Kentucky line in Tennessee, two small forts had been erected to guard these rivers: Fort Donelson on the Cumberland and Fort Henry on the Tennessee. They were but twelve miles apart. On these forts Johnston must rely for protection against

approach by way of the rivers. Therefore, through Hopkins-
ville he stretched his thin line away toward its anchor post at
Columbus. Situated on a formidable bluff overlooking the
Mississippi twenty miles below Cairo, Columbus was the
northernmost defense point on the river. It had already
been occupied by General Leonidas Polk, and the heavy guns
he had placed upon the bluff defied the passing of Union gunboats and transports. Besides, Columbus was the northern
terminus of the Mobile & Ohio Railroad, which reached all
the way to the Gulf and connected with all important railroads in that direction. At Humboldt in Tennessee it crossed
the Memphis & Ohio* which ran northeast from there to
intercept the Louisville & Nashville at Bowling Green. Thus,
by way of Humboldt, Johnston was provided with railroad
communication between his center and his extreme left. In
the long run, however, it was unfortunate for the Confederacy
that this road crossed both the Cumberland and the Tennessee
rivers at points behind his defense line.

During the autumn and early winter Johnston, brilliant
veteran of the United States Army, gave all that he had of
energy, intelligence and devotion to building an adequate
organization. Henry and Donelson were improved, extended
and reinforced;[8] more guns were mounted on the Columbus
bluff and more men sent to Polk's command. Hardee was
brought from Arkansas to strengthen Buckner at Bowling
Green.[9] By the time the blow fell, early in 1862, the Kentucky
line was no longer a mere mask.

With less alacrity Union commanders prepared to occupy
the whole of Kentucky, clear the Mississippi to Memphis and
carry the war to Tennessee, key state of the Confederacy in
the West. On September 5, Grant seized Paducah and took
control of the mouths of the Cumberland and the Tennessee.
The two great water gateways to the heart of Tennessee stood
wide open to the fleet of Federal gunboats and transports
built and building on the Ohio.

---

* This name is used to designate the entire line between Memphis
& Bowling Green.

Disappointed with the motley contingents of raw recruits sent him and disgruntled by the lack of support he felt he was receiving from Cameron, Sherman fretted over his task of preparing an invasion army in the environs of Louisville. Even more than Buckner overrated Sherman's strength at the center, Sherman overrated Buckner's at Bowling Green.[10] While Johnston's purpose went no further than to forestall Sherman's use of the L.&N. for a swift thrust at the weak Confederate center,[11] Sherman was confident Buckner was ready to use the same railroad to overwhelm him and take Louisville.[12] When Buckner's scouts burned the Rolling Fork bridge on September 17, the frustrated Sherman swallowed without a struggle the unsupported rumors that they were the advance guard of a force of 15,000 men then well on their way to Louisville.[13] As far as Sherman was concerned, Johnston's bluff was working perfectly.

At Cairo, on the Union right, Grant calmly went about his business of developing his army, undisturbed by rumors of an impending advance by Johnston. At Camp Dick Robinson, on the extreme Union left, Thomas had seen through the Johnston mask and entertained no apprehensions over an early Rebel offensive.[14]

On the contrary, his interest centered in an offensive project of his own, which, had it been successfully developed, would have dealt a staggering blow to the Confederate line from Centerville to Columbus. Nashville had become a major depot of supplies for the Confederate army in Virginia. With keen perception of railroad significance not yet common to Union commanders, Thomas saw a chance to accomplish the sort of thing Lee earlier had feared McClellan might do if he defeated Garnett in West Virginia. Thomas reasoned that, by sideslipping Zollicoffer's little army, he could readily advance to Knoxville, cut the East Tennessee & Virginia Railroad, a vital link in the South's only east-west trunk line, and with this one blow both isolate Confederate supplies at Nashville and destroy rail communications between Richmond and Johnston's army.[15] The proposal came too early in the war. Thomas' capacity was still unknown and the Union authorities had not yet come to grasp the railroad's importance in military strategy. Thomas had come under the command of the bewildered Sherman, who at Zollicoffer's first jab at Union outposts had ordered Thomas to retire.

As the year ended, Union gunboats cruised the Ohio at will, nosed into the lower reaches of the Green River and moved up and down the Cumberland and the Tennessee as far as the unusually low water stage would carry them. Grant was master of the situation on the south bank of the Ohio opposite Cairo. Buell had replaced Sherman in command at Louisville and a much larger and more efficient army occupied the country thereabouts. Skirmishing columns had been pushed out as far as the Green River. Thomas, free of Sherman's timidity, harassed Johnston's right in the Cumberland country. The L.&N. served two masters, with its longer reach in the hands of the Confederates. A decisive battle was in the making.

CHAPTER IX

AT THE END OF '61

I

To the inadequately financed railroads of the South, war brought quick distress. The swift blockade of the Southern ports by the Union Navy immediately dried up the cotton carriers' chief source of revenue. The speedy decline in general business which followed the end of cotton export worked a similar result on those roads which were dependent on miscellaneous sources of income. Whereas in April 1861 the Southern roads had enthusiastically volunteered to serve their new government without charge, they found themselves in December compelled to look to the government for revenue. With the war scarcely begun, financial starvation was on them.

Rates for the transport of civilian passengers and freights had been sharply increased but produced far more public indignation and resistance than revenue. The demands of the government had become so heavy that little capacity remained for such civil business as was available, and the near-capacity load of military business by no means met the need for cash income. On the contrary, it made the situation more difficult. Rates for military transportation had been fixed by the Montgomery Convention. Payment was in government bonds and not in cash. Money was required to defray the costs of operation and supplies and such costs were rising rapidly. To make matters worse, rolling stock and track were deteriorating ever more rapidly under the relentless pounding of the military service.

The light iron with which most track originally had been laid was poorly adapted to carry the heavy traffic imposed by the war. Trouble quickly appeared. To procure, at any price, rails with which to make necessary repairs and extensions presented a problem quite as tough as that of finding money with which to pay for them. With the Northern rail supply entirely cut off and blockade practically preventing any importation from Europe, the outlook for keeping track in good repair was extremely dark, even before the first winter came to add its bedevilment.

There was some iron in Savannah which the importers offered to sell "for cash."[1] To most roads this condition made it unavailable. The Virginia Central had on hand sufficient rail to lay nine miles of track.[2] In New Orleans there was a small supply.[3] At Selma, Alabama, there was a small iron-works which was capable of turning out some rails, but its entire capacity was under contract to the government for the manufacture of ordnance. The Tredegar Iron Works at Richmond could have made rails, but there also guns had a higher priority.

Under such limitations the railroads of the Confederacy faced the task of maintaining 9,000 miles of track in a service far too heavy for it even in favorable circumstances.

The North had even tighter control of the manufacture of locomotives and cars. How poorly off this left the Southern roads is well illustrated in the records of three important lines in Virginia. In 1861 the Virginia Central operated slightly more than 200 miles between Richmond and Jackson's River in the Upper Shenandoah. Its rolling stock consisted of 27 engines and 241 cars of all classes. With much of this equipment already old and in need of repairs[4] when the war began, the problem of replacements immediately stumped the line's management. From Richmond to Aquia the Richmond, Fredericksburg & Potomac operated approximately 75 miles of vital track with 11 engines and 134 cars of various types.[5] The Manassas Gap, little more than half as long as the Virginia Central, owned 223 cars but had only 9 engines.[6] The total number of engines owned by all three roads was less than the number seized from the B.&O. by Jackson in his scoop at Harper's Ferry.

Few if any roads in the South were better equipped with rolling stock than those cited and most were unable to count a comparable number of engines or cars per mile of road operated. Before the first snow fell in the camps of Johnny Reb, this shortage of rolling stock began to work its war-long curse on his military operations. It was only September when W. S. Ashe, Assistant Quartermaster General, was ordered to procure from other roads six locomotives and seventy box-cars and turn them over to the management of the East Tennessee & Virginia. Ashe went first to the Western & Atlantic. His orders were to purchase the rolling stock, if possible; otherwise to impress it and have it appraised.[7] Apparently the War Department had overlooked the fact that the Western & Atlantic was owned by the State of Georgia. Ashe met a sharp rebuff. For having issued this order, Judah P. Benjamin, newly appointed Secretary of War, promptly apologized to Governor Brown, but in his letter of apology he asked Brown for voluntary assistance. Said Benjamin: "Without some additional rolling stock on the Virginia and East Tennessee road it is utterly impossible to transport the troops and supplies required for public defense."[8]

Brown's reply to this appeal graphically summarizes the sad outlook in the autumn of 1861.

We have let the East Tennessee roads have the use of our cars and engines this summer, and they have abused and broken them until we shall be very hard pressed for motive power and rolling stock to do our winters business. If we could get material for the repair of our engines it would be possible for us to repair them and still accommodate, but much of the material necessary can not be had in the Confederacy. . . . We now have three or four of our engines in the shops badly broken up by them and we lack material to repair. Some fifty or more of our cars are in like broken and injured condition.[9]

In specific form the same story is told in the report of General Albert Sidney Johnston on the movement of Hardee's command to the support of Buckner at Bowling Green. Johnston wrote: "Deficiency of rolling stock did not permit me to make his [Hardee's] movement more compact."[10]

Though apparent from the first months of the war, the distress of the Southern railroads seemed a matter of small consideration to the Confederate government. No satisfactory explanation of this attitude appears. Perhaps too many influential officials still clung to the notion the war would be won quickly; it may have been part of the price paid for the expensive victory at Manassas. Perhaps the leaders had not yet grasped the military potential inherent in the railroads. Possibly too few foresaw that in the end valor and enthusiasm would be no substitute for food and iron; that in a war of motion ill-shod feet would be no match for locomotive wheels.

To railroad executives the attitude was puzzling and vexatious. They saw clearly that if the roads were to continue to operate in the service of the government, the government in turn must do something for their relief. It was not in their power to bring the necessary railroad equipment and supplies through the Union blockade. As long as the government monopolized the output of limited home manufacturing, no relief could be had from that source. Without money or rails they could not lay the missing track connections for which the military was calling. Without the aid of military guards, they could not guard their tracks and bridges against hostile depredations.

In directing the attention of the government to these dilemmas, no one was more alert and active than Peter V. Daniel, Jr. In April he had prepared a conservation and safety code for all railroads, but, though it was endorsed by Lee, the government failed to pursue it. Two months later he wrote directly to President Davis explaining why the railroads could not construct the terminal connections at Richmond and Petersburg. In July he provided the Secretary of

War with an estimate of the cost of building the Richmond connection and a proposal that it be financed through government aid.[11] Later in the same month he wrote the Secretary that a light temporary connection sufficient to move cars by horsepower might be cheaply constructed and asked to be notified if the government was interested.[12] In November he minced no words in telling Secretary Benjamin what he thought of the treatment accorded the railroads that ". . . are and have been making sacrifices for the public good which have no parallel in the country." His letters went unanswered. He dismissed the men he had privately employed to guard the tracks of the R.,F.&P. because the company could no longer endure the expense. Though there were camps of idle soldiers all along the line, his requests that some be detailed to patrol the road had been ignored. The government had ". . . declined to defray any part of that cost or even to furnish arms or ammunition for those guards." In closing, he warned that the railroads ". . . may exhaust their means of maintenance before the end of the existing war."[13]

Despite these and many other such warnings, nothing important in the way of railroad relief or track extension was undertaken in 1861. A measure of railroad supervision had been vested in Quartermaster General Abraham C. Myers, and an assistant, Mr. Ashe, President of the Wilmington & Weldon Railroad, was assigned to the particular task. Myers' authority, however, went no further than to contract for transportation of troops and supplies and to see that they were carried at the rates agreed on. He could arrange for the use of such facilities as existed but had no power to extend or improve them. In the office of President Davis and the War Department much talk and correspondence went on about the building of connections but within the year nothing was done. For the particularly important connecting tracks at Richmond and Petersburg, Lee had to wait.

During that first summer and fall of the war, the Confederacy let precious months slip by without paying real heed to the warnings of its railroad men. Much was lost to it that never could be regained, and when at last it was obliged to set about in earnest to make the most of its limited rail system, the circumstances in which it labored had become infinitely more complicated and difficult.

Strangely enough, army officers as a class were lamentably backward students in the schooling of the country to the use of the railroad in war. Lee and Jackson, Thomas, Grant and Frémont were notable exceptions. Possibly the reason may be found in the fact that so great a proportion of the officers in both armies came directly from civilian pursuits and knew little or nothing about either military duties or railroading. Whereas the professional soldier had to learn only the application of the railroad to his profession, the civilian-trained officer first had to learn how to be a soldier. Throughout the first months of the war the railroad remained to the average officer only a factor of accommodation to be used as and when it could be made to serve his own immediate convenience.

This general attitude is well illustrated by an incident of troop movement in Virginia during the first summer. Pulled by an Orange & Alexandria engine, a trainload of Southern soldiers from Lynchburg steamed into Gordonsville. Riding in the cab were two armed soldiers who held the engineer under arrest and, regardless of the danger of collision, required him to operate the train as ordered by the officer in command of the troops, rather than in accordance with the instructions of the railroad. At Gordonsville a Virginia Central engine replaced the one from the O.&A., but the Central engineer bluntly refused to submit to military arrest or turn a wheel of his engine until the soldiers were removed from the cab.[14]

During the early part of the war these annoying and dangerous instances of officers assuming train control occurred with great frequency in both armies. Gradually the evil was reduced, but it was never entirely eliminated. Commanders were slow to comprehend the railroad as a mobile base, a factor in strategy, or an element in maneuver; slow to understand that while serving the Army, train operation was a thing for the railroads and must not be interfered with or appropriated by troop commanders.

2

In the North the railroad situation at the end of 1861 stood in sharp contrast to that in the South. Surplus trackage had come into full operation. Roads hard pressed before the war for sufficient business to warrant operation had stepped up to the class of prosperous carriers. Approximately 500,000 soldiers were in the service of the Union.[15] Their camps dotted the war frontier from Washington to Cairo, with others scattered from New England to the Missouri River. Assembling these men and moving them hundreds of miles toward the combat zones put cash in the treasuries of the needy roads as well as the more prosperous ones. Thousands of tons of food, hundreds of cars of livestock, long trains of forage, and countless carloads of clothing, munitions and miscellaneous supplies rolled night and day over the Northern railroads. It was cash business. Manufacturing and agriculture were stepped up under the impetus of war and, aside from the purely military business of the roads, general freight and passenger service was in greater demand than ever before. While the Southern roads were starving for lack of cash returns, those north of the Potomac and the Ohio were reaping a harvest. In fact, it is difficult to specify a single particular in which the roads of the North held no advantage over those in the South.

There is little evidence that Northern people were then conscious of their railroad superiority or of its significance. Few had yet observed the long shadow it cast across the Confederacy.

Despite this superiority, the North was not without grave railroad difficulties of its own—not vital problems of physical properties and financing such as threatened the South, but rather of control and operation. The public was aroused over the manner in which its military and civilian shipping was

being handled, and its protests led to early correction of evils
which otherwise might have nipped the fruits of advantage.
No single event or group of events was responsible for the
public reaction. It was the accumulation of irritations and
unexplained annoyances that sharpened tempers and exhausted
patience. Not only had rates risen far beyond apparent justification, but lack of freight-carrying capacity in east-west
civilian shipping was hurting business badly.

Why had the War Department not protected the B.&O. or
cleared it so as to restore service? At a time when the
Pennsylvania was publishing notice in the West that no more
consignments to the seaboard cities could be accepted,[16]
hundreds of B.&O. engines and cars stood idle and appeals to
the Secretary of War went unanswered. Why was Simon
Cameron urging Congress to authorize government aid to a
company which proposed to build a brand-new road which
would by-pass Baltimore and give the already glutted Pennsylvania and Northern Central a direct connection with Washington? Eastern newspapers published charges that Cameron
was manipulating military shipping to favor his Northern
Central against other roads. In the Northwest, scandal was
spreading in connection with contracts made by quartermasters for the transportation of troops and supplies. Suspicion
was ripening into conviction that responsibility for the
lengthening list of railroad aggravations rested with the War
Department, and that within its organization existed a cabal
bent on turning civilian as well as military shipping to
personal profit.

For the transportation of troops and supplies it had long
been the department's practice to advertise for bids from all
available carriers. Contracts were then let in accordance with
the recommendation of the quartermaster involved in the
movement.[17] During the brief tenure of Frémont as Commander of the Military Department of the West, ugly rumors
drifted eastward charging his quartermasters with graft. A
Congressional Committee on Government Contracts went to
St. Louis to investigate. It was immediately discovered that
the practice of seeking competitive bids had been abandoned.

Instead, a schedule of rates applicable to all roads had been put into effect by Edward H. Castle, in charge of railroad transportation in the department. Two cents per mile per man for carrying soldiers and local rates on all government freights were specified.

An examination of claims filed under this arrangement promptly uncovered startling abuses. During the examination even the claimants admitted that the two-cent fare had proved profitable in handling large bodies of men, and that the freight rates were substantially higher than their ordinary "through freight" charges. The committee reported that on a shipment of horses the government had paid a "per car" excess of eighty per cent over the average to ordinary customers. In another case an excess payment of $20,000 came to light.[18] Such disclosures could not fail to lend credence to rumors that quartermasters were lining fat purses with the returns from preferential contracting, that things had come to such a pass that even regimental commanders were selling the privilege of transporting their men and equipment. There was plenty of profit for a handsome bonus.

The origin of this schedule was traced to Tom Scott, who had sent it out from Washington in July. Called on for an explanation, Cameron brusquely informed the committee it was by no means intended as a schedule of rates to be applied uniformly, but was, in fact, a specification of maximum charges which were not to be exceeded.[19] This explanation satisfied no one. It was consistent neither with the use of the schedule nor with Scott's instructions to the Quartermaster Department when it was first presented. Scott had written Major Sibley: "In making settlements with railroad companies for transportation of troops and supplies, please observe the following as a general basis." This preface was followed by definite specification of "first-class local rates" and no mention was made of any "maximum" charges to be observed.[20]

Doubtless Cameron's weak reply to the committee only hastened ready appreciation of how the Northern Central would profit immensely by the application of Scott's schedule. By collecting "local freight" rates from Harrisburg to Baltimore on government shipments originating at Pittsburgh or beyond, the Northern Central would enjoy a savory differential as against sharing in the customary "through freight" charges. The committee later would report flagrant frauds in connection with the shipping, at "local rates," of beef cattle from the Northwest to feed the army about Washington.

Except for those roads which had been seized as the nucleus of the system of United States Military Railroads, Cameron had no authority over railroad operations. For coordination of military shipping he was obliged to rely on negotiations and persuasion, and in dealing with the railroads Scott had acted from near the beginning as his agent and mouthpiece. In August, Cameron had in no wise diverted public suspicion of his administration by manipulating the appointment of Scott to the post of Assistant Secretary of War. Scott's dislike of Garrett and bitter opposition to him were well known, and his appointment immediately accentuated the B.&O. controversy. With his authority and prestige greatly enhanced in the department, little hope could be entertained for more vigorous military aid in reopening the shattered main stem of Garrett's road.

Felton, the only man in the original transportation cast who was not involved in the Pennsylvania-B.&O. competition, had broken with Cameron over his attempt to force military traffic between Philadelphia and Baltimore to be routed via Harrisburg and the Northern Central rather than over the shorter and more direct Philadelphia, Wilmington & Baltimore. Cameron sent Scott to induce Felton to lift his barrage of newspaper attack on the War Department's connivance in diverting business from the P.,W.&B. to the Northern Central. This resulted only in convincing the public that Scott, too, was a willing participant in an audacious scheme to manipulate military shipping.

By his early appointments and orders after becoming Assistant Secretary of War, Scott helped things none at all. One of his first moves was to open a through passenger service between the capital and New York via the Washington branch of the B.&O. and the P.,W.&B. To supervise it he called Thomas H. Canfield, former president of the Washington & Rutland.[21] Under Scott's authority Canfield retained operating control over the B.&O. segment of the route while merely supervising the service over the P.,W.&B. The arrangement neither appeased the outraged Felton nor weakened public opinion that the War Department coterie meant to keep Garrett on a short leash whatever the cost to the war effort or to civilian shipping.

Another incident of the autumn reacted badly against Scott and Cameron. Little more than a month after his promotion Scott had selected R. N. Morley to act, under his authority, as manager of the military railroads. Morley was commissioned a disbursing officer in the quartermaster division with the rank of captain. The appointment drew no criticism, but the early report he made to Cameron in November was a strange and revealing document. Though signing as "General Manager, U. S. Military Railroads," it clearly appears Morley had received from Scott no authority over the transportation of troops or military freight. Despite his high-sounding title, Morley's job seems to have been only that of looking after repair and construction details and signing a report to the Secretary. The strangest thing about this wholly strange report is that it should have been made at all. In the short time elapsing between his appointment and his filing of the report, nothing of sufficient importance had happened to warrant a report to the Secretary. Indeed, it contains little reference to any operation for which Morley was responsible or in which he was involved even remotely. Instead, it is composed of a summary of Scott's activities from the time of the army concentration on Washington through the Bull Run campaign. Morley recounts the seizure and operation of the Washington branch of the B.&O. and the Annapolis & Elk Ridge with which he had nothing to do. To this story he appends the following unrelated but highly significant statement about a matter in controversy: "Previous to this period the enemy destroyed seven bridges upon the Northern Central Railroad north of Baltimore, which were immediately rebuilt by the company, protected by the Government."

It may have been by accident rather than design that this statement was placed on file at the very time Felton was charging that the engineering expense of rehabilitating the Northern Central was borne by the government though like aid in rebuilding the burned bridges of the P.,W.&B. had been refused. In any event, the Northern Central was no part of the system of military railroads, and if its bridges were "rebuilt by the company" one is hard put to find any reason for the "General Manager of U. S. Military Railroads" to report that fact to the Secretary of War. If the words "protected by the Government" are relied on for an explanation, the question immediately arises why similar protection was not extended to the B.&O.

In the well-known circumstances, if the critics chose to regard this as nothing more than a self-serving plea made under the guise of an official report and authored by someone other than the newly appointed quartermaster captain who signed it, Cameron and Scott had no one but themselves to blame.[22]

With one such incident following another in rapid succession, it is not surprising that when Congress met in December a committee was appointed to investigate the whole business of military transportation.

CHAPTER X

THE ROADS IN THE TENNESSEE FIGHTING,
SPRING '62

I

The year 1862 was to disclose with what foresight Mc-
Clellan had spoken when he counseled President Lincoln not
to ignore the importance of the new element the railroads had
introduced into war. The wisdom of that counsel became
apparent at the outset of the spring campaign of the Federals
in Kentucky and Tennessee.

It opened on February 2, with Grant's thrust at Fort
Henry. Four days later the fort was his and at his request
the gunboat *Carondelet* "ascended the Tennessee River and
thoroughly destroyed the bridge of the Memphis and Ohio
Railroad."[1] At the time little note was taken of this seemingly
unimportant bit of work but Grant knew what he was about.
The *Carondelet* had broken Johnston's line of communication
between his center at Bowling Green and his left at Columbus
and thus laid a tremendous handicap on his subsequent operations.

Without waiting further orders from General Henry W.
Halleck, his department commander at St. Louis, Grant set
out immediately on an eleven-mile march across the narrow
watershed to strike Fort Donelson on the Cumberland. After
two days of bitter fighting, it surrendered to him on February
16. Meantime, General Buell, who now commanded the
Department of the Ohio, was moving southward along the
L.&N. Railroad, intent on breaking through the Confederate
line at Bowling Green. This was the Federal approach
Johnston had most feared from the beginning.

Torrential rains had filled the rivers and greatly increased the cruising range of the Federal gunboats. The Tennessee was now open to them all the way to northern Alabama where the Memphis & Charleston Railroad so closely paralleled its southern bank as to be vulnerable to attack from the river side. On the Cumberland the reduction of Fort Donelson had brought Nashville within their reach. Unable, through the loss of the M.&O. bridge, to co-operate with Polk's army at Columbus, and with Grant and the gunboats free to strike in his rear, Johnston saw there was nothing to be gained by fighting Buell at the Big Barren. Suddenly his long defense line had become untenable. Without waiting for Buell to attack, he abandoned his fortified position at Bowling Green and retreated across the Cumberland.

The first phase of the campaign was over. Although Grant and Foote had been obliged to beg of the reluctant Halleck permission "to go up the Tennessee and take Fort Henry as a base for further operations"[2] and all the rest had been accomplished without orders or directives from him, Halleck claimed credit for the brilliant successes and as a reward received the coveted appointment as supreme commander in the West. All the troops in the contested area fell under his control. How well did he understand the "new element the railroads had introduced into war"?

However much Johnston was disappointed by the Federal successes he was neither taken by surprise nor frustrated by them. At the outset he had decided to make his defense of Nashville at Fort Donelson because he considered the city otherwise indefensible. Should this plan not succeed, he knew his next stand must be at some point behind the Tennessee River where he could restore co-ordination between his left and center. So it came about that when he failed at Donelson he immediately directed his retreat toward Murfreesborough. When they learned their city was to be left to the mercy of the Federals, panic swept the population of Nashville.

Because of wild rumors the citizens clogged the highways and railroads in their desperate attempts to get out of town.[3] There were but two railroad outlets to the south. One was

the Nashville & Chattanooga through Murfreesborough to
Stevenson, Alabama, where it turned east to Chattanooga; the
other was the Alabama & Tennessee, which had not been
completed to the Tennessee River and had no connection at
its southern terminus. Drenched by a cold winter rain, the
people fled to the two railroad stations and jammed into and
atop every available car that could be attached to a movable
train.[4] They pressed private conveyances of every sort into
service, and paid fabulous prices. Into the midst of this confusion marched the retreating columns from Bowling Green.
Up the river came the boats bearing the wounded, the sick
and the survivors from Fort Donelson. Bedlam prevailed.

Nashville was one of the key cities of the Confederacy.
She not only manufactured ordnance and a wide variety of
army supplies but contained huge depots of army stores on
which the armies in Virginia as well as those in the West
depended. The loss of much of this military property could
have been prevented had Johnston, at the first sign of panic,
seized the railroads and placed them under military control
as Ben Butler had done in Maryland. Employment of troops
to bring things under control and take over the railroads for
use in evacuation of stores came too late to accomplish much.
Trains which had gone south packed with civilians and their
belongings were ordered returned at once. They must be
used first for moving out the sick and wounded of the army.
As trains became available, hundreds of the unfortunates were
placed aboard them and dispatched to Chattanooga. Through
freezing winter weather they rode unattended in unheated
boxcars. Of the 300 men on the first train, three were dead
before arrival and two more died immediately after.[5] Hospital
trains would come, but no one had yet forseen the railroad
cast in such a role.

It was not until Sunday morning, February 23, an entire
week after the panic started, that Buell's pickets first appeared
on the riverbank opposite the city. Meantime, on the nineteenth, the two bridges across the Cumberland had been
wrecked to prevent their use by the Federals. One of these
was the fine new bridge of the L.&N., only lately completed.

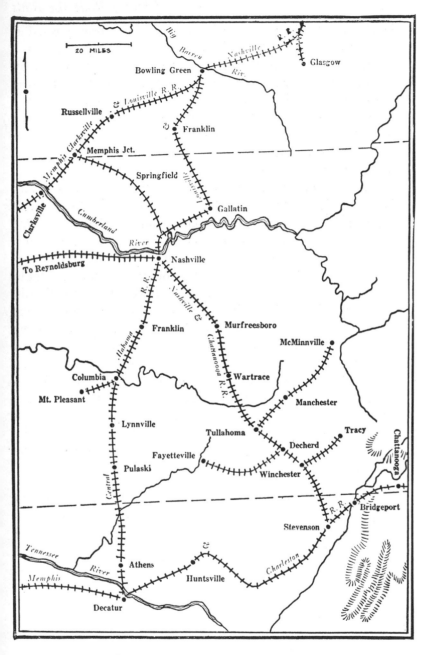

LINES IN THE NASHVILLE AREA

During the week, removal of army stores had been pushed as rapidly as confusion and crippled transportation would allow. A fresh deluge of rain on Saturday washed out two near-by bridges on the Nashville & Chattanooga and put an end to the work of evacuation. Some stores had been saved but they were only a small part of those which could have been removed had the railroads been taken.in control sooner. On the twenty-third the last of the Confederate soldiers passed out of Nashville, never to return.

Deprived of communication with the troops which had formed his left, Johnston at Murfreesborough was precariously exposed. The surrender at Donelson had so reduced his force as to make a stand against Buell entirely too dangerous. Beauregard, who had lately come out from Virginia to command west of the Tennessee, was not strong enough to hold if Grant should undertake to drive between them. Obviously the safety of both depended on a speedy concentration. Since he could not hope to defend both middle Tennessee and the line of the Mississippi, Johnston decided it was more important to concentrate to protect Memphis and the river and so notified President Davis on February 27.[6] It afforded a chance for him to reach Beauregard, then at Jackson, Tennessee, in time for their combined forces to attack and defeat Grant before he could be reinforced by Buell.

Robert S. Henry vividly points out the significance of the point selected for the concentration.

A few years before, Corinth had become a railroad junction of importance, at the crossing of the Mobile & Ohio Railroad, north and south, and the Memphis & Charleston, east and west. Through connections at Grand Junction, rail transportation reached southward to New Orleans, and at Chattanooga to all of the eastern South. For that reason, Corinth was chosen by Albert Sidney Johnston as his place of concentration for making a stand below the Tennessee River.[7]

Fortunately for Johnston, Halleck was still quibbling over matters of authority and procedure instead of pressing his advantage. This gave Johnston time to retire in good order to the line of the Memphis & Charleston near Huntsville, Alabama, whence he was to move westward behind the Tennessee to Corinth. From examination of the maps of the area, one may well wonder why, instead of marching from Murfreesborough via Shelbyville and Fayetteville, he did not move by rail over the Nashville & Chattanooga to Stevenson, Alabama, and thence westward by the M.&C. The answer is found in a letter which was written after the war by General Jeremy F. Gilmer to General Johnston's son and which further illustrates the tragic lack of capacity and efficiency of the railroads:

As to the movements by rail from Murfreesborough to Stevenson and thence to Corinth by the Charleston and Memphis Railroad [sic], it was simply impossible without sacrificing the supplies and munitions on which the subsistence and armament of the command depended. The entire transportation capacity of the railroads was taxed to the utmost and even then immense quantities of meat and other commissary supplies were left at Nashville, Murfreesborough, Shelbyville, Fayetteville and Huntsville. Again, the movement was made over the roads leading to Shelbyville, Fayetteville and Huntsville as expeditiously, considering the number of troops to be transported, as it could have been by rail, with the imperfect organization of the railroads as it then existed.[8]

In justice to the railroad management it must be remembered that the Confederate government had no co-ordinator of transportation. The panic at Nashville and the frenzied flight of citizens had come without warning, and in the midst of the confusion army officers had impressed rolling stock with which to salvage army stores. With no one in authority to organize rail transportation, it is no wonder railroad management was unable to handle it.

On his arrival in Corinth, Johnston found most of his troops already assembled. Columbus had been evacuated, and down from the north over the Mobile & Ohio had come the troops from the Columbus, Humboldt and Jackson areas. Over the Mississippi Central, General Daniel Ruggles had brought up

5,000 men from New Orleans. With 10,000 more General Braxton Bragg came up the M.&O. from Mobile and Pensacola. All of these were joined by smaller groups collected from along the line of the Memphis & Charleston. Except for the concentration of the Union Army at Washington the previous April, Johnston's move to Corinth involved the most extensive use of railroads for military purposes then known to history.

It nowhere appears that serious consideration was given to a very grave danger inherent in this procedure. Should the concentration at Corinth draw the full strength of the Federal armies of the West to that vicinity and should Johnston be defeated there, the entire transportation system of the Confederacy west of Chattanooga and north of Vicksburg would be paralyzed. The life of the Confederacy in the West was the stake in the game Johnston was playing.

More than a month had elapsed since the fall of Nashville, yet Halleck had in no wise interfered with the assembly, within thirty miles of the Tennessee River which he controlled, of the largest army the Federals were ever called on to face west of the mountains.

2

Polk's troops had been gone from Columbus more than a week before Halleck moved. Johnston was safely across the Tennessee and heading west from Decatur. Ruggles and Bragg were pouring thousands of men into the vicinity of Corinth. Halleck was still engrossed in petulant correspondence with Washington over a fancied insubordination of Grant. At last he sent some units steaming up the Tennessee aboard transports. Sherman, restored to the command of a division, led the way and was under orders to precede the main body of troops to Eastport, Mississippi, land there, march across the narrow strip of land and cut the Memphis & Charleston. Just what Halleck thought to accomplish by this maneuver is not clear. Eastport is too near Corinth for a break at that point to have had any serious effect on Johnston's plans. Any damage Sherman could have done would have been easily repaired as soon as he withdrew and there was no chance for him to remain there and prevent repairs. Besides, Johnston was in no sense dependent on the railroad east from Corinth for supplies or troop transport. In any event Sherman's little expedition was a failure because the heavy rains had so swamped the low country thereabout that he could not reach the railroad and had to return downstream. At Pittsburg Landing, seven miles above Savannah, he disembarked his division and went into camp on the rolling ground which bordered the river on the west.

Finally rid of the restrictions Halleck had placed on him, Grant arrived at Savannah on March 17 to resume command of the entire army which he found scattered on both sides of the river from Savannah to Pittsburg Landing. On Sherman's recommendation he selected the Pittsburg Landing campsite as the point at which to gather his forces.

Apparently it had at last dawned on Halleck that his situation and Johnston's had been reversed. It was his turn to develop co-ordination between widely separated armies. Buell was ordered to march through railroadless country south of Nashville and join Grant at Savannah on the Tennessee. Whatever may have been Halleck's ultimate objective, Grant knew precisely what should be done next. Because of its railroad significance he regarded Corinth as "the great strategic position at the West between the Tennessee and Mississippi Rivers and between Nashville and Vicksburg."[9] If he could obtain possession of Corinth, the enemy would have no railroad for the transportation of armies or supplies until that running east from Vicksburg was reached. He meant to strike there as soon as Buell joined him.[10]

But Johnston had not come to Corinth merely to await attack. If possible he meant to whip Grant's Army of the Tennessee before Buell could arrive and for that purpose, on April 3, he set 40,000 men moving toward Pittsburg Landing. He had only twenty-three miles to travel, but somehow he

spent three days on the march and it was Sunday morning
April 6 before he struck the first blow at the Federals in the
neighborhood of Shiloh Church. By two untoward events a
great victory was snatched from the grasp of the Confederates.

While the tide of Sunday's battle was running strongly in
his favor, the bullet destined for Albert Sidney Johnston
found its mark and for him the war was at an end.

Despite his late arrival at the field and his untimely death,
success for his men seemed certain, for when night came to
silence the guns of Shiloh, Grant's army was in desperate
plight. Shattered and exhausted, it lay cornered atop the
muddy bluff between the river and rain-swollen Snake Creek.
Then, at Monday's dawn, the men from Corinth were called
on to pay an appalling price for the time wasted on their
twenty-three-mile march to the field. On Sunday afternoon
while they were driving Grant, and had victory almost won,
Buell's Army of the Ohio was completing its long march to
the east bank of the river. In the night it crossed, and on
Monday the combined Federal armies savagely ripped the
Confederate lines and sent them reeling back on Corinth.
Johnston was dead and his hopes had been in vain.

Halleck's ambitions were flowering and he was quick to
take personal advantage of the successes won by his subordinates. Four days after Shiloh he arrived at Pittsburg Landing
from St. Louis and "immediately assumed command in the
field." Although promptly reinforced in numbers more than
twice the casualties suffered at Shiloh,[11] he made no move to
pursue the defeated enemy until the last day of April. Had he
not yet comprehended the staggering blow that might be dealt
the entire Confederacy by the swift reduction of Corinth?
Was he afraid to risk the prestige won for him by his subordinates in a quick stroke of his own to capture that railroad
prize?

After a long delay which distressed his corps commanders
he moved on, but at a snail's pace while constructing a network of roads and entrenchments over every mile advanced.

Discouraged by the slow progress, Grant and others sought to convince him that time was far more important than trenches, but he stubbornly stuck to his policy, literally digging his way across the intervening miles. At last, in the morning of May 30, fifty-three days after Shiloh, he faced Corinth in full battle formation and waited to receive the attack he expected from the Confederates. Instead of an attack he received embarrassing news. Corinth had been evacuated.

If Halleck had hoped to win glory by personally leading his troops to a spectacular victory in the West, he had frittered away his opportunity with a month of digging useless trenches through the Mississippi woods. Not only had the Confederates escaped him but they had used the abundance of time to ship out their sick and wounded, their ordnance, their accumulated stores and all their equipment. Corinth's railroads had served them well, both before and after their defeat at Shiloh. They were, of course, a great prize left to Halleck when he occupied the place without opposition, but he had let Beauregard, the new commander, get ready to fight another day.[12]

So it was, at the end of May 1862, that Union forces held a firm grip on a vital part of the Confederates' one line of railroad between Virginia and the Mississippi River. They, instead of the enemy, now had an east-west rail line across the tops of Alabama and Mississippi. The full length of the L.&N. was now in their possession. They held the Nashville & Chattanooga as far as Stevenson, Alabama, and the junction with the Memphis & Charleston. The Mobile & Ohio all the way from Columbus, Kentucky, to Corinth was in their hands. They held the Mississippi Central between Grand Junction and Jackson, Tennessee, and the Memphis & Ohio which, with its L.&N. connection at Bowling Green, provided a direct line between Louisville and Memphis.

Not all of these roads were in good condition. For example, Confederate Colonel Robert W. Wooley wrote of the Memphis & Ohio at the time Fort Donelson fell:

The railroad was almost bare of transportation. The locomotives had not been repaired for six months and many of
them lay disabled in the depots. They could not be repaired
at Bowling Green, for there is, I am informed, but one place
in the South where a driving-wheel can be made and not one
where a whole locomotive can be constructed.[13]

But when the Federals took possession of roads, the shortage
of rolling stock was quite readily solved. They had engines
and cars brought down from the North, and if their supply
was not sufficient they placed orders for more with the
manufacturers. They had a far greater supply of trained
workmen to replace or repair damaged and worn-out track.

While the battlefield of Shiloh was twenty-three miles
from the nearest railroad and the sole objective of Johnston's
attack was to destroy Grant's army, the result proved one
of the greatest railroad victories of the war. Leading directly,
as it did, to the occupation of Corinth, it did precisely what
Johnston had risked happening when he concentrated there:
it paralyzed the entire rail transportation of the Confederacy
west of Chattanooga and north of Vicksburg. It set up for
the Union a network of rail communications which permitted
operations as far south as Alabama and Mississippi and as far
east as Stevenson, Alabama, without fear of overstretching
supply lines.

All of the Northwest was within speedy reach of the Ohio
River at Cincinnati, Louisville, Madison and Cairo. From
that river, men and cargo could be put ashore at railheads
for Nashville and Stevenson, for Humboldt and Jackson, for
Corinth and Memphis. Then via the Memphis & Charleston
they could be shuttled back and forth between east and west,
south of the Tennessee, and all this regardless of the water
stage in the upper reaches of the Cumberland and Tennessee
rivers.

Before the year end we shall see with what savagery the
soldiers of the South fought to recover control of these rail-

roads and with what determination the Federals fought to keep what they had won. However, with few exceptions, there is little to indicate that at the time the North understood or appreciated what, besides a battle, it had won at Shiloh, or that the South realized what it had lost when, throughout Kentucky and Tennessee, its engineers were replaced at the throttles of the locomotives by men from north of the Ohio.

CHAPTER XI

Stonewall Jackson Knows How to Use a Railroad

I

Before March 1862 the Manassas Gap Railroad well might have been referred to as the Meat Line of the Confederacy. Beside its track at Thoroughfare Gap the army had built an extensive meat-packing plant, and during the fall of 1861 and the winter which followed, the road carried there great quantities of livestock from the Shenandoah farms for slaughter and processing. Over the lower end of the same railroad both fresh and cured meat was then shipped on to supply the army of General Joseph E. Johnston, which lay in winter quarters about Centreville in front of Washington. The rail haul, first from farm to packing plant and thence to commissary, was short and direct. As long as the Army of Northern Virginia occupied the old Manassas line, no more effective or convenient arrangement could have been wished for. The plant was only thirteen miles west of the Orange & Alexandria junction, by way of which its products could be readily shipped to troops in central Virginia.

As spring approached, a large surplus of cured meat was accumulating, yet livestock by the thousand head continued pouring into the slaughter pens. No one seemed disturbed by the fact that this large and extremely important operation was located very near enemy lines or that the railroad on which it depended was quite vulnerable to enemy attack. Nothing should have been more obvious than the certainty that if expediency or necessity required Johnston's retirement even

The Famous Potomac Creek Bridge on the R., F. & P.
Herman Haupt built this bridge in nine rainy days from standing timber. Lincoln said,
"There is nothing in it but beanpoles and cornstalks."

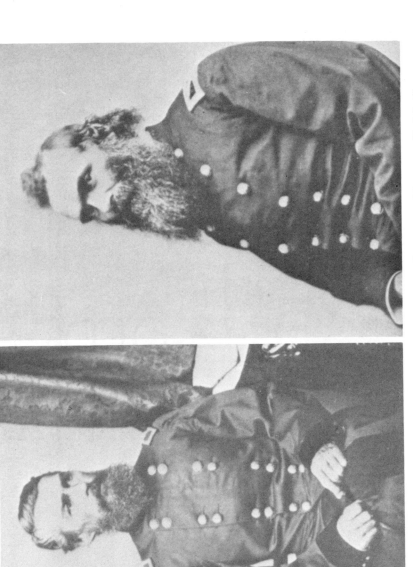

Brigadier General Herman Haupt,
Union Railroad Genius

Brigadier General Daniel C. McCallum,
Director and General Manager of the

for a short distance, the entire plant would fall into the hands of the Federals.[1]

Meat was not the only surplus which piled up in Johnston's immediate rear. Huge depots of stores had been accumulating at Manassas Junction. It was as though commissary and quartermaster officers had suddenly found the railroads an effective means for silencing the traditional abuse to which their like had been subjected since soldiers first went to war. Into the Manassas depots they poured trainloads of excess stores in utter disregard of the proximity of a great Union army. After the war Johnston was to say he had repeatedly sought to have this shipping halted but over his protests more than three times the carloadings he needed continued to come forward.[2]

A vast amount of matériel belonging to the separate states had been shipped to Manassas where it was stored in charge of their agents. And that was not all. The soldiers had come to Manassas by train, and since there was no limit on the amount of baggage each might carry, "a trunk came with every soldier." Johnston described this accumulation as "such a quantity of baggage as no such army had ever before collected together."[3] He might well have added that never before had any such army been served by railroads operating in its immediate rear. Perhaps this prodigal massing of supplies too near the enemy was due to men in high places having assumed from their success at Manassas the previous July that this line was firmly established.

Johnston held no such optimistic view. He had watched the steady development of the vast army McClellan was assembling and training in his front, and correctly assumed its purpose to be a determined spring offensive. Repeatedly he expressed his opinion that the Manassas line could not be held in event of an all-out attack. Already at odds with President Davis and Secretary Benjamin, he was summoned to Richmond for a conference on February 19. On arrival he found the President conferring with the Cabinet on the late him to confer on the question of withdrawing his army from the Manassas line—whether it should be done and, if so, when and how. Johnston offered his opinion that since McClellan could advance along so many lines of his own choosing, the Confederates should not attempt to maintain their position but should pull back farther south.[4] However, he stoutly maintained that because of muddy roads and the tremendous amount of property to be moved, the withdrawal should not be undertaken until winter was over. Otherwise, large losses of equipment, guns and stores would be certain.

Questioned by Davis, Johnston was unprepared to recommend a specific line to which the army should retire.[5] The President irritably insisted that in any event the heavy guns in the Potomac batteries and those emplaced about Manassas must be brought out, while Johnston argued they could not be moved until the roads settled in the spring. Other than increased tension between Davis and the general, little came of the discussion. Johnston returned to his command with no orders more specific than to lead his army southward to a more secure front as soon as practicable. Could he and the President agree on the interpretation of such general terms?

Geographically the Army of Northern Virginia then occupied three distinct military districts. The main body occupied a line north of the Manassas Gap Railroad and roughly extending from the Blue Ridge Mountains to Occoquan Creek. On the left the District of the Valley was commanded by Jackson with headquarters at Winchester. On the right the troops in the Potomac District which lay north of the Rappahannock and included the northern terminus of the R.,F.&P. Railroad, were under the command of General T. H. Holmes.

Within this sprawling and vastly important area extending from the Shenandoah to Aquia Creek Landing lay three railroads which inevitably would become involved in the retirement of the army to a "more secure position." The story of what happened to these roads and how they were employed sheds much light on the early Confederate approach to the railroad as a military adjunct as well as on the structural weakness of the roads themselves.

After much controversy between President Davis and General Johnston, an early retirement of the army was ordered. On February 22 the Quartermaster and Subsistence Departments ordered the removal of all military property from the depots at Manassas and environs to Gordonsville as rapidly as possible and appealed to President John S. Barbour of the Orange & Alexandria to operate the railroad to full capacity for that purpose.[6] No military man seems to have anticipated the difficulties involved in speedily moving the incredible mass of accumulated property over a single-track railroad which had only very limited sidetrack facilities.[7] Under severe criticism from Richmond for delay in getting under way, Johnston wrote President Davis on February 28, blaming the "wretched management" of the railroad.[8] Again, on March 5, he complained to Davis that great sacrifices of property must be made because there were not enough engines and cars available.[9]

On behalf of the President, Quartermaster General Myers replied explaining that there were too many trains on the road already; that for lack of sidings they were unable to pass, and for that reason some engines had spent thirty-six hours making the sixty-mile run from Manassas to Gordonsville. He pointed out that all available engines and cars of the O.&A., the Manassas Gap and the Virginia Central were already engaged in the operation and no additions could be made.[10] Of the effort to move this property, Douglas Southall Freeman says: "The operation of this railway during the first days of March, 1862, was an early classic example of the manner in which a single-tracked line that lacked adequate sidings could be overcrowded with trains."[11]

On March 7 the main body of the army started moving southward, and three days later the rear guard applied the torch to the depots in the Manassas area. Such supplies as had not been moved out were destroyed, and with them went the packing plant at Thoroughfare and a large quantity of fresh and salt meat. Such a loss was appalling and it seemed to the people wholly unnecessary. Stung by the criticism heaped on him, Johnston undertook to shift the responsibility to President Davis for having ordered the move made too early, to the Commissary Department for having overstocked the depots, and to the railroads for their failure to carry the supplies with dispatch.

The reply of Colonel L. B. Northrop, Commissary General, is a contribution to the record of how the railroad was used.

Two weeks before his [Johnston's] move, he promised my officer, Major Noland, the transportation deemed sufficient and of which he had assumed direct control. Empty trains passed the meat which had been laid in piles, ready for shipment. Empty trains lay idle at Manassas for days, in spite of Noland's efforts to get them. General Johnston says the stores of other departments were brought off. Eight hundred new army saddles, several thousand pairs of new shoes and a large number of new blankets were burned.[12]

Considering his conduct during this retirement and his extensive writing on the subject, one may find it difficult to escape the conclusion that at that time Johnston had little appreciation or understanding of the railroad potential in military affairs. By his criticism of the O.&A. he clearly disclosed his ignorance of how to use the railroad and what was to be expected of it. Not until February 22 was the road informed that what he repeatedly described as a formidable accumulation of army stores and baggage was to be shipped to Gordonsville, yet he complained that it was not all moved out by the end of the first week in March. At no time did he show the slightest concept of how the capacity of the road was limited by its single track and inadequate switching facilities.

According to Northrop, he had assumed direct control of the road, yet he complained of its "wretched mismanagement." Obviously the general had not yet learned that efficient railroad operation is accomplished only through direction by skilled railroad executives unhampered by military field commanders. It took a long time for some high-ranking officers to learn that elementary lesson.

In his *Narrative*, written after the fact, Johnston tells of his analysis of the probable invasion routes to be used by the Federals, but not once does he mention the service to which they might have put the railroads. Neither does he refer to the consequences of abandoning the railroads of northern Virginia to the enemy. If, in early 1862, the field commander of the greatest Confederate army had as yet conceived the military significance of railroad transportation, he disclosed it by neither word nor deed. Nowhere was his disregard of it more clearly demonstrated than in his relations with General Holmes.

Despite the fact that within the district commanded by Holmes lay the northern terminus of the R.,F.&P. and its track between Fredericksburg and the Potomac, Johnston's orders left Holmes entirely in the dark as to when he should fall back, the line to which he would withdraw, or what should be done about the railroad.[13] From the time he left Manassas until safely behind the Rappahannock, Johnston was completely out of touch with Holmes and, so far as Johnston knew or seemed to care, the R.,F.&P. was to be a gift to the Federals as a link in the most direct route to Richmond.

On March 11, while Johnston's army was on the move and its location or destination unknown to either Holmes or the War Department, Adjutant General Cooper sent Holmes this word:

Mr. Daniel, President of the Richmond, Fredericksburg and Potomac, has been advised by the Secretary of War to cause that part of the road between Aquia Creek and Fredericksburg to be broken up and the rails to be removed to some place of safety. You are requested to give such facilities in men and means as may be in your power, to accomplish this object.[14]

In the previous spring the Confederates had lost the Alexandria, Hampshire & Loudoun short line between Alexandria and Leesburg. Now, by their retirement, they were abandoning the Manassas Gap, the R.,F.&P. north of Fredericksburg and the Orange & Alexandria as far south as the Rappahannock. It was only spring of 1862, yet, out of their limited rail facilities, the Confederates already had lost all those in Kentucky, western Tennessee and northern Virginia. Only such Confederates as Robert E. Lee and Stonewall Jackson understood the magnitude of that loss.

Johnston took up his new station behind the Rappahannock and its tributary Rapidan. Almost parallel with his line, and not more than.twenty-five miles behind it, ran the Virginia Central, one of the most important railroads in the South. At Gordonsville it intercepted the O.&A. which passed through his left center. From Fredericksburg, the R.,F.&P. gave his right wing a direct rail connection with Richmond, only fifty miles away. At Hanover Junction it crossed the Virginia Central which also turned south to Richmond from there. Thus was formed a parallelogram, three sides of which were first-class railroads and the fourth the army's new defensive line. To what extent, if any, Johnston took into account this remarkable railroad potential in selecting his new position does not appear. In fact, one may search in vain for any evidence that he attached to it any importance whatever. His one purpose seems to have been to put the Rappahannock River between his army and the enemy.

The relation of the railroads to the Army of Northern Virginia appeared soon enough. Less than a month from the time it arrived on the Rappahannock, McClellan's campaign on the Peninsula was developing threatening proportions. Three divisions of Johnston's command were detached and ordered to join Magruder. Now we have the first friendly reference from Johnston to transportation of troops by rail. We have his rather boastful word for it that 18,000 men were sent from his army to the Peninsula "as fast as the railroad trains could carry them."[15]

Had it never come to his mind that over these same rails and at like speed, reinforcements could have reached him had the blow fallen on his front instead of at Yorktown? It seems unlikely, because shortly thereafter the Peninsula was added to the area of his command, and before being wounded at Seven Pines he was preparing to abandon the Virginia Central west of Hanover Junction.[16] This would indeed have been a great mistake.

About this time an unfortunate occurrence on the Virginia Central demonstrated the danger of army officers' interference with train operation. While reinforcements were being hurried to Richmond, a heavily loaded Orange & Alexandria troop train was being shunted to the Virginia Central track at Gordonsville at the same time a similar Central train was preparing to leave for the same destination. When the question arose which train should take precedence, a pompous Louisiana colonel ordered the O.&A. train ahead, climbed into the engine cab and bellowed, "Let 'em roll." Soon after these trains left Gordonsville it became necessary to send out a special westbound train from Richmond. Its conductor was ordered to run to Hanover Junction and report. Assuming that the eastbound Central train would stop at the junction for orders, the train dispatcher expected to arrange a meeting of the trains at that point. He had no reason to anticipate the conduct of the army officer who, aboard the O.&A. engine, demanded of the engineer the greatest possible speed and passed Hanover Junction without a pause.

On a curve which ran through a cut near Little River, the troop train smashed head on into the westbound train and one of the worst wrecks suffered by the railroads during the entire war resulted. The old wooden cars were telescoped and split apart, and the fragments were strewn along the right of way and driven into the banks of the cut. Among them lay the mangled bodies of a trainload of Confederate soldiers. They had met death at the hands of one of their own officers, who never lived to learn that interference with train operation was no part of his—or any other army officer's—job.[17]

2

At last the harried Baltimore & Ohio was to have a respite from the raids of Jackson's men who regularly came up from Winchester way to smash its tracks and bridges. It had been one of Stonewall's cherished objectives to destroy that railroad and reclaim northwestern Virginia; but when the main army retired from the Manassas line, he was allotted a very different task.

While he was wintering at Winchester, a Federal army far outnumbering his own and destined for the command of General N. P. Banks was assembling in his front. Jackson's new assignment was entirely defensive in nature. As the main army moved southward east of the mountains, he was to retire up the Valley, at all times keeping his forces so interposed between Banks and Johnston as to prevent the Federals from crossing the Blue Ridge and turning Johnston's flank.

Falling back from Winchester, first through Strasburg, then through Mount Jackson, he started a campaign of maneuver and surprise harassment against the pursuing enemy so bold in concept and effective in execution as to remain to this day a fascinating study for students of military tactics the world over. By April 21 Banks had reached Harrisonburg, forty-five miles south of Strasburg and within twenty-five miles of Staunton on the all-important Virginia Central Railroad. Though somewhat south of Johnston, he was still in the Valley with Jackson interposed. Quite unlike Johnston, Jackson understood the importance of the Virginia Central and was determined Banks should not cut it at Staunton. Though strongly reinforced, he was still too badly outnumbered to risk a full-fledged battle with Banks. He resorted to maneuver on a larger and bolder scale.

As far as Mount Jackson, Banks's supplies were coming in over the Manassas Gap Railroad, then carted the rest of the way. Jackson reasoned that if this road were cut at Front Royal, Banks would be forced to rely on a long wagon haul from Winchester; that such a supply line through such a

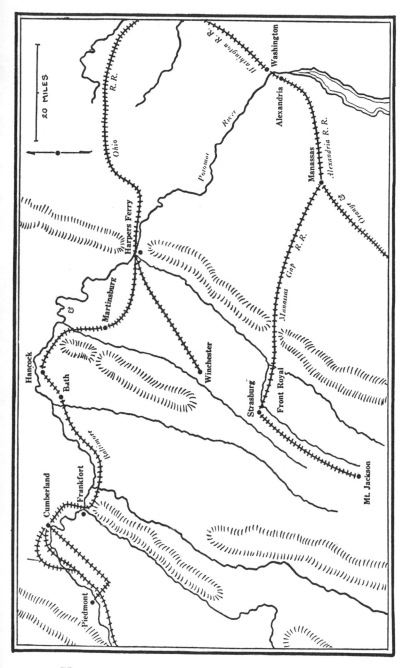

THE SHENANDOAH AND NORTHERN VIRGINIA

country would be so vulnerable to cavalry forays he could force Banks to fall back down the Valley. Success in the venture would relieve the pressure on Staunton and the danger to the Virginia Central. The scheme Jackson devised contemplated taking advantage of the peculiar geography of the Valley region, with every mile of which he had made himself familiar. The upper Valley is split in two by a short but rugged mountain range, the Massanuttens, extending from Harrisonburg down to Front Royal and Strasburg. The narrower valley east of the Massanuttens through which flows the South Fork of the Shenandoah River is known as the Luray. He calculated that by using the Massanuttens as a screen he might send a swiftly moving expedition down the Luray and strike the Manassas Gap Railroad at Front Royal before Banks became aware of his purpose.

Unexpectedly Banks retired from Harrisonburg and started retracing his route along the Valley pike on the west side of the mountain screen. For this strange movement the Confederates saw no explanation except that he was getting out of the Valley in order to join McClellan in the drive against Richmond. The sly fox of the Shenandoah straightway decided the time had come for him to take the offensive. With part of his force Jackson dogged Banks's heels as far as New Market while he dispatched Ewell's division rapidly down the Luray Valley. Then, by shifting troops back and forth over the little-known roads across the Massanuttens, he so deceived Banks that on May 23, in full strength, he swept out of the wooded hills above Front Royal and routed the Federal contingent left there to guard Manassas Gap and the railroad. By this brilliant maneuver Banks's supply line was broken and the whole of Jackson's army was on the flank of his long-drawn-out retreating column. How Jackson pressed his advantage until Banks was driven on through Winchester and finally across the Potomac is a great story but it is without railroad significance.

It is most unlikely that the people of Front Royal understood how Jackson's recapture of their little town and its railroad spelled disaster for Banks. Their interest was in the sudden reappearance of their own soldiers and that was sufficient to set them celebrating their "deliverance." Their joy was unbounded. A young lady of the town wrote in her diary:

The New Orleans Tigers played a most amusing prank on the Yankees today. It seems that in their hasty flight yesterday they left arms, ammunition, and clothing, tents, wagons and a large amount of commissary stores in our possession. The Tigers doffed their uniforms and donned the Yankee blue—then they got on the cars and steamed off to Markham where the news of the fall of Front Royal had not arrived and the Federal troops of course took them to be some of their own men and coming out of quarters at the invitation of the Tigers a number of them concluded to "take a ride up the road a little way." The hospitable Rebels not only extended the ride to Front Royal but also gave them lodging and board there au gratis [sic].[18]

A few days later Jackson's men were resting at Charlestown, a short distance from Harper's Ferry. Shocked by the defeat of Banks and the sudden reversal in the Valley, and overestimating Jackson's strength, Washington was in a dither lest this deadly and elusive wraith of the mountains swoop down on the capital. To forestall such an attack, the Federal command ordered Shields to cross the Blue Ridge from the east and co-operate with Frémont, who had been sent into the Shenandoah from the west in an attempt to trap Jackson where his chase of Banks ended. The cunning, courage and endurance that Stonewall showed in escaping from "the snare of the fowler" have no equal, but it was not until after he had made incredible marches, fought bloody battles and was safely back in Staunton, that the railroads re-enter his story.

3

North of the Rappahannock, McDowell commanded the Federal army which occupied much of the territory abandoned by Johnston in his retreat. Lee, who had succeeded to

field command when Johnston was wounded, was more than a
little concerned lest McDowell join forces with McClellan
and add a new complication to the defense of Richmond.
Well aware of Washington's fear of an attack by Jackson,
he reasoned that a good way to dispose of the McDowell
threat would be to reinforce Jackson, let him make another
march down the Valley and thus revive the fear of him in the
Federal capital. He collected a division of first-rate troops,
put them under General W. H. C. Whiting and sent them to
join Jackson.[19]

Meantime, a column from McClellan's right wing had made
a foray into the neighborhood of Hanover Court House and
burned the long bridges of both the Virginia Central and the
R.,F.&P. over the South Anna River. The reinforcements
for Jackson were unable, therefore, to go from Richmond

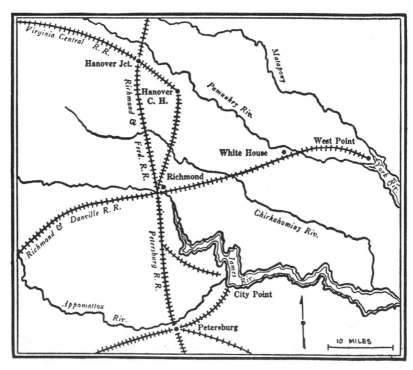

LINES IN THE RICHMOND AREA

directly via the Virginia Central. They had to be put aboard the Danville line, transferred at Burkeville to the South Side and taken to Lynchburg, where, because of the difference in gauge of the South Side and the O.&A., they were obliged to detrain. Confusion and delay resulted. The O.&A. had no passenger cars at Lynchburg, and trains to carry the troops to Charlottesville had to be made up of freight cars, work-train flats, cabooses and anything that could be found "with wheels on it."[20]

Before Whiting could complete the journey and report to Jackson in the Valley, Lee changed his plans. Instead of an attempt to draw McDowell back by a threat against Washington, the time had come to call Jackson from the Valley and, with the combined armies, take the offensive against McClellan on the Peninsula. Finding that Jackson liked the plan, Lee ordered him to bring his men out of the Valley. Ever the mastermind in the technique of deception and surprise, he readily understood the necessity for secrecy and devoted himself to maintaining it. Never a word of what was afoot did he speak to his staff or subordinate officers. Even after the troops were under way, their division and brigade commanders were left completely in the dark as to their destination. Other than that they were concentrating about Mechum's River Station and moving eastward along the Virginia Central, they knew nothing. The newly arrived Whiting was ordered to retrace his steps to Gordonsville. In his attempt to discover where he was supposed to go and what he was supposed to do, he became so mixed up and disgusted he declared of Jackson, "I believe he has no more sense than my horse."[21]

Officers, soldiers and railroad men entertained a common surmise that a movement toward Washington was in preparation. This seemed the more likely when Whiting's division arrived at Charlottesville and trains were made up to carry it on to Mechum's River Station; especially when these trains were unloaded and sent farther west to pick up and bring back the troops remaining around Staunton. Speculation turned entirely from destination to route. One question was settled when the trains returned to Mechum's and it was found that other trains had loaded everything there and were on the way back to Charlottesville. "Old Jack" was not going to hoof it down the Valley. He was going to ship north via the Orange & Alexandria Railroad on the east side of the mountains. But what about this? Before night, instead of passing through Charlottesville, the troops were debarked there. The men began to ask why, if they were shipping north, they were detraining at the junction.

Meantime, Superintendent Whitcomb of the Virginia Central had been collecting at Charlottesville everything in the way of rolling stock that could turn a wheel and ordering all train-operating personnel to report to him there. Some of these men, caught in Richmond when the South Anna bridge was destroyed, had come out with Whiting's division. As they reported, Whitcomb ordered them to arrange train crews to suit themselves but added to his instructions: "In consideration of the enormous task of moving such an army with so limited power, I would be glad to have one sober man in each crew and think it best not to put all the whisky men together." He could tell them nothing about where the army was to be moved. They could only "stand by" and await further orders.

The next morning the crewmen were told to take the infantry on to Gordonsville. Cavalry and artillery were taking to the country roads and moving in the same direction. There was not enough rolling stock to haul the entire army; not even enough to carry all the infantry. That was why Jackson applied the "riding and tying" plan. One group would occupy the trains for a time while the other group marched. Then the trains would unload, push back, pick up the marching group, pass the troops who had been first to ride, and repeat until the entire army was collected at Gordonsville.

This accomplished, the trainmen were ordered to load all trains and head them north toward Orange Court House. Definitely that was movement toward Washington and neither soldiers nor railroaders longer doubted where they were bound, but there was much delay and the soldiers fretted while the train crews swore. All day the crowded trains stood still or crept from one stop to another. Something had gone wrong. At nightfall other orders came. All trains must be unloaded and returned to Gordonsville. There they stood until morning, while the soldiers marched back to the campsites they had occupied the night before. Could there be truth in the rumor that Jackson was "crazy"? To many it began to look like it.

Very early in the morning an agent of the Virginia Central awakened the train crews by thumping a brake stick along the sides of the cars in which they were sleeping and bellowing an ominous announcement: Any engineer not ready to move his train in forty-five minutes would be shot.

The conductor of one of the trains was Charles S. Anderson. After the war he wrote the story of what happened that morning and for some days following. No record in print gives a better picture of military train operation in the Confederacy at the time. Anderson's engine was the "Monroe." His engineer was John Whalley, a big, hard-drinking man, loyal to the South, of inimitable good nature when sober but surly when drunk. The fireman Anderson describes as a "gingerbread free negro named John Wesley." The wood in the tender of the Monroe was sorry stuff—half-seasoned four-foot lengths they had picked up the day before from ricks beside the tracks. With it John Wesley could not get the boiler to steam, and with no better success Whalley took a hand at it. Soon all the other engines were ready to go and the deadline was creeping up on Whalley. Waiting troop officers, failing to grasp what was wrong, became suspicious of him and started accusing him of purposeful delay. Anderson knew the man well, understood his trouble and, feeling sorry for him, undertook to help. Behind a near-by building he found some empty barrels, rolled them to the stubborn engine and broke them up while John Wesley crammed the dry staves into the firebox. With them went all the waste in the cab. Off came the greasy coat of the engineer. He grabbed his greasier seat cushion and flung both coat and cushion into the firebox. The fireman's coat followed them in. Over the lot Whalley poured all the oil he could lay hold of, and in a few minutes the Monroe's steam gauge registered 140 pounds. He made the deadline by a hair's breadth and the soldiers cheered him as a hero.

This time when the trains were loaded, they headed east on the Virginia Central instead of north over the Orange & Alexandria. They were to run to Louisa Court House but no farther. Betting among the soldiers now ran strong with big odds: they were on their way to Richmond to help Lee whip McClellan. In a few hours, however, the odds were on the other side. The foremost trains were unloading at Louisa. One after another they pulled up to the station and the soldiers were ordered off. No, they were not going to Richmond. "Old Jack" was playing a game of riddles with the Yankees. They were going to Washington and the march from Louisa would be much shorter than from Gordonsville. Why else would they detrain at Louisa?

It was Saturday. On four miles of track through and on either side of Louisa the trains stood parked and empty over Sunday. On Sunday morning a revival meeting was held in camp, but the tired and baffled railroad men were not interested. They could find little to eat because the soldiers, now on short rations, bought up all the extra food available. Hoping for news of what they were supposed to do and when they might get out of Louisa, the hungry railroaders congregated about the telegraph office. There was no more news than food, but of one commodity there was an abundance in the neighborhood: it was not long before many of them were drunk from too much new apple brandy.

Near noon their curiosity was aroused by the screaming whistle of a locomotive coming from the east. How could that be when every Virginia Central engine west of the burned South Anna bridge was headed in the opposite direction? The noisy puzzle turned out to be a queer-looking little engine of the R.,F.&P. with a single car attached. It must have run the gantlet of Yankee pickets about Hanover Junction and be doing its level best to carry some important personage to Gordonsville or beyond. But how was it to pass the four-mile-long string of trains standing on the single track?

No engineer was too drunk to know the answer. All knew they would be ordered to fire up their cold engines, push the trains back past the opening of the one short sidetrack so the westbound nuisance could get in the clear. Then they would have to pull the trains forward to clear the switch and let the troublemaker out.

Half the afternoon the crews worked to open the track for the westbound train. His part of the job finished, John Whalley returned to the siding, eyed the little R.,F.&P. engine, compared it with the Monroe and contemptuously found it amusing. He offered to bet that he could pick ten men and hold the car so tightly the engine could not move it until he gave the order to let go. The bet was quickly covered. A pompous officer came up and ordered the engineer to take him to Charlottesville as fast as he could run. John and his men laid hold of the car and dug in their heels. The engine was stalled. When the cheering spectators made it clear John had won his bet, he reversed the pressure, shoved the little train onto the main track and gave it a running start for Charlottesville.

Sunday passed with no inkling of news about the next move. The railroad men hoped the soldiers were correct that when they left Louisa they would march on Washington. This would take them away from the railroad and put an end to the exasperating and seemingly senseless business of loading, unloading and reloading of which they had had more than plenty. But there was more to come. Monday morning brought orders to load every available car and engine to capacity. The trains would leave Louisa at thirty-minute intervals. Each was to be kept well in control at all times. Brakemen were to be posted at front and rear to keep a sharp lookout for preceding and following trains. All use of whistles and bells was strictly forbidden. Death for the entire crew was the penalty prescribed for any train causing a collision.

These orders came from the military and not from the railroad. When President Fontaine of the Virginia Central heard of the movement, he immediately notified the government that the railroad would not take responsibility for running the trains farther east. If the government cared to take it he would not object. The army promptly took over and under the direction of its officers the order was put into effect.[22]

Just before dark, in a drizzle of rain, the loading began. There were ten trains of eighteen or twenty cars each. An average of 2,000 soldiers piled into and on top of each train. Anderson's train was second in running position. As he was ordered to move his train up to the loading area, he found himself in trouble. John Whalley was drunk and John Wesley was drunker than Whalley. While the troops were coming aboard, Anderson quickly consulted the crew of the train next behind. They told him that if he would ride in the cab of the Monroe and keep Whalley from running into the train ahead they would take care not to run into him.

Anderson climbed into the cab. His first act was to silence the whistle by tying a heavy knot in the cord. Then he ordered Whalley to get under way. For a time things went well enough. Then they were coming close to a long, steep downgrade which would be ticklish for a train so heavily loaded even if the engineer were sober and careful. As they approached it Whalley was gathering speed. Suddenly with the toe of his boot he kicked the firebox open and ordered John Wesley to "fill 'er up." Too drunk to know what he was about, the fireman started feeding wood toward the rear of the tender instead of into the firebox and Whalley was in no condition to notice the difference.

As the track dipped into the downgrade they were running much too fast. Anderson ordered Whalley to "shut 'er off" and get the train under control. Instead, the drunken engineer pulled the throttle wide open and reached for the whistle cord. Anderson's heart came into his mouth when he saw Whalley yank it hard, but the big knot he had tied stopped it at the guide. As the train fully entered the downgrade running at dangerous speed, Anderson snatched up a stick of wood and threatened to brain Whalley unless he slowed down. He had barely got the train down to a manageable speed when they rounded a sharp curve and saw the road lights of the first train a short distance ahead. Into the engineer's fogged brain some memory must have come of the penalty he would have to pay for a collision. The sight of the train ahead so frightened him that he sobered immediately. On the rest of the run John Whalley made no more trouble.

For the soldiers the hazardous railroad journey ended at Beaver Dam Station. As each train unloaded there, it was pulled ahead to permit the one behind to haul up. Anderson's parking spot was in the woods about a mile and a half down the track. The moment they reached it he and Whalley, side by side, stretched out on the floor of the caboose—a wet and muddy freight car—and fell sound asleep. Next morning they wakened chilled to the bone. John said he was going back to the station to find himself a "warm-up dram." Later, when he came plodding back, it was clear he had found his dram. He was wearing the gray dress coat of a Confederate officer![23]

As the soldiers detrained at Beaver Dam Station, they marched quietly away to the southeast. Doubt had vanished now about where they were going. Very soon McClellan was to discover that Jackson's Army of the Valley was nowhere near the Shenandoah but instead was bearing down on his right flank north of Chickahominy.[24]

CHAPTER XII

THE NORTH FINDS AN ENGINEERING GENIUS

I

Spring of 1862 marked the beginning of a long series of feats by which the Yankees repeatedly demonstrated how they outclassed the Confederates in replacing the railroad facilities destroyed by the enemy. The South's lack of equally expert engineers and construction personnel was as great a handicap as its lack of materials. The North had the all-important know-how and first put it to work in a large way in the speedy reconstruction of the R.,F.&P., which General Holmes had thoroughly wrecked when the Army of Northern Virginia abandoned the Manassas line to withdraw behind the Rappahannock.

The first demonstration was the indirect result of an important change in the Lincoln cabinet. Because of growing complaint against Simon Cameron, the President had relieved him and on January 11 appointed Edwin M. Stanton to succeed him as Secretary of War. By this appointment General McClellan was both surprised and greatly displeased.[1] Immediately there developed an unpleasant tenseness between him and the administration which worsened with subsequent events.

While McClellan was engaged in his campaign on the Peninsula, General McDowell commanded a strong corps concentrated in the territory north of Fredericksburg and which, until detached to form the new Army of the Rappahannock, had been a part of McClellan's command. In compensation for the resented loss of McDowell's corps, McClellan demanded reinforcements and persisted in pressing his claims on the President and the War Department. To mollify the disgruntled McClellan, Stanton ordered McDowell to move directly southward and threaten Richmond from the north while McClellan hammered at her defenses on the Peninsular side. McDowell, however, made it clear he could not move until he had established a supply line. He dared not move his army with its thousands of necessary animals fifty miles into enemy territory until arrangements were made for providing subsistence. This would necessitate the opening of the R.,F.&P. Railroad from Aquia Creek to Fredericksburg.

McDowell had studied the wreckage made of this stretch of road by the Confederates and knew its early restoration was no job for an amateur. The terminal dock at Aquia Creek, comprising a surface of more than an acre, and all the buildings connected with it had been burned. Though not all of it had to be restored, some wharfage had to be built. Along the first three miles from the dock not a vestige of track remained. All rails had been taken up and carried away, the ties piled and burned. Softened by the excessive spring rains, the low grade was no more than a muddy trail churned by the hoofs of enemy cavalry horses. Of the bridge across Ackakeek Creek nothing remained except such debris as would not burn. Then came a stretch over which the destruction was a little less complete.

At Potomac Creek a seemingly unsolvable problem presented itself. There the railroad crossed the little stream which at that point ran through a deep ravine nearly a hundred feet below the level of the bordering hills. The old bridge had been 400 feet long but Holmes's men had left nothing of it except the rubble of its stone piers. It had taken almost a year to build it. How could it be replaced, even temporarily, in time to comply with Stanton's order? Certainly by nothing less than a genius.

The North had that genius!

By wire, on April 22, Stanton asked Herman Haupt to come from Boston to confer with him and McDowell. Haupt was forty-five years old and perhaps the foremost railroad construction engineer in the world. While yet in his twenties he had distinguished himself as a bridge designer and builder. At thirty-five he was Chief Engineer for the Pennsylvania Railroad, a job he had given up to build the famous Hoosac Tunnel in Massachusetts. On Thursday April 24 he listened to Stanton explain the plan for Mc-Dowell's operation and the necessity for speed. On Friday he visited McDowell at his headquarters not far from Aquia Creek and studied the details of the miracle he was asked to perform. On Saturday he returned to Washington for another conference with Stanton, and when he left the Secretary's office he was Colonel Herman Haupt, aide-de-camp on the staff of General McDowell.[2] He had agreed to put the R.,F.&P. back in service.

Stanton had no organization to place at his disposal, nor could he supply any equipment other than such simple hand tools as could be collected in Washington. No bridge timbers were available, but there were plenty of iron rails and a cargo of them was hustled aboard a river boat and sent down the Potomac. Only a small staff of assistants could be assembled, and of workmen experienced in track laying or bridge building none was to be had. Haupt would have to get along with the three companies of soldiers McDowell detailed to serve as workmen.

Before noon on Tuesday he was unloading his insufficient collection of tools and cargo of rails at Aquia Creek. He sent a crew of soldiers at once into the near-by woods to cut and bring in crossties. Another crew shoveled at the trampled grade. Over all an unfriendly sky spread sheets of cold April rain. Darkness brought no halt in the work. By the glimmer of lanterns the ties cut during the daylight hours were laid in mud and the rails spiked in place. At daylight McDowell came out to inspect. He shook his head disconsolately and rode away, declaring that an engine could never run over such a track. Haupt looked up from his work only long enough to say, "Come back tomorrow."

The green, crudely cut crossties varied from four inches to a foot in thickness. He had invented his own machinery to bore through Hoosac Mountain,[3] and now Haupt made leveling instruments from poles and pushed ahead. Despite rain and mud and darkness the work went on for three days and nights. On Friday morning an engine passed over the three miles of track where only the remnants of a trampled grade had been on Tuesday. On Saturday morning it brought up a car loaded with lumber for the Ackakeek bridge. On Sunday afternoon the astonished McDowell rode it across the new bridge, 150 feet long and 30 feet high.

The forbidding chasm of Potomac Creek was not far ahead, and already Haupt knew precisely what he was going to do about it. While laying track in mud and rain, the master engineer, who in his youth had delighted in exploding accepted concepts of proper bridge construction, had worked out to the last detail the structure he meant to throw across the yawning gorge. He had no carpenters, insufficient tools and no timbers with which to build bents. Perhaps no other man then living would have believed it possible to build a bridge there of sufficient strength to carry a loaded train or to resist a freshet. Haupt knew himself; he was undismayed, and by this time he knew his men. They were from the Northwest.[4] Among them would be some who knew how to build a log house and would, therefore, know how to cut and notch logs to build cribbing. The superstructure would rest upon a first story of cribwork. While McDowell was taking his Sunday afternoon ride across Ackakeek, men sent out in advance were felling trees and shaping logs on the hills above Potomac Creek.

Hardy as they were, the soldier-workmen found the terrific pace set by their forty-five-year-old leader beginning to tell on them. Sickness and utter exhaustion took a heavy toll of the crews, whose numbers were further depleted because guards had to be detailed to protect them from Rebel snipers.

On arrival at the site, Haupt spent three days sorting out the ablest men, organizing crew units and explaining their assignments. Seldom at any one time were more than a hundred and twenty men fit to work on the bridge, and of these only a few were reasonably adept at it. Sunshine broke through to give relief from the bone-chilling rain, but it lasted only a day or two. No sooner had work been resumed in earnest than a steady drizzle returned to torment the miserable men.

While one crew hoisted and locked up the notched crib logs, others went into the dripping woods to cut and trim selected saplings and fetch the long poles to the bridge site. Men, tools and time were too scarce to strip them of their bark. Above the cribs three stories of trestlework were to be erected, and for these an enormous number of poles would be required. The steps of the wet and weary workers lagged, but they had come to have boundless faith in their leader and they slogged ahead. At the second-story level of the trestle a new difficulty presented itself. Very few of the men had the ability or the courage to clamber about on the wet and slippery ropes and poles so far above the rock-strewn bed of the gorge. As the structure grew taller, the number became smaller until only a squad could be mustered for the terrifying tasks at the eighty-foot level. But somehow men who worked alongside Haupt became imbued with his passion for doing the impossible and, despite the danger, there remained a few willing to risk their lives.

Nine days after the cribs began to take shape, the last trestle was raised and Haupt crossed the bridge on foot. Three days later the track was laid, and in the evening of May 15 an engine was pulled across with ropes. As it crept along, the architect of this incredible structure studied it for any evidence of weakness disclosed by the strain. All was well. When the engine rolled off the bridge onto firm track beyond, there rose from the throats of the jaded men such a shout as comes only from soldiers who have won victory against appalling odds. Four days later, trains were running between Aquia Creek and Fredericksburg. From timber growing at the site and with no machinery more effective than simple hand tools, Potomac Creek bridge was built in twelve days by untrained soldiers, who came to the task already weary and worn from backbreaking labor in laying the track which approached it. Less than a month had elapsed since Haupt first talked with McDowell.

Meantime, the Confederates had abandoned Fredericksburg, and Daniel Stone, acting under instructions from Secretary Stanton, had repaired the railroad bridge across the Rappahannock.

On May 23, exactly one month after his first talk with Stanton, Haupt met President Lincoln with some members of his cabinet at Aquia Creek and accompanied the party on a trip over the reconstructed railroad to visit McDowell at his Fredericksburg headquarters. When the party returned over the same route, to Washington, Lincoln said to the War Committee, "I have seen the most remarkable structure human eyes ever rested upon. That man Haupt has built a bridge across Potomac Creek 400 feet long and nearly 100 feet high, over which loaded trains are running every hour and, upon my word, gentlemen, there is nothing in it but beanpoles and cornstalks."[5]

In view of the sacrifices made by the men and the ingenious devices of their leader, it seems unfortunate that their spectacular success should have brought no greater reward. It contributed nothing to the campaign against Richmond because McDowell went no farther than Fredericksburg. On the very day Lincoln and his party were visiting McDowell, Stonewall Jackson was repossessing the Manassas Gap Railroad at Front Royal. While the President was commenting on Haupt's remarkable bridge, Banks was in full flight toward Winchester with Jackson at his heels. The War Department sent new orders at once to McDowell, who had completed all preparations to move toward Richmond on Monday May 26.[6] Now he was to go at top speed across country in almost the opposite direction through Front Royal, trap Jackson in the lower Valley and destroy him.

McDowell protested on the ground that Jackson's move was entirely diversionary and constituted no threat against Washington; that because of comparative distances over which he must advance and Jackson could retreat, the odds were three to one Jackson would escape before he could reach Front Royal.. Despite his protest, the order stood, and on Sunday May 25 Haupt sat down with him to plan another supply line.

Alexandria would serve as a base. Transportation would be via Manassas Junction over the O.&A. and the Manassas Gap lines, and since forced marches were ordered, all baggage and equipment which could be spared on the march would be shipped back to Alexandria over the river and rail line just opened. There would be trouble on the outer portion of the Manassas Gap road because it was in control of Jackson's men. Since they did not control its eastern terminal at Manassas, the road was of little use to them, and certainly they would not leave it intact for the Federals to use as Banks had used it. The next morning Haupt set out for Alexandria with part of his crew. There he arranged with Colonel J. H. Devereux to manage transportation while he went on toward the Valley to put the track in order.

Applying the same tireless effort and inventive skill that had restored service over the R.,F.&P., Haupt repaired the Manassas Gap line so quickly it was in operation to Piedmont almost as soon as the army got there. On June 1 he rode an engine into the village of Front Royal, where he met McDowell. In spite of continuous rain and roads of sticky mud, the march from Fredericksburg had been made in good time; but as McDowell had correctly predicted, Jackson was already safely out of reach and on his way to help fight McClellan, leaving the Army of the Rappahannock helpless in the Valley, while the Peninsular campaign collapsed.

Twice within a month Haupt's construction crew had demonstrated the astounding capacity of the North for speedily restoring damaged railroad communications. So rapidly had they worked, awed contrabandists were led to remark that "the Yankees can build bridges faster than the Rebs can burn them down."[7]

2

Before the spring campaigns opened, the Federal government had taken a long step ahead of the Confederacy in railroad controls. On February 4 Congress passed an act authorizing the President of the United States to take possession of any or all railroads and telegraph lines, if and when in his judgment the public safety should require it. The authority extended to all rolling stock and equipment and enabled him to place under military control all officers, agents and employees and operate the lines as a part of the military establishment.[8]

Little time was lost in implementing this authority. On February 11, D. C. McCallum was appointed military director and superintendent of railroads in the United States. He would, of course, be responsible to the War Department and report directly to Secretary Stanton.

It is a bit difficult to reconcile Stanton's later conduct toward Herman Haupt and Daniel Stone with the scope of the order appointing McCallum.[9] How was McCallum to exercise his authority "to enter upon, take possession of, hold and use all railroads, engines, cars, locomotives, equipments, appendages and appurtenances that may be required for the transport of troops, arms, ammunition and military supplies" if like authority was given other men with respect to particular roads? However, if any question as to the propriety of these appointments arose before the opening of the road to Fredericksburg, it does not appear in the record. It was not until the morning of May 26 that Haupt found himself in trouble because of Stanton's conflicting orders and instructions.

Before leaving Fredericksburg for Alexandria to restore the Manassas Gap, Haupt was giving instructions to some of his men for rebuilding the bridge across Massaponax Creek, which had been burned during the night before. Daniel Stone, who had supervised the rebuilding of the bridge across the Rappahannock, objected to the instructions and confronted Haupt with a surprising letter from Stanton of which Haupt had no previous knowledge.[10] The letter, a month old, was written to Stone and said:

This may certify that Daniel Stone is authorized to do anything he may deem expedient to open for use in the shortest possible time the Richmond and Acquia Creek Railroad and all Government transports are required to transport free of charge any men or materials he may require for that purpose.[11]

Here, indeed, was a fine predicament. The authority of McCallum had first been invaded by the assignment of Haupt to open the R.,F.&P., and now Haupt discovered a third man holding written authority to disregard or alter any orders or instructions either he or McCallum might give. Immediately Haupt pointed out to McDowell the utter futility of attempting to run the railroads under such conflicting authority.[12] His letter contained no complaint but stated his belief that his mission there was ended.

McDowell must have acted quickly, for two days later Haupt had a "by order of the President" communication from Stanton appointing him Chief of Construction and Transportation in the Department of the Rappahannock. Because the terms of this appointment supplied the background for the formation of a permanent construction corps, the remainder of the text is here set out in full:

You are authorized to do whatever you may deem expedient to open for use in the shortest possible time all military railroads now or hereafter required in said Department; to use the same for transportation under such rules and regulations as you may prescribe; to appoint such assistants and employees as you may deem necessary, define their duties and fix their compensation; to make requisitions upon any of the military authorities, with the approval of the Commanding General, for such temporary or permanent details of men as may be required for the construction or protection of lines of communication; to use such Government steamers and transports as you may deem necessary; to pass free of charge in such steamers and transports, and on other military roads, all persons whose services may be required in construction or transportation; to purchase all such machinery, rolling stock and supplies as the proper use and operation of the said railroads may require, and certify the same to the Quartermaster General, who shall make payment therefor.

You are also authorized to form a permanent corps of artificers, organized, officered and equipped in such manner as you may prescribe; to supply said corps with rations, transportation, tools and implements by requisitions upon the proper departments; to employ civilians and foremen and assistants, under such rules and rates of compensation as you may deem expedient; to make such additions to ordinary rations when actually at work as you may deem necessary.

You are also authorized to take possession of and use all railroads, engines, cars, machinery and appurtenances within the geographical limits of the Department of the Rappahannock, and all authority granted or instructions heretofore given to other parties which may in any way conflict with the instructions herein contained are and will be without force or effect in the said Departament of the Rappahannock from and after this date."[13]

The effect of this order was to carve out of McCallum's jurisdiction an important geographical area at the very heart of things. However, the specifications of authority were so inclusive that if exercised by a competent man, the maximum advantage of rail transportation within the department was assured to the departmental commander. On any theory other than that Haupt's work had established him with the high command as a rare genius, it is difficult to explain his appointment to independent command within an area over which McCallum had held jurisdiction. It must have been true, also, that the handicaps under which he had accomplished his feats impressed the War Department with the necessity of creating a separate corps to be trained and serve under an independent authority. The administration, too, deserves credit for recognizing thus early in the war that to be effective, the commander of the construction corps must have full authority in all railroad matters.

McCallum himself was an able engineer and administrative officer. It happened that before Haupt was called in he had not had time to organize his department and adjust himself in his new job, nor opportunity to demonstrate what he too could accomplish under pressure. While, at the time, Haupt's appointment may have looked like taking from McCallum a pound of flesh, ultimately he was to enjoy the results of the education Haupt had given the War Department. It follows, therefore, that though McDowell's supply lines to Richmond and into the Shenandoah contributed nothing to the cause, they opened the way for the formation of the great system of military railroads which had much to do with the downfall of the Confederacy.

Haupt's service in that spring of 1862 was not confined to demonstrations of the rebuilding ability available to Union armies. Supplying McDowell during his brief stay in the vicinity of Front Royal gave him opportunity to prove further the efficacy of full authority over railroad affairs. Good train operation was quite as vital as quick track construction, and quite as impossible unless kept free of interference from army officers. On May 28 McDowell included in general orders that all persons connected with railroads, either in construction or transportation, would receive orders from Haupt as if they were given directly by McDowell himself.[14] The wisdom of this order was soon shown. When the Manassas Gap line was opened to Piedmont Station, Haupt found a paymaster who had appropriated a boxcar standing on the main track and was using it as an office. When he refused to obey orders to vacate, Haupt called up a detail from the guard, carried the money chests, records and furniture to a near-by house and directed the paymaster to follow them.[15]

Just as soon as trains began arriving at Piedmont, another blockade formed because of the failure of subordinate officers to unload the cars promptly as Haupt had ordered. When

McDowell heard of the jam he decided on an object lesson. His chief quartermaster and commissary officers were at Rectortown, four miles from Piedmont. It was an extremely dark night and rain was pouring down in torrents. McDowell ordered these two officers to proceed at once to Piedmont and personally superintend the unloading of the cars. It is unlikely that they permitted Haupt's orders to be ignored again.[16]

Unfortunately there were many other offenders who must be taught that railroads were not to be used for their personal convenience or operated in accordance with their individual ideas of military requirements. The abuse persisted for a long while, though Haupt did much to stamp it out.

In another way he improved things at this time. Train operation on the Manassas Gap line had been handled exclusively by telegraph with aid of neither schedules nor timetables. Haupt found this arrangement most unsatisfactory for a military railroad. In a letter to Stanton dated June 6 he gave his reasons for changing the system and issuing orders to operate all trains on schedules which he devised.[17] To cut a telegraph wire was the work of only a minute for a lone enemy sympathizer and could be accomplished safely under cover of darkness. When the telegraph line was out of commission trains stood still, and when breaks were mended the line was so congested with army business that there was little or no opportunity to send train orders over it.

Haupt reported an instance in which he walked eight miles to order forward supply trains which had been held up by the glut of army business on the telegraph. In another case he traveled eighteen miles before he could get into wire communication with Superintendent Devereux at Alexandria. He said: "A system which admits of such irregularities is not safe and reliable. To require trains to lie for hours, perhaps for days, upon sidings waiting for instructions when there is no possibility of communicating with them, I cannot approve of and it was under the pressure of such an exigency that I assumed the responsibility of suspending the use of the telegraph."

So he put his trains on schedules, sometimes running them in sections and sidetracking empties that were going in the opposite direction, so that when there were delays the empties rather than the loaded trains absorbed the time loss. It was his policy to keep all supply trains moving toward their destination. He would, if necessary, send out relay runners with flags; the trains could move no faster than the men could run but they kept in motion until the danger point was passed.[18] While he considered the telegraph valuable as a sort of reserve aid, he thought it entirely inadequate as a major means in handling trains under emergency conditions or in hostile country.[19]

Before the middle of June, McDowell's army was on its way back from the Shenandoah and moving south to re-occupy the line of the Orange & Alexandria north of the Rappahannock. The pressure on Haupt was relieved and opportunity given him to devote some time to the permanent organization of the Construction Corps, which up to then was still composed of soldiers detailed to the service. Under date of June 11 he issued the first set of regulations specifying the structure of the new organization and setting forth the basic rules under which it was to function. The "constitution" he then wrote formed the base on which was built one of the most effective and efficient organizations to serve the Union cause throughout the war. Nothing even remotely similar to it ever existed in the Confederacy.

Thinking he had now performed the duties for which he was summoned from Boston, he asked to be relieved, but he received no answer to his written request. Three railroads were now running within his immediate jurisdiction. While waiting for a reply, he continued his efforts to prevent army officers from interfering with rail transportation. On June 25 he published regulations striking directly at the evil and sparing no rank. Quartermaster and commissary officers were "positively forbidden" to load cars without proper authority. Sutlers had to look to the quartermaster general for their transportation. The shipping of articles or materials by officers for their own private use would not be permitted.

Any officer who lent his name to others for the purpose of
procuring transportation would be guilty of "conduct un-
becoming an officer and a gentleman." There were rules for
the inspection of consignments and the confiscation of
baggage or other property shipped contrary to the regulations.

Even to a stupid man it should have been apparent that in
little more than two months' time a pattern had been set to
secure maximum military returns from the railroads within
occupied areas. It happened, however, that when the army
was reorganized, General John Pope took command. He
refused to recognize Haupt as part of the army organization
and declared that "a separate and independent department
for the construction and operation of the railroads was unnecessary."[20] Pope contended that since the railroads were
used for the transportation of army supplies they should be
under the control of the Quartermaster Department. Haupt
went to Washington, explained things to the War Department
and renewed his request to be relieved. This time it was
granted, and the man who could build railroad bridges of
"beanpoles and cornstalks," run supply trains where others
said they could not go, and organize a corps that performed
miracles of construction and operation, went back to his home
in Massachusetts. Whatever other mistakes may be charge-
able against John Pope, none was made with more arrogance
or less reason than his dismissal of Herman Haupt. Soon he
would regret his error and learn an expensive lesson.

3

Had Confederate Intelligence been reasonably alert to railroad significance in early 1862, it surely would have discovered in Baltimore Harbor a key to McClellan's plan for
the Peninsular campaign. In March he had told McCallum
to have five locomotives and eighty cars loaded on vessels at
Baltimore and held subject to his orders for shipment.[21] There
they lay aboard ship until May. Since there was but one railroad on the Peninsula, anyone might have guessed from the
moment he landed at Fort Monroe that he contemplated

moving up the York River and occupying West Point; else he would have had no use for railroad engines and cars. But one conclusion could be drawn: McClellan meant to establish his base of supply at or near West Point, the eastern terminus of the York River Railroad, which ran to Richmond. It was a newly built road with only thirty-eight miles of track, but, clearly as lines could be drawn, it pointed out McClellan's intended route to the capital of the Confederacy.

If further evidence were needed of General Johnston's depreciation of the railroad as a weapon, it would be found in his decision to withdraw his army from the lower Peninsula and establish his line for the defense of Richmond only a few miles outside the city. With scarcely a struggle to preserve the line for his own use and without lifting a hand to destroy it, he abandoned more than three fourths of the York River Railroad to the Federals. It seems never to have occurred to him that without this railroad every mile McClellan marched toward Richmond would have lengthened a tortuous supply line over wagon roads through bush and swamp, in comparison with which the roads about Manassas were veritable boulevards.

By the first of May, McClellan had forced the opening of the York River and stocked a huge depot at White House on the Pamunkey near West Point. McCallum forwarded the engines and cars he had purchased from Northern railroad companies and shortly after added a sixth engine to the collection.[22] Thus, as McClellan's great army closed in on Johnston's defense line, the York River Railroad stretched back from the marching front to White House and, unmolested, wheeled up subsistence, ammunition and all manner of supplies. It is estimated that while the army lay at its nearest point of approach to Richmond, 600 tons of supplies were being carried to it daily by this road.[23]

At Savage Station west of the Chickahominy River, and still farther west near Fair Oaks, advance depots were established. To these, great quantities of artillery ammunition were shipped. Beside the track at Savage, an extensive and well-equipped hospital was set up under canvas. The railroad kept the hospital well supplied, and it quickly evacuated hundreds of seriously sick and badly wounded soldiers to base hospitals.

When Lee took command of the Confederate forces after Johnston was wounded at Seven Pines, the York River Railroad was immediately recognized as a menace to his position. In planning the offensive by which he hoped to drive McClellan back from Richmond, Lee counted the railroad as one of his major objectives. If he could hit McClellan's right wing hard north of the Chickahominy, then swing south, cross the river and cut the railroad, the Federals must either retreat, change base or fight where they were and on such subsistence as was at hand.[24] Any one of these alternatives would give Lee an opportunity to take the pressure off Richmond.

First, he must ascertain the composition of McClellan's right wing, the disposition of its units and particularly how far west it had been extended on the north side of the Chickahominy. To secure this information would be the task of the intrepid Jeb Stuart. No assignment could have been more to his liking. Before his carefully selected cavalry units had been an hour in the saddle, he was dreaming of the ride around McClellan's army which was to crown him with undying fame. Though not contemplated in his orders, it would bring him to the railroad far in McClellan's rear. With such adventure ahead, he found plausible excuses for not turning back when he had the information Lee wanted. Choosing roads which led southeastward along the Pamunkey River, he was soon in the neighborhood of Tunstall's Station. The great depot at White House was no more than five miles away, but infantry was there and a raid in that direction would certainly fail. Better to turn south and strike the railroad at Tunstall's. What glory would be his if with a small body of cavalry he should destroy McClellan's communications and disrupt the plans of the great Army of the Potomac!

The small guard at Tunstall's was easily routed, and Stuart's cavalrymen went to work. They would have to work fast, for the alarm had sounded and the pursuing Federals would soon be on them. Scarcely had they started chopping at the telegraph poles when a train was heard approaching from the west. Without proper tools to tear up track quickly, the best they could hope for was to derail the train. They were too late. The obstructions hastily thrown across the track were insufficient and readily swept aside by the locomotive. Behind it was a string of flatcars loaded with soldiers. As the train swept past, the cavalrymen had to be content with peppering it with bullets before they mounted their horses again and headed for a distant bridge across the Chickahominy. Stuart's attempt to cut the railroad had failed, but the Federals were to pay handsomely for the ideas it planted in the minds of the brilliant young cavalry leaders who rode with him on his great adventure. In Virginia, Union leaders could no longer feel secure and complacent in their possession of railroad supply lines.

Lee's drive down the north side of the Chickahominy ended successfully with the bloody battle at Gaines's Mill on June 27. The next morning he was surprised to discover that during the night the enemy had left the field and withdrawn across the river. What next? Whether McClellan was in full retreat or massing for an attack on Richmond, one of the first things to consider was the railroad. Before making any other plans, Lee called Stuart and sent him galloping down the river with orders to get astride the Federal supply line and destroy the railroad. Stuart struck the road at Dispatch Station, set the place on fire and, with conditions much more favorable than at Tunstall's, put his men to cutting the telegraph and tearing up track. Unknown to him, he was receiving excellent help from the enemy, for down the road only a few miles a Union artillery officer was, at the same time, burning the railroad trestle bridge across the river.[25]

Soon convinced the Federal retreat was genuine, Lee organized for pursuit. On the twenty-ninth he was crossing the river, and next day one of his columns was fighting the rear guard at Savage Station in an action more spectacular than deadly. The Federals there had a double duty to perform. While fighting a delaying action, they had to burn the great quantity of stores accumulated in depot. That was simple enough, but to destroy the tons of ammunition which otherwise would fall into the hands of the Confederates was a different matter. To explode it at the site would not only endanger the troops who must remain to the last, but would rain shell fragments on the 2400 sick and wounded men in the field hospital. With all possible speed they loaded boxcars with the shells and put an engine behind them. When the train got under way the engineer pulled the throttle wide open and jumped from the cab. One after another the cars plunged from the burned trestle into the Chickahominy River.[26]

The battle at Savage Station supplied the setting for something new on rails. While the Federals were struggling to hold off the attackers until they could complete the destruction of their stores and ammunition, shells far too heavy to be fired from any ordinary fieldpiece began falling upon them from the direction of Richmond. It was soon discovered that through a railroad cut about a mile west of the station a locomotive was moving slowly toward them, pushing an armored car upon which was mounted a heavy naval gun, firing as it came. This was the debut of the railroad battery, brand-new and built by the Confederate Navy Department at the request of Robert E. Lee.[27]

Next morning, when the Federal troops withdrew, the York River Railroad from Richmond to the Chickahominy was in possession of the Confederates. They would not have to fight for the rest of the line. McClellan was through with it. He was abandoning his base at White House and the railroad which had made it possible, and was on his way to the James River, which he meant to use as an all-water supply line. It was White Oak Swamp and Frayser's Farm and Malvern Hill which interfered with his plans and sent him to Harrison's Landing. The transports waiting there finally carried the Army of the Potomac back to northern Virginia.[28]

CHAPTER XIII

THE SAGA OF THE "GENERAL"

Attached to Buell's Army of the Ohio at the time it occupied Nashville were two strange individuals who collaborated in parlaying bizarre military concepts and a locomotive into the most dramatic railroad adventure of the war. One of these men was the vain poseur and college professor turned soldier, General Ormsby M. Mitchel; the other, a heavily bearded quinine peddler named James J. Andrews.

When Buell was ordered west to join Grant before the battle of Shiloh, not all of his army went with him. A garrison remained at Nashville, and a small force operating above the Cumberland was left there to continue the watch over Cumberland Gap. To guard against possible raiding south of Nashville, a third force of about 8,000 men under Mitchel's command was left behind. Since Halleck's orders had put a stop to Buell's plan to move against Chattanooga after Johnston turned west toward Corinth, the mission of troops he left behind was purely defensive. His instructions to Mitchel were quite general in nature and left much to discretion. He was advised to take position at Fayetteville, twenty-eight miles north of Huntsville, Alabama, and from there operate "according to circumstances." The sole specific was a reminder that he should occupy the Memphis & Charleston Railroad at Huntsville or Decatur should opportunity offer.[1]

But to sit idly on the defensive at Fayetteville offered Mitchel no opportunity to win either publicity or glory. Heroes are not made by waiting for something to happen. In Buell's absence he was largely on his own and meant to make the most of it. He knew that Lincoln and Stanton had their hearts set on the occupation of East Tennessee and the "liberation" of its loyal population. Chattanooga was the key to that objective and it was lightly garrisoned. Why wait for Buell to return and harvest all the credit for capturing it?

The stage was perfectly set for the entree of the quinine peddler. Andrews was a civilian spy in Buell's employ who used his quinine traffic as an excuse for moving about the country. That he was a loyal man of limitless courage there can be no doubt, though Buell doubted his value as a spy[2] and had refused to approve some of his wild proposals for sabotage within enemy lines. Perhaps that is why Andrews called on Mitchel as soon as Buell went away. Out of their conferences came an audacious scheme to isolate and capture Chattanooga in Buell's absence. Andrews proposed that he take twenty men through enemy lines to Marietta, Georgia, 200 miles away on the line of the Western & Atlantic Railroad. Somewhere near there he would steal a train, cut the telegraph line, run the train northward to Chattanooga and burn the railroad bridges behind him. On the same day Mitchel would occupy the Memphis & Charleston at Huntsville, and with its communications cut both west and south, Chattanooga could be taken easily.

Co-ordination was essential to the scheme, and timing, therefore, was important. Friday April 11 was the date agreed on for the theft of the train, and that meant Mitchel must strike the Memphis & Charleston the same day. Precisely on schedule he reached Huntsville at 6:00 A.M. of the eleventh, routed the small guard he found there, captured fifteen locomotives, together with an assortment of cars, and placed his force astride the railroad. He was strictly within his orders, complete master of the situation and unthreatened from any direction.

But he had not come there merely to "occupy" the railroad. He meant to do much bigger and more important things. Next morning he sent a detachment of troops eastward along the tracks, destroying bridges and capturing five more locomotives before they turned back four miles short of the bridge across the Tennessee River at Bridgeport. At the same time he had set another detachment working westward, which returned eleven days later after burning the bridge at Decatur. Not satisfied with this destruction, he followed with a personally led expedition to Bridgeport where he arrived in time to see a small band of Confederates wreck the east span of the long bridge and run away. He demolished the remaining span and returned to Huntsville. So hungry was he for War Department recognition, he reported directly to Stanton instead of to Buell as he should have done. Pompously he wrote: "This campaign is ended and I can now occupy Huntsville in perfect security while all of Alabama north of the Tennessee floats no flag but that of the Union."[3]

Truthfully and much more properly he might have told Buell that he had, without reason, burned both bridges across the Tennessee, and all the other important bridges in this section; that he had taken twenty locomotives which were useless because he had ripped up the track upon which they might have been operated or run out of danger; that with no enemy in sight he had ruined his own communication lines and was now sitting isolated in Huntsville waiting for applause from Washington.

What had Andrews been doing while Mitchel was so absorbed in destroying bridges that the Federals would soon have to rebuild under difficulties and in writing Stanton about his "campaign"? Mitchel had failed to notice that Andrews had neither returned nor reported. The fact was that Andrews had met with no difficulty in getting his men through to Marietta. After exchanging their uniforms for clothing appropriate to the hill country, they made their way in small groups to various railroad stations and took different trains to the place of rendezvous. Questioners seemed satisfied when they said they were Kentuckians on their way to join the Confederate Army, and none was delayed. At the appointed time and place they met Andrews who then made the fatal mistake of postponing action until the next day.

At exactly six o'clock in the morning of April 12, Conductor W. A. Fuller signaled Jeff Cain at the throttle of the "General," the locomotive of the northbound passenger train, to pull out of the Western & Atlantic depot in Atlanta.

Rain had started to fall and a far less pleasant run than the previous day's was in prospect. Besides, the train was heavier than usual. Directly behind the General were three empty boxcars Fuller had been ordered to deadhead to Chattanooga. As the train covered the twenty miles to Marietta, Andrews' men were straggling into the ticket office there, and each bought his own ticket to some station north of the Etowah River. There was nothing unusual about the looks of these passengers. Distributed through the coaches, they attracted no particular attention during the eight-mile ride to Big Shanty Station.[4]

Andrews had selected this as the place to take possession of the train. On his way down to Marietta he had noted that an unusual number of trains were on the road, many carrying soldiers, and that at Big Shanty a body of Confederate troops had made camp across the track from the station. The idea of stealing a train before their eyes only heightened his spirit of adventure.

As the train ground to a stop, Fuller sent the usual call through the cars: "Twenty minutes for breakfast!" All the crew and many passengers hurried off to the restaurant about forty feet away. Pretending to follow, Andrews and his men quietly dropped off on the opposite side. As soon as Fuller and his crew sat down to breakfast, the well-trained enginemen Andrews had brought with him climbed into the cab of the General while the other men scrambled into one of the three boxcars and closed the door. When all were aboard, Andrews uncoupled the other cars from the train, joined his men in the engine cab and they were off with the boxcars. Everything was working out precisely as planned. Not a shot was fired by the soldiers who idled about. Fuller looked up from his breakfast only when startled by the sound of the snorting engine. With Jeff Cain at his heels he started in pursuit, but Andrews' engineer had made a good start and soon outdistanced the men on foot.

As Fuller later told the story, he had no idea at the time that the offenders were Federals. There had been a series of desertions from the camp at Big Shanty and Fuller had been asked to keep a sharp lookout for men boarding his train there. At the start of the chase he assumed that the men making away with his engine were a group of deserters who would abandon it as soon as they were safely away from the camp. In pressing his pursuit he had in mind not only to recover his engine but to capture the deserters as well.

Andrews was an inventive genius with unfailing memory and a penchant for details. He had familiarized himself with every mile of track he was to cover, carried copies of all train schedules and understood precisely the normal hazards to be expected. On his run he must meet three trains. Two were regularly scheduled runs and the places where they would meet the northbound passenger were well established. The third was an unscheduled local freight which kept out of the way of the northbound schedule. It followed, therefore, that if he held to the schedule of Fuller's train, he would be safe from collision with trains running in the opposite direction. By pulling out of Big Shanty immediately he had gained the twenty minutes the schedule allowed for breakfast there. A few miles on he used this period to stop, tear a rail from the track, cut the telegraph wire and load crossties for use in burning the bridges he planned to destroy.

Soon the raiders were passing through Etowah Station. There, with steam up, the "Yonah," an old engine owned by a mining company, stood on the sidetrack. Should they stop and disable her? The local freight could not be far away, and Andrews wanted no alarm spread until that unscheduled train was behind them. Besides, the Yonah was old and too slow to catch the General should anyone try to use her in pursuit. Quickly he decided to leave her alone and keep moving.

It was at Kingston, thirty miles from their starting point, that things began to go wrong. There a short line branched off to Rome, and on the track stood a Rome train, waiting the arrival of Fuller's northbound passenger and mail. When, in its stead, a train of three boxcars arrived in charge of a strange conductor, explanations were demanded. The quick-witted Andrews provided them. He was running extra with three carloads of powder for Beauregard at Corinth and must not be delayed. And where was that local freight? Told it was expected at any minute, he pulled into a siding and waited. Soon it came up, but to Andrews' chagrin it carried a red flag on its engine, indicating another train behind it. Without a moment's hesitation he accosted the conductor and started berating him in language loud enough for all to hear. "What does it mean that the road is blocked in this manner when I have orders to get this powder to Beauregard?" The answer was a shock to Andrews, a stunning disclosure of his own mistake in postponing his venture until the twelfth: Mitchel had captured Huntsville, was threatening Chattanooga, and the Confederates were running everything out of there as fast as the trains could carry them. No use trying to get through to Corinth. Mitchel had cut the M.&C.

The poise and commanding appearance of Andrews began to pay off in this desperate crisis. He was all apology. Would the conductor of the local please pull his train down the track some distance away from the powder cars? This was done, but from the talk of the railroaders at the station Andrews knew suspicion had been aroused. Who were these strangers who composed the crew of the special? None of the regular employees had ever seen them. It seemed "mighty funny" they would put the General on a job like this. That was Jeff Cain's engine, and who was "that feller settin' in Jeff's seat?"

The bearded raider made no effort to avoid them. Instead, he paced among them and stuck close to the telegraph office in the station pretending exasperation that no message came through to clear the track for him. They never guessed his real purpose was to see that they sent no message out questioning the authenticity of his story. At last the second section of the southbound train arrived and it, too, carried a red flag! To pull out onto the main track between the second and third sections would be suicidal. There was nothing to do but wait, and with the same story Andrews persuaded the second train to move on down the track, safely away from the "explosives."

For an hour and five minutes the raiders in the boxcar huddled in breathless silence. Unable to see what was going on, they knew from the voices they heard that trouble was brewing. They were not surprised when, through one of their two engineers, their leader managed to send them a cautious warning to be ready to come out fighting should the gathering crowd decide to investigate the contents of the cars. They could hear enough to understand that the men outside were wanting to know why Fuller's long-past-due train had not arrived. Their confidence in Andrews was tremendously increased when he succeeded in keeping the people gathered about the depot from investigating until the third section of the local had finally pulled past the end of the siding and their "powder train" got under way once more.

Four miles beyond Kingston the raiders made another stop, cut the telegraph line, and were busy prying a rail from the track when they were startled by the whistle of an engine coming from the south. They abandoned their work, scrambled aboard their cars and made all haste to reach Adairsville. There, according to schedule, the south-bound express should have been waiting for them to pass. Instead, the siding was occupied by a mixed train, and the express was not in sight. Obviously it, too, was running late. Andrews had no choice. Nothing remained for him except to make a run for it. Maybe he could make Calhoun, nine miles off, without smashing head on into the express. Staking everything on luck, he stepped up the General to a speed of more than sixty miles an hour. Luck was with him. The express was at Calhoun, and when he told the powder story to explain his haste, the raiders were soon again in the clear.

So far as his party knew, the last of the southbound trains was now behind them and the track was open to Chattanooga. If they could make one more break in the track they would have plenty of time to burn the Oostenaula bridge and then they would be safe. They could burn other bridges below Chattanooga and before nightfall they would be back within Mitchel's lines. Once more they paused to cut the telegraph and rip the track. Without proper tools the lifting of a rail was a difficult business, and before it could be done they were again forced to run for their cars and be off. The rail was badly bent, but not far away a screaming locomotive was bearing down on them at full speed.

Andrews could not account for the way he was being pressed. He had broken the track just beyond Big Shanty and again below Adairsville. How had that pursuing engine crossed those gaps? How could an engine be so near he could see its streamer of smoke trailing above the timber and distinctly hear its whistle? Unless that bent rail ditched the locomotive chasing them, they had no chance to get to the river bridge soon enough. The bridge timbers were soaked with the rain which had been falling steadily since they left Marietta, and they wouldn't catch fire quickly.

Fuller could have explained how the chase had kept up. He was aboard the engine which was pressing the raiders, and the pursuer was no less determined and little less astute than the pursued. Though he had been left on foot at Big Shanty, he had not given up.

Not far from the starting point he, Jeff Cain and a passenger had grabbed the handcar of a track crew and pushed on until it struck the first break the raiders had made in the track. It went into the ditch. In a few minutes they had it back on the rails and were on their way to Etowah. They found the Yonah still steaming on the sidetrack just as Andrews had left her. To board and run her out on the main track was the work of moments only. Pressing the old engine to the fullest speed she could develop, they reached Kingston less than five minutes after Andrews departed!

By only that narrow margin had Andrews waited out the third freight and regained an open track north. Otherwise the venture would have collapsed within thirty miles of its beginning. Unintentionally, however, Andrews had set up an effective road block. The three freight trains he had persuaded to move down the track away from the "powder cars" now stood between the Yonah and the General, which was speeding on toward Adairsville.

Fuller was equal to the occasion. Fortunately for him, the

train blockade was below the Y which connected the Rome branch with the main line. He abandoned the Yonah, raced on foot along the track to where the Rome train waited, uncoupled the engine and one car, and with about forty armed men aboard was off again in pursuit.

On that fateful day luck was playing no favorites. Fuller's engineer saw the break in the track below Adairsville in time to reverse his engine and stop short of derailment. Was that to be the end? Not for the irate and physically powerful Fuller! He leaped from the cab and again took up the chase, on foot and alone. A short distance ahead he met and flagged down the mixed train Andrews had met at Adairsville. He had the train backed into the switch track it had left only a few minutes earlier, uncoupled the engine and, with it still running backward, carried on the race at the cost of little more time than Andrews used in his attempt to break the track beyond Calhoun. Fuller was aboard the "Texas" now, an engine of the same class as the General.

Beyond Calhoun they came on the damage done the track by Andrews' men. Bouncing and swaying, the Texas struck the bent rail but in some inexplicable manner righted itself and passed safely over. Fuller was gaining now and soon succeeded in closing the distance to rifle range. Andrews was not only surprised but amazed. To impede his pursuer he ordered the rear car uncoupled and let it fall behind. The ruse accomplished little. Seeing the loose car ahead, Fuller reduced speed and fell away only long enough to pick up the still rapidly rolling car and push it ahead of him. A bit farther on Andrews dropped a second car. It, too, was successfully picked up, but the General had won a slight advantage. Running backward and pushing two cars ahead of its tender, the Texas could not keep the full pace. As the two trains approached the Oostenaula, the gap between them was widening, but Andrews had not gained enough time to stop and fire the bridge. Soon he would have to pull up to take on wood and water. There was nothing to do except hold his speed across the high wooden structure and leave it intact behind him.

At Resaca, Fuller stopped long enough to push the two box-cars onto a sidetrack. This gave Andrews an interval to cut the telegraph line. He dared not let a message of warning get through ahead of him. And he knew that unless he could get far enough in front to burn the Chickamauga bridges, his venture would end in utter failure. Already he had missed his chief objective—the destruction of the Oostenaula bridge.

Once more the General was pressed to the greatest possible speed. The end of the remaining boxcar was broken out and dropped on the track. The crossties the Federals had hoarded for bridge burning also were dropped as they ran. This accomplished the desired result: the Texas was obliged to reduce speed and fall behind. Andrews' party had not succeeded in derailing it, but they could venture to halt long enough on a curve to place a rail diagonally across the track with the hope it would send the Texas into the ditch. Had they been equipped with a few proper tools for lifting spikes, they could have soon made themselves safe from further pursuit, but the need had not been anticipated when they had been thinking only of burning bridges. The Texas struck the loose rail at full speed but, though it suffered a terrific jolt, it miraculously held the track and came on.

At the rate the General was then running, Andrews would be passing Dalton before long. Beyond that station he would have to make another stop to cut the telegraph and prevent a warning message being sent ahead. Fuel was running very low, the tank was almost empty and rain continued to fall. His men were giving up their last hope of burning the Chickamauga bridges. They were now thinking less of the success of the raid than of escaping with their lives. They knew what to expect if they were captured within Confederate lines dressed in civilian clothes. A number of times the Texas had been sufficiently near for them to see that both engine and tender were loaded with armed men. Unanimously they urged Andrews to stop on a curve, use the engine as a blockade, ambush the pursuers and fight it out at short range. But their leader clung to the hope for victory at the next bridge.

When they stopped to cut the wire beyond Dalton, they piled a barrier on the track made of anything they could grab. Then they hastened on. Andrews was drawing on the General's last remaining power in a desperate attempt to get to the covered bridge not many miles ahead. The men were set to work ripping boards from the sides and remaining end of the car and piling them in the middle of the floor. They brought blazing brands from the engine firebox, and despite the rain the rush of air soon set the timbers flaming. They clambered atop the tender. The timing had been perfect. They came slowly into the covered bridge. The burning car was pulled to the middle of the span and uncoupled. As the flames licked at the roof and sides of the bridge, each of them knew the issue would be settled there. The General retained a fair head of steam, but there was no more fuel and no chance to maintain the long race. All now depended on whether the Texas was far enough behind to permit the fire to render the bridge impassable. The suspense was soon ended. They heard the pursuer coming, and as they pulled away they watched the Texas move cautiously into the blazing, smoke-filled structure and push the burning car out into the open and to the next sidetrack.

Fuller stopped only long enough to leave the burning car, then came on with a fresh burst of speed. Meantime the raiders watched the steam gauge of the General gradually fall as they sped over the last few miles of their journey.

When there was no longer any hope, Andrews ordered his men to jump, take to the woods and each try to save himself. Before he and the engineer jumped they reversed the engine, hoping the General would work up enough speed to wreck the Texas and give the men a good start toward escape. But Andrews had postponed his last effort too long. The General had not enough steam left to gather speed, and the Texas easily backed away until the General could be stopped without damage. The race was over.[5]

In the rough and wholly strange country the raiders had little chance to get away. The alarm was spread and the wooded hills filled with soldiers. One at a time the fleeing

Federals were picked up and all were held as spies. A Confederate court-martial was promptly convened, and it speedily tried and convicted Andrews with seven of his men. In Atlanta on June 7, 1862, they were put to death. The trial of the remaining twelve, and of two others who had joined the party but failed to board the train at Marietta, was postponed. With a display of the same daring that marked the entire enterprise, they attacked their guard in broad daylight and made off. Eight succeeded in reaching the Union lines, but six were recaptured and remained prisoners until exchanged in March 1863.[6]

Death and imprisonment for Andrews and his courageous followers were the sole proceeds of the wild adventure, but the story will live as long as railroads are run by Americans.

CHAPTER XIV

THE RAILROADS AND BRAGG'S INVASION, 1862

I

While Halleck spaded his slow way through the woods from Shiloh to Corinth, Admiral Farragut opened the lower Mississippi with victories at New Orleans and Baton Rouge, and six days after the bloodless occupation of abandoned Corinth, Union naval forces took Memphis. Since Mobile was effectively blockaded, these victories left the western Confederacy clinging to Richmond by a tangle of circuitous railroad connections which depended on a single line running eastward from Vicksburg. In these developments Grant saw an opportunity to dispossess the enemy of his entire railroad potential west of Chattanooga, clear him out of the Mississippi Valley, and confine the war to the territory east of the mountains.[1]

That this great chance was lost he attributed entirely to Halleck's failure to press his advantage. In his opinion, "Corinth could have been captured in a two-day campaign commenced promptly on the arrival of reinforcements after the battle of Shiloh."[2] Had this been done before Beauregard had time to reorganize his defeated forces, ship out his equipment and supplies and consolidate a new position, Halleck's army of 120,000 would have been strong enough to protect the territory already won and push on to cut the Southern of Mississippi and isolate Vicksburg. It was for this that Grant contended. But who was Grant? Only a newly promoted major general who had stolen the spotlight from his department commander and been sent off to cool his heels while Halleck shoveled on and built miles of useless fortifications about Corinth.[3]

As a unit, the huge army headquarters at Corinth was never brought to bear upon the enemy. It was soon divided into two major forces. Whether this was done on Halleck's initiative or because of pressure from Washington is difficult to ascertain. That the high command still cherished the hope of a successful campaign against Chattanooga and East Tennessee is certain. That Halleck had continuously stressed the importance of operations along the Mississippi is equally certain. In any event the movement Buell had started toward Chattanooga before being ordered west to join Grant was resumed on June 11. The Army of the Ohio was detached and turned back in the direction from which it had come to Shiloh.

In the same manner that he had frittered away his opportunity before Corinth, Halleck now chose for Buell the slow and tedious approach to Chattanooga. His orders were to base on Memphis, follow the line of the Memphis & Charleston Railroad and repair the road as he went. What was obvious to Buell from the start would soon be disclosed to all— that Memphis was not his proper base, and the Memphis & Charleston was neither necessary nor suitable as a supply line for operations in middle or east Tennessee. It was too long and too susceptible to interruption by cavalry patrols and guerrilla bands who could approach it safely from unoccupied territory. Besides, to repair it and put it in shape for use as he advanced would entail long and needless delay in the movement of the whole army. In addition to the damage done the road by the enemy, Mitchel's bridge burnings had greatly increased the difficulty of reaching Chattanooga by this route. From his former supply line based on Louisville, Buell had marched swiftly west and arrived in time to turn the tide at Shiloh. Only Halleck's orders prevented his returning to that line in the same fashion.

To account for these orders is most puzzling. One must assume either that Halleck had no enthusiasm for the Chattanooga campaign, that he failed to comprehend the handicap placed on Buell, or that he had supreme confidence the enemy would in no way interfere. In any case he was to learn soon how seriously he had erred.

General Braxton Bragg, who had replaced Beauregard in command at Tupelo, quickly and correctly diagnosed the Buell movement and ordered Forrest, then at Chattanooga, to strike out with his cavalry, harass Buell and delay him as long as he could. Meantime, Buell had worked his way slowly along the Memphis & Charleston to where he encountered the heavy damage done the railroad by Mitchel. At that point he assumed the responsibility for changing the procedure. He sent detachments north to put the Nashville & Chattanooga in condition so that he might proceed to Stevenson and resume his old supply line from Louisville through Nashville. On July 12 the necessary repairs were completed to Bridgeport and the road was open to within thirty miles of Chattanooga. He had wasted a month repairing a railroad for which he now had no use and which was already broken behind him.

July 11, 12 and 13, 1862, were three momentous days in the life of the commander of the Army of the Ohio. On the eleventh the man who had given him his impossible assignment was called to the command of all the Union armies and ordered to headquarters in Washington. On the twelfth his former supply line was re-established to within a day's march of Chattanooga. On the thirteenth Bedford Forrest swept down upon Murfreesborough, captured the small garrison and rode back to McMinnville, leaving behind him a devastated stretch of the newly repaired railroad.[4] Buell's glimpse of success, despite the handicap laid on him, faded with that raid. Of it he later said:

The consequence of this disaster was serious. The use of the railroad from Nashville, which had been completed the very day before and which I was depending on to throw supplies into Stevenson for a forward movement, was set back two weeks; the force of Forrest threatened Nashville itself and the whole line of railroad through Tennessee.[5]

But that was not to be all. On July 21, while the Murfreesborough break was being repaired, Forrest again rode out of McMinnville in a circling swoop which brought his troopers within sight of Nashville. They cut the railroad in a second place and delayed Buell's advance another eight days.[6]

Bragg had gained the time he needed. On the same day that Forrest broke the Nashville & Chattanooga the second time, Bragg began to shift the main body of his army from Tupelo to Chattanooga.[7] Leaving General Earl Van Dorn with one independent command to defend Vicksburg, and General Sterling Price with another to watch Grant and hold him on the Memphis-Corinth line, he loaded his infantry on Mobile & Ohio trains and started them toward Mobile. His cavalry and artillery horses were set on the march across country and with them went his supply trains. On arriving at Mobile, the infantry was ferried across the bay and up the Tensas River to the head of the new Alabama & Florida Railroad, which carried them to Montgomery. From there the Montgomery & West Point took them on to Atlanta via Opelika, and from Atlanta they rode the same rails over which Andrews and his raiders had sped to fame if not to fortune.[8] It was a long, tedious route, but Forrest had held Buell in check at Huntsville and the trip was made in safety.[9]

On August 15 Bragg was writing from Chattanooga to General Kirby Smith in Knoxville: "My infantry is all up, the artillery coming in daily and part of my train is arriving."[10] By a comfortable margin he had won the race with Buell for Chattanooga, and the consequences can be measured in the loss of an untold number of lives and the indefinite prolongation of the war. Left to his own devices, Buell easily could have reached the Nashville & Chattanooga Railroad long before Forrest could have interfered. What might have happened had Buell been sent from Corinth to Chattanooga as rapidly as he could march is, of course, matter for pure speculation, but in later years Grant was moved to say that the bloody battles of Stones River, Chickamauga and Chattanooga might well have been avoided.[11]

Halleck, seemingly forgetful that it was he who had ordered Buell to repair the M. & C. Railroad instead of marching with all speed to Chattanooga, was now using the telegraph from his new office in Washington to tell Buell of the great dissatisfaction there with the slow progress of his army. To this Buell promptly replied that his lines of communication had been "constantly beset by a vastly superior cavalry force. They had been twice seriously broken in that way just as they were finished. The army could not be sustained in its present position, much less advanced, until they were made secure. We have therefore found it necessary to fortify every bridge over more than 300 miles of road."[12] By Bragg's use of the railroads offensively and Forrest's defensive tactics in destroying the enemy roads, the Confederates stopped the Federal campaign against Chattanooga in its tracks, and Buell's army was left to swelter in the midsummer heat of northern Alabama.

2

In the four months after February 12, 1862, the Federals had driven the enemy from Kentucky, middle and western Tennessee and a strip along the northern borders of Alabama and Mississippi. The Union front roughly paralleled the Memphis & Charleston Railroad for nearly 300 miles between Memphis and Stevenson, Alabama. Behind that front lay a vast area of vital military and political importance to both sides. Within it were more than 1,300 miles of railroad, approximately ten per cent of the total trackage controlled by the Confederates at the beginning of the war. It contained no less than a dozen railroad junctions, and over this rail network flowed munitions and supplies for nearly 200,000 soldiers and forage for their thousands of horses and mules. Not a single north-south line west of Virginia and north of Mississippi and Alabama remained in control of the Confederates.

Despite the Secessionist sympathy of the population of the territory through which these railroads ran, and the consequent necessity of detailing large numbers of soldiers as bridge and track guards, Grant held the opinion that Halleck could have continued the offensive to Vicksburg had he chosen to do so. But when Halleck lost time at Corinth and then divided his forces, and the campaign against Chattanooga bogged down for lack of transportation, the great, slashing columns which had driven relentlessly from the banks of the Ohio to the rim of the cotton states surrendered their initiative and willy-nilly went on the defensive. Instead of the irresistible force they once had been, the united and victorious divisions Halleck had commanded at Corinth became a scattered and harassed army of occupation.

When Halleck received his appointment as supreme commander, no reason remained to keep Grant in the background. He was immediately summoned from Memphis to Corinth and placed in charge of the District of West Tennessee.[13] Since no superior was appointed to succeed Halleck, Grant became, in fact, commander of the Department of the Mississippi, although he was not given that title until the following October. At Corinth he found only a comparatively small part of the great army which, two months earlier, had been assembled there. Not only had the Army of the Ohio departed, but from the force he had previously led, troops had been lavishly distributed along the Mobile & Ohio from Columbus to Corinth, along the Mississippi Central from Jackson to Grand Junction, and along the M.&C. all the way from Iuka to Memphis.[14] Small garrisons had been scattered throughout the territory from the Mississippi line to the Ohio River. Price and Van Dorn were in strength on his front and their cavalry was operating in his rear. With the striking force under his orders so reduced, the opportunity for a vigorous offensive to isolate the enemy in the west was gone. It was not Grant's kind of war; but nothing remained for him except to prevent a break-through by Price and Van Dorn, protect the captured railroads in his rear and wait for another chance.

These were anxious days for the new commander of the Department of the Mississippi who had no liking for defensive operations.[15] His first object was to dispose the main body of his troops so as to provide a maximum of defensive strength at whatever point an attack might fall. In this, mobility was a prime consideration, and fortunately he found a ready-made pattern at hand. Ninety-three miles of the Memphis & Charleston between Corinth and Memphis formed the base of a railroad triangle with its apex at Humboldt, Tennessee. The left leg was eighty-four miles of the Memphis & Ohio from Memphis to Humboldt, and the right leg was the Mobile & Ohio between Humboldt and Corinth. From Jackson on the right leg, the Mississippi Central crossed the base at Grand Junction, forty miles west of Corinth, thus forming a smaller triangle within the larger one. Strong detachments at Grand Junction, Memphis, Humboldt and Jackson were each provided with alternative rail connections with the others and with Corinth. A fifth force was located at Bolivar on the Mississippi Central, twenty miles above Grand Junction. By this distribution of troops Grant was not only prepared to protect the roads within the area but to use them most advantageously. He could effect a consolidation at any one of the several points where the enemy might choose to attack. Moreover, with the roads open, the garrison troops outside the Memphis-Humboldt-Corinth triangle would be available if needed.[16]

3

Now began one of the strangest large-scale campaigns of the war. Kirby Smith, Confederate commander in East Tennessee, was at Knoxville facing no immediate opposition. When Bragg arrived at Chattanooga the two district commanders held a conference and agreed on plans for an immediate joint offensive by which they hoped to drive all Federal forces out of Kentucky and Tennessee. It was a bold scheme which, executed boldly by a single commander, might well have restored to the Confederates everything they had lost since Grant struck Fort Henry. Bragg was one of many highly placed Southerners who still believed that Kentucky had been bludgeoned into remaining with the Union; given the opportunity, her people would rise en masse and help drive the Union "invaders" back across the Ohio. The plan of campaign, therefore, contemplated a twofold purpose and a two-pronged attack.

While Bragg worked his way into Buell's rear, Smith was to march across the mountains from Knoxville, occupy the rich bluegrass region of Kentucky, recruit and organize the "delivered" Kentuckians and incorporate them into his Army of East Tennessee. When Buell was either defeated by Bragg or forced to retire, the two armies would meet at Frankfort, install a Confederate governor in the Statehouse and complete the expulsion of the Federals from Kentucky. Grant would then be obliged to retire or allow himself to be caught between Bragg and Smith on the one side and Price and Van Dorn on the other. Early in August they were ready for the jump-off.

At that time Buell's supplies came over a single line of railroad 350 miles long. To remain in northern Alabama, Buell had to keep this line in operation; otherwise he would be obliged to move nearer his base. To start him in that direction and keep him on the move was Bragg's first job. Following Forrest's July raids, Buell had made the portion of the rail line south of Nashville safe from depredations by covering its length with heavy guards. But Forrest was not the only troublemaker in Bragg's service. North of the Cumberland, John H. Morgan was operating quite as effectively on the Louisville & Nashville part of the line as Forrest had done on the Nashville & Chattanooga. Morgan's assignment was to destroy bridges and stretches of track between Nashville and Bowling Green. However, a few miles north of Gallatin, Tennessee, was something more difficult to repair than any bridge. He made for it. There the L.&N. passed through twin tunnels. Both bores were shored up and lined with wooden timbers. On August 12 Morgan captured the small

guard and set fire to the timbers. The resulting rock falls
so completely disabled the tunnels as to stop all traffic to
Nashville for an indefinite period.[17]

To make matters worse, Buell's railroad guards were showing little disposition to fight off the raiders. More than once
he found it necessary to issue general orders stressing the
seriousness of this poltroonery and citing specific instances
where, with disastrous results, guards had fled their posts at
the first threat of attack by inferior numbers.[18]

By August 30 his troops were reduced to a ten-day supply
of rations.[19] North of Nashville his supply line had been
broken for more than two weeks, and the destruction of the
Gallatin tunnel left no hope for prompt restoration of service.
Bragg had crossed the Tennessee River and was on the move,
probably headed for Nashville. Just as Bragg had planned it,
Buell was forced to take the first step backward. He ordered
a concentration of his mobile forces on Murfreesborough.
His scouts soon reported that Bragg was skirting Nashville
and apparently going toward Bowling Green. Ten days
later Buell was across the Cumberland. If Bragg were allowed
to reach Bowling Green, he would not only be astride the
L.&N. but would control the junction with Grant's Louisville connection through Clarksville. As rapidly as possible
Buell pressed on and by the middle of September was back
in Bowling Green, his first objective in the previous February.

Bragg's campaign was working out exactly as planned.
With nothing more serious than slight cavalry brushes and
repeated cutting of the railroad, he had brought Buell all the
way from Alabama to the Big Barren. But Bragg was not at
Bowling Green. On September 2 Morgan had finished his
job by burning the L.&N. bridge across Salt River, only
seventeen miles south of Louisville, and thrown that city into
near panic. Smith was in possession of the Bluegrass and
living fatly off the country. His near approach created such
a furor in Cincinnati that business was suspended while
citizens prepared hastily contrived defense works.

Buell's situation was little less than desperate when, moving
on beyond Bowling Green, he encountered Bragg deployed

across his front at Munfordville. The Confederates had surprised and captured the garrison of more than 4,000 men there and taken up a strong post behind the Green River. Buell's rations were at the point of exhaustion. Nothing remained but to fight his way through. In the evening of September 20 he prepared to make his bid the following morning. Could his weary and discouraged men whip the confident Johnnies on ground of their own choosing?

Then came a strange and inexplicable development. In the morning of September 21 Buell found himself facing only a rear guard of Bragg's army. He quickly pushed it aside, and with that the road was open to Louisville where he arrived safely four days later. Since leaving Corinth on June 12, he had marched along 530 miles of railroad track which now lay broken in segments behind him, with most of it in possession of the enemy. At the end of September he was back where he had started in February. He had taken part in one major battle, the victory at Shiloh, yet, with the exception of Nashville, the territory embraced within his command was in possession of the Confederates. An explanation of his ill fortune will be found in the inept handling of the railroads which fell to the Union forces before Halleck learned how to use them either offensively or defensively.

What happened to Bragg at Munfordville? As one of his officers later put it, he had Buell "in the hollow of his hand,"[20] then, without a battle he shifted out of the way and allowed him to reach his base. Apparently the political aspect of the campaign suddenly overwhelmed his military judgment. In the night of September 20 he left the line of the railroad and turned northeast to Bardstown, where he established headquarters. On the twenty-eighth he and his staff left Bardstown for a meeting with Kirby Smith at Lexington. The two commanders rode on to Frankfort where, on October 4, they installed the Honorable Richard Hawes as Confederate Provisional Governor of Kentucky. It was a feeble gesture, for Hawes was powerless.

Except for the huge quantity of stores accumulated during his stay in the rich agricultural area of Kentucky, Smith had accomplished nothing of value to the Confederate cause. The number of recruits obtained failed by far to replace his casualties and losses suffered through defections and sickness. The expected uprising of citizens against the "invaders" failed to develop and the political balance remained unchanged. "I regret to say we are sadly disappointed in the want of action by our friends in Kentucky," gloomily reported Bragg to his government.[21]

As far as Munfordville, Bragg's part in the campaign had been a complete success. Had he pressed his advantage over Buell there, he might have left a different story for historians to tell. But when he chose to sacrifice his military success in order to bolster Smith's political failure, his strategy collapsed and the tables quickly turned. In his new position at Louisville, Buell was unassailable. With heavy reinforcements and an abundance of supplies, he was much stronger than when the campaign began. While Bragg and Smith were engaged with the empty ceremony of inaugurating a provisional governor, the rejuvenated Army of the Ohio took up the offensive. Before the forces of the two Confederate commanders were effectively united, Buell had reached Perryville. Far from any base, with no supply line available and much weaker than when they started, the Confederates were in a hazardous fix. On October 8 they were brought to battle at Perryville. It was a fierce but poorly managed and indecisive struggle, a stalemate. But it produced thousands of casualties and convinced Bragg that, for him, Tennessee was a safer place than Kentucky.

CHAPTER XV

JACKSON, HAUPT AND SECOND BULL RUN

I

Dawn of June 25, 1862, saw the empty trains which had brought Jackson's army from the Valley parked below Beaver Dam Station. The soldiers had marched away toward the Chickahominy, leaving behind them the weary railroaders who had slept but little and had not eaten a decent meal in many days. Among them was no one in authority, and, except for Jackson's request that no whistles be blown east of Louisa, they were without instructions. There was no more food at Beaver Dam. Holding a council among themselves, they decided to take the trains back to Charlottesville.[1]

For more than a month, none of the engines had been near a shop. Since they would have to back to Gordonsville before they could be turned around, the engineers set about examining each engine carefully before they started. To illustrate the handicaps under which these faithful servants of the Confederacy kept trains rolling, the case of the engine "C. R. Mason" is sufficient. This was a mountain climber, usually assigned to special duty west of the Millsboro tunnel, and was designed to pull four passenger cars over a grade which rose 360 feet to the mile. Its tanks were mounted on its sides and had too little capacity to permit running between water stations out on the line. But when the movement to Beaver Dam started, the need for power was so great that a captured B.&O. tender was attached to the C. R. Mason and, along with the others, it pulled a train to the end of the run. The examination at Beaver Dam disclosed that one of her drive

189

wheels had come loose. Improvising a blacksmith's forge with charcoal fired in an iron kettle, one of the crew shaped up a piece of scrap iron and tightened the wheel enough to permit the Mason to haul back its train.[2]

In the movement of Jackson's army not a soldier was hurt through any fault of the railroad. Despite the overtaxed and worn condition of all the motive power, no train halted because of breakdown or accident. When the trains returned to Charlottesville in safety, the engineers were told to take all the engines to an improvised shop at Shadwell where they could be overhauled and made ready for their next job. No one then surmised how quickly it was to come.

Meantime, track and bridge crews of the Virginia Central worked at full speed. Except for the structure across the South Anna, the burned bridges below the R.,F.&P. junction were quickly made passable. By using the R.,F.&P track from the junction to the South Anna, transferring across that stream and reloading, service to Richmond was soon restored. While the Seven Days' Battles raged, workmen engaged on the South Anna bridge were pushed to the limit of endurance, and other workmen struggled to build track connections through Richmond, the lack of which had been a handicap and was now a grave danger.

The South was in a fair way to pay an appalling price for the prewar obstinacy of the city. Without connecting tracks, no way existed to shunt the rolling stock of the Virginia Central and the R.,F.&P. to lines running south. If McClellan reached Richmond, all these locomotives and cars would fall into his hands. If he forced the evacuation of the city, the Petersburg line was the natural escape route and it would be in desperate need of rolling stock. Without the connecting track, none of the Virginia Central or R.,F.&P. equipment would be available.

In this emergency Richmond built its first north-south connection through the city. Tracks were laid on the ground through the streets. They were too light to carry trains but strong enough to permit single units to be drawn by horses or pushed by man power. Unfortunately the terminus of the Petersburg line was at the top of a hill and the Virginia Central track ended at its foot. The grade of the street-laid track was too steep to be negotiated by a locomotive, and it was therefore necessary to rig tackle by which both engines and cars could be pulled up the hill. One mishap after another beset and discouraged the workers until the project came near being abandoned, but in the end it was made to work.[3]

By the time the railroads had subdued the Richmond hill, Lee's soldiers had taken Malvern Hill, fifteen miles down the James, and the pressure on the city was relieved. Immediately the railroad executives shifted their concentration to the completion of the South Anna bridge and the repair of rolling stock.

In the midst of this hurried activity, the workmen in the Richmond shops of the Virginia Central went out on strike for higher wages. So rapidly and so steeply had living costs risen that President Fontaine recognized their need. Despite the financial difficulties which confronted all Southern roads, he granted the increase and the men went back to work. Before the middle of July the road was in operation over its entire length and ready for the next military task.

2

Scattered over northern Virginia were three idle corps of the Federal army. To employ these troops in the campaign to reduce Richmond while maintaining a strong defense of Washington, Stanton planned a consolidation of the three corps into a new army under one command. He reasoned that a large force demonstrating northwest of Richmond would not only be prepared to intervene should the enemy attempt an attack on the Union capital, but its presence on the upper Rappahannock would compel Lee to weaken his opposition to McClellan by withdrawing troops to guard against the threat in his rear. This was, of course, the revival on a much larger scale of the plan he had worked out for McDowell at the time he called on Herman Haupt to restore the R.,F.&P. Railroad between Aquia Creek and Fredericksburg.

Though outranked by each of the three corps commanders, Frémont, Banks and McDowell, John Pope was called from Tennessee, and on June 27, while McClellan was fighting desperately at Gaines's Mill, was put in charge of the 50,000 men composing the new Army of Virginia. To the corps commanders orders were soon on the wires directing a concentration of forces. As it neared completion, Pope was at Culpeper with the larger part of his army camped within the triangle formed by the confluence of the Rappahannock and the Rapidan. Contrary to the new commander's wishes, Stanton insisted that King's division of McDowell's corps be left at Fredericksburg.

So in July Pope occupied much the same position as that to which Johnston had retired from Manassas in the early spring. In his possession and control as far south as the Rapidan, the Orange & Alexandria Railroad provided him rail communication with Washington and points between. At Manassas Junction, where, a year before, Confederate supplies had accumulated in such mass as to embarrass Johnston, a vast depot of Union stores was now established. Roughly paralleling his front and twenty-five miles distant, lay the Virginia Central, Lee's only rail route to the Shenandoah Valley.

Pope was now in a position to show whether he had a truer appreciation of the military value of railroads than Johnston. They had a greater potential for offense, his reason for being there, than for defense, Johnston's reason. His view of the railroads was equally myopic. In his new command was a master of railroad construction, maintenance and operation. If Pope had had any conception of the significance of the Orange & Alexandria to the operation on which he was launched, he would have hung onto him at any cost. He dismissed him as an unnecessary encumbrance. If Pope had had any understanding of what the Virginia Central meant to the Confederacy, he would not have stopped at Culpeper. By marching only twenty-seven miles farther along his own

Wreckage Left Behind by Pope in Retreat from the Rapidan to Manassas

CONSTRUCTION CORPS IN ACTION

The bearded man on the bank at the right is General Haupt supervising in person.

well-established supply line, he could have reached the Gordonsville junction and struck a stunning blow at Lee's communications. Evidently he failed utterly to evaluate the railroad as a new and great weapon.

What might have happened if the Army of Virginia had been organized a month earlier and if Pope had taken his position before the battle of Malvern Hill must remain a matter for speculation. As it transpired, Lee learned of Pope's arrival at Culpeper on July 12. By that time McClellan had retired to Harrison's Landing. While by no means relieved of anxiety as to the future intentions of his old adversary, Lee was now able to give studied consideration to the new development on the Rapidan. Quickly he concluded that, whatever McClellan intended, the Virginia Central Railroad must not fall into the hands of the enemy.

So fixed was his determination to avoid this disaster that he waited only until the next morning to take the first step in one of the most daring maneuvers of his military career. Naturally he turned to Jackson, a man intimately acquainted with the country and noted for swift, secret action and daring tactics. On July 13 Jackson with his own and Ewell's division was detached from the Richmond defenses and ordered to move by train to Louisa Court House, leaving sufficient cavalry at Hanover Junction to cover that most important point on the railroad. If, on arrival at Louisa, he found that Pope had not already taken Gordonsville, Jackson was to proceed there immediately.[4] Thus, without sending Jackson and Ewell beyond reach, should the assault on Richmond be renewed, Lee was demonstrating his theory of how best to defend a railroad. It was the direct opposite of that held by the man who within the month was to become general in chief of all the Union armies.

In the West Halleck was attempting to protect his newly captured railroad properties by the use of a multitude of small garrisons and by scattering infantry details along the tracks—a procedure so extravagant of man power as greatly to reduce the striking power of his mobile army. Lee could not spare the men required for anything like that. Besides, he believed "it is easier to defend a railroad by massing troops at salient and commanding points to repress the attack of the enemy and strike him if he advances, than to extend the force along the whole line." [5]

Over the same rails that his men had ridden eastward from the Valley shortly before, Jackson returned to Gordonsville with equal secrecy and much greater speed. Pope was unaware that the railroad he had failed to occupy was now bringing troops from Richmond. McClellan was no longer in condition to take advantage of the reduction of the forces confronting him, as Stanton had hoped. Jackson could do much more effective work at Gordonsville. As the days passed, Lee watched and waited for further development of Federal plans. Evidence was accumulating that McClellan's troops were leaving the Peninsula. But Burnside, coming up from the south, was reported to be aboard transports off Fortress Monroe. What was he up to? What of the force of unknown strength that lay at Fredericksburg? Was it likely to move southward along the R.,F.&P. and strike the Virginia Central at Hanover Junction?

Then suddenly came an event which determined Lee's next move. Jackson learned that advance units of Pope's army were moving southward. Without waiting for orders he struck out from Gordonsville to meet them with the hope they might be defeated before the main body could move to their support. On August 9 the two forces clashed in bloody battle at Cedar Mountain,[6] some ten miles south of Culpeper and near the O.&A. Railroad.

Of this battle Dr. Freeman says that it "exposed much and decided nothing."[7] Certainly it exposed to the surprised Pope the presence of a strong force in his front and to Lee the necessity of sending reinforcements to Jackson. By now he was convinced the movement from the Peninsula was a genuine evacuation, that McClellan's troops were shipping north, ultimately to join Pope, and that Burnside was planning to move up the Rappahannock for the same purpose. Pope must be crushed before this huge concentration could be accomplished. Lee prepared to strike.

To prevent any interference with the railroad east of Louisa, he dispatched two brigades to Hanover Junction. As rapidly as trains could be supplied, the men of Longstreet's corps were put aboard and hurried off to Gordonsville. When they had unloaded there, the engines were turned and the empty trains went back to Richmond to load up again with as many men as could get inside and atop the cars. Day after day this process was repeated until Longstreet's ten brigades with their field equipment were transferred from Richmond to the new theater. Too little credit has been given the railroadmen who accomplished such feats. They never undressed and slept only while trains were being loaded and unloaded. Enginemen slept in their cabs, and other members of the crews napped wherever they could drop down for a few minutes. As if their fatigue was not enough to jangle their frayed nerves, the equally tired and sleepy soldiers chose the occasion to display obstinacy and ill humor.

Anderson tells of one car in a crowded train which was disabled when its drawhead pulled and how the soldiers in it refused to rouse up and shift to another car. It happened that near by was a little sidetrack, built to hold a piledriver. Spotting it, the harassed conductor cut the disabled car from the train, kicked it into the siding and left it there with its stubborn occupants.[8]

To the same author we are indebted for another story, which illustrates the way officers demanded the impossible from the railroaders. The efficient general yardmaster of the Virginia Central at Richmond was one Cornelius Tyler. He took his job most seriously and resented any interference from outsiders. While Longstreet's corps was being moved, Tyler had just completed loading out the last available engine and car in the yards. For respite when the task was done he stepped into the Antitotti Bar in the depot for a sociable drink. Before long he went back to the platform and stood looking over the cleaned-out yards. A hard-riding cavalry officer came dashing down Broad Street and drew up beside him.

"Where can I find the superintendent?" he demanded.

"I am he, sir," Tyler replied politely.

"Well," snapped the officer, "I want ready here in twenty minutes three trains of twenty cars each to load those soldiers coming down the street."

"Well, General," said Tyler, "I have sent out every single engine and car that can turn a wheel. But alight and be seated. I will go up and order Master Mechanic Freeman to build three engines and I will have Master Carbuilder Childs put up sixty cars and have them here in twenty minutes."

Over the railroad which Johnston would have abandoned and which lay for days lightly defended within a day's march of Pope's headquarters, Lee moved a formidable army to Pope's front, and on August 15 he boarded a train for Gordonsville to take personal command in the field. He found Pope's army pleasantly encamped on open, level ground facing the Rapidan, with the Rappahannock in its rear and dependent for all its supplies on the Orange & Alexandria, which entered the area over the bridge at Rappahannock Station. To quote Dr. Freeman: "Pope's ignorance of Lee's movements had caused him incautiously to present his adversary with as fair an opportunity as ever a soldier was offered." [9]

3

It will be remembered that when Pope took command he found no use for Herman Haupt and transferred the maintenance and operation of the railroads within his department to the Quartermaster. The magnitude of this blunder was disclosed by a telegram sent to Haupt by Assistant Secretary of War P. H. Watson after the battle of Cedar Mountain: "Come back immediately; cannot get along without you; not a wheel moving on any of the roads." [10] At no time had the railroad situation with which he had to deal been so completely bungled by an army commander. With characteristic speed and directness Haupt went about untangling the mess made of things during his brief absence from the service.

From Washington he took an engine and sped to army headquarters near the Rapidan. There he found Pope so ready
and anxious to restore to him the authority of which he had
been deprived that he was invited to dictate in the name of
the commander any orders he considered advisable.

There was no delay. On August 18 Pope issued "General
Order No. 22" as Haupt dictated:[11]

All railroads, and especially the Orange and Alexandria
Railroad, within the limits of the Army of Virginia, are
placed under the exclusive charge of Col. Herman Haupt.
No other officer, whatever be his rank, shall give any orders
to any employe of the road, whether conductor, engineer,
or other agent. No orders regulating the running of trains,
construction or repair of the roads, transportation of supplies
or troops shall be given except by authority of these Headquarters through Colonel Haupt.

All persons now employed in any way on these railroads
will immediately report to him and will hereafter receive
instructions from him only.

All requisitions for transportation and all applications for
construction or repair of roads will be made direct to him
at Alexandria, Va.

All passes given by him to employes will be respected as if
issued from these Headquarters.

The next day Stanton extended the authority previously
granted Haupt "to embrace all the railroads which are or
may hereafter be included within the lines of operation of
the Army of Virginia."[12]

A quick survey disclosed to Haupt that the confusion on
the O.&A. was due to causes with which he was quite familiar. He cites them as "military interference, neglect to unload
and return cars, too many heads, and, as a consequence, conflicting orders."[13] Before Haupt could do anything toward
re-establishing orderly operation, Pope followed his discovery of Lee's army in his front with an order for immediate
retreat across the Rappahannock. He called on Haupt to

remove the large supply of stores which had been collected at Culpeper. In this Haupt succeeded through the use of rolling stock already accumulated thereabouts.

For the complete story of Lee's efforts to dislodge Pope from his strong position on the north bank of the Rappahannock, the reader may turn to the books of general war coverage.[14] The point here is to explore the relation of the railroad to the progress of the campaign and its ultimate result. First it must be said that by sending a cavalry detachment secretly across the Rappahannock to cut the railroad in Pope's rear and burn the Rappahannock bridge, Lee hoped to trap him in the triangle between the rivers. Unfortunately for Lee, the cavalry was delayed for two days, and before it could strike, Pope was safely across the river and in position on the north bank. Lee considered it too hazardous to force a crossing in the face of such opposition. Instead he resorted to a series of thrusts, feints and flanking movements designed to confuse Pope and throw him off balance.

4

Meanwhile Haupt was bringing order out of the chaos into which Pope's rail communications had fallen. Pope wished no depot established at Rappahannock Station. Instead he wanted Haupt to see to it that a train of twenty cars be kept running regularly according to orders as a means of providing daily subsistence for the troops. He asked also that "nearly the whole of the rolling stock of the road be switched off on the side-tracks either at Catlett's or Warrenton Junction, so that in case of necessity I can carry off all the baggage and material of the army by railroad at the shortest notice."[15] The amazing speed and foresight that marked Haupt's work was again displayed. Before nightfall of that same day he not only assured Pope that sixty cars would be at Warrenton Junction "tomorrow" for use in case of need, but advised him as to the disposition of forage and stores Pope had not mentioned. He warned the commander against concentrating too many locomotives at the south end of the line. This, he said, would leave him short at Alexandria if reinforcements were to be forwarded.[16]

But that was not all he did that day. He ordered the siding at Rappahannock Station immediately extended to hold twenty cars of commissary stores and arranged for twenty more to be held at the next station back to replace the first when empty. Then he found time to advise Halleck of what he had done and asked to be advised of any contemplated troop movements in order that transportation for them might be arranged without delay.

Under terrific pressure and vexed by all sorts of surprises and annoyances, he worked for six days and nights. If he managed to get any sleep there is no record of it. No man of less physical strength or mental imperturbability could have endured the strain or avoided hopeless snarling of the transportation. Back and forth he shuttled between Alexandria and the front as the fighting intensified. From Pope, Halleck, field generals, Watson, Devereux and railroad employees, telegrams and courier-borne messages followed him ceaselessly wherever he went. Trains were wanted of him which could not possibly be supplied. He was berated for not running them in both directions over the single track at the same time, and the heavier the fighting grew the more he was bedeviled by men who had given no thought to the railroad until the emergency was on them.

While he was returning from Rappahannock Station to Alexandria on the twenty-second, his train was fired on by enemy cavalry at Catlett's and the train following was captured there. Lee was determined to cut that vital railroad and shut off Pope's subsistence and reinforcement, but the carefully planned raid by Stuart's cavalry failed. The blackness of the night kept him from tearing up track and a torrential rainstorm made the bridge across Cedar Run too wet to burn.

When Haupt reached Manassas he was handed a telegram from Pope, asking him to retire all rolling stock from the south end of the line. It was too late. An enemy force was now between Haupt and the large number of engines and

cars Pope had ordered sent to the front. The flood of telegrams continued to pour in: The army is changing its position. Push troops forward to Catlett's. Keep your rolling
stock above Catlett's and out of danger. Let no trains pass
Manassas except those bearing troops. Tell General Heintzelman, Cox and Sturgis to detrain at Warrenton Junction
and take position there. Send forward the provision trains.
Such was the substance of the messages which came to Haupt,
who through all the criticism and confusion kept the wheels
rolling, wisely apportioning the available transportation between troops and subsistence.

About midnight on the twenty-third, Haupt was waiting
in Alexandria for the arrival of four long-overdue trains
from the south when into the station stamped one of the
conductors. He indignantly reported that the trains had
been stopped four miles from town by General Sturgis who
had taken possession of them and refused to allow them to
proceed. Sturgis had been demanding transportation for his
troops. Haupt immediately set out for headquarters. When
he got there Sturgis undertook to place him under arrest.
Haupt presented his authority from Halleck and ordered
Sturgis either to release the trains at once or himself submit
to arrest. Upon examining the credentials Sturgis sullenly
replied, "Well, then, take your damned railroad."[17] Of the
Sturgis incident Haupt wrote: "This interference deranged
the trains for some time and kept at least 10,000 men out of
the battle." Watson wired Haupt to "be patient as possible
with the generals; some of them will trouble you more than
they will the enemy."

Trains were still running as far south as Warrenton Junction, and all available rolling stock, loaded to capacity with
troops, subsistence and ammunition, was kept moving. The
maintenance of this railroad service was Pope's only hope of
holding on in the Rappahannock country until the thousands
of troops arriving in Alexandria from McClellan's army could
join up. On the twenty-fourth, Haupt advised Halleck that
in favorable circumstances he could move 20,000 troops per
day, but that accidents and detentions were certain to reduce

the number. Constant bickering went on between field officers and railroad men over which units should have preference in transportation, and out of it came fresh nightmares for Haupt. He could not understand why troops should be permitted to wait for rail transportation when they could march to their destinations sooner than cars could be provided to carry them.

Haupt's telegrams of August 24 and 25 give a vivid picture of an indomitable railroader fighting to sustain a hard-pressed army. Here are some excerpts from typical messages:

To P. H. Watson, Assistant Secretary of War:
. . . none of the engines sent to Catlett's with troops have returned. I have ordered an empty engine to go forward cautiously, ascertain cause of detention and report.

If you can find General Hooker, . . . please say to him that we expect to carry his whole force to-morrow; but, to do it, the trains must be loaded in 15 minutes, and everything should be beside the track.

Another day is lost in our transportation by the neglect of General Sturgis' officers to load the cars furnished to them. . . . I have seen General Sturgis and informed him that no more cars can be furnished him until others are supplied.

I ordered back nearly all the trains, and will load them to-night with supplies and ammunition, and send forward as fast as possible in preference to troops.

To General Kearny:
You telegraphed to-day for another battery; it cannot be sent in morning, as it is not unloaded from boats.

To Major General Halleck:
The Quartermaster informs me of 20,000 more troops by transport, and also a lot by rail. . . . If the troops are to go by rail, I should know the order in which they are to go, and the points of destination.

Despite his remarkable foresight and careful arrangements, best results repeatedly were prevented by failure of officers to load or unload cars as he ordered. Cars of forage and supplies were detained needlessly. It seemed all but a hopeless struggle to teach army officers not to obstruct or interfere with railroad operation on which the very lives of their men depended. Many an officer forgot that rail service was for the benefit of the army as a whole and continued to regard it as something he could appropriate for himself or his own unit at will.

"I am just informed that the four trains following the engine Secretary are captured and that the rebels are approaching Manassas with artillery. These may be exaggerations but the agent and operator are leaving." This was the ominous message sent on August 26 by the tireless Chief of Construction and Transportation to General Halleck in Washington. There was no exaggeration. On the contrary, at half past four o'clock the next morning President Lincoln got a dispatch from Haupt, reading: "Intelligence received within twenty minutes informs me that the enemy are advancing and have crossed Bull Run bridge; if it is not destroyed, it probably will be."[18] Something quite unexpected had happened. How could the enemy be in force at Manassas when only the day before trains had been running to Warrenton?

5

For four days after Lee's arrival at the south bank of the Rappahannock he maneuvered by right and left flank, up and down the river, seeking an opening. Twice he failed to cut Pope's supply line—first at Rappahannock bridge and again when Stuart's raid on Catlett's Station was unsuccessful. But on that raid Stuart had captured Pope's dispatch book which disclosed his purpose to hold the line of the Rappahannock until joined by McClellan. Possessed of this information, Lee knew he must find a way to get at Pope quickly. Should a junction of the two Federal armies be accomplished, he would be hopelessly outnumbered and could do nothing else than retire and abandon the campaign. In fact, Pope alone was too strong and too well positioned for

Lee to hazard a direct attack. His only hope was to execute a master stroke of tactics which would force Pope either to change his position or divide his forces.

Again Lee called in the intrepid Jackson and out of a hurried conference the afternoon of August 24 came a plan to cut the railroad far to Pope's rear and interpose a force between him and Washington. At that time Jackson had moved by the left flank up the river until his men lay at Waterloo Bridge, six miles west of Warrenton. The plan was for him to march northward next day at dawn, proceed behind the Bull Run Mountains, turn eastward through Thoroughfare Gap and strike full speed for the railroad in the Manassas neighborhood.[19] Pope anticipated an attempt to outflank his right but expected the move to come through Warrenton. Jackson slipped quietly past him. He passed through the lightly defended Gap, and the famous "foot cavalry" stepped off the miles in swinging strides. At mid-afternoon they were at Gainesville. Jackson was obliged to choose now between two routes to the railroad. An important consideration was to reach a bridge, the destruction of which would halt operation of the road for as long a time as possible. Near Bristoe Station, four miles below Manassas, such a bridge spanned Broad Run. At a little greater distance above Manassas was another, but to get to it would mean a longer march over a more difficult road. He would strike at Bristoe.

Near sunset the weary men, who by that time had guessed their destination, were electrified by the whistle of an engine. Then by another. Running in close order, Haupt's empty trains were rushing back to Alexandria to pick up new loads of troops and supplies. With a whoop and a rush, Jackson's men ran for the track as a second train came on. In a frantic effort to stop it they threw debris upon the track, but they were too late. The speeding engine plowed through and the disappointed soldiers could only pour into it an ineffective stream of bullets. They would get the next one. They found a derailing switch, opened it and prepared to fire a volley into the engine cab. They had but a few minutes to wait for the third train. The unsuspecting engineer drove full speed into the blast of fire, struck the derail and, with his engine and half his train, went crashing down an embankment. A few more minutes and another train of twenty cars crashed into the wreck of the first. The right of way was piled high with the debris, and the jubilant Johnnies, who in two days had marched fifty-four miles to surprise the Yanks with this smashing show, stood by to watch the wreckage pile still higher. But the fun was over. The engineer of the next train saw the mess in time to stop, reverse his engine and back his train out of danger. What next?

From residents of Bristoe, Jackson learned of the huge depot at Manassas. The train which escaped to the north would carry the news of the attack to Alexandria. The one which backed away from the wreck would spread the alarm to Pope. There was no time to waste. Although his men had dropped from near exhaustion and fallen asleep where they lay, Manassas would have to be taken before morning. Two regiments of infantry and part of Stuart's cavalry were aroused and pushed forward through the dark to rout the small guard posted at the supply depot and climax "one of the greatest marches of history"[20] with the capture of a prize beyond the capacity of the captors either to consume or carry away.

Leaving Ewell with three brigades at Bristoe, Jackson moved early in the morning to Manassas. To the hungry and poorly clad Confederates, the magnitude and variety of stores found there seemed incredible. Warehouses crammed with such staples as meat, flour, sugar and good coffee stood beside others filled with clothing which ranged from shoes and over-coats to linen handkerchiefs. There were barrels of whisky, cases of cigars, and luxuries which many of the soldiers had never hoped to see. Cakes and canned lobster, candy and soap, French mustard and Rhine wine drew their attention away from fine saddles and fancy underwear. In addition to the warehouses, the railroad yard was crowded with loaded cars. According to General A. P. Hill there were two miles of them.[21] When Jackson saw that all these goods and edibles could not be hauled away, the men were allowed to help themselves. Not until each man had chosen what he would eat and what he would carry was the torch applied to the remainder.[22]

In the neighborhood of Alexandria were strong units of McClellan's army. Pope would be rushing up from the south. Jackson thought it high time he was getting out from between the two Federal armies. On the twenty-eighth he marched away to the northwestward and took position on the Warrenton Pike near Groveton, and close by the old Manassas battlefield. From there he could retire if necessary or join Longstreet who, if Lee's plan was working out, should soon be coming through Thoroughfare Gap. Longstreet was on time. The maneuver was working out precisely as planned. Instead of facing Pope across the Rappahannock, Lee's reunited army was resting on the fringe of the field from which McDowell had been driven in July of 1861.

From the day Jackson left Richmond until his withdrawal from Manassas to Groveton, the control of two railroads had been the determining factor in every major move made in the campaign. Preservation of the Virginia Central had motivated its initiation. The use of that road had made it possible for Lee to take the offensive, and the cutting of the Orange & Alexandria at Bristoe had forced Pope to retreat from his strong post on the Rappahannock and give battle where he had least expected—on a field chosen not by himself but by the enemy. Lee's Virginia Central was safe and Pope's Orange & Alexandria was useless below Bull Run.

Though clipped to a mere stub below Alexandria, the O.&A. played a part in the bloody battle which raged through the remaining days of August. Pope's army was out of rations for men and of forage for the overworked horses.[23] Haupt undertook to haul supplies as far as the burned Bull Run bridge, but they were delayed by a rear-end collision which blocked the track near Union Mills. Word came to him that enemy cavalry and guerrilla bands were riding as far up the line as Burke's Station. He applied himself to bringing off wounded who had collected at Burke's and Fairfax. His trains got through though they were fired on promiscuously at various points.[24] Then he wired his agent at Burke's: "At least one of the bridges beyond Fairfax is destroyed, perhaps others. It is not probable that we can use the road again for some time, and the army must cut its way through."[25]

Despite his gloomy prediction, Haupt's men worked unceasingly to repair the road as fast as the enemy damaged it. By evening of the twenty-ninth the prospect was much more encouraging. The Federals were again in possession of Manassas and Bristoe and as yet there seemed no fear of disaster to Pope. Halleck was taking most seriously the matter of restoring and maintaining the railroad and promptly met Haupt's requests for troops to protect his working parties and for strong track and bridge guards. Next day the track was open to Sangster, four miles from Centreville by wagon road, and eighty-eight cars of subsistence and ammunition were delivered there. This was sufficient to supply the immediate demands. The tension was easing a bit, and on the thirtieth Haupt telegraphed Lincoln: "Our telegraph operators and railway employes are entitled to great credit. They have been advanced pioneers, occupying the posts of danger, and the exploit of penetrating to Fairfax and bringing off the wounded when they supposed that 20,000 rebels were on their front and flanks, was one of the boldest performances I have ever heard of."[26]

Other developments of that eventful day included the opening of the track to Bull Run, the assignment of an entire division to strengthen the guard over railroad repairs, property and operations, and the discovery of two attempts at sabotage. Before noon Haupt wired Watson to arrest one William Hook, employed in the machine shop, believed to be a Rebel and charged with secreting parts of engines in order to make them unfit for service. Later in the day he sent Watson another message, telling how the master machinist in the Fredericksburg shop of the R.,F.&P. had discovered a loaded shell placed in each of the forges.[27] He got news from the lower end of the line that crews were repairing the bridges between Catlett's and Manassas and would shortly be able to pass trains over them. Haupt, in turn, notified Washington that Bull Run bridge should be passable the morning of September 1. The savage battle to restore transportation over the Orange & Alexandria seemed almost won.

Then came the worst of bad news. The work on Bull Run bridge was abandoned. Engines and cars caught south of the broken bridge at Bristoe were being burned by Union troops. Pope was defeated. Soon his shattered brigades came slogging through mud and rain back to the railroad east of Sangster. Nothing remained for Haupt except to rescue his rolling stock, bring out as many wounded as he could, and burn the supplies he must leave behind.

One of the greatest railroad fights of military history was over.

With the picture fresh of fast-moving trains hitting a derail switch opened by Jackson's men and plunging down an embankment to oblivion, it is time to pause and pay a little of the credit long due to the railroaders on both sides not only in the turbulent days of Second Manassas but throughout the

In the many chronicles of the Civil War too little has been written about the men who operated the railroad trains. Despite their bravery and almost incredible feats they are, to people today, a group almost forgotten. Unarmed and defenseless, engineers and firemen were favorite targets for snipers and bushwhackers. Hundreds of them, whose names appear on no honor roll, indeed on no enlistment roll of either army, died in their engine cabs. Still other hundreds were maimed or killed in the countless wrecks caused by worn-out and broken-down track or by enemy raiders. For engineers and firemen who started a run within a combat area there was no such thing as safety. They invited a cab full of bullets, a crash off a curve where a rail had been removed, or a plunge through a burned bridge into a stream.

The service they rendered was quite as essential as the soldiers'. Their chance of surviving a run was little greater than a soldier's chance of coming out of a battle unharmed.

Working for their chosen side, blue or gray, they responded to orders with the same alacrity and bravery that marked the men who carried guns. Sherman said of his railroaders: "I am convinced that the risk of life to the engineers and men on that railroad fully equaled that on the skirmish line, called for as high an order of courage and fully equaled it in importance."[28]

Early in the war the Federals began equipping many of their engines with armored cabs which would usually ward off a bushwhacker's bullets but were no safeguard at all against a plunging locomotive when it left the rails. Because of the casualties there were times when a lack of experienced men to operate trains threatened to halt traffic. Always, however, replacements stepped up, willing to learn to drive an engine or fire a boiler.

Then men of the Construction Corps were every bit as useful, as willing and as brave as the trainmen, and just as deserving of recognition. They, too, faced danger without flinching. They, too, were the targets of bushwhackers and raiding cavalry. Much of their work was performed high atop flimsy structures where a slip or misstep meant certain death. No soldier marched longer or fought harder than the railroaders worked when necessity called. They well deserved Sherman's meed of praise, given long after the war was over: "The Atlanta campaign would simply have been impossible without the use of the railroad from Louisville to Nashville—one hundred and eighty-five miles—from Nashville to Chattanooga —one hundred and fifty-one miles—and from Chattanooga to Atlanta—one hundred and thirty-seven miles. Every mile of this single track was so delicate that one man could in a minute have broken or removed a rail."[29]

Under enemy fire, in mud and rain, under scorching sun or in freezing cold, in daylight or dark, they worked to maintain tracks and bridges where military trains must run. Large numbers of them were civilians, not soldiers subject to military orders. It would be a pleasant thing if one might say of the thousands of soldiers assigned to guard the tracks and bridges, and to man the blockhouses at the more vulnerable structures, that they showed the same devotion to duty, the same courage and fortitude as those who served in their building, maintenance and repair. But one cannot. As a rule they served in small detachments, frequently posted in lonely places far from the front lines with only the passing trains· to relieve the monotony. In all too many cases the service developed a morbid fear of cavalry raiders. It was not unusual for them to flee at the first shot or surrender at the first demand. Then the Construction Corps would have to repair the damage.

In the Atlanta campaign the Construction Corps developed such a reputation for speed that it acted as a substantial deterrent to the enemy. Why risk riding a hundred miles to tear up a stretch of track or burn a bridge when it seemed inevitable the damage done would be made good almost as soon as the raiders could return to their base?

On a hot day a group of Confederates were resting in the shade of a tree overlooking Sherman's camps about Big Shanty. One soldier said to another: "Well, the Yanks will have to git up and git now, for I heard General Johnston himself say that General Wheeler had blown up the tunnel near Dalton, and that the Yanks would have to retreat, because they could get no more rations."

"Oh hell!" said the listener. "Don't you know that old Sherman carries a duplicate tunnel along?"

After the war was over, General Johnston expressed to Sherman his admiration for the Yanks' feats of bridge-building and railroad repair. He cited the instance of an officer bringing him news that Wheeler's cavalry had made a bad break in the railroad about Tilton's Station which would take at least a fortnight to repair. While they were talking they saw a train coming down the road.

Victories traveled on the rails these men laid.

CHAPTER XVI

THE RAILS IN THE ANTIETAM CAMPAIGN AND AFTER

I

For the second time since the war began, a September sun shone down on a victorious Confederate army facing Washington from near-by Virginia. But what a different army it was! And what a different Virginia! Lee's veterans bivouacked where Johnston's newly made soldiers had frolicked through the previous autumn, but the feet of thousands were bare, their clothing was in tatters and they were hungry.

For more than a year the fields of northern Virginia had been trampled and fought over by armies clad in blue and in gray. Where Johnston's men had fed on the fat of a healthy land, neither meat nor grain remained to revive the spent strength of Lee's hard-fighting, hard-marching soldiers who had rested scarcely at all since the Seven Days. Stretching away to the southwest, the Orange & Alexandria Railroad was broken and stripped of its rolling stock. Westward to the Shenandoah, where there was food but no ammunition, ran the recaptured Manassas Gap line, ripped and useless. By destroying a railroad Lee had won a battle but left himself without a supply line.

In front of him lay the forbidding defenses of Washington within which Pope's beaten army and thousands of McClellan's men from the Peninsula had taken refuge. Already the Army of Virginia and the Army of the Potomac, victualed and munitioned by the great network of Northern railroads, were being welded into one mighty force under the command of McClellan. Against such odds Lee dared not move farther in pursuit. Neither was it safe for him to linger in this advanced position until McClellan was ready to take the offensive. Lee must move. But where should he go? To return to the Rappahannock line would mean the loss of much he had gained and only invite another thrust against Richmond. The same would be true of a move to the Shenandoah. Thus far, he had won through skillful maneuver. Was there not still more to be gained by the same process?

Across the Potomac the rich farm lands and towns of Maryland had not been touched by war and contained food and forage in plenty. If he could get to them without fighting a major battle he could live for a time off the country, and when the Federals came to drive him out he would have ample room in which to maneuver. Perhaps he could cut them to pieces in detail after the manner in which he had defeated Pope. Moreover, elated by the news of the victory at Manassas, Southern newspaper editors were clamoring for an invasion.[1] What influence they had on Lee's decision is difficult to determine. Certain it is, however, that he turned an attentive ear to those of his people who argued that, given a fair chance, Marylanders as well as Kentuckians would rise in support of the Confederacy. So at the very time Bragg and Kirby Smith were pursuing this phantom in Kentucky, Lee turned the faces of his men toward Maryland.[2]

Across the Potomac there would be no doubt about subsistence, but how to procure ammunition was another matter. There was but one route over which it could reach him. From Staunton on the Virginia Central it would have to be carted down the Shenandoah and into Maryland via Shepherdstown. But before wagon trains safely could operate over the Valley Pike, the Federal garrisons at Winchester, Martinsburg and Harper's Ferry must be removed from the lower Valley. Lee had good reason to hope his presence in Maryland would cause them to be withdrawn without a fight.

Although undertaking an invasion far beyond the reach of rails, he took the precaution to prepare a railhead to which he could retire in case he should be forced to give up his plans.

He would return to Warrenton—and with that possibility in
mind he asked President Davis to order the repair at once of
the Orange & Alexandria bridges across the Rappahannock
and Rapidan.[3] Then he headed his columns toward White's
Ford near Leesburg, eleven miles south of Frederick, Maryland. Measured in miles it was neither a long nor difficult
march, but the tired, shoeless and hungry men were in no
mood for taking the road again so soon after their fight at
Manassas. Except for green corn and some ripening fruit,
they could find little or nothing to eat. They were attacked
by a serious diarrhea, and in their physical misery and mental
disturbance, their straggling and desertion came near putting
an end to the invasion before it got under way.

By September 7 the Potomac was behind them and the head
of the column rested comfortably in Frederick. Once in
Maryland with a full belly and a pair of shoes on his feet,
Johnny Reb felt his spirits rise rapidly. He was ready for new
adventures, but his commander was sadly disappointed. Of
the troublesome Federal garrisons in the lower Shenandoah,
only the one at Winchester had withdrawn. To detach troops
to clear Martinsburg and Harper's Ferry would be delaying
and dangerous if McClellan should pursue Lee, but if the
larger scheme which had by that time evolved in his mind
was to be carried out, his wagon road to Staunton must first
be made secure. Already it seemed that the political aspect of
the invasion was a failure. Maryland showed no disposition
to leave the Union, and there was no rush of citizens to
enlist under the Confederate flag.

Lee's plan called first for moving the main body of his army
to Hagerstown as a base of operations. Hagerstown was
located on the turnpike which would be his line of supply.
Also, it was the southern terminus of the Cumberland Valley
Railroad which connected it with Harrisburg. Twenty-two
miles north of Hagerstown the Cumberland Valley line connected with the York & Cumberland, which ran from
Chambersburg east to meet the Northern Central at York.
Good wagon roads led deep into Pennsylvania.

Lee counted heavily on McClellan's well-known disposition to procrastinate. He decided that he could detach forces to clear Martinsburg and Harper's Ferry; their missions could be completed and the army reunited at Hagerstown before McClellan would take the field. That done, he would start maneuvers, not against McClellan but against the railroads on which Washington and its defenses were dependent for supplies.

He could destroy the Cumberland Valley or occupy it and turn it to his own use in a thrust against the Pennsylvania trunk line at Harrisburg. In an operation in that direction, the first objective would be the destruction of the Pennsylvania's very long and expensive bridge across the Susquehanna. To the south he would strike against the defenseless B.&O. and keep it out of service as long as might be necessary to accomplish his major purpose. By disabling these two trunk lines, he would have the Northern Central and all lines west of Philadelphia within his grasp, and Federal communications between all the East and the Ohio Valley would be cut except for the long way round via New York and Lake Erie. He would have nearly 50,000 men between the B.&O. and the Pennsylvania railroads and be in control of both. His men could be faced east with their left flank within reach of the Susquehanna and their right on or near the Potomac. In that happy position he would make his bid for negotiations to end the war.

For the first time the Confederates were in force north of the B.&O. tracks. Considering his former exploits in connection, with that railroad, Jackson must have found some satisfaction in being chosen to recross the river, take Martinsburg from the north, cut the railroad there and then turn eastward along the track and approach Harper's Ferry from the rear, while two other columns struck from the heights on opposite sides of the little town. He lost no time in reaching Martinsburg. The blue garrison learned of his approach and fled to join their comrades at Harper's Ferry. Stonewall was back at the scene of his first devastating stroke at Union transportation; back where, more than a year before, he had given the B.&O. shops and great quantities of rolling stock to the flames.

The story of how Harper's Ferry was captured, of how Lee went to Sharpsburg and how the scattered and delayed columns rejoined the main army barely in time to receive the shock of unexpected battle is not for these pages. Nor is it to be told here how McClellan learned the details of Lee's plans before they were put in effect and how he took advantage of the division of the Confederate forces, fought his way through Turner's Gap in South Mountain and fell on Lee on the banks of Antietam Creek to end the invasion in one of the bloodiest battles of the war. Because the railroads were not directly involved in this struggle, it is sufficient to say that in the night of September 18 the invading army left on the field of Antietam its terrible toll of dead and started its retreat across the Potomac.

Except for the destruction of the B.&O. bridge across the Monocacy River on the march to Frederick[4] and the brief occupancy of that line by Jackson at Martinsburg and Harper's Ferry, not a railroad was touched. Not a carload of troops, munitions or supplies moved into the campaign area by rail. Despite this, the campaign had much railroad significance, not only because of its origin but because its objective involved control of railroad operations the potential of which remain beyond measure or estimate. That Lee's plan was no idle dream is evidenced by the fact that before he was cut off at Antietam his purpose had been divined, and Harrisburg, Philadelphia, Baltimore and Washington were in near panic.

Again it must be said that speculation is idle occupation; yet who can fail to wonder what course the war would have taken had Lee's soldiers reached the Susquehanna bridge!

2

For more than six weeks after Lee's retreat across the Potomac, McClellan's army remained in the vicinity of Sharpsburg. Since this position was no nearer than a day's wagon haul to any railroad, it posed a problem in supply. Fortunately a good wagon road ran through Sharpsburg south to Harper's Ferry and north to Hagerstown, making the army campsite accessible from the B.&O. on the south and from the Cumberland Valley line on the north. But wagon trains sufficient to supply an army of nearly 90,000 men, together with its animals, even though coming in from both ends, would tax the capacity of any road. The problem, therefore, was to manage transportation on the railroads so as to distribute the load and keep a steady and uninterrupted flow of supplies to the wagon trains. Herman Haupt wrote a detailed record of how these lines managed to supply McClellan until he was ready to cross into Virginia, and how the military railroads then took up the task of feeding the Army of the Potomac on its way to the Rappahannock.

In recognition of distinguished service during Pope's retreat, Haupt had been commissioned a brigadier general. When Lee crossed into Maryland, Haupt promptly set about repairing the Orange & Alexandria to Bristoe Station. He was thus engaged when, immediately after the battle of Antietam, Halleck directed him to give his attention to expediting the transportation of supplies to the army at Sharpsburg.[5] Three difficulties were confronted. The B.&O. bridge was out at Harper's Ferry. Because of the break in the B.&O., the Northern Central was again clogged with traffic. The Cumberland Valley line seemed unable to function effectively.

Despite the fact that shipments via the B.&O. had to be pontooned across the Potomac to Harper's Ferry and the wagon road, Haupt's first order required that all military shipments from Baltimore and points south be forwarded over that road, while those originating north of Baltimore must go via the York & Cumberland through Chambersburg to the Cumberland Valley and thence to Hagerstown.[6] He went direct to Hagerstown and found five or six trains stranded there, the main track blocked with unloaded cars, no adequate siding available and no warehouse facilities arranged for. He took immediate possession of that portion of the road below Chambersburg and placed it under control of a man of his own choosing. Then he sent W. W. Wright, a member of his own corps, to Chambersburg to ferret out the trouble with the Cumberland Valley and, if necessary, to assume control of all train movements over it. At the same time, however, he reminded Wright that if it was possible to get results through the regular officials of the road, it was preferable to leave the management in their hands. In either event three points must be given special attention: No supplies must be forwarded to the advanced terminus until actually required and only in such quantities as could be promptly removed. Prompt unloading and return of cars must be insisted on. No delay of trains beyond the time fixed for starting must be permitted.[7]

From the outset of his service Haupt had emphasized that violation of these three basic rules was the principal cause of the frequent and embarrassing jams in handling military supplies by rail. After personal attention to raising the Hagerstown blockade, he made an inspection trip over the York & Cumberland and found no serious complaint to make of the management. The only trouble there came from the fact that the amount of business to be handled exceeded the capacity of the road for prompt transportation. To facilitate matters he ordered all private sidings vacated and required that all cars belonging to individuals and all cars not used for military purposes be run off the tracks or removed where they would not stop traffic. On his way back to Baltimore he found about 200 loaded cars which had been standing on the B.&O. siding near Monocacy for nearly a week. These he ordered unloaded and the cars returned at once.

In Washington again on September 23, Haupt was informed that operations on the B.&O. were being embarrassed because of the failure of other roads to return their cars. Of all the causes of delay in military shipments, neglect to return empties was a fault he could neither tolerate nor forgive. Forthwith he sent out, over the Northern Central, the Pennsylvania and connecting roads, two experienced train dispatchers from the Orange & Alexandria to locate Mr.

Garrett's missing cars and return them promptly. Next day he went to Harper's Ferry to see what assistance might be given the B.&O. to finish the reconstruction of its bridge over the Potomac. Finding the supply of materials insufficient there and the force of workmen far too small, he telegraphed the Construction Corps, then at work on the O.&A., to report at Harper's Ferry with 150,000 feet of long, square timbers he had accumulated at Alexandria against just such an emergency.[8] There seemed no limit to the capacity of this versatile expert. Through his supervision McClellan's men were adequately supplied while they remained in Maryland.

General Haupt's handling of the supply lines to Sharpsburg by no means ended his service to the Army of the Potomac. His correspondence shows that as early as October 11 he anticipated McClellan's purpose to launch a campaign against Lee in Virginia and began a careful survey. As a result, he was ready with the answers before the questions were put to him. When McClellan asked for the reconstruction of the Winchester & Potomac with T rails, he promptly advised that it was inexpedient. The road was too lightly constructed, too poorly equipped and had suffered too much damage from Jackson's men who had battered it to pieces in their retreat. To procure rails and ties and make necessary repairs would take two months, and when completed, the road would have a capacity of no more than sixty cars per day. Furthermore, it would be of little or no use unless McClellan meant to expel the enemy from Winchester and remain there. If he meant to push farther into Virginia, the proper supply line would be the Manassas Gap, and the Winchester line would be of no importance.

Since McClellan planned to move southward on the east side of the Blue Ridge along Pope's old route to the Rappahannock, he readily conceded the soundness of Haupt's reasoning and withdrew his request. On October 26 he telegraphed Haupt:

I have the honor to request you to ascertain how far the Leesburg Railroad is practicable. I have also to request you to be ready to supply this army, via Orange and Alexandria and Manassas Gap Railroads, and to take steps at once to re-establish the wharves, etc., at Aquia and to be prepared to rebuild the railroad bridge over the Rappahannock at Fredericksburg, and to supply that road with rolling stock.[9]

Nothing more clearly demonstrates the comprehensive scope of railroad information available to the War Department and its field commanders through General Haupt's office than the reply sent to McClellan on the same day:

Your commands will receive prompt attention. I have the honor to report that from Alexandria to Difficult Creek, a distance of 18 miles, the Leesburg Road is in running order. From Difficult Creek to Leesburg, about eighteen miles of track have been destroyed, cross ties burned and iron scattered through the woods. Spans of bridges, most of them 150 feet in length, in six different localities, require to be constructed before the road can be used. The reconstruction of this road beyond Difficult Creek in time for any immediate advance will be impracticable.

Manassas Gap Railroad: General Siegel reports this road in running order to Front Royal. In case of an advance the enemy will no doubt endeavor to destroy the Goose Creek bridges, and I have ordered material to be prepared for their reconstruction. The capacity of this road, with present equipment, is about 700 to 900 tons per day, if cars are promptly returned and no accident occurs. Please report the probable demands upon this line, and how soon.

Acquia Creek and Fredericksburg Railroad: The destruction of this road was an unfortunate piece of vandalism on the part of our troops.[10] I reported to General Halleck that the destruction of this road was unnecessary, and highly censurable. The Potomac Creek bridge was nearly 80 feet high and 400 feet long. Nearly all the available timber within reach was used in its construction. This bridge was blown down, then burned.

The reconstruction of the Rappahannock bridge at this season will be difficult, and the structure, if rebuilt, precarious. Timber at this time is very scarce. Would it not be best to rely on boat and pontoon bridges at Fredericksburg?

The wharf at Aquia Creek was a very complete affair, covering an area of nearly an acre and a half, with double tracks, and commodious buildings. It cannot be reconstructed as it was in four months. The material cannot be procured in any reasonable time.

The cars on this road, some 60 in number, were all destroyed at the time of the evacuation.

If it is absolutely necessary to use this road, extraordinary efforts will be required to reconstruct it in time to be available, and I respectfully request instructions as to the relative military importance of these roads and the order of priority in which they should be prepared for service.[11]

The speed and effectiveness of campaign planning made possible by Haupt's independent corps appears from the cipher message McClellan sent Haupt within forty-eight hours after his first inquiry about the condition of the Leesburg Railroad:[12]

Please take immediate steps to enable you to forward supplies via Orange & Alexandria and Manassas Gap Railroads for this army, at rate of seven hundred tons per day. Also, be prepared to repair the Orange & Alexandria Railroad beyond Manassas Junction wherever it may be damaged.

McClellan seems not to have been informed of the extent of the damage suffered, nor to know, as Haupt did, that the Confederates had repaired the track, were running trains to Bristoe, five miles south of Manassas, and were carrying off the disabled engines and salvaging the car wheels, axles and other metal parts left along the road during Pope's retreat. Haupt understood that before repairs could be completed, possession must be regained.

At the end of October the Army of the Potomac recrossed the river and marched to the line of the Manassas Gap Railroad. With a supply line already established and subsistence rolling toward the new position, McClellan was soon prepared to take off in pursuit of Lee, who was retiring toward the Rappahannock. The series of episodes beginning with Haupt's arrangements to supply the army at Sharpsburg and continuing through the new offensive demonstrates more clearly than any other in the entire war the tremendous advantage gained by having rail transportation planned and handled by an able railroad man with authority rather than by military commanders in the field.

Unfortunately, the education of subordinate officers and soldiers in the use and protection of railroad property seemed next to a hopeless task. Speaking of operations on the Manassas Gap, Haupt said: ". . . more trouble was often given by our own soldiers than by the enemy." Where camps were near the road, the soldiers persisted in tearing up sidings, breaking switch stands and burning the wood gathered for the engines. Washing person and clothing with soap in the springs and streams which supplied the stations frequently caused engines to be stopped on the road by boilers foaming from soapy water. Such disturbances were not confined to the Manassas Gap. At Camp Upton on the Loudon & Hampshire, the sidings were destroyed, while on the O.&A. water was drained from the tanks and engine wood carried off for camp and cooking fires. Officers insisted on stopping trains and holding them on the main track while they examined passes. So annoying was this needless delay that a special order had to be issued to stop it. Besides all this, there was the habitual failure to unload and return cars.

Most difficult of all was persuading officers to provide adequate track and bridge guards and see to it that the men performed their duties. Anxious for the safety of the Orange & Alexandria, Haupt complained to General Heintzelman: "There is not a guard on the road between Fairfax and Union Mills, although we have five bridges in that interval." As for the Manassas Gap, not a guard was to be seen between Gainesville and Manassas despite the fact enemy partisans were known to be riding there. Haupt was not concerned for the safety of track and bridges alone, but for the protection of engine crews as well. Riding unarmed and helpless in their cabs, they provided excellent targets for any sharpshooting guerrilla. Too many of his men had been killed in this fashion for Haupt to take the lack of guards complacently. Heintzelman's only reply was that he thought "the officers sent to guard the roads would no doubt attend to their business." But from experience Haupt knew they would do no such thing unless they were given specific assignments and were carefully watched and supervised.

Haupt found out before long that whereas he had estimated the capacity of the Manassas Gap at 900 tons per day, McClellan's demands would exceed 1,500 tons. "We will have tough times on the railroad," he wired the War Department. "You recollect the difficulty of supplying General McDowell's army and the confusion that reigned for some time. That was in June, when grass could be obtained; now 60,000 animals must be fed exclusively by rail, and General McClellan's requirements for transportation are four or five times as great as McDowell's. Never before, perhaps, has a single-track railroad, of such limited capacity, been so severely taxed."[13]

By November 6 Lee had moved back to Culpeper and McClellan's men pushed forward to Warrenton. Emphasis on transportation of supplies was shifted from the Manassas Gap line to the Orange & Alexandria below Manassas Junction. Then came a sudden and unexpected development which was to change the whole procedure. McClellan was ordered to transfer his command to General Ambrose E. Burnside. On November 9, the day Burnside took over, Haupt warned him fully of the transportation difficulties likely to be encountered if the campaign continued along the line of the Orange & Alexandria. He pointed out that the railroad by which his army must be supplied was a single track, newly restored and without sidings sufficient to accommodate long trains; the road was inadequately furnished with either wood or water, and its normal capacity was less than half what was required to supply an army of the size Burnside commanded. From the left, the road would be exposed to enemy raids, and the farther he advanced the harder it would become to prevent breaks in the line by the enemy or as a consequence of overloading. In his opinion the O.&A. alone would provide a very insecure reliance. Possibly, he thought, by a combination of good management and good fortune it might be made to suffice, but he quite frankly stated the minimum conditions: a well-filled depot at Manassas, together with advance depots at intervals of thirty or forty miles to guard against line breaks. Not only must these depots be heavily guarded, but at each must be maintained a force of sufficient size to unload all cars at the same time as soon as they pulled in. There must be no interference from local quartermaster or commissary officers; all cars must be promptly returned when unloaded. Tracks and bridges must be alertly watched and adequately guarded, but in no circumstances must the guards be allowed to interfere with train operation. Orders to this effect and so strict that no man dare disobey them must come directly from the army commander. "Without this," said Haupt, "the supply of your army is impossible. No man living can accomplish it."[14]

The difficulties Haupt foresaw in supplying Burnside via the Orange & Alexandria alone convinced him that the reconstruction of the R.,F.&P. from Aquia to Fredericksburg was immediately called for, and he so reported to the War Department. Before the middle of the month the work was under way and was rapidly pushed forward. Whether by the O.&A. alone the Army of the Potomac could have been supplied in a further advance was never put to the test, for the entire plan of campaign was suddenly revised. To what extent Haupt's boldly expressed forebodings influenced the War Department and Burnside is not known, but all had learned that his unerring judgment was not to be taken lightly. In any event, the advanced positions on the Orange & Alexandria were abandoned, and the army marched cross-country to take up a new position on Stafford Heights, across the Rappahannock from Fredericksburg.

Damage done the R.,F.&P. by the retreating Union soldiers in August was found more readily repaired than that done by the enemy in April. Dockage at Aquia Creek was extemporized, the track restored and the high bridge across Potomac Creek replaced with a truss structure, most of which had been prefabricated. Rolling stock was shipped down the Potomac on river barges from Alexandria, and by the time the army was collected at Falmouth the road was in full operation. Meantime Lee had anticipated Burnside's purpose and shifted his own army to the formidable heights behind Fredericksburg, where it was readily supplied by the lower section of the R.,F.&P. Supplied by different sections of the same railroad, the two armies faced each other across the narrow valley until December 11, when Burnside sent his divisions across the river to the futile slaughter which was the Battle of Fredericksburg. When it was over, Burnside withdrew to the position from which the hopeless attack was launched, and from the heights on either side the two armies looked down on the battered city and waited while the year 1862 passed into history.

CHAPTER XVII

FORREST FINDS GRANT'S ACHILLES' HEEL

I

With his wagons loaded full of the stores Kirby Smith had foraged in the rich fields of eastern Kentucky, Bragg was bearing off southeastward by roads which led through the hill country east of Nashville. Now and then his cavalry turned to sting the front of the blue column which followed; but Buell had no intention of penetrating too far into the rough country of East Tennessee. He meant to march directly to Nashville where he had left 12,000 men in garrison, consolidate there and get ready for a drive against the all-important railroad junction of Chattanooga. Already he had detachments at work repairing the Louisville & Nashville Railroad behind him. As repairs progressed, the wagon haul would be shortened and when the railroad was running again, he would accumulate a depot of supplies in Nashville before he pushed on.

So he marched the main body of his army to Bowling Green while a separate column saw to it that the retreating Confederates kept on the move. He got no farther, for at Bowling Green, on October 30, he received an order from Halleck to turn the army over to General William S. Rosecrans. When Buell explained his plans to the new commander, Rosecrans thought them excellent and adopted them as his own.

He had no more than taken command when Morgan and his elusive, hard-riding cavalrymen, who had wrought such

THE NASHVILLE DEPOT OF THE NASHVILLE & CHATTANOOGA

This picture was taken while Sherman was preparing for the Atlanta campaign.

The Famous General

damage to the railroad in Buell's rear, made a sudden sortie in Rosecrans' front. Unable to halt the well-protected repairs which were being pushed rapidly forward from Louisville, Morgan took a different turn in his attempts to cripple Federal rail communications. Several hundred L.&N. cars had been left stranded between the Gallatin tunnels and the bridge across the Cumberland River at Nashville, both of which had been wrecked. These cars had been collected and stood idle at Edgefield on the north bank of the river. Morgan cut in ahead of Rosecrans and made a swift dash into the yards on November 5, but met with such unexpected resistance from across the river he had to gallop off before he had done much damage.[1]

Obviously Morgan was evaluating the cars in Confederate terms, else he would not have taken such a risk. To the Confederates the loss of even 100 cars from their dwindling supply would have been a very severe blow. But had the entire collection at Edgefield been destroyed, the shortage would not have been serious or more than momentary. The North was building cars faster than the enemy could destroy them, and replacements could have been sent down from Louisville long before Rosecrans was prepared to use them.

Precisely as Buell had outlined, Rosecrans moved on to Nashville, where he halted until rail communications with Louisville were re-established and the depot was sufficiently stocked to make him independent of day-to-day train arrivals. Essential as this pause was, it gave Bragg time to make extensive plans to meet the expected thrust at Chattanooga. He well understood that if and when the Federal commander undertook the attack, possession of the Nashville & Chattanooga Railroad would be just as necessary to him as it had been to the maintenance of Buell's army in Alabama. Bragg, therefore, skirted Nashville, turned west, and set his troops astride the railroad at Murfreesborough before Rosecrans completed his repairs on the L.&N. Only thirty-five miles separated the two camps. The armies spent Christmas Day of 1862 with battle imminent.

2

Though the most desperate fighting of that fateful September and October had occurred beyond Grant's jurisdiction, he was by no means neglected. Price was prowling south of Corinth. Grant called in the few troops left along the Memphis & Charleston between Corinth and Iuka. Just what Price had in mind was not clear, but on September 13 he occupied Iuka. Grant was apprehensive lest his purpose was to side-step Corinth on his way to join Bragg. Grant also saw another possibility. Van Dorn with a large force was within four days' march of Corinth, and the plan might be to attack him there, with Price coming in from the east and Van Dorn coming up from the south.[2] In either event Price must be driven back before co-operation between the two could be effected.

Not enough men for such an undertaking could be taken away from the defensive works about Corinth. At once Grant's disposition of troops in relation to the railroads became effective. All spare forces at Jackson and Bolivar were ordered to Corinth. So quickly were cars concentrated at Jackson that within twenty-four hours from the transmission of the order, the entire command arrived at its destination— this, despite derailment of the leading train which caused a delay of four hours.[3] Meantime a column had been set marching cross-country to strike Iuka from the south. When the troops came in from Jackson and Bolivar, they went aboard cars of the Memphis & Charleston for Burnsville where they detrained and approached Iuka from the north. After stubborn fighting, Price was forced to give up the town and retreat. Grant's railroads had worked fast and effectively— so much so, indeed, that their destruction thereafter became a major objective of the Confederates.

On September 19, the day the Army of the Ohio found Bragg squarely across its path at Munfordsville, General George H. Thomas was ordered east to reinforce Buell, and Grant's army was thereby greatly reduced. Except at Corinth

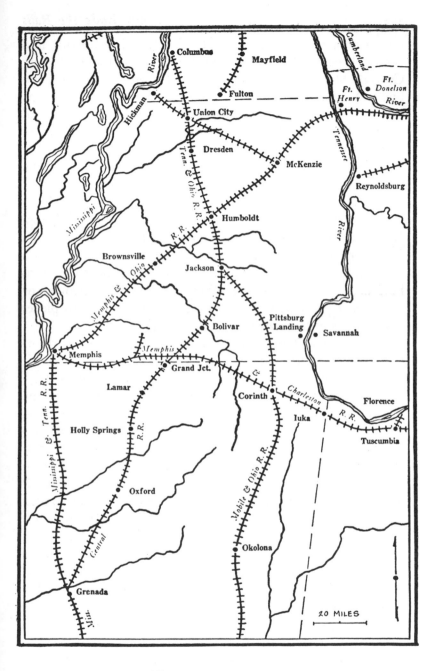

THE MEMPHIS AREA

he abandoned the Memphis & Charleston Railroad, and Bolivar became his most advanced position on the Mississippi Central. Should he be forced out of Corinth, the vital trunk line to Virginia would be back in Confederate hands. On the thirtieth Grant discovered that Van Dorn and Price had crossed the railroad west of Corinth and were massing in great strength inside the large railroad triangle. The next day he could see that they planned to attack Corinth from the northwest. Once more, troops from Jackson were hurried southward over the east leg of the triangle while reinforcements from Bolivar were marching from the Mississippi Central ahead of the oncoming enemy. On October 4, when Van Dorn made a slashing assault, Corinth was strong enough to shake him off. Again the railroads had enabled Grant to hold his position. Only his subordinates' mismanagement of the pursuit prevented him from cutting Van Dorn to pieces within the smaller triangle.

Despite Van Dorn's escape, Grant reckoned the battle of Corinth a decided victory.[4] At the same time he regarded it as a wholly unnecessary battle. On the blundering of the high command in Washington he placed the responsibility for the danger to which he had been exposed, the more than 2,000 casualties suffered, and, in fact, the very presence of the Confederates north of the Memphis & Charleston Railroad. Grant, it will be remembered, had attributed the Union's failure to take Vicksburg in the spring or early summer to Halleck's dalliance after Shiloh. To the same source he now traced another failure. While Van Dorn and Price were operating against him at Iuka and Corinth and holding him to a hazardous defensive, they were dependent on the lower portion of the Mississippi Central for supplies. Without it they could not have kept their armies in northern Mississippi long enough to be a serious threat. During the period of greatest danger a strong Union force lay unthreatened at Helena, Arkansas. It would have been a simple matter to bring these troops across the Mississippi River and break up the Mississippi Central far to the south. Then Van Dorn would have been compelled to fall back and maintain so strong a defensive force to protect his line of communications as greatly to impair his mobile striking power. But these troops at Helena were on the wrong side of the river to be within Grant's jurisdiction, and Halleck left them idle there while Grant fought off the fierce enemy thrusts at his own life line to Columbus.[5] To think of Lee neglecting such an opportunity is quite impossible.

Soon after the battle of Corinth things began looking up for the Federals in western Tennessee. With Bragg marching out of Kentucky and the crisis on the left of the long Federal front over, reinforcements started pouring into the Humboldt-Jackson-Corinth area. Grant's long anxiety for the safety of his jurisdiction was relieved.[6] On October 25 he was placed in authoritative command of the Department of the Tennessee and at once began preparations to resume the offensive which had been surrendered by Halleck in early June.

Never since Shiloh had he wavered in his opinion that the reduction of Vicksburg was the most important Federal objective in the West. Not only would it remove the last Confederate bastion on the Mississippi but it would put an end to enemy rail communication between East and West. Accordingly, on November 2, he telegraphed Halleck: "I have commenced a movement on Grand Junction. . . . If found practicable, I will go to Holly Springs and, maybe, Grenada, completing railroad and telegraph as I go."[7] At this time his command held the Mobile & Ohio from a point twenty-five miles south of Corinth northward to Columbus, Kentucky; the Mississippi Central from Bolivar to its junction with the M.&O. at Jackson; the terminus of the Memphis & Charleston and a few miles of that road east of Corinth, as well as the Mississippi River from Cairo to Memphis.[8] Without sufficient troops to guard all this mileage closely and at the same time take the offensive, he acted on the theory, also held by Lee, that the best way to defend a railroad is to hit the enemy who threatens it. For that purpose he began to concentrate his forces in the apex of the "iron triangle."

General John C. Pemberton, who had taken command of the troops assigned to the defense of Vicksburg, was entrenched across the Mississippi Central Railroad on the south bank of the Tallahatchie River, some thirty-five miles south of the Memphis & Charleston, with advance posts at Holly Springs and Grand Junction. On the eighth Grant's advance units occupied Grand Junction, and five days later his cavalry took Holly Springs as the enemy fell back behind the Tallahatchie. Then in possession of the railroad all the way from Holly Springs to Humboldt and thence to his supply base at Columbus, Grant halted while necessary track repairs were made below Grand Junction.

While there, he decided to establish at Holly Springs an extensive depot of supplies and munitions, all of which were coming to him by rail from Columbus. His supply line was long to maintain in enemy country. He was meticulous in his care that it be put and kept in good repair. Further to concentrate his striking power, he ordered Sherman to bring two divisions from Memphis and join him on the Mississippi Central. Instead of two, Sherman brought three divisions. It was while these troops were on their way that Halleck, after the greatest need had passed, ordered the troops in Helena to cross the river and cut the railroad in Pemberton's rear.[9] They had no difficulty reaching their objective, but, once there, were content to do so little damage that Pemberton quickly repaired the track and got the trains running again.

Water in the Tallahatchie was very high, and Pemberton had destroyed the railroad bridge across the stream. Grant regarded a crossing in the face of a fortified enemy as impossible.[10] He sent his cavalry farther up the river where they got across safely. When Pemberton found this force on his right flank and the railroad raided in his rear, he promptly withdrew to Grenada, behind the Yalobusha River. Pemberton's men had botched the job of wrecking the Tallahatchie bridge and the Federals easily restored it to service for trains. That done, Grant moved on to Oxford, forty-six miles north of Pemberton's new position at Grenada. The campaign was progressing nicely, but with each mile of advance toward Vicksburg the Federals' bread-and-bullet line back to Columbus was growing longer and longer.[11]

Before Grant could reach the Yalobusha, he would have 200 miles of single-track railroad between him and his base of supplies. Undoubtedly that was why he halted at Oxford long enough to collect large stores at his advance depot in Holly Springs. Undoubtedly, too, he felt anxiety over the vulnerability of his long supply line and was eager to get to Grenada, for from there he meant to cut loose from the railroad, establish a new base on the Yazoo River and rely on the Mississippi for transport of supplies.[12]

Christmas was approaching. Hundreds of the boys from Indiana, Illinois, Wisconsin and other states of the Northwest held furlough papers in their pockets and waited their turns to board the empties daily rolling northward. Christmas at home was to be their reward for a job well done. Some of these men were coming into the yards at Jackson, Tennessee, when suddenly the entire picture changed. Snatched from the cars, they found themselves prisoners of Bedford Forrest. They stood helplessly by to see this scourge of Buell's transportation rip up the railroad by which they had been fed and munitioned since Shiloh and over which they had been on their way home. They did not know that on this very day, the twentieth of December, Van Dorn's cavalry cut in behind them, captured the garrison at Holly Springs, burned the depot and destroyed all the food, forage and munitions. Though they did not know it, the twin strokes of this day put a sudden end to Grant's overland campaign against Vicksburg by the simple process of severing the railroad in his rear.

This seemingly incredible stroke by Forrest was one of the great exploits of his ingenious military career. Ten days before his appearance at Jackson he left Columbia, more than 100 miles away, with a small and poorly equipped command. He crossed the swollen and well-guarded Tennessee River, swooped down on Jackson, and so deceived and outmaneuvered more than four times his number that before morning of December 21 he had cut all three railroad approaches to the city. On the twenty-first, his men spent the day tearing up Mobile & Ohio track over a seventeen-mile stretch to the north. Still farther north the railroad crossed both forks of

the Obion River and for fifteen miles ran through swampy
bottom lands over a succession of short bridges and trestles.
Forrest's men spent the twenty-second and half the twenty-
third burning and wrecking this stretch, a section very difficult
to reconstruct.

Relentlessly Forrest pushed forward the work of destruction until he reached Union City, only twenty-four miles
below Columbus. There his troopers were allowed to rest on
Christmas Eve, and next morning the weary raiders rode out
through cold rain in a desperate and successful venture to
win their way back to the safety of Bragg's lines. Their work
was done. Few though they were, they had got to the life
line of an army and frustrated the campaign of a great commander. Through the genius of an incomparable leader and
by their own physical endurance and invincible spirit they
fought their way through the traps laid for their capture, and
recrossed the Tennessee. From the safety of Columbia
Forrest might well have reported in the terse terms of the
modern airman, "Mission accomplished."

Out of communication with Sherman and his other commanders north of the Memphis & Charleston, the stores in his
advance depot destroyed and his supply line shattered, Grant
moved back to Holly Springs. From his headquarters he
arranged for the repair of the railroad between Memphis and
Corinth and the transfer of his supply base to Memphis. He
and his staff were there on January 10. His overland campaign against Vicksburg was in the discard. Supported by a
railroad, it collapsed when the railroad was broken.

CHAPTER XVIII

GOVERNMENT RAILROAD POLICY, SOUTH AND NORTH

I

Whatever railroad policy the Confederate government displayed was formulated during 1862. Except in a few particulars this policy is difficult either to recognize or define, for it was in no sense comprehensive and its inconsistencies frequently cast doubt on its actual existence.

Of first consideration was the need of track extension and connections between key railroads. With the realization, late in 1861, that the war was not to be confined to northern Virginia, the deficiencies became too obvious to be longer ignored. Admittedly, something had to be done to close the vital gaps, but it could be seen from the impaired financial status of the roads, the lack of iron and the shortage of labor that if any improvement was to be accomplished, the government would be obliged to participate.

Months earlier Lee had called attention to these necessities, and since mid-1861 appeals from railroad executives for aid in track extension and maintenance had been piling up in the offices of the President and Secretary of War without action. Suddenly, observing neither long-range plan nor studied policy and seemingly actuated more by fear than considered judgment, Congress initiated a series of resolutions and appropriations which thrust the government into a miscellany of railroad-building projects for which it was wholly unprepared. The first was an act passed on February 10, authorizing President Davis to close the gap between the

Richmond & Danville and the roads through the Carolinas. This act contemplated the building of a new road between Danville and the outer terminus of the North Carolina Railroad at Greensboro, appropriated $1,000,000 for the purpose, but left to the judgment of the President the location and manner of building the road.[1]

Only five days later another act was passed, authorizing the President to advance $150,000 to the Alabama & Mississippi Railroad to complete a connection between Selma, Alabama, and Meridian, Mississippi.[2] Again, on April 19, the President was authorized to contract with the New Orleans & Texas Railroad to finish its line from New Iberia, Louisiana, to Houston, Texas. For this the sum of $1,500,000 was appropriated with terms and conditions to be negotiated by the President.[3] Then in October came a similar appropriation of $1,122,482.92 to build an entirely new road from Rome, Georgia, to Blue Mountain, Alabama.[4]

For all these projects, ranging from Virginia to Louisiana and from outright building to mortgage loans, "military necessity" was advanced in common justification. But for evidence of any fixed policy or process by which that necessity was determined or the relative needs appraised, one seeks in vain. Manifestly it was impossible at that late date to weld all the loose ends of the Southern roads into a well-integrated and efficient system. What, then, was the process by which Congress arrived at the selection of undertakings for which it made appropriations? Naturally these appropriations, huge for the time, and the common justification offered did not go unobserved by those railroad executives and promoters throughout the South who had been unable to complete building projects launched before the war. One after another they sought aid from the government, each urging the completion of his road as an absolute "military necessity."

Some of these proposals had merit; some had none. Doubtless some of the petitioners were earnest but honestly mistaken as to the service their roads could render if finished, while others seem to have been motivated entirely by competitive and purely selfish business interests. Local politics and business favoritism unquestionably played a part in selecting the projects, but how far they influenced final decisions is unknown. For instance, A. H. Garland, member of Congress from Arkansas, persistently sought support from Secretary Randolph for a bill designed to provide a loan to build sixty miles of track on the Little Rock & Memphis, declaring its early completion to be a "military necessity" for the protection of his state from Federal invasion. Garland's bill failed. On the other hand, the request of A. M. Gentry for an appropriation for the Louisiana project was supported by a fervid petition from the New Orleans Board of Aldermen and was granted. Yet necessities as obvious as the Selma and Danville connections had been voted only over substantial opposition in the Congress.

A study of the outcome of these various hasty attempts to extend transportation facilities discloses how faintly the government understood the ventures on which it had embarked. The Rome-Blue Mountain operation was designed to establish a new route from northern Georgia through the coal and iron sections of Alabama and on to the Mississippi River.[5] Built in time, the road would have been of enormous value in preparing the South for war, but the effort came too late. For lack of rails the beginning of construction was long put off and the road was not carried through until after the war. Likewise, nothing came of the Louisiana enterprise. The argument that building this road would make available the incalculable military resources of Texas, with enough beef to subsist the entire Confederacy, ignored realities. Presented at the proper time it might have been logical, but it, too, came too late. Six days after the appropriation was voted, New Orleans and the lower Mississippi were in Federal hands.

A start on the Danville-Greensboro connection was postponed by the indecision of Jefferson Davis as to the best supplementary route from Richmond to the Carolinas. Instead of proceeding at once in accordance with the authorization of Congress, he listened overlong to the protestations and representations of Henry Wood and Thomas T. Giles, who had a different idea about how best to accomplish the purpose

Congress had had in mind. Wood was president of the Roanoke Valley Railroad and had much at stake. He pointed out to Davis that before the war began, his road was engaged in building an extension from its outer terminus at Clarksville to the Richmond & Danville at Keysville. Much work had been done before the job was halted for want of money and rails. Keysville, he argued, was only half as far as Danville from Richmond, and the distance from Keysville to Clarksville was only thirty miles as against the forty-eight miles between Danville and Greensboro. Furthermore, the route via the Roanoke Valley to Weldon would offer more and better connections with the roads to the south than the route via the North Carolina Railroad from Goldsboro. If the government would supply the rails and lend its financial support, a connection between the Danville line and the Carolina roads could be achieved via the Roanoke Valley more promptly and more cheaply than in any other way.[6]

While Mr. Wood may have been entirely sincere in his representations, it seems unlikely he was overlooking the possibility of procuring government aid to extend his road by a program it could not have financed alone and he had an eye on the competitive situation which would arise from building a line between Danville and Greensboro. The supporting arguments presented by Giles, who had the President's ear, were far from subtle. They lead one to suspect something more than devotion to the Confederacy lay behind this effort to persuade Davis to substitute the Keysville-Weldon route for the Danville-Greensboro line voted by Congress.[7]

Whatever their motives or the merit of their arguments, Wood and Giles so influenced Mr. Davis that he referred the matter to A. L. Rives, Chief of the Bureau of Engineers, for a thorough investigation. Rives, in turn, delegated A. M. Dupuy, "a civil engineer of experience," to do the investigating. Sometime later, Dupuy reported to Rives that he found the Roanoke Valley Railroad "in very bad condition," and if the Wood plan was to be adopted, extensive repairs on the finished part of the line would have to be made before the proposed extension would serve its purpose. He considered the work already done on the extension beyond Clarksville faulty in many respects, and the plans for necessary bridging particularly inadequate. To complete the job would take no less than three months' time, and the cost would amount to at least $540,000. Besides all this, the track gauge of the Roanoke was different from that of the Danville line, and its use would therefore require the reloading of all shipments at Keysville.[8] Certainly there was little here to recommend the Keysville route, yet, in advising the Secretary of War, Rives attempted to minimize the difficulties pointed out by Dupuy and added, "An examination of the map will at once convey a clear idea of the importance to be attached to this work."[9]

Quartermaster General Myers read the map quite differently. He had made his own investigation and his military analysis led him to warn the President that, in view of actual and threatened Federal operations in eastern North Carolina, the Roanoke Valley road might well become useless by the time it could be made ready. Vigorous in his opposition to any scheme for extending and rehabilitating it, he reported all track and bridges in very bad condition, the rolling stock to consist of only two engines and no more than five or six cars, all in a bad state of repair. The company, he said, was financially embarrassed, unable to pay the interest on its bonds, and had earnings barely sufficient to meet its small operating expenses.[10]

Two months and more were wasted with such business before the President finally instructed the Engineer Corps to select the most practical and economic course and locate the line between Danville and Greensboro.[11] Because of the rapidly increasing scarcity of labor and supplies, the road was not finished until May 20, 1864.[12] No case better illustrates the weakness of policy, the lack of organization in co-ordinating transportation and the general incapacity of the Confederate government to cope with its railroad problems.

The sole tangible result accomplished in 1862 through the policy of paper expansion was the completion in December of the Selma-Meridian connection; but the difficulties encountered are worth relating in further illustration of the weakening railroad position of the South. At the time Congress made the appropriation for this work, part of the line was nearing completion, part was graded and some bridges had been built. On other sections little or no work had yet been done. Efforts of the private interests involved to get the job done had bogged down for want of rails, lack of funds and scarcity of labor. Perhaps the fall of Fort Henry and the opening of the Tennessee River to Federal gunboats brought Confederate congressmen to realize that their one through line of rail communication between Virginia and the West was in grave danger. At any rate, typical of legislators suddenly alarmed and knowing nothing of the problems involved, they started pressing for completion in a hurry.

In an effort to comply with Congressional wishes, the Secretary of War ordered Captain A. S. Gaines to the scene to supervise the work and make arrangements, "upon terms not embarrassing or expensive to the Government," which would permit "through transportation without change of cars." More specifically his orders read:

> You will see that proper arrangements are made and suitable rolling stock provided for transportation over the road of troops, munitions of war, provisions and passengers, and that suitable arrangements are made for crossing the Tombigbee River until the company shall construct a bridge across the river. . . . It has been suggested that a part of the iron necessary to complete the road from Reagan to Meridian is now in New Orleans and that difficulty has existed in regard to its transportation to Meridian, growing out of the fact that the New Orleans and Jackson Railroad is in the employment of the Government. Instructions will be given authorizing its transportation over the road at the expense of the company.[13]

All this the government proposed to accomplish at an expenditure of $150,000.

The response to Secretary Randolph's confident instructions to Gaines came quickly. He was advised that if the work was to be completed within the next few months, it would be

necessary to increase the government appropriation to $500,-
000.[14] This was but the beginning of controversy and delay
which beset the project through the remainder of the year.
In June, G. G. Griffin, president of the Alabama & Mississippi,
advised the War Department he was out of spikes, chairs and
bolts, and the tires on the engines used to haul materials were
worn out. The Shelby County Iron Manufacturing Company
could, he said, supply the needed iron provided it were released from its obligation to turn over its entire output to the
government; but direct instructions from the War Department would be necessary.[15]

It seems beyond doubt that only because of the loss of the
Memphis & Charleston, the stunning successes of Federal
arms and the threat against Vicksburg, was sufficient pressure
brought to bear to get the job done before the end of the year.
It was becoming evident that very soon the road must be
made available not only for the transport of "troops and
munitions of war" but for transport to the east of coal and
iron ore from the Alabama fields as well as foodstuffs to points
of need.

In the government's attitude toward railroad labor, rolling
stock, supplies and train operation, traces of a fixed policy are
more discernible. While almost wholly negative, it was at
least consistent. It was a do-nothing policy apparently based
on the refusal of Congress in 1861 to pass a law authorizing
the President to assume control of the railroads where military
expediency required it.

Not only was the supply of rolling stock still diminishing
but the depreciation was distressing. Superintendent Whitcomb of the vital Virginia Central reported to his Board of
Directors: "The locomotives are constantly used with loads
to the extent of their capacity and cannot be spared [for]
repairs; they are run until they can run no longer. Many of
them are old and constantly out of order."[16] In reporting the
status of power on a single road, Whitcomb tersely sum-
marized the situation throughout the South. On some roads
conditions were even worse, and on only a few were they any
better. Overworked engines were running on worn-out tires;

boiler tubes and fireboxes were burning out, and axles and other parts constantly needed replacement though new materials could not be obtained. Month by month the supply of serviceable engines was growing smaller.

From constantly running overloaded and without overhauling, cars, too, were wearing out at a great rate. Much damage was done to the best of them by overcrowded and battle-weary soldiers on such journeys as that of Jackson's men from the Valley to the Peninsula. Some replenishment came through capture, but destruction by the Federals offset the gains. Both military and civilian shipping were suffering acutely from lack of facilities. It is by no means clear just how the government calculated to equip the additional trackage for which it was appropriating money when there was not enough rolling stock available to supply the existing roads even moderately.

To the harried railroad executives it must have brought some measure of satisfaction to discover they were no longer alone in their efforts to impress on the government the gravity of keeping the railroads alive. Awakened civilians such as Neill S. Brown, former governor of Tennessee, were beginning to speak up in their support. Said Brown, in a letter to the War Department: "To keep up the roads is now a means of defense second in importance only to supplying munitions of war. . . . Under the enormous pressure of freight the locomotives and cars are rapidly wearing out and the period is not far distant when transportation upon the roads will be exceedingly difficult, and on many routes impossible."[17] Bluntly he declared the situation to be such as to "admit of no delay or evasion," and said the government either should construct manufacturing plants equipped to build new engines and cars or finance the roads to do it. The latter plan, he thought, would be more desirable.

Meantime Walter Goodman, president of the Mississippi Central and a friend of Jefferson Davis, was in Richmond urging on the President an elaborate scheme for relieving the shortage in rolling stock. He argued that the government should supply its own engines and cars and pay the railroads on a mileage basis to operate them. To procure the needed equipment he would have the government contract with the stronger roads to build it in their own shops. He specified five such roads, whose shops were scattered from Holly Springs, Mississippi, to Charleston, South Carolina, all of which, he contended, could manufacture cars "if springs or materials for springs" could be secured. "Wheels and axles," he said, "can be obtained in reasonable time from Lynchburg, Richmond and Knoxville." As for locomotives, "there are but few railroad shops on long roads but what are capable of turning out engines with a small increase of mechanical force if materials can be procured." Materials most needed, of course, were steel boiler plate, sheet iron and boiler flues. To provide all the materials except steel, he proposed construction by the government of a number of rolling mills, one of which should be located at Huntsville, Alabama, because of its proximity to a supply of good iron ore and coal. For the same reason Decatur and Nashville should be considered as likely sites.[18]

The Goodman recommendations well illustrate the impractical and immature thinking so often applied to the industrial problems newly confronting the South. For too long it had been content to buy industrial products from the North, paying for them with the proceeds of a cotton economy, rather than making them for itself. There was real significance in the contempt of a Union soldier when he noticed that the simple ironwork on the Vicksburg courthouse steps was manufactured in Cincinnati.[19] The futility of Goodman's proposal should have been apparent from his first "if." There was no steel in the Confederacy and the sheet iron, wheels and axles of which he spoke were no more than ore yet to be mined. The equipment and machinery for his rolling mills would have to be fabricated from metals not yet refined.

Ignoring the realities of war in progress, he was proposing to roll back the calendar to lost yesterdays and start a building program which could have solved the problem at hand only if it had been accomplished before the war began. The irony of his recommendations is seen in the fact that long before they could have been put in effect, many of the sites for shops and buildings he recommended were in Federal hands.

Maybe the government could have done little at that late date to replenish the dwindling rolling stock; but it could have done much to help the railroads solve other vital questions with which they were struggling. Without constant repairs and replacements, the light construction of the Southern roads could not take the beating to which they were subjected by war traffic. The soft iron rails were wearing rapidly, ties were rotting away, and the fragile bridges and other wooden structures were growing precarious. Rails, labor and money, all essential to the maintenance of track, were becoming more and more difficult to obtain. To buy rails abroad and try to run the Union blockade involved more money and more risk than the individual roads dared hazard.

Early in 1862 a convention of railroad executives assembled in Richmond to devise some method of obtaining rails and other necessities. At that time Mr. T. D. Bisbee was proposing the formation of a large English trading corporation to be participated in by the government, the manufacturers and the railroad companies. He believed that with its credit backed by cotton and with shipments carefully planned and protected by the Confederate Navy, the pooled strength of the government and private business would enable it to deliver to the South large quantities of supplies otherwise unobtainable.[20] There may have been merit in Bisbee's plan. The railroad convention approved it and sent Edmund Fontaine to present the approval to the War Department.[21] The government refused to co-operate and thus brought it to a sudden end. The reason? It was no proper function of the government to support private enterprise. One is moved to wonder who was responsible for the failure to comprehend that starvation of the railroads meant death to the government.

Still another example of the crippling do-nothing policy occurred during the year. For the railroads the problem of procuring skilled and unskilled labor notably increased during 1862. Slaves had been the reservoir from which they had drawn common labor; but as the war went on, slaves were harder to get and still harder to keep. Some were owned by the railroad companies;[22] others were hired by the year from planters along the routes. Not only did railroad work offer excellent opportunities for escape, but Negro work crews were being drained off by bushwhacker and Federal raids, and owners sought to keep their slaves as far as possible from the railroads. In Virginia an attempt was made to impress slaves into the service of the railroads, but it was unsuccessful. Then came conscription, and not until 1864 were the railroads able to persuade the government to exempt railroad laborers. An aversion to lending any sort of aid to the railroads seemed manifest.

To make all these handicaps the heavier, the financial condition of the roads was growing steadily worse. Maintenance and operating costs skyrocketed as labor and materials became scarcer and more expensive. Though going at full capacity, that capacity became more and more absorbed by military transport, for which they were paid at low rates in Confederate bonds which were rapidly depreciating. Such cash commercial business as remained available was being crowded from the roads by the increasing demands of the military. Repeated attempts to procure higher rates for government shipping were brushed aside. Expressions of fear and discouragement became more frequent.

Typical of these was a letter to the Secretary of War from Thomas C. Perrin, president of the Greenville & Columbia Railroad in South Carolina. Reluctantly he announced that his road could no longer abide by the rates previously agreed on. It could not, he said, "earn interest on our debt and expenses. . . . We are compelled to advance our charges or cease altogether to run our trains." Thereupon Perrin ordered his agents to charge the Confederate States three cents per mile for carrying soldiers, and the regular rates on freight.[23]

In proportion to their deserts, pitifully small credit has been given the courageous and determined railroad men who made the most of the little they had and kept trains rolling though ever so slowly and intermittently. Devising all manner of

expedients for maintenance and repair, they kept up the
struggle to stave off the collapse of rail transportation in the
South. Near the close of 1862 President Fontaine reported to
his stockholders:

Much anxiety is felt to know whether our railroads can be
kept in safe running order if the war shall continue a few
years longer, and it is hardly to be doubted that the rapid
decline in the efficiency of our roads is soon to diminish our
means of successfully maintaining our struggle for independence. . . . If the speed of our trains is judicially reduced,
with reference to the depreciation of the rails, our roads will
last many years longer. In conformity with these views, the
speed of our trains has been much lessened and, if necessary,
will be to a greater extent.[24]

No doubt officials of other roads, if they had read the
Fontaine report, would have been quick to remind the government and the public that the Virginia Central, though hard
hit, was more fortunate than most roads since it was one of
the most sturdily built lines and enjoyed the support of the
State of Virginia, the largest holder of its securities.[25]

If ever complete government control of railroads, including
maintenance and operation, can be justified, certainly no
better proving ground could be selected than a country resist-
ing invasion by a hostile army. It is impossible to say whether
the railroads would have had greater or less difficulty if the
government had seized and operated them at the beginning
of the war. Evidence is abundant that from temperament,
disposition and capacity the Confederate government was
entirely unfitted for the job. Time after time it demonstrated
its failure to understand the problem, its lack of industrial
comprehension, and its inability to deal in a practical manner
with the mechanics involved. Possibly it might have achieved
a greater measure of co-ordination, but it could have offered
no substitute for the tireless energy, the sense of responsibility,
and the personal pride the Southern railroad man had in the
performance of his road. These were the qualities which
blacksmithed into crippled locomotives the power to pull

grotesque trains of shattered cars, improvised audacious equipment, coddled worn-out tracks, and kept unbalanced wheels rolling.

During 1862, however, it grew increasingly apparent that a measure of control more effective than that given the Quartermaster General was badly needed. Even though his authority over the railroads did not amount to much, Myers seemed reluctant to delegate any of it. Despite the railroad training and experience of his assistant, W. S. Ashe, Myers persisted in using him largely as a traveling agent to make inspections, investigate complaints, co-ordinate timetables and train connections, and make recommendations, while reserving to himself all power to make decisions and issue directives.[26] So little was accomplished through this arrangement that it was given up.

On December 3 the Secretary of War nominated William M. Wadley, president of the Vicksburg & Shreveport, to take supervision and control of transportation for the government on all railroads in the Confederate States.[27] Wadley was not subject to Myers' orders but reported directly to the Secretary of War. His authority covered control of government agents, railroad employees and rolling stock while engaged in government transportation, but stopped short of management.

Vigorously, but with no success, Myers protested against this arrangement on the same theory that led Pope to set aside Herman Haupt in the North. Transportation was the quartermaster's job. When Wadley sought to speed up shipping by getting all railroads to agree to operate under his direction and supervision, he promptly ran into trouble. Under his plan the superintendent of each road would act as his assistant and make weekly reports to him. One specific objective was to initiate a through train schedule between Richmond and Montgomery, Alabama. Naturally the roads refused to surrender operating control to a man with no authority or power to protect their property or to discipline violators of the agreement. Failing to procure the agreement, Wadley recommended to the War Department that the government take control of and manage any road that failed to perform its full duties.[28] In this he was coming close to the Federal policy of control, but the vital question remains: Could the Confederate government have managed its railroads? At any rate it was not willing to try. Other than to approve a new schedule of rates adopted by the roads and assist some destitute ones to obtain a bit of rolling stock, Wadley accomplished nothing. He disappeared from the larger scene when, on May 1 of the following year, the Senate refused to confirm his appointment.[29]

Thus it was that the railroads of the South tottered through the critical year of 1862. With hundreds of miles of tracks they had owned at the start now lost to the enemy, tortured and racked by the overheavy burdens of war, moneyless and destitute of supplies, they came to the new year determined to give all they had left to the Confederate States of America, which had done so little to ease their distresses.

2

— By far the most significant railroad event of 1862, if not of the entire war, was the act of the United States Congress authorizing the President to take possession of the railroads if and when, in his judgment, the welfare and safety of the country demanded it. As the new Secretary of War, Edwin M. Stanton thereby became the administrator of presidential policy. He forthwith appointed D. C. McCallum, the experienced railroad executive, to be Director and Superintendent of U. S. Military Railroads. All this was accomplished before the middle of February. When the Federal armies opened their spring campaigns in Tennessee and Virginia, the law was in effect and the War Department was prepared to administer it. —

Like any other law, the efficacy of this one was to depend on the manner of its administration. As it happened, both Lincoln and Stanton were experienced railroad lawyers before they went to Washington. They understood thoroughly the problems of railroad transportation. Fortunately neither carried with him into public office any illusory notions of governmental superiority in the management of public utilities. Fortunately, too, neither suffered from any itch to exercise this immense railroad authority for the enhancement of personal power, profit or prestige. Consequently the policy adopted by them was so logical and simple that it can be defined in few words. It was this: so long as any railroad in the loyal states operated effectively and without prejudice to the war effort the government would not interfere with its internal affairs. In any case where, from inability or unwillingness, a railroad failed to perform its full duty to the military service, swift and effective action would be taken. To any worthy and needy road important to army aims, aid would be given in such matters as reconstruction, repairs and track protection.

Though never promulgated in exact words, this policy was clearly understood and results were instantaneous. Except for the disloyal or mismanaged road it held no threat, yet the incentive not to tempt the exercise of Federal authority was ever present. A high degree of co-operation between the government and the railroads was the thing sought for, and it was promptly secured. To understand how effectively it was accomplished demands observation of developments in relation to no more than two important roads.

First, there was the unusual case of the Louisville & Nashville. At the outbreak of the war the L.&N. was operating 286 miles of road, 45 miles of which lay in Tennessee. Its rolling stock consisted of 37 engines, 9 baggage, 22 passenger and 260 freight cars: a small complement indeed in relation to the importance the road was about to assume. Moreover, it was heavily in debt.[30] Its president, James Guthrie, of Louisville, has been described as "self-willed, dominating and masterful"; also as "one of the most energetic and persistent businessmen of ante-bellum days."[31] In bitterly opposing the election of Lincoln he made many public speeches, all of which indicated that if war came he and his railroad would be found supporting the South. Instead, when hostilities opened, he stoutly advocated the policy of neutrality for

Kentucky. Casting no reflection on his loyalty, one may fairly say that he would have been less the businessman than his reputation indicated if he had failed to foresee that, should Kentucky become a belligerent state, a railroad running from the Ohio River to Nashville would be fair game for the stronger side and probably would be ruined in the fight for its control.

When neutrality failed and Guthrie was obliged to choose between the Union and the Confederacy, he already had a foretaste of what he might expect from the South. Buckner had given it to him in the previous September when, on moving to Bowling Green, he had seized the road to within thirty miles of Louisville, together with the larger part of its rolling stock. Nothing less than a defiant reaction to this move could have been expected from a man like Guthrie. It came quickly. Whether from sudden conversion to the Union cause or from resentment and keen business perception, he sought out Union authorities in Louisville and gave counsel on the formation of plans for a campaign against Nashville. Perhaps he was interested only in the recapture of his railroad; but, whatever his motives, his help contributed much to the success of the undertaking. Instead of taking possession of the road, Stanton took advantage of Guthrie's managerial skill and turned it to good account in the very first step of the campaign. It was the effective co-operation of the L.&N. that made possible Buell's prompt advance to Bowling Green. Without it there would have been much delay, because the rains had made most wagon roads impassable for any kind of vehicle.

In their retreat from Bowling Green the Confederates burned many bridges, tore up a deal of track and ran off or destroyed a large part of the rolling stock in their possession. Guthrie estimated the damage at $668,000—a staggering sum for a road already in debt and with its equipment shattered. Luckily for him and for the Union army, Federal policy was ready. Army engineers were rushed forward to aid in replacing bridges and repairing damaged track. To replace some of the lost rolling stock, a number of shorter Kentucky roads of the same gauge and lesser military importance were placed under military control and some of their engines and cars were transferred to the L.&N. without delay. As rapidly as they could be adjusted to five-foot gauge, 15 engines and 400 freight cars were diverted from Ohio roads to Guthrie's service. By March 26 the L.&N. was again operating trains to Nashville.

As the beneficiary of such speedy restoration, Guthrie continued to devote his extraordinary energy and executive ability to giving Buell's army efficient service. He could not afford to risk having his road taken over by the government. Yet he risked nothing in vigorously protesting the going rates for the transportation of troops and army freight. Quartermaster General Meigs listened to his argument that the L.&N. should be exempt from the general agreement to carry soldiers at two cents per mile and government freight at ten per cent off regular rates. With no freight moving north over the line, Guthrie said government business would not pay expenses, especially since the army had reached the Cumberland and much of the supply load other than pork and hay was moving up the river by boats. Most of his road lay in contested territory and required the maintenance of expensive guard. Ultimately he won his point, conditioned on the railroad's paying the expense of restoring the Cumberland River bridge at Nashville. Thus, early in the year, a good example in cooperation was being set.

At midsummer, devastation returned to the road with Bragg's Kentucky campaign. From the time Morgan blocked the Gallatin tunnels until near the end of the year, there was little traffic, and the damage to track and to rolling stock exceeded the entire amount previously received from handling government business. But Guthrie had won the full confidence of the War Department, and once more, with government aid, the road was restored. Shortly after Rosecrans reached Nashville, the L.&N. was serving as his main supply line precisely as it had served Buell earlier in the year. Until the end of the war the Louisville & Nashville remained a key factor in Union military operations in the middle South, with James Guthrie maintaining a standard of private management which would not have been improved and probably could not have been equaled by government control.

The second of the two roads referred to was the Baltimore & Ohio, the neglect of which had brought a storm of criticism down on Cameron and which, on his retirement, lay in wreckage for 100 miles west of Harper's Ferry. Having come from Ohio, Stanton was well acquainted with the traffic congestion this produced in the Ohio Valley. Immediately on taking office he arranged for the repair and reopening of the B.&O. under adequate military protection. At last Mr. Garrett had a friend instead of an enemy at the head of the War Department. With Stanton's co-operation, track and bridge repairs were speedily made. On March 21, five days before Guthrie resumed operations to Nashville, the B.&O. was open from Baltimore to the Ohio. In unprecedented volume, freight started moving over its rails and the resumption of through passenger service followed on April 1. Public reaction to this reversal of the Cameron policy found expression in a large and enthusiastic celebration at Wheeling.[32]

At about this same time, rabidly partisan members of the railroad's board of directors took an unfortunate step. Against strong and well-reasoned opposition they managed to force the adoption of a resolution which required the United States flag to be flown over all their important station houses.[33] Realizing the B.&O. was lost to them, the Confederates looked on this flaunting of flags as a deliberate taunt and missed no chance to retaliate. Virginians were especially galled. In his message to the House of Delegates, Governor Letcher said:

The Baltimore and Ohio Railroad has been a positive nuisance to this State from the opening of this war to the present time; and unless its management shall hereafter be in friendly hands, and the government under which it exists be a part of our Confederacy, it must be abated. . . .[34]

But abating the "nuisance" was more easily threatened than accomplished. Except for Jackson's cavalry patrols which touched at Martinsburg and Black Creek during the Valley campaign, the Confederates were held at a distance all summer and the road ran at capacity until Lee invaded Maryland in September. The invasion brought another serious interruption of through service. While substantial damage was done as the Rebel soldiers crossed the line on their way to Antietam, the most effective demolition was accomplished in the course of the retreat. From the Virginia side of the Potomac, detachments from Lee's army raided the railroad at will until late October when McClellan belatedly crossed the river and took up the pursuit.[35] Thirty-five miles of track, together with the telegraph lines, water tanks, sand houses and most of the fixed equipment at Martinsburg were again destroyed.[36] Relief from these depredations came as Lee retired deeper into Virginia and the Federals reoccupied Winchester. The work of restoration began at once. At the time of the invasion, Garrett was preparing to double-track the Washington branch and had at hand the necessary rails, ties and other equipment. He quickly diverted them to use in repairing the main line. The job was done in six weeks and through traffic was resumed on January 6, 1863.

Had nothing more been accomplished in that first year of new presidential authority over the railroads, the Federal policy would have justified itself by restoration of these two vital railroads and by its winning the loyal co-operation of two of America's most able railroad executives—men whose prewar sympathies had been with the South. But that was not all. Stanton had put out the fuse which was sizzling toward an explosive charge of indignation in the North at the time he came to office. The Committee on Government Contracts was still investigating complaints that military shipping was being manipulated to serve the personal interests of Cameron and his friends; that civilian shipping was being smothered through their attempt to eliminate a competitor. Scott was only making things worse in his attempts to protect Cameron. Perhaps the committee went too far in its merciless castigation of the Cameron administration of the War Department. It may be its final report was distorted by politics and a growing prejudice on the part of certain agrarian leaders of the Northwest against railroad corporations in general.[37] However that may be, it cannot be denied that intolerable situations were exposed and resentment was high. But the report was not made until July and by that time Stanton had removed the causes of complaint and left it all thunder and no lightning.

Especially clever was his handling of Scott's case. Because of Scott's part in the Cameron administration it seemed doubtful he could be retained as Assistant Secretary. Stanton appreciated the railroad advantage held by the North and was determined to preserve it. He realized that it derived from a well-trained force of executives and skilled mechanics who knew how to build railroads, operate and maintain them. In this particular, Scott had an enviable reputation and had been subject to no criticism. Stanton wanted to use his capabilities, and evaded the ticklish problem involved by changing his relation to the department. Procuring the appointment of Peter H. Watson as an added Assistant Secretary, Stanton transferred to Watson all of Scott's administrative and organizational duties within the department and assigned to Scott the function of translating railroad policy into action, thus shearing him of power to determine what that policy should be. Scott went immediately to the West and was in Louisville at the time the Tennessee campaign was planned and executed. It was he who supervised and managed government aid in restoring the broken L.&N. He was the man who exercised the authority to impress rolling stock for the use of that railroad. He established the co-operation with Guthrie and solved the problems of military transportation which were beyond the reach of an executive not vested with government authority. In all this he did a masterful job. Before the summer ended he resigned and returned to his post with the Pennsylvania.

Properly to evaluate Scott's over-all war service is not easy. So stanch was his friendship for and support of Cameron he cannot be dissociated from the faults of the Cameron administration. On the other hand it must be said for him that once free from Cameron's influence he served faithfully and expertly in implementing the government's new railroad policy.

As enemy roads were captured in the spring campaign there was no waiting on authority, no political debating and no delay. Stanton's administrators simply moved in on the heels of the soldiers, took possession of the roads, restored them to running order and started operating them in the service of the army. With like directness and precision the policy was applied on Northern soil at the first invasion. There was no hesitation in sending Wright to Harrisburg after the Battle of Antietam with peremptory instructions either to straighten out the snarls in operation of the Cumberland Valley Railroad or take it over and run it himself. It was doctrine with McCallum and Haupt that needed trains must run—preferably under company management, but they must run.

In point of railroad mileage taken from the Confederates, no other year until the ultimate surrender equaled 1862. At one time or another the Federals occupied the Manassas Gap line, the Orange & Alexandria as far as Culpeper, the R.,F.&P. to Fredericksburg, the York River, the Winchester & Harper's Ferry, and parts of the Norfolk & Petersburg and of the Seaboard & Roanoke. In the West the enemy was ousted from all or substantial portions of the Memphis & Ohio, the Tennessee & Ohio, the Memphis & Charleston, the Central Alabama, the Mississippi Central, the Louisville & Nashville and the Nashville & Chattanooga. Though much of this mileage was retaken by the Confederates, the year's end found the Federals back in control of almost all. Some portions were so badly damaged they were abandoned until after the war. Some roads were better stocked and had more capacity than they had ever had while serving the Confederacy. For example, while the huge Army of the Potomac remained in the neighborhood of Warrenton after its return from Antietam, the restored Orange & Alexandria was able not only to supply its men but to carry forage for its 52,000 horses and mules.[38]

To be sure, all this had not been achieved without severe

loss in the military reverses such as Pope's defeat. No less than 11 engines and some 400 cars had been captured or destroyed, and enormous quantities of railroad supplies had been consumed in the repair of tracks and bridges destroyed by the enemy. Only the power of the North to maintain a steady flow of newly manufactured equipment kept such losses from slowing down the whole war effort.

Contrary to the situation in the South, Northern roads approached 1863 in good condition both physically and financially. Many had added to their rolling stock through purchase and manufacture, tracks were kept in repair, and sidetrack facilities expanded rather than diminished. They had moved more than a million men to the various fronts and transported an unending stream of ammunition, provisions, clothing, wagons, artillery and small arms from places of production to supply depots, and from the depots to the points of distribution or to the boats and captured railroads which carried them on into enemy country.

Reporting to Stanton, Quartermaster General Meigs said the railroads had done such a good job it had been unnecessary to invoke the control law except as to those roads within the limits of an insurgent state. He said, "No other mode of transportation could have accomplished so much," and he claimed for the companies due credit for the patriotic manner in which they had performed service to the government.[39]

As the decisive struggles of 1863 drew near, the long shadow cast on the Confederacy by the Northern railroads rapidly grew darker.

CHAPTER XIX

THE RAILROADS IN THE VICKSBURG CAMPAIGN

On New Year's Day 1863 Bragg and Rosecrans fought desperately on the banks of Stone's River near Murfreesborough. Dead and wounded, more than 18,000 men fell there[1] before Bragg left the field, retired to Tullahoma and gave Murfreesborough to the Federals. The losses were appalling but it marked the beginning of the end in the long struggle for possession of the railroad junction at Chattanooga.

From Corinth to Huntsville, thence via Nashville to Louisville and back again to Murfreesborough, the Federal army had marched and fought throughout 1862. To refute Grant's argument that all this could have been avoided is far from easy. Other than Halleck's order to reconstruct the Memphis & Charleston, nothing appears which would have made it difficult for Buell to reach Chattanooga well ahead of Bragg. Had he done so, he would have been between Bragg and Kirby Smith and their Kentucky campaign could not have been launched. In that event there would have been no Perryville—no Stone's River. While it is idle to speculate what turn events might have taken had Buell been allowed to march swiftly from Corinth to Chattanooga, it seems safe to say that many months of fighting along hundreds of miles of railroad tracks would have been spared. As it transpired, Bragg still was entrenched between Rosecrans and the goal. Thirty-seven miles apart and each supplied by different sections of the Nashville & Chattanooga Railroad, they faced each other in comparative quiet until July.

During this period the North sought to emulate Forrest, master of the long raid behind enemy lines. In April the

most famous of these attempts was launched by Colonel
Abel D. Streight of Rosecrans' command. His plan was to
circle Bragg's fortified position at Tullahoma, ride through
northern Alabama into Georgia and destroy the Western &
Atlantic by which the Confederates were drawing supplies
from Atlanta. With four regiments of infantry mounted on a
motley assortment of horses and mules, Streight struck out
from Nashville on a circuitous route which called for nearly
1,000 miles of travel.² But Streight was no Forrest, and his
poorly mounted and inexperienced infantrymen were no
match for Forrest's hard-riding troopers who soon were on
their trail. Steadily gaining on Streight, Forrest chased him
diagonally across upper Alabama to Gadsden, where Streight
turned northeast toward Rome, Georgia. From utter exhaustion of men and animals he was obliged to surrender at
Rome without having come in sight of the railroad he sought
to destroy, although the raiders outnumbered their captors
three to one.³

In the Union army there were good cavalrymen but no
Forrests. Never were they able to outwit, outride or outfight
him, and railroads were the meat on which he fed. Because
of him the Western & Atlantic continued to supply the troops
defending Chattanooga while Grant floundered in the Mississippi River bayous because Forrest had destroyed the
M.&O. between Jackson, Tennessee, and Columbus,
Kentucky. By his incredible railroad raids he had changed
the whole aspect of the war in the West.

The problem with which Grant struggled in the early
months of 1863, however, was not one of transportation.
When obliged to give up his original plan to approach Vicksburg along the rail line through Grand Junction, Holly
Springs, Oxford and Grenada, he adopted the alternative of
moving by the Mississippi. This involved no hardship in
transporting men, equipment or supplies. His difficulty was
to find a place near Vicksburg where he could put his army
ashore.⁴ 'Unprecedented late winter rains raised the water
level and flooded the bayous and bottom lands on both sides
of the river above the Vicksburg bluffs from which heavy

Confederate guns defied the passage of Union transports. Already, Sherman had demonstrated the futility of landing on the east bank and attempting to reach high ground by way of the sluggish Yazoo. Unassailable from the river side, Vicksburg could be approached on its land side only from below, and the only way to get below it was to cross the long, low spit of land which lay within the hairpin bend of the river directly in front of the city. Consequently troops were put ashore on the west bank wherever campsites could be found above water.

With the movement fairly under way, Grant returned to Memphis to complete the details of his plan. With the exception of those at Columbus, all river garrison troops were withdrawn, as were those along the line of the wrecked M.&O. Railroad. The Mississippi Central was likewise abandoned and the guarding force added to the others who were sent down the river to join the main army.[5] Only that portion of the Memphis & Charleston west of Corinth was retained and left under guard.

For three miserable months Grant's men ate, slept, wallowed and worked in water and mud, seeking to find or devise some way by which they could by-pass the formidable batteries that covered the river at the bend. How they explored the far-reaching bayous, tore down levees, struggled to cut canals and at last, with the aid of the navy, which had boldly run by the batteries, reached Bruinsburg on the east bank far below Vicksburg is not a part of the railroad story. However, it is important to remember that all this was brought about by Forrest's devastation of the M.&O.

It was not until April 17 that the railroads again became a factor in the Vicksburg campaign. As will be remembered, in the previous December the Selma-Meridian link had been completed, thus giving Vicksburg a direct rail connection with the eastern Confederacy. At Jackson, Mississippi, this facility was supplemented by a southern connection via the New Orleans & Jackson, while at Meridian it was crossed by the M.&O. then in operation between Corinth and Mobile. Aside from lack of equipment on these roads, the great weak-

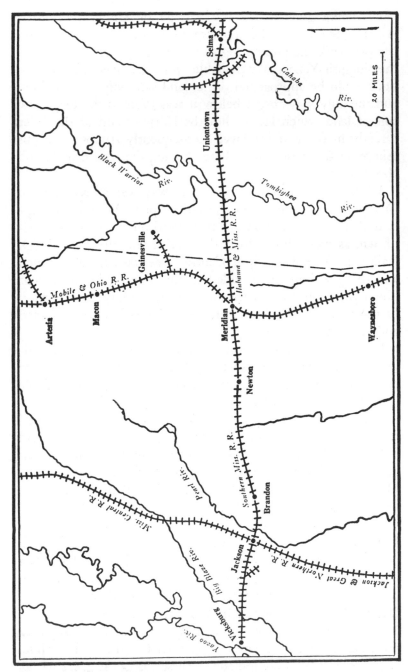

VICKSBURG AND NEAR-BY RAILROADS

ness in Pemberton's rail supply system was the fact that west of Jackson it was wholly dependent on a single track.

Mindful of the discomfiture Forrest had caused Grant through destruction of the M.&O. between Jackson, Tennessee, and Columbus, Kentucky, Union Colonel B. H. Grierson set out to perform a similar raid on the Confederate end of the same road. This was the second Union attempt to apply the railroad tactics Forrest used so effectively against the North. On the same day that Streight left Nashville on his impossible venture, Grierson rode out from LaGrange, a village on the Memphis & Charleston three miles west of Grand Junction. With him he took 1,700 troopers and led them southward along a route just west of the M.&O.[6] At a point about opposite Columbus, Mississippi, he detached 700 under command of Colonel Hatch and sent them to wreck the railroad at or near Columbus.[7] After a sharp fight Hatch completed his mission, then retreated northward breaking the road again at Okolona and a third time at Tupelo.[8]

Grierson was pushing on to cut the Vicksburg line west of Meridian. Turning southwestward, he destroyed the Jackson & New Orleans and came safely to Baton Rouge, Louisiana, on May 2. He had been out only sixteen days, had ridden the length of Mississippi, broken the M.&O. in three places, cut the east-west trunk line, shut off rail communication to Louisiana, and left Pemberton with no rails open except the track to Jackson.[9] It was the nearest the Federals ever came to matching Forrest's feats of speed and devastation. When Grant learned of Grierson's success he was highly pleased. He later declared the raid had been of "great importance" for quite another reason than the damage done the railroads. It had, he said, "attracted the attention of the enemy from the main move against Vicksburg."[10]

By the first week in May, Grant had a large part of his army on the east side of the river and was driving northeastward behind the strongly fortified Confederates on the bluff at Grand Gulf. Fighting back the detachments Pemberton sent out to harass and delay him, he made steady progress up the Big Black River toward a position which, if attained, would enable him to envelop Vicksburg from the rear.

Joseph E. Johnston, recovered from the wound suffered at Seven Pines, had come out from Virginia in December to take command of all Confederate troops west of the mountains. So alarming were Grant's movements that in obedience to a wired order from Richmond, Johnston rose from a sickbed in Chattanooga and set out for Jackson, Mississippi, to take personal charge of the Vicksburg defenses. Once it would have been a simple matter for him to have taken the Memphis & Charleston to Grand Junction, thence to Jackson via the Mississippi Central with a single change of cars. But in May 1863 he was obliged to ride the "war-racked railroads" the long way around via Atlanta, Montgomery, Mobile and Meridian.[11] By the time he arrived at Jackson in the night of May 13, McPherson's corps of Grant's army had reached Clinton on the railroad between Jackson and Vicksburg and torn up the track there.[12] The troops being hurried to Pemberton's support were cut off and could not reach him.

With that accomplished, Grant suddenly made a most unorthodox move. Turning his back on Pemberton, he struck out full speed with the corps of Sherman and McPherson for Jackson and the next day drove Johnston's force from the city. That night, May 14, he slept in the room Johnston had occupied the night before.[13] Then he reversed his course, and with McPherson's corps he headed straight west along the railroad for Vicksburg, forty-four miles away. Sherman was left to destroy Jackson "as a railroad center and manufacturing city of military supplies." This he did most effectually before he rejoined the main body of the army.[14] Readjusting the lines of his other corps, Grant pushed forward with characteristic vigor. At Edward's Station he met Pemberton's advance units coming out, as they thought, to strike him in the rear and drive him into Johnston's hands. For three days it was march and fight, one battle after another, until Pemberton's main defense lines were reached on May 19. Unable to carry them by assault, the Federals settled down to siege operations. With the Navy now effective on the river side and Grant's reinforced army, 100,000 strong, entrenched in double lines, Vicksburg was completely invested. Final surrender was only a matter of time.

Johnston, also heavily reinforced by troops from as far away as the Carolinas, failed in repeated efforts to force Grant to raise the siege. Ultimately he collected a force of 24,000 men behind the Federal lines, but Confederate rail transportation was inadequate to bring him the necessary guns and cavalry horses.[15] How the Confederates, constantly bombarded from land and river, went underground to cling to Vicksburg through more than forty days of gruesome siege is one of the best-known stories of the war. When, on July 4, Pemberton surrendered and quietly marched his starving but heroic soldiers unarmed through the Federal lines, the issue of who was to control the Mississippi River had been decided.

In no great campaign of the war did the railroads become less involved or play a smaller part in the final outcome. Except in a few particulars, such as Grierson's raid and the destruction of the rail connections at Jackson, it was conducted in the same manner it might have been in pre-railroad days. Its major railroad significance lies in the fact that with the fall of Vicksburg the Confederates lost their last through rail connection to the Mississippi and the Southwest. Without it their two main north-south connections in the Mississippi Valley, the M.&O. and the Mississippi Central, were reduced to minor importance on the outer fringe of the remaining struggle.

To the day of his death Grant contended all this could have been accomplished more than a year earlier had Halleck followed Shiloh with a prompt and vigorous pursuit of Beauregard. But Halleck then dreamed of glory in opening the Mississippi and thought in terms of a direct approach via the river itself. Grant, on the other hand, believed the logical way to reduce Vicksburg was to occupy the railroads in her rear. As it worked out, the city proved invulnerable against attack from the river alone and in the end had to be taken from the direction Grant had thought right in the spring of 1862.

Should it be argued that the failure of Grant's first campaign proved Halleck right in stopping at Corinth, it must be remembered Halleck's army was twice the size of that with which Grant made the attempt, and that in April neither Forrest nor Van Dorn was prepared to do what he did in December. Regardless of whether it was done at the earliest possible time or in the easiest way, the capture of Vicksburg brought the result Grant most desired. The Confederacy was cut in two, her railroads in the Mississippi Valley captured or neutralized, and the burden of enemy defense shifted to the East where it must be continued, if at all, without benefit of the vast quantities of supplies produced in the Southwest.

Once more Grant was to find his plans to follow up a great victory frustrated by Halleck's strange concepts of strategy. Having cleared Vicksburg and vicinity of regular Confederate forces within a radius of 100 miles,[16] Grant proposed to take advantage of the demoralized enemy by an immediate move against Mobile, which at that time could have been taken with ease. In terse and logical explanation we have Grant's own words:

Having that [Mobile] as a base of operations, troops could have been thrown into the interior to operate against General Bragg's army. This would necessarily have compelled Bragg to detach in order to meet this fire in his rear. If he had not done this the troops from Mobile could have inflicted inestimable damage upon much of the country from which his army and Lee's were yet receiving their supplies.[17]

To place himself in this enviable position with little bloodshed would have demanded the prompt and vigorous action slow-thinking Halleck seemed never able to comprehend. Had it been taken, either there would have been no Chickamauga with its consequent battles or Grant would have cut the heart from what remained of the Confederate railway system.

With the Mississippi open and "commercial cargo" from far up-river being discharged at New Orleans docks, Halleck adopted another pet notion. It was the subjugation of the trans-Mississippi—a procedure comparable to standing on the tail of a serpent while it coils for another strike. In the same way as at Corinth, he held Grant at Vicksburg and started breaking up his powerful and successful army. Large detachments were sent to Banks for the trans-Mississippi campaign, others were ordered to Missouri to fight Price, and the remainder kept on the piddling business of chasing guerrilla bands and destroying property that might be of use to the enemy. By these orders Grant's striking power was dissipated. Again he was left on the defensive precisely as in the previous summer in West Tennessee.

CHAPTER XX

GETTYSBURG—AND HAUPT AGAIN

I

A short distance inland from Pamlico and Albermarle sounds on the east coast of North Carolina lies a belt of rich farm lands which extends northward beyond the Virginia border. In early 1863 this was a country of "corn and hogs" where tons of good bacon and an abundance of grain were produced. Farther east, along the shores of the sounds and tidal rivers, countless barrels of fish were cured and packed for shipment each year. Eastern North Carolina constituted a vast food reservoir of incalculable value to the Confederacy.

Some sixty miles back from the shore the Wilmington & Weldon Railroad ran due north to connect at Weldon with the Petersburg line for Richmond, and these two lines formed the backbone of north-south rail transportation east of the Blue Ridge. Within carting distance of their tracks lay food and forage for a larger army than Lee could muster. At Goldsboro, eighty-four miles north of Wilmington, the W.&W. was supplemented by two connections, one running east to Beaufort, the other west to Greensboro. The Seaboard & Roanoke came in from Norfolk through Suffolk to connect at Weldon. By these well-placed roads the Richmond commissariat was given access to a mammoth storehouse of army supplies.

Threatening this important food-producing area, Union arms in 1862 had gained footholds at Suffolk, Virginia, near the North Carolina border and at New Bern on the Neuse River east of Goldsboro. Shortly after the battle of Fredericksburg the Confederates observed heavily loaded Union transports steaming out the mouth of the Potomac obviously heading south. The movement provoked wild speculation as to their probable destination and where the next attack would fall. Would it be Wilmington? Charleston? Perhaps Savannah. Beauregard, then in command at Charleston, suspected a move against Weldon via Hampton Roads and Suffolk and was anxious over the defense. He told Richmond it would not be easy to bring up troops by way of Wilmington because the railroad was in such wretched condition it had taken forty-eight hours to move 1,000 men in the opposite direction.[1]

In winter quarters on the hills behind Fredericksburg, Lee differed in opinion with his lieutenants commanding in the coast cities. He believed the next Union move in force would be another attempt by the Army of the Potomac to cross the Rappahannock. In his opinion the transports carried only a diversionary force, most likely to go ashore as reinforcements for the Federal troops at Suffolk. However, he conceded the possibility of a Federal move up the James in an attempted surprise attack on Richmond and considered the situation grave enough to warrant careful attention. Early in January he detached Longstreet with two divisions of his corps to take defensive positions along the Blackwater River between Petersburg and Suffolk. The other two divisions he sent to the Richmond area where they could be drawn back or sent on to Longstreet as occasion might demand.

From Lee's position at Fredericksburg the R.,F.&P. ran directly south to Richmond and should have provided an adequate line over which to bring up subsistence shipped to the capital from North Carolina. Yet before the middle of January his men and horses were hungry, with rations steadily being reduced. The R.,F.&P. was proving unequal to feeding an army and its animals. With no co-ordinator of transportation such as the North had in Haupt, the railroad was unable to maintain any regularity in the delivery of supplies, and as the demands became heavier the tangle of its trains grew worse.[2] Nor was this condition limited to the R.,F.&P. Wadley was complaining to James A. Seddon, the new

Secretary of War, about utter confusion on the Carolina roads, particularly on the Wilmington & Weldon and the North Carolina to Greensboro.[3] Since the State of North Carolina owned a controlling interest in both these roads, Seddon warned Governor Zebulon Vance that Lee's army might soon be wholly dependent on supplies from his state and asked if something might not be done to procure more efficient management of the roads.[4] So distressing was this state of affairs that on January 25, Lee wrote to President Davis:

Unless regular supplies can be obtained, I fear the efficiency of the army will be reduced by many thousand men when already the army is far inferior in numbers to that of the enemy. I do not know whether the difficulty arises from want of provisions in Richmond or from delay in its transportation to this point, but the result is that there is a scarcity of food for the men. If the provisions are in Richmond, I think, by energetic operation of the railroad, they can be readily transported. Great delay in the running of the freight trains has been reported to me which could be avoided by zeal and energy on the part of the agents.[5]

February brought more rain and snow and less food and clothing. Failing to supply the men, the railroad was even less able to carry fodder and grain for the starving horses. The cavalry was foraging its mounts on the distant flanks of the main position, but the wagon train and artillery horses were in a pitiable plight. To save them, Lee sent hundreds farther south to be fed until grass should grow again.[6] In fact, much of the artillery was sent all the way to the North Anna, but that did not reduce the suffering of the men who, barefoot and half clad, paced the frozen hilltops and watched the observation balloons ride high above the Union army beyond the river. They knew the Federal army was now commanded by Joseph Hooker, who had replaced Burnside, and wondered whether they could remain strong enough to fight off another attempt of the Yanks to cross the Rappahannock. Freeman says, "Before the winter was to end, the danger of starvation and of immobility resulting from a collapse of transportation was to be plain to every private in the ranks."[7]

With his job of speeding up supplies, Wadley was getting nowhere. The worn-out railroads, stripped of help and left by the government to fend for themselves, floundered in confusion. Tons of bacon, rice, sugar and other perishable foods spoiled in accumulated masses while soldiers in near-by Virginia famished for want of them.[8] The frustrated Wadley was helpless. His only recommendation was that mechanics be released from military service to work for the railroads, and that the government take control of any road which, once supplied with help, failed to do its duty.[9] Nothing came of his recommendation.

Hearing there was plenty of meat in Atlanta and in Tennessee, Lee suggested to Seddon that energetic agents of the Quartermaster Department be detailed to go out along the railroads and attempt to expedite its shipment, and that less important freight be held up until it was in the hands of the Commissary General in Richmond.[10] At a prior date he had proposed to Davis that all spare wagons in the towns along the line of the Virginia Central be collected and set to hauling grain to the railroad for transportation to Richmond. Nothing happened. The hope he had entertained of taking the offensive against Hooker rather than waiting to be attacked at a time and place of Hooker's choosing was almost gone. With Longstreet absent, the soldiers weakened from lack of food. His horses unfit for duty and no relief in sight, he could do nothing except wait, watch and hope Hooker would stay quiet.

In March, Seddon admitted that Lee's shortage of supplies was due chiefly to lack of railroad capacity or failure to make proper use of it.[11] This was in spite of the fact the army could not have been located in a spot more convenient to railroad supply. Once more rations were cut, then cut again and again. From Lee another appeal came to Seddon to send men out along the roads to untangle traffic and speed up the movement of supply trains.[12] Both Seddon and Lee urged on Commissary General L. B. Northrop the danger of further reduction in rations and the necessity for better-managed transportation. Nothing came of it. Not Seddon or Lee or anyone else could move the stubborn, ill-tempered Northrop from his contrary way, yet he remained a favorite with Jefferson Davis. His delight seemed not in feeding hungry soldiers but in quarreling with field commanders who sought food for their men.[13]

Firmly entrenched on high ground in a position so strong that Burnside's divisions were shattered in futile attempts to dislodge them, Lee's men were being sapped of vigor, not by acts of the enemy, but through their own people's inept handling of transportation. They were within fifty miles of Richmond with a railroad actually within their lines. Richmond lay at the upper end of a railroad running the length of one of the most productive agricultural areas in the South, and was served by two other roads which tapped country by no means short of supplies. Yet, only fifty miles away, the army on which Confederate hopes were pinned was slowly being reduced to starvation. This was the incalculable price paid for the government's policy—or lack of policy—in dealing with the railroads.

On April 15, General Imboden, who as a militia captain had led the expedition against Harper's Ferry in April 1861, set out on a daring raid into West Virginia. His avowed purpose was to destroy the B.&O. Railroad through the mountain country and hamper the movement of supplies to Hooker's "fat and sassy Yankees" who were well supplied because of Herman Haupt's management of the northern end of the same railroad that had failed Lee. However, in approving Imboden's plan, Lee made it quite clear that bringing in a supply of horses and beef cattle would be of even greater service than breaking up the railroad.[14] Ultimately Imboden did both.

Then Lee wrote Seddon a final letter of warning. Of his soldiers he said:

Their ration consists of one fourth pound of bacon, eighteen ounces of flour, ten pounds of rice to each hundred men about every third day, with some few peas and a small amount of dried fruit occasionally as they can be obtained. This may give existence to the troops while idle, but will certainly cause them to break down when called upon for exertion.[15]

His last chance to put Hooker on the defensive was gone. Nothing remained except to outfight him when he attacked: 63,000 gaunt and ragged men against twice their number of well-fed, well-equipped and eager soldiers of the Union. But the 63,000 knew they held one great advantage: if and when Hooker chose to strike, they would be led by Lee and Jackson.

At last signs of spring began to show in the woods, and with its coming the spirits of the haggard men began to rise. As the weather warmed, squads from each regiment were detailed for one of the strangest duties they were ever to know. Scurvy had appeared in the camps, and to fight it these details were sent into the woods to collect sassafras buds, wild onions, lamb's-quarters and other green things as quickly as they appeared.[16] While they worked, the blue horde on the hills across the river began to stir. Surely the men picking buds and poke sprouts must have chuckled at the irony of it, if they had known General Stoneman was moving out on a cavalry raid to cut their railroad supply lines.

More balloons could be seen. Hooker was moving. Lee's cavalry discovered long blue columns marching up the north bank of the Rappahannock and crossing the fords. The time had come. Obviously the attack was to fall on their left flank. They gathered up their equipment and struck out along the Culpeper road to meet it. Ten miles west of Fredericksburg, the unevenly matched armies clashed on May 1 in one of the most tragic battles of the war. On the second day of it, Jackson made his historic, secret march around Hooker's right and at nightfall delivered the vicious surprise attack which sent Hooker reeling back across the Rappahannock in utter defeat. The confidence of the 63,000 in their leadership had not been misplaced.

Beside that Culpeper road one still finds among the trailing honeysuckle vines, broken remnants of foundation on which stood the sturdy brick house that was Chancellorsville. Near by on the same side of the road a heavy stone marks the spot on which Jackson fell mortally wounded in the night of May 2, 1863. A few miles to the southeast on gently rising ground overlooking the tracks of that same R.,F.&P. Railroad at Guiney's Station, still stands the little frame house in which Stonewall Jackson died. These things remain mute testimonials to Confederate government folly in the management of its transportation; to the failure of its railroads which held Lee tethered on the Fredericksburg hills while his chance to take the offensive starved and died. Chancellorsville was a battle devised by civilian stupidity but won by a soldiery which would not be defeated either by starvation or by the guns of the enemy.

2

While smoke from the burning underbrush still hung over the field of Chancellorsville, Hooker led his bewildered columns back to Falmouth and Stafford Heights. Back to the hills whence they came to stifle the fourth cry of "On to Richmond" marched the tattered Gray. Across the rooftops of Fredericksburg the two armies again watched each other, and between them the graceful spire of St. George's Church pointed skyward just as it does today.

While the positions of the opposing armies remained the same as before, the Confederates had attained much more than their success in stopping Hooker at Chancellorsville. It was May and the sun was shining warmly. Their hungry horses were feeding ravenously on the springing grass. Now they were strong enough to draw wagons, and the roads had settled. Such provisions as remained in the surrounding country could be carted into camp. Some improvement in rail transportation had been accomplished. Though still on very short rations, Lee's men, flushed with victory, could live tolerably. Now the cold was gone, they could get along better without shoes and blankets. It was time to move. Lee knew that the countryside was rapidly being stripped of its last subsistence, and that the army could not long remain at Fredericksburg.

The picture that confronted the Confederate high command in the early summer of 1863 was not pleasant. In Tennessee, Bragg was pinned down by Rosecrans and had accomplished nothing since Stone's River. Pemberton was besieged in Vicksburg, and Johnston could not open a road for his escape. D. H. Hill's army was held fast on the Carolina coast by threats of invasion from the sea. Lee was again confronted by Hooker's huge army on the Rappahannock. On May 14 Lee was called to Richmond for a conference with President Davis and his cabinet about what should be done next.

From the beginning of the war Davis had opposed any strategy contemplating the sacrifice of territory in order to concentrate power. As a result his troops were now scattered from the seaboard to the Mississippi, not strong enough at any point to force the issue. On the contrary, Lee favored enough concentration to strike decisively, even though it might mean giving up territory for the time being. Apparently Davis was now beginning to see that in widely dispersed fighting, the side with the better railroad system had an automatic advantage—something new in strategic considerations. Since this advantage increasingly favored the North, the South was not going to get anywhere by defensive fighting all over the map. Somewhere it must take the offensive, with vigor and decision. How and where to strike was the question before the conference.

Some argued for sending troops to Mississippi to rescue Pemberton by forcing Grant to lift the siege of Vicksburg. Longstreet preferred to reinforce Bragg and drive Rosecrans back to the Ohio. He thought this would force Grant to give up his siege and go to Rosecrans' rescue, and so serve a double purpose. In neither proposal could Lee see hope for the Confederacy. Each contemplated taking large detachments from the Army of Northern Virginia, and without them he could not stand against Hooker. When it was suggested he might retire and await developments, he pointed out that he would have to go all the way to Richmond and invite disaster by besiegement. He contended the only hope for substantial results lay in concentration for an invasion of Pennsylvania.[17]

Despite the bitter memories of Antietam he had not lost faith in the enormous possibilities of another campaign with the same objective he had envisioned for the previous autumn's invasion. After all, his defeat at Antietam came about from circumstances that could now be avoided by first driving the Federals out of the lower Shenandoah and clearing a supply line as he advanced. He still believed that if he could destroy the rail lines from the West to Baltimore, Washington and Philadelphia and occupy the territory between the Susquehanna and the Potomac, he would be in excellent shape to negotiate for an ending of the war. The time was ripe. The "peace party" in the North was rapidly gaining strength and stirring up no end of trouble for the administration. Already newspapers were predicting that Lincoln could not be re-elected. With rail communications cut and an invading army in Pennsylvania, the influence of the malcontents would be tremendously increased.

Lee's reasoning held strong appeal for Davis. He had great faith that, properly and vigorously promoted, the Copperheads in the North would ultimately disrupt the war effort. In the end, he and all members of the cabinet save one supported Lee's proposal. With this agreement the conference ended.

Lee hurriedly returned to his headquarters and plunged into the task of preparing for the great undertaking. Because he could not afford to fight another battle on the Rappahannock, his plans must be complete and he must be on his way before Hooker made another move. Instead of promoting a new man to take over the whole of the fallen Jackson's command, he reorganized the army into three corps, left Longstreet in command of the First, gave the Second to "Dick" Ewell, and called A. P. Hill to command the Third. Then came the tedious business of recalling Longstreet and his scattered divisions. There were endless details to be worked out while he kept an anxious eye on Hooker. If this elaborate and complicated maneuver was to succeed it must be thoroughly understood, perfectly timed and flawlessly executed.

This was the plan as finally developed.[18] The route would lie through Culpeper. This would take them across the O.&A. Railroad, but it was not to be disturbed. Ewell would take the lead, Longstreet would follow, and Hill would stay at Fredericksburg to mask the withdrawal. From Culpeper, Ewell would cross into the Shenandoah, turn toward the Potomac, and clear the Valley of all Federal troops. Longstreet would parallel Ewell's column, marching north on the east side of the Blue Ridge with Stuart maintaining a cavalry screen on his right. When Ewell reached the Valley, Hill would move out of the Fredericksburg defense line and follow Ewell's route. Lee calculated that if he gave the First and Second Corps a long start across Hooker's right flank, the discovery would revive the chronic alarm for the safety of Washington and bring the Army of the Potomac hurrying back within its outer defenses.

Meanwhile the Army of Northern Virginia would destroy the B.&O. Railroad, cross the Potomac into Maryland, and march toward Hagerstown. Ewell, well in advance, would then divide his corps. One column would head for Harrisburg and wreck the Cumberland Valley Railroad. The other, moving on the east side of the northern spur of the Blue Ridge, would strike for York and break up the Northern Central. This would leave Longstreet free to demolish the Pennsylvania main line and set the scene for negotiations with isolated Washington.

The morning of June 3 Ewell took to the road. On the ninth Hill started. For better or worse the army was on its way to Pennsylvania. When Hill had crossed behind Longstreet and entered the Valley to follow Ewell, Longstreet turned west through Snicker's Gap, leaving Stuart to guard the Blue Ridge passes. Probably no more plausible plan for ultimate victory was at any time conceived within the Confederacy. Perhaps the South then was nearer success than ever before or afterward. Certainly the North was never more vulnerable politically, and it is difficult to overestimate the consequences had Washington been confronted with the situation Lee set out to produce. And what was to prevent his success? On June 25 his army was crossing the Potomac at Shepherdstown and Williamsport. Through Hagerstown they moved on toward Chambersburg. Still out in front, Ewell reached Carlisle, and Longstreet was ready to drive for the great railroad bridges across the Susquehanna.[19]

Thus far the campaign had developed precisely as planned. With one exception every man had executed his assignment with admirable skill and promptitude. The entire army was on Union soil, and in its rear many miles of the B.&O. Railroad lay in ruins, while the other great trunk line, the Pennsylvania, was only a short day's march ahead. But where was "Jeb" Stuart? His job was to screen the right and keep Lee posted on Federal movements. Before crossing the Potomac, Lee had sent him riding off toward Washington to discover the whereabouts of Hooker and what he was doing. For almost a week there had been no word from him. In fact, Lee had neither seen nor heard from him since crossing the river. Day by day the pressure of uncertainty was bearing more heavily on Lee. At every bivouac he paced back and forth, baffled by Stuart's failure to report. What had happened to him? Had Hooker failed to follow northward? Had he turned to march on Richmond?

Artfully concealing his extreme anxiety from his subordinates, Lee went to his tent on the night of June 28. Shortly after ten o'clock he was roused by an officer who came to announce the arrival of one of Longstreet's scouts with a startling story. Lee ordered the man brought to him at once, listened to all he had to tell. The Federal army was north of the Potomac. In fact, it had advanced to Frederick, Maryland, and at least two corps had reached South Mountain. Hooker had been relieved. George Meade was in command of the Army of the Potomac. As Lee listened he was analyzing the situation and setting a course of action. With George Meade close in his rear there was but one thing to do—concentrate his force on the east side of the ridge and keep Meade out of the Cumberland Valley behind him. Otherwise the game was up.

At full speed he dispatched couriers to the corps commanders. All previous orders were canceled. With all haste they must move at once toward concentration in the neighborhood of Cashtown, east of the divide. Two days later Lee watched with high satisfaction as his swiftly marching divisions topped the ridge and debouched onto level ground. Some units pushed on to where the Chambersburg road crossed Willoughby Run. But where was Stuart?[20] Without him how was he to know the dispositions of his old comrade, George Meade, and what he was up to? Then he paused to listen. Guns! The sound of the firing was coming from the east—about where Harry Heth's division would be. More guns! The grim salute for the thousands who were to die at Gettysburg.

3

Lee's prediction of what Hooker would do when the Confederate movement was discovered proved entirely correct. Shortly after Hill's corps left Fredericksburg, Hooker abandoned Falmouth and marched northwestward to the line of the Orange & Alexandria Railroad. This placed the Army of the Potomac on the inner line between Lee and the city of Washington. Once more Herman Haupt was called on to supply the massive army by means of the vulnerable O.&A. He was immediately confronted with all the difficulties against which he had warned Burnside in the previous autumn. Roving guerrilla bands started firing on trains, burning bridges and obstructing track. To operate with any safety each train had to carry a guard of thirty to fifty men.[21] Haupt gave the management of the line to Adna Anderson, his very capable chief engineer of military railroads in Virginia. Anderson kept the essential trains running while Hooker cautiously crept forward toward the Potomac, seemingly doubtful of what to do or where to go.

Through most of June, Hooker annoyed Washington far

more than he disturbed Lee. He could not agree with Lincoln or Stanton or Halleck as to the proper use to be made of the Army of the Potomac. He wasted time quibbling over orders and arguing petty questions of procedure. Though moving along the inner and much shorter line, he fell so far behind the swiftly marching enemy that on June 27, while Ewell was passing through Carlisle, only eighteen miles from Harrisburg, Hooker was still on the Potomac below Harper's Ferry. That was when Meade replaced him. On the same day Haupt's authority was extended to cover all railroads in Maryland and Pennsylvania.[22]

From his experience in supplying McClellan after Antietam, Haupt well knew how hard it would be to supply Meade where he would be moving. Perhaps no Union man grasped more clearly than he the desperate peril if the enemy reached the Pennsylvania trunk line and laid waste to it as he had already done to the B.&O. Haupt had divined Lee's purpose in the invasion and entertained no doubt of the consequences should he be allowed to destroy the railroad communications. Meade's men must not be delayed for want of provisions. Time was of the essence of success in preparing transportation for supplies. To study the situation at first hand, Haupt made ready to leave at once for Harrisburg.

For some unaccountable reason never disclosed, Halleck detained him for two critical days in Washington while Meade was moving deeper into that part of Maryland reached by no railroad. When permitted to leave, he found the Northern Central broken at numerous places. He had to detour via Philadelphia, and arrived in Harrisburg late in the evening of June 30.[23] There he held hurried consultation with Tom Scott. Out of concern for the safety of the Pennsylvania, Scott set up his own scout service and kept in close touch with all Confederate movements since the enemy had crossed the river. He told Haupt how Ewell had countermarched hurriedly through Carlisle; that at the same time Early had scurried away from the line of the Northern Central and was then heading west toward Chambersburg.[24] Scott felt much relieved. In all this strange hurry he saw preparation for Lee's

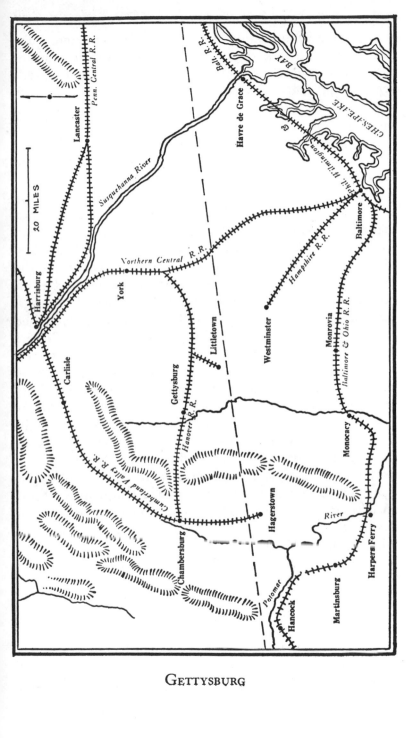

GETTYSBURG

retreat from Pennsylvania. Haupt read the same signs quite differently. To him there was an obvious explanation for this sudden reversal of course. Lee had learned of Hooker's replacement and discovered that Meade was on the move. Lee was not retreating but concentrating in anticipation of a fight. Unless Meade halted or changed his course, a battle was imminent. Late in the night Haupt telegraphed Halleck what he had learned and set out immediately aboard an engine for Baltimore. Not a minute was to be lost.

Having lived for some time in Gettysburg, he was familiar with the wagon roads and rail facilities on which he must depend to get supplies to Meade. From Baltimore the all-rail route to the general area lay over the Northern Central to Hanover Junction, Pennsylvania, thence westward via the York & Cumberland. But Early's men had burned bridges on both roads and they were useless until repaired. The B.&O. was open to Frederick, but from there to the army would be a long, tedious wagon haul. The nearest rail approach then open would be over the Western Maryland to Westminster, some twenty miles short of the point where supplies must be delivered. On July 1 Haupt set out to appraise the possibilities of adopting this route as a supply line. The Western Maryland was only twenty-nine miles long. He found it a pitifully weak little road, in poor condition, with no experienced executives and far short of the required capacity. It was a single track without a single siding long enough to pass a full-length train. There were no water stations and no turntables. It had no telegraph line and could run only three or four trains a day.[25] Of what use could it be? Haupt would need at least thirty trains each day.

At Westminster he found himself in the midst of howling confusion. Hundreds of Meade's wagons were collecting there. The disappointed quartermaster officers were clamoring for supplies. Was this to be the end of Haupt's incredible record in the solution of military transportation problems? To escape the ill-humored crowd and gain a few minutes alone in which to think, he crept into a covered wagon and hid himself from the yowling teamsters. In these few minutes he devised a complete plan. Had he told it then, most likely he would have been thought insane. Without a word to anyone he slipped out of the wagon and hurried away to the nearest telegraph station.

Next morning answers to his telegrams began to arrive in Baltimore. But they were neither spoken nor written. Up from Alexandria came Adna Anderson with 400 members of the Railroad Construction Corps. They brought with them their tools and equipment, and many lanterns and water buckets.[26] Another train bore a number of full train crews and cars loaded with an abundance of good split wood for engine fuel. Impressed rolling stock rapidly accumulated in the Baltimore yards. Promptly on Anderson's arrival repair crews were dispatched to open the Northern Central to Hanover Junction and then work westward along the York & Cumberland toward Gettysburg where the fighting had now started. Other crews were distributed along the track of the Western Maryland, instructed to keep it in running order at any cost. Trains were being made up in the Baltimore yards and loaded with provisions. Haupt notified the Quartermaster Department he was ready; the adequacy of supplies delivered at Westminster would now depend entirely on the speed and regularity with which that department loaded and unloaded cars. It should have enough men so they could load or unload all the cars of a train at once.

There would be no train schedule. With no facilities for passing, trains would run in convoys of five each. These convoys would be spaced at intervals of eight hours, giving each departing one time to unload and return before the next one started. That was why there could be no delay in loading or unloading.

By July 3, while the battle of Gettysburg was at its height, Haupt was moving supplies over the Western Maryland at the rate of 1,500 tons daily, and his returning trains were bringing out thousands of wounded to the Baltimore hospitals. The scheme devised so speedily while he lay hidden in the army wagon at Westminster was working perfectly. For lack of turntables the trains ran backwards from Westminster,

five in close order. When they cleared the track, five others
started in the opposite direction. The lack of water stations
was overcome by stopping the trains at streams. Waiting
crews filled the tanks with the buckets Anderson had brought
from Alexandria.[27] By such devices the capacity of the little
road was increased tenfold.

At four o'clock next afternoon Haupt telegraphed Stanton
that the Northern Central was in order to Hanover Junction,
and the Gettysburg line open as far as Littleton. He had
found General Sickles there, badly wounded, and was sending him to Washington by special train. A second supply line
was now running, and trains loaded with wounded already
were moving out via Hanover Junction. At 11:00 P.M. he
sent another wire, this time from Oxford, seven miles east of
Gettysburg, saying two hours' work the following morning
would complete the road to the battlefield.[28]

So it was that by the time Lee started his retreat, rail supply
lines to the Union army were delivering subsistence beyond
the daily requirements.[29] Considering all the circumstances
in which it was accomplished, this feat rarely if ever has been
surpassed. It is farther from Baltimore to Gettysburg than
from Richmond to Fredericksburg, yet in four days during
the heat of desperate battle Haupt accomplished for Meade
what the Confederate organization could not do for Lee in
four months of quiet.

How Meade failed to follow up his victory and pursue Lee
to the Potomac when he might have destroyed the Confederate army is a story familiar to all students of the war.
His neglect to do so left Washington aghast and ultimately
led to Grant's being brought in above him.[30] During the ten
days Meade faltered before taking up the pursuit, Haupt
restored the Northern Central over its entire length and put
the Cumberland Valley line back in operation as far south
as Chambersburg. On July 14, Stanton ordered him to
abandon further work in Pennsylvania and return at once
with his men and equipment to Alexandria. Lee had escaped,
recrossed the Potomac and was now safe in the Shenandoah
Valley.

Slowly the two armies retraced the routes by which each had come up from the Rappahannock. Again it became Haupt's job to feed the Federals via the exposed and harassed Orange & Alexandria, a task to dismay a man of less courage. In Pennsylvania he had hoped it would not be necessary. He had foreseen the danger of Lee's escape and on the night of July 5 had hurried to Washington on an engine to plead for a peremptory order for Meade to move at once.[31]

While the army was north of the Potomac, both the O.&A. and the Manassas Gap roads had suffered much at the hands of guerrillas. To restore them to good running order was a very considerable job. Large cavalry patrols had to guard the Blue Ridge passes and prevent Lee's horsemen from swooping down out of the Valley and destroying the tracks as rapidly as they could be repaired. From Alexandria southward to Warrenton the country was infested with night-riding partisans who specialized in breaking tracks and wrecking trains. To be contended with was the intrepid and mysterious Colonel Mosby, whose fierce raiders were omnipresent yet never to be found or identified. He kept track guards in terror. Haupt had so much trouble procuring the assignment of enough soldiers to guard his railroads that he sought and was granted authority to expand his own corps and make it able to defend itself.

Notwithstanding all these difficulties, August 1 found the Manassas Gap line open to Front Royal, and O.&A. trains were running with reasonable regularity as far as the Rappahannock. Lee retired across the Rapidan. Once more the Army of the Potomac and the Army of Northern Virginia rested, facing each other no more than a day's march from Fredericksburg. For the second time Lee's hope for peace through invasion had been thwarted because he was brought to battle before he reached the position he aimed at. For the second time he had escaped through the failure of dilatory Federal commanders to exploit their victories. The war must go on.

CHAPTER XXI

Transportation Feats in the Chattanooga Campaign

I

August was slipping away. Soon the third autumn of the war would come and, save for the expensive victory at Chancellorsville, only misfortune had been the lot of Confederate arms throughout 1863. Once more, Lee was called to Richmond for conference with President Davis.

One distinct advantage remained theirs—they held the much shorter, interior line. It was hinged on the right. The far left had swung deep into the South until now it extended in a southwesterly direction from northern Virginia to middle Mississippi. On the right Lee was resting quietly at Orange Court House behind the Rapidan where his men recovered swiftly from the exhausting and fruitless Gettysburg campaign. At the center Bragg was in Chattanooga whither he had retired when Rosecrans maneuvered him out of his fortified position at Tullahoma. The left of the grand line of defense was a frayed end floating in the woods of Mississippi because of the loss of its anchor at Vicksburg.

The high-ranking Confederate generals agreed that they could not win the war by pursuing a strictly defensive policy. How, where and when to strike an offensive blow before they lost the advantage of the inner line was the question before the Richmond conference.[1] As at the similar conference in May, there were wide differences of opinion, but it was readily agreed that strong reinforcements must be sent to the army selected to take the offensive. In the end they decided there was greater promise of success in a blow at the center where the forces of Bragg and Rosecrans were about evenly matched. Many reasons led to this decision. Far from the least was the fact that in a few days troops from the Army of Northern Virginia could reach Chattanooga by rail via Lynchburg and thence down the Tennessee Valley over the Virginia & Tennessee Railroad. Bragg had also an excellent supply line in the Western & Atlantic direct to Atlanta. Perhaps Longstreet was the man most pleased with the decision, for it was he who in May had argued this strategy as against the invasion of Pennsylvania.

Lee agreed to send two divisions from the Rapidan, and Johnston would start two more marching across country from Mississippi. Considerately Lee gave Longstreet the opportunity to participate in the undertaking for which he had so stoutly contended and let him take two divisions from his own First Corps of veterans. The distance to Chattanooga via Lynchburg, Bristol and Knoxville was approximately 500 miles. Longstreet expected to cover it in four days. But he had no Herman Haupt to perform miracles of transportation. Under the ineffective policy of the Confederacy, the job of moving his divisions fell to Quartermaster General Lawton, who was to find it complicated in the extreme. While the move was still under consideration, the entire situation changed. Burnside came charging over the mountains from Kentucky, took Knoxville and closed the direct rail route from Lynchburg to Chattanooga.

Then followed another demonstration of the difficulty that the lack of east-west railroads created in Southern troop movements. Plans for the campaign had gone too far to be shelved. Nothing remained for Longstreet but to take the long way round via Richmond, Wilmington, Augusta and Atlanta. Lawton's task was immediately magnified many times. Nearly 1,000 miles must be covered and no less than ten different railroads would be involved. This route would double the distance, and the constant transfers from train to train where lines met but did not connect would lose time and cause trouble. With no authority to take possession of the roads and their rolling stock, Lawton had an immense, laborious and vexatious piece of work before him.

It was September 9 when the first trains started rolling on the Virginia Central tracks, which had carried Jackson's men from the Valley to Beaver Dam. As one followed another into the Richmond yards, the detraining soldiers were greeted with wild enthusiasm. These were the men who had fought at Gettysburg, and in spite of the fact they had lost, they were heroes nonetheless. Below Richmond the trip degenerated into a home-coming celebration mixed with a burlesque of a movement of an army by rail. G. Moxley Sorrel, Longstreet's Chief of Staff, said: "Never before were so many troops moved over such worn-out railways, none first-class from the beginning. Never before were such crazy cars—passenger, baggage, mail, coal, box, platform—all and every sort, wabbling on the jumping strap-iron—used for hauling good soldiers."[2] But to dampen the spirits or curb the humor of the veteran Confederate soldier required more than discomfort or the memory of fruitless charges at Gettysburg. Most of the men lived in parts of the Carolinas and Georgia through which they were riding the "crazy" assortment of bouncing cars. They turned the trip into a lark.

Through the countryside and at every village and town "home folk" gathered beside the tracks and cheered until hoarse. Flags and handkerchiefs waved, and hats sailed into the air. Every car of every train was crowded with all the soldiers who could get inside, climb atop or cling to the outside. The boys who rode outside were having all the fun. The men inside were swearing and railing at their misfortune. However, these pent-up soldiers soon solved the inequitable distribution of the carnival-like hilarity. With axes they chopped and pried off the side walls, leaving the framework to support the crowded roofs of the cars while they enjoyed the shaded, rolling amphitheaters. Now they, too, could wave to the girls and answer the yells of the men and boys.[3] Unfortunately a new stripping job had to be done each time they changed to a different railroad.

That two divisions of infantry and a battalion of artillery

ultimately arrived at Ringgold, Georgia, twenty-two miles south of Chattanooga, is a tremendous tribute to Lawton and the courageous railroaders who made up trains from anything that would roll and kept them moving over tracks scarcely worthy of the name. Not in magnitude or in speed but in sheer stubborn accomplishment of so much with so little, the transfer of Longstreet's corps from the Rapidan to Ringgold was the outstanding operational feat of the Confederate railroads during the war.

The long journey of these veterans from the Army of Northern Virginia ended amid circumstances far different from those anticipated when the move was planned. About the time they left the Rapidan, Bragg was again diverted by the crafty Rosecrans, who, instead of following him to Chattanooga, halted at Bridgeport, some thirty miles down the river. Rosecrans reasoned that it would be easier and safer to maneuver him out of the coveted city than to fight him out of it. The Union commander crossed the Tennessee, marched directly east across two mountain spurs and took positions from which he could either proceed down the narrow, sheltered valleys and pin Bragg against the river or cross another ridge and destroy the Western & Atlantic Railroad, Bragg's sole source of supplies. When the ill-tempered Bragg, notorious for his disdain of the intelligence service,[4] discovered what had happened, it was too late for him to do anything except give up Chattanooga and retire to Dalton in order to cover his rail communications. Instead of waiting there for the arrival of the reinforcements he knew to be on the way, he turned to an immediate offensive, hoping to catch the Union corps scattered out and defeat them in detail. He missed his opportunities though skirmishes became more and more severe until he attacked in the heavy oak and hickory timber that bordered Chickamauga Creek.

About three o'clock in the afternoon of September 19 the first of Longstreet's trains stopped within sound of the battle at a little flag station called Catoosa Platform.[5] Longstreet leaped from the train, coaxed his horse to jump from the car in which it had been shipped, and in a matter of minutes

was riding through the woods in search of Bragg's headquarters. With him rode Sorrel and two other staff officers.
The quarrelsome and disgruntled Bragg had left no directions
by which he could be located. The search did not end until
after ten o'clock that night when they found him asleep in
an ambulance.[6] When the battle was renewed on the morning
of the twentieth, five of Longstreet's ten brigades had arrived
and were marched directly to the field. Of the two divisions,
these five brigades were all who completed the trip in time to
participate in "the Great Battle of the West."

The artillery units under the command of E. P. Alexander
had followed the infantry all the way from Richmond and
arrived at Dalton, twelve miles from the Chickamauga field,
at two o'clock in the morning of September 25, five days
after the fight was over.[7]

With the bitter controversies over generalship, mismanagement, lost opportunities and needless slaughter at the Battle
of Chickamauga, we have no present concern. To say that
Rosecrans, narrowly saved from rout by Thomas' stubborn
defense, was defeated, suffered ghastly losses and retreated
into Chattanooga is sufficient to the railroad story.

2

By his retreat to Chattanooga, Rosecrans fell into the trap
he had set for Bragg. After their Chickamauga victory the
Confederates moved up to occupy a strong line extending
from the northeast end of Missionary Ridge to Lookout
Mountain southwest of the city. On the heights they emplaced field guns, and across the valley they deployed infantry.
Their supply line was secure behind them.

On the narrow plain between Missionary Ridge and the
unbridged Tennessee lay the camps of the disorganized and
badly mauled Federals. Past the precipitous nose of Lookout
Mountain the sharply bending river conceded barely enough
passageway to accommodate the Nashville & Chattanooga
track and the wagon road to Bridgeport. Occupation of Lookout thus made it a simple matter for Bragg's men to deny Rose-

crans the use of road, river and railroad to bring up supplies. The Army of the Cumberland had come to the end of the long and rugged road to Chattanooga to find only the promise of starvation. Rosecrans was besieged.

Except for Halleck's repetition of an earlier blunder, Sherman might have been there to ease things. From Vicksburg via the Mississippi to Memphis, the red-whiskered fighter had started east with a sizable army to reinforce the Cumberlanders. From Memphis he meant to use the badly damaged Memphis & Charleston as far as possible, then march the rest of the way along its line. Scarcely had he started when Halleck's obsession over the use of that railroad as a supply line to Chattanooga again found expression in orders, and Sherman was hobbled with the same gear Buell had worn. He was told to repair the railroad as he went east and prepare it for shipments from Memphis. Obediently but disgustedly he set about wasting precious days spiking down rails and building bridges on an unnecessary railroad which the Federals could neither protect nor maintain once it was reconstructed.[8] So, while Rosecrans was being routed from the field at Chickamauga, the tragedy of Halleck's fatal orders to Buell was being re-enacted in northern Mississippi.

In the evening of September 23 Stanton received the following ominous telegram from his Assistant Secretary of War, Charles A. Dana, then in Chattanooga:

No time should be lost in rushing twenty to twenty-five thousand efficient troops to Bridgeport. If such re-inforcements can be got there in season everything is safe and this place indispensable alike to the defense of Tennessee and as a base for future operations in Georgia will remain ours.[9]

This was not Stanton's first news of the alarming situation there, but it was confirmation and dispelled any doubt that prompt action was necessary.

No one in Washington could have foreseen how desperate Rosecrans' position was to become before the most hurried relief could reach him. In Bridgeport was an abundance of supplies and a railroad to bring up more when those were exhausted, but the only way to get them to Chattanooga was to cart them over a wagon road which wound sixty miles through the rough mountain country north of the river, and ferry them across. Hard use and the early autumn rains soon converted that road into a channel of churned mud. Over its slimy length bedeviled teamsters screamed curses on the jaded and starving animals which at snail's pace drew slithering wagons until they could no longer keep their feet. When they could no longer stand they were dragged to the roadside and left to die. Before long the route was lined with their stinking carcasses. Remnants of broken wagons, overturned to get them out of the way, also marked the route from plenty to famine. Meanwhile in Chattanooga sick and wounded men died for want of medical supplies and the well fell sick from lack of food. In their camps was no fuel with which to cook such rations as could be found, or to build fires to dry their clothing or dispel the bone-shaking chill of the autumn nights. Without hope of early relief and with winter coming on, it is little wonder Rosecrans was threatening to abandon Chattanooga, try to cross the river and escape into the mountains. Fortunately such a foolhardy attempt was averted through what Festus Summers has called the "accomplishment par excellence in Civil War logistics."[10]

Upon receipt of Dana's telegram of the twenty-third, Stanton summoned Halleck to his office, and by hurried messengers urged President Lincoln and Secretaries Seward and Chase to join them there at once. When the solemn group assembled in the dimly lighted room, Stanton explained the emergency at Chattanooga. He pointed out that Sherman was too far away to march to Bridgeport in time to relieve the situation; that Burnside could not be sent to Rosecrans' support without abandoning Knoxville and all of east Tennessee. Then he made the startling proposal that 30,000 men be sent by rail from the Army of the Potomac to break the siege of Chattanooga, and to jar his listeners further, he estimated it could be done in five days. When Halleck heard such a preposterous idea seriously advanced by his chief, his

TYPICAL RAILROAD SCENE
The O. & A. near Union Mills.

FINAL TOUCHES ON ONE OF GENERAL HAUPT'S
PREFABRICATED TRUSS BRIDGES

STRAWBERRY PLAINS BRIDGE NEAR KNOXVILLE
This bridge was destroyed and rebuilt four times. Note earthworks at right.

protruding eyeballs must have popped still farther from their sockets. He was quick to express his disapproval. He was still fighting the war according to the rules of strategy laid down in the old texts he had studied in his youth.

So skeptical was Lincoln that he said to Stanton, "I will bet that if the order is given tonight the troops could not be got to Washington in five days."[11] But Stanton had unshakable faith in the railroads. Supported by Seward, he argued so persistently that when the conference ended he had approval to send the Eleventh and Twelfth Corps west under Hooker. He was confident that with perfect planning and the exclusion of all other business from the railroads it could be done in time. No sooner had the door closed behind his departing confreres than the telegraph wires came alive with messages of preparation. Throughout the remainder of the night orders to the military and instructions to railroad officers poured from the office of the Secretary of War as they had rarely done before.

At noon next day Samuel M. Felton, Tom Scott, John W. Garrett and William P. Smith were poring over maps in that office carefully calculating equipment, time, distances and routes. Stanton's able board of strategy for transportation was hard at work. The familiarity of these executives with the capacity, condition and connections of the available roads enabled them to designate a route promptly. Starting at Culpeper, the line of travel would lie through Washington where the trains would be picked up by the B.&.O. Washington branch and taken to Relay House near Baltimore. There they would be shunted onto the main stem of the B.&O. which would carry them without change all the way to Benwood on the Ohio River. At Benwood the troops would detrain and be ferried over to Bellaire, Ohio. Then connecting Ohio roads would supply transportation via Columbus to Indianapolis. From Indianapolis they would travel to Jeffersonville, Indiana, and recross the Ohio River to Louisville. From Louisville the route would be via the much fought-over L.&N. to Nashville, thence over the vital N.&C. through Stevenson, Alabama, to Bridgeport.

Lincoln did not wait for a specification of the roads but issued a blanket order authorizing Hooker to take military possession of all railroads and their equipment "which may be necessary to execution of the operation."[12] He quite well realized that from start to finish Stanton's plan contemplated the exercise of the President's power to control the needed railroads, and that without it there could be no hope of success. Before nightfall of the twenty-fourth, it was arranged that Colonel McCallum would supervise the original loadings and transportation as far as Washington. From Washington to Jeffersonville the responsibility would rest with that dauntless veteran of railroad emergencies, John W. Garrett. Below Louisville Scott would have charge. With the further understanding that the B.&O. would supply McCallum 420 "cars with seats," these men separated, each to plunge into his allotted task.

Meantime, Stanton was reeling off military orders at amazing speed and crackling with terse finality. McCallum would have charge of all loading, and officers of whatsoever grade were to obey his orders. Troops were to be ready to move the minute cars were ready.[13] Artillery would travel with its respective corps. Cars loaded with five days' forage for artillery horses would join the trains at Alexandria. Artillery units would take 200 rounds of ammunition for the guns. Each man would carry cooked rations for five days. Coffee and sugar would be supplied along the way. Infantry would carry 40 rounds of ammunition per man and take along a minimum of camp equipment, no hospital tents and only such medical supplies as might be needed en route.[14]

Nothing was left to chance. So completely were the plans worked out that at five o'clock in the afternoon of September 25, two trains composed of 51 troop cars and 4 cars loaded with field guns passed through Washington, with other trains following close behind. Less than forty-eight hours had elapsed since Dana's message arrived. Later in the evening came an illustration of the meticulous care exercised by the railroad men. When the first trains reached Relay House, W. P. Smith, Master of Transportation for the B.&O., wired

McCallum asking that he limit his trains to twenty or twenty-two cars so that when they reached the mountainous country on the main stem their engines would not be overloaded and the running speed needlessly reduced.[15]

Phrased in the crisp style of a train dispatcher, bulletins of progress began coming over the wires to the delighted Stanton. On September 26, he read:

9:45 A.M. Three trains of more than sixty cars with more than 3,000 troops have passed Martinsburg in good order.[16]

11:00 A.M. Twelve trains with 7,000 men have passed Relay. Everything working smoothly. Transportation through Ohio all arranged.[17]

4:00 P.M. First three trains have passed Cumberland.[18]

6:00 P.M. Arrangements for transfer at Indianapolis and ferriage at Louisville all complete.[19]

At 9:00 on the twenty-seventh, trains bearing 12,600 men, 33 cars of artillery and 21 cars of horses and baggage formed a great wheeled caravan traveling steadily westward between Washington and Benwood. Now reconciled to the plan, Halleck made his contribution. To General B. F. Kelley, commanding in West Virginia, he telegraphed the information that troops were coming over the B.&O. and ordered him to exercise all possible precaution to protect the trains.[20] Later in the day he sent another dispatch ordering Kelley to close all saloons and drinking places in the neighborhood of Benwood.[21]

Railroad and army personnel were working in perfect coordination to set an amazing new world's record in military transportation. Major general or humble station agent, each had his assignment and neither interfered with the other except at his peril. It was General Carl Schurz who first felt the heavy hand of the Secretary of War. It so happened that

Schurz found himself aboard a train well in rear of the leading elements of his command. His German military instinct revolted against such violation of priority. He telegraphed the station agent at Grafton to hold the trains carrying the Third Division of the Eleventh Corps until its commanding officer arrived. But the agent was working for John Garrett and had been told that train operation was not to be interrupted by anything less than orders direct from the War Department. When the division's trains arrived at Grafton they were promptly dispatched in order.

Schurz was furious. That an ordinary railroad agent should defy a major general of the army was beyond his comprehension. Anger turned to frustration when he received a telegram of reprimand from Stanton threatening his arrest and removal from command for having attempted to delay the movement of the trains.[22]

This was the sort of authority, foresight and organization that brought the first troops to Bellaire in the morning of September 27. The long caravan had now stretched itself from the Rapidan to the Ohio. More than 20,000 men were moving. All except 3,300 members of the Twelfth Corps were on their way and by noon of the twenty-eighth all of Hooker's command was wheeling it for Bridgeport. Had anyone covered Lincoln's proffered bet, the President would have been due to pay. It was the fifth day and at 3:00 P.M. the first trains were passing through Columbus, Ohio. Two hours later 200 carloads of troops had left Bellaire.[23] W. P. Smith telegraphed Stanton:

So far not one out of thirty trains of nearly 600 cars has been delayed improperly. The only thing we have to regret is that the actual movement exceeds the requisitions by nearly 20% in men and more than 50% in horses.[24]

It was inevitable that at some point on so long a route a movement of such size and complexity should lose speed. That point proved to be Indianapolis. Because of the different gauge of the Jeffersonville Railroad the entire force had to be detrained and reloaded there. Moreover, the five days' cooked rations were exhausted. On the bank of White River, a mile west of where the trains stopped, stood the Soldiers' Home. As the men detrained they were marched there to be fed. On the average, six hours elapsed between arrival and departure on the next leg of the journey. Despite that delay the head of the column passed through Louisville on the twenty-ninth, only a few hours after the last train left Washington.[25] For those who led the way the journey ended two days later near the banks of the Tennessee. Nine days had elapsed since Lincoln had offered to bet that the troops could not be brought to Washington in five days. In eleven and one-half days the troop transfer was completed.[26] In that time two army corps traveled 1,200 miles, much of the distance over a railroad four times crossed and devastated by the whole of Lee's Army of Northern Virginia and as often reconstructed. Throughout 300 miles it had been broken time and again by enemy raiders. The first fifty miles of the journey were over a line completely wrecked the previous autumn; the last 300 were over two roads to which Morgan and Forrest had done their worst during the summer of 1862. Yet without mechanical difficulty almost 25,000 men, 10 batteries of artillery with their horses and 100 cars of baggage were brought safely to their destination in Tennessee.

Behind the troop movement followed with equal precision a second stream of trains bearing more than 1,000 horses and mules, spare artillery, wagons, and equipment for field transportation, additional baggage and all the impedimenta requisite to the operation of an army in the field. When all these trains had delivered their cargo, the cars and engines were returned promptly to their owners and the railroads resumed their normal operations. An incredible thing had happened. American railroads, not yet of military age and still widely referred to as "contraptions," had accomplished an unparalleled military feat.

Only a few years before this an Indiana Congressman had required more time to travel from his home to Washington than it had taken the young railroads to carry an army from the Rapidan to Indianapolis and supper at the Soldiers' Home. While the direct purpose of this unprecedented undertaking was to relieve Chattanooga, its success brought far-reaching results. The remnants of an earlier disposition to discount the railroad as a major factor in strategy and tactics were practically tossed overboard. The proof that it was and would remain an important implement in warfare was overwhelming. Of the soundness of Federal policy no further proof was needed. The movement had been a magnificent demonstration of co-operation between military and railroad personnel at all levels. Only through the sagacious use of the railroad authority temporarily vested in the President could it have been accomplished.

The arrival of Hooker's command on the Tennessee set the stage for operations which were to relieve the siege of Chattanooga. In the first place, it reduced the grave danger that Confederate cavalry raiding below Nashville might break the N.&C. Railroad, stop the shipment of supplies to Bridgeport, and make the relief of Rosecrans impossible. And it furnished ready man power with which to strike.

The administration now turned to Grant for generalship to recoup its lost initiative at the center of the Confederate line. Stanton came out from Washington to meet at Louisville the newly appointed commander of all Union armies west of the Alleghenies.[27] During their conference Stanton received another startling telegram from Dana: unless peremptory orders were issued at once, Rosecrans would try his threatened retreat.[28] The orders quickly dispatched were nothing if not peremptory. They relieved Rosecrans of his command and replaced him with General George H. Thomas. The "Rock" wired back: "We will hold the town till we starve."[29] On the next day Sherman was made Grant's successor as commander of the Army of the Tennessee.

It was October 23 when Grant reached Chattanooga via Bridgeport over the terrible wagon road through the mountains north of the river. A few moments' survey was enough to prompt him to send a courier flying to Sherman, then at Iuka. He was to stop work on railroad repairs and bring his command full speed to Stevenson. Still nettled by the memories of Forrest and Van Dorn, Grant was acutely sensitive to the possibility of Rebel raids on his supply line. With Thomas, Hooker and Sherman concentrating on Chattanooga, nothing less than disaster would result should enemy cavalry slip through and destroy the railroad below Nashville. There was the probability, too, of his having to supply Burnside's command of 25,000 by the same route. Even if the N.&C. remained undisturbed, the load certainly would be too great for a single track to bear.[30]

Grant puffed hard on his cigar and recalled that coming with Sherman was General G. M. Dodge, excellent soldier and experienced railroad builder.[31] Grant snapped an order off to Sherman—halt Dodge and his command at Athens, Alabama, to repair the Central Alabama Railroad below Nashville, extend it to the Tennessee River at Decatur, then repair the M.&C. between Decatur and Stevenson. This would give Grant a supplementary supply line below Nashville.[32]

The task assigned to Dodge was no less trying than some of the worst undertaken by Haupt on behalf of the Army of the Potomac. He had with him no tools except the axes, picks and spades of the pioneers. Aside from those he could detail from his own command, he had neither skilled mechanics nor common laborers. He was obliged to live off the country, and that in itself required no small effort; but in a manner reminiscent of Haupt at Potomac Creek he went to work. Axmen were set to getting out bridge timbers and cutting fuel for locomotives. Blacksmith shops in the surrounding country were seized, dismantled and, with all they contained, moved up to the line of the road where smiths were detailed to hammer out tools for the work ahead.

All bridges on the line had been destroyed and the rails taken up, heated and twisted around trees in accordance with Confederate practice. All cars not carried off had been burned, and all engines damaged beyond the possibility of immediate use. Dodge distributed among his 8,000 men the assignments of foraging for supplies, fighting off marauders, building bridges and replacing track, while Grant assumed the responsibility of providing from other roads the necessary rails, cars and locomotives, some of which came all the way from Vicksburg.[33] Within forty days after receiving his orders, Dodge completed his work. He had built or repaired 102 miles of track and 182 bridges and culverts. Grant was no longer wholly dependent on the single track of the Nashville & Chattanooga. For the armies of the West he had found a Haupt of his own.

By continuous operations between October 28 and November 23 Hooker drove the enemy from Lookout Valley, cleared them off the heights of Raccoon and Lookout mountains and opened the supply line to Bridgeport. The left jaw of the great vise in which Bragg had held Rosecrans so firmly was snapped off and tossed back on Missionary Ridge. In the interim Sherman arrived.

Grant was now ready for the final blow to break the impasse at Chattanooga. With the Cumberlanders recuperated, reorganized under new leadership and eager for revenge, it was time to strike. On his right he had the veterans from Gettysburg; on his left the fierce fighters from the Army of the Tennessee. For leaders he had the ever-dependable Sherman, the indefatigable Thomas and "Fighting Joe" Hooker, who had done well as a subordinate. In the last days before winter they went to work in earnest on the boys who had driven Rosecrans from Chickamauga. It began on November 24, and at the close of two days' fighting marked by galling Union fire from both flanks and terrifying assaults up the steeps at the center, Bragg's men fled from Missionary Ridge and retreated to the neighborhood of Dalton, Georgia. At last Lincoln's dream of the redemption of east Tennessee was realized and Chattanooga was secure.

CHAPTER XXII

Wounded and Disabled Ride Away

I

Although the railroads' main job was to carry men and supplies to the battle fronts, very early in the war they began to have other tasks thrust on them. Every car that came up to the front lines had to go back. Usually it went back empty, but it was available for a load.

Before the fighting was six months old, the returning cars got a new job: transporting the wounded away from combat areas, where they were a nuisance, to points in the rear where they could be more adequately cared for. Crude at first, this service was gradually refined and improved as the war proceeded and as specialized equipment was devised. It began in the west, and, significantly, on Union railroads.

In the heat of an August day in 1861 a history-making train pulled out of Rolla, Missouri, the outer terminus of the Southwestern Railroad. There was nothing unusual about its outward appearance. Bound for St. Louis, it was made up of ordinary boxcars which had come out to Rolla loaded with supplies for General Lyon's army and was pulled by an ordinary eight-wheeled wood-burning engine. Doubtless those who saw it pass thought it only another string of "empties" returning for more provisions. They could not have been more mistaken.

The train carried a capacity load of badly wounded survivors of the battle of Wilson's Creek. They lay in rows on the bare floors of the cars. Still wearing the fouled emergency dressings hastily applied to their wounds at the crowded and poorly equipped field hospitals, these men with shattered limbs and shot-torn bodies endured the agony of the hours through which the cars jolted and swayed over 110 miles of new, unsettled track. There were some attendants, but since they could not pass from one car to another while the train was in motion, fresh hemorrhages went unstanched, and agonizing positions remained unrelieved, while the bouncing floors added new miseries and sapped the men's waning strength. Except for what they could administer to one another and what orderlies could give during train stops, the sufferers received no care en route. Terrible though the journey was, it ended in fresh, clean beds in St. Louis hospitals with doctors and nurses in attendance.

This was the first organized railroad hospital train. Crude and cruel as it was, it marked the opening of a new era in the relations between field armies and their sick and wounded men. It was the beginning of modern practice in the disposal of disabled personnel from combat areas—practice that never ceased to develop until helicopters came to pick up wounded men from dressing stations in the mountains of Korea and hurry them by air transport to base hospitals in Japan.

The thought of wounded soldiers riding unattended for hours on the bare floors of bouncing boxcars was revolting, but the idea of their swift removal to base hospitals for treatment appealed to the imagination. Although wholly unanticipated, in the North this potential of rail transportation was recognized with surprising promptness and challenged the development of facilities. Because of their constant use in bringing supplies to combat areas, boxcars were far more frequently available than any other type. Naturally, attention was first directed toward making transportation by boxcar more comfortable. At first the floor was covered with a thick bed of straw or fresh hay on which the men were laid at properly spaced intervals. Then well-filled bed sacks were placed on top of the floor padding and when these "nests" were carefully prepared they so absorbed the shocks as to make travel quite comfortable for many of the unfortunates and tolerable for all. This is about as far as improvements went. The system continued in use to the end of the war. Often, however, it was difficult or completely impracticable. After severe engagements with heavy casualties, sufficient hay or straw was frequently unobtainable, and in certain areas and at certain seasons there was none at all. A case is reported in which the field hospital bed sacks of an entire corps were emptied in order to supply floor cover for a train of its badly wounded men.[1] While as many as twenty men could be crowded onto the bare floor of a car, the space would accommodate only nine recumbents properly padded for comfort. That was not enough. Something had to be done to increase the capacity.

The boxcar of average size had an inside length of only twenty-five feet two inches and a width of seven feet eight inches. The interior height was about six feet nine inches at the center. What could be done to utilize the space above the floor? Ingenious soldiers and medical officers invented all sorts of devices to suspend beds. Hanging them in tiers directly from the roof resulted in the transmission of road shocks comparable to those suffered when the patient was laid on the bare floor. To overcome this difficulty tent poles were shaved down to give them the maximum of elasticity consistent with safety. They were laid crosswise beneath the roof by inserting the ends in auger holes bored in the side studs of the car. Ropes were then attached to the poles at the top and to the floor directly beneath. Two tiers of field stretchers were lashed between these rows of vertical ropes. This whole contrivance was intended to afford much relief from shock, but it was a slow and tedious process to rig, the stretchers swayed, the lashings slipped, the ropes stretched and, while the capacity of the car was doubled, the whole scheme proved impractical. Next a double row of stanchions replaced the vertical ropes. By placing them at intervals of seven feet and lashing on three tiers of litters, the capacity of the car was again enlarged, but at increased expense to comfort because road shocks were transmitted through the rigid stanchions.

The number of stretcher cases to be transported by rail increased rapidly. The ever-enlarging armies, the growing severity of the engagements, as well as a fuller appreciation of the advantages of removing disabled men from the combat areas to base hospitals far away, absorbed car space as fast as it could be created. The comfort of the well-padded floor was again sacrificed to capacity when lines of wooden bunks were built in tiers along the sides of the cars and the wounded laid on them like merchandise on shelves. The cycle had been completed from rigid bare floors through varying degrees of elasticity back to rigidity.

Dr. Elisha Harris of the Sanitary Commission came up with a novel invention which promised both capacity and comfort and immediately appealed to the imagination of all concerned. It involved the use of stanchions, but, instead of the tedious and unstable lashings, elastic rubber rings were hung on pins inserted in the stanchions at regular intervals. When the litter was carried in, its handles were passed through the rings, and with no other effort on the bearers' part, the patient lay suspended in all the resilience provided by the rubber connections between his bed and the body of the car. Boxcar doors were five feet wide. Dangerously wounded men could be moved on and off the train on their original hospital litters without being moved from one bed to another. This procedure seemed so logical and impressive that orders were issued to equip a large number of cars.

But Dr. Harris' idea proved a great disappointment. Excellent in theory, it turned out to be quite impractical in use. The reason was tersely stated by a prominent army surgeon: "The Harris car does not work well in practice. The elasticity of the rubber rings keeps the bed in constant vibration while the car is in motion. This annoys the patient who objects to riding in a capering bed."[2] Too much elasticity had been attained.

The boxcar, with or without rigging of one style or another, never was abandoned as a vehicle for the evacuation of disabled men. In emergencies, such as those met at Gettysburg and about Richmond, no other cars were available, and the capacity of the special cars later developed was all too often quite unequal to the need.

From the outset common passenger cars were preferred for the transport of wounded who could sit up, but they were often scarce when needed most. Until converted they were of no use for stretcher cases. The lack of passenger cars for dispersal was not so unfortunate as at first it might look. Since it was the car of greatest capacity and provided the most freedom to move about en route, the tendency of both soldiers and medical officers was to overcrowd it. Many men who should have been transported as recumbents suffered terribly during the period of travel and afterward, because of having to sit up in a passenger car during long trips to the hospitals. Even after the converted passenger car came into use, the aisles were often filled with men sitting on camp chairs, men who would have been far better off lying at full length in a rigged boxcar.

The first method of converting a passenger car for litter patients was to remove alternate seats on each side of the aisle and to erect a stanchion at the end of each remaining seat. A lower tier of beds was laid on the backs of the seats which remained in place and directly above them a second tier was provided by attaching litters to the stanchions. The Harris rubber-ring suspension was commonly employed, so that there was a great difference in comfort as between the man lucky enough to draw a "lower" and the comrade who drew the "capering bed" above him. These cars ranged from forty-five to fifty-five feet in length and, when converted, would accommodate an average of thirty bed patients in addition to the nonrecumbents crowded into the aisles.

Variations in converting passenger cars were soon as wide and numerous as those used in rigging the boxcar. Fitting out hospital cars became a popular project among benevolent societies, and each of them was likely to introduce its own pet scheme for adding to the comfort of "the poor boys." Often as not the innovations proved instruments of torture rather than contributions to comfort. Anyhow, from the day that first trainload of wounded from Wilson's Creek arrived in St. Louis, the removal of disabled soldiers by rail continued to interest practical-minded military men and railroad executives of the North as well as an emotionally stirred public.

In 1863 President Felton of the Philadelphia, Wilmington & Baltimore Railroad brought out a specially designed "hospital car" which was, indeed, a hospital on wheels. It was arranged with two tiers of beds much after the fashion of the later sleeping car except that the berths were portable, slipped in and out of their suspensions, and could be carried on and off the car through extra-wide end doors without removing the occupants. Each car carried fifty-one berths, and seats at the ends accommodated traveling nurses or attendants. There was a stove on which light food could be prepared, a locker, a water tank and a toilet. Designed as self-contained units for attachment to regular passenger trains, a goodly number of hospital cars were soon in operation about Baltimore, Harrisburg, Philadelphia and New York.

Reports in the Surgeon General's office indicate that regular operation of solid hospital trains was first instituted by the army in Tennessee. About the time Rosecrans pushed on from Murfreesborough toward Chattanooga in the autumn of 1863, the Medical Director of the Army of the Cumberland organized a regular train service exclusively to transport the disabled to the rear. Though not so well equipped as those of a later date, the trains made regular runs to Nashville and Louisville, and in reasonable comfort evacuated thousands of men who would otherwise have placed a heavy burden of care on the army. This service was especially effective in evacuating the overcrowded hospitals in the Chattanooga area when it became almost impossible to supply them even in the most meager fashion.[3]

A typical train was made up of converted passenger cars for recumbent cases, common passenger cars for those able to sit up, and a boxcar with a door cut in the end and rigged as a kitchen. Each train was in charge of a medical officer and carried a detail of nurses and cooks. The service so impressed General Thomas that, when he took command of the Army of the Cumberland, he assigned to the hospital trains the very best locomotives available and manned them with the most efficient crews. The smokestacks, cabs and tenders of the engines were painted a brilliant scarlet, and when running at night three red lanterns hung in a row beneath the headlights. On each side of the cars the words HOSPITAL TRAIN were painted in large letters.

There is no record of any train so marked being molested intentionally by the Confederates. On the contrary it is known that General Forrest gave strict orders to his troopers not to interfere with their operation, and to make every effort to keep a hospital train from running into a break in the track. It is said that John Morgan once stopped a train to ask whether there were enough food and stores aboard to care for the men until repairs could be made in the track. Answered in the affirmative, he ran the train into a siding, tore up the main-line track and remained on the scene to rifle and destroy five supply trains when they came to the break.

At no other time or place was the dispersal of sick and wounded by rail better organized or more conspicuous for its success than during the operations about Chattanooga and the subsequent Atlanta campaign. In 1864, as Sherman drove the Confederate army southward along the Western & Atlantic toward Atlanta, the hospital run was gradually extended to keep pace with him. Behind the lines temporary hospitals were set up at points on the railroad and disabled men collected there. At least once daily a hospital train of ten or twelve cars left the collection points loaded with men whose condition warranted their removal from the combat area. Even when Sherman reached Atlanta the trains were running regularly from the front to base hospitals, some of which were 472 miles away. The three connecting railroads which formed Sherman's long supply line were employed in the service. Dr. Barnum reported that he had supervised the transport of 20,472 patients over these lines with the loss of only one man en route.[4]

In both east and west equipment and facilities continued to develop until the end of the war. During the last eighteen months of fighting a great many individual and highly improved hospital cars were to be found attached to regular passenger and freight trains. A highly improved complete hospital train came into common use in the East. As a rule it was made up of ten patients' cars, a surgeon's car, a combination kitchen and dispensary car, and on long trips a boxcar carried in front for extra supplies and equipment.

The new patients' car was forty-five feet six inches long, eight feet six inches wide, and six feet eight inches from floor to roof. End doors were three and one-half feet wide to accommodate the passage of stretchers. Many features of the Felton car were incorporated. An important advantage of a train made up of such cars was the ability of surgeons, nurses and cooks to move from one end of it to the other while the train was running.

Usually carried at the rear end, the surgeon's car was fitted with a bed, toilet facilities, a desk, table, chairs, storage space for instruments and supplies, and a small dispensary—all so grouped as to leave open space in which to perform emergency operations.

The kitchen and dispensary car was divided into two compartments. The kitchen unit was equipped with a cooking stove, wood box, water cooler, icebox, a sink, table and pantry. Along one wall were cases of drawers and shelves, and it carried, of course, the necessary supply of cooking utensils. The dispensary unit had a heating stove in one corner with the indispensable wood box beside it. In the opposite corner was a toilet. Cases for supplies were ranged on one side, and opposite them was a couch. A table, a washbasin and chairs completed the standard furnishings. Room was left in which to work.

To appreciate the contribution of the railroads to the mobility and striking power of the Union armies through the removal of the disabled, one need only consider a few notable incidents in which large numbers of sick and wounded were involved. At the close of the Battle of Gettysburg the medical officers of the Army of the Potomac were confronted with the stupendous problem of caring for 20,344 wounded men of both armies, who lay on the field or staggered and crawled aimlessly about the neighborhood. Without rail facilities for them, Meade would have needed no other excuse for not pursuing Lee. He could not have carried them with him, and to abandon them would have been unthinkable. To care for them in the combat area would have either held his army immobile for a long time or dangerously reduced its fighting strength because of the large number of men necessarily detailed for their care and the vast amount of equipment diverted to their use.

It will be remembered, however, that during the battle Herman Haupt opened rail service to the very scene of the fighting and was bringing up hundreds of tons of supplies daily. By loading the returning supply trains with wounded, he evacuated 15,425 of them, within two weeks' time, to hospitals in York, Harrisburg, Philadelphia, Baltimore and New York.[5] Whatever other reasons there may have been for Meade's long delay in following up his victory, the encumberance of the wounded was not one of them. Their removal by rail becomes the more significant when it is considered that, while Meade waited, Lee's retreat to the Potomac was being fearfully hampered and confused by his efforts to carry back as many of his wounded as possible. With no railroad to serve him, his long train of horse-drawn vehicles, overloaded with wounded men, made slow, circuitous way through pouring rains over the muddy roads that wound through the hills between Gettysburg and the river.[6]

Another instance in point is found in connection with the battles of the Wilderness and Spottsylvania Court House. Because of better rail facilities, Grant's thousands of wounded were removed even more rapidly than their comrades had been evacuated from Gettysburg. From battlefield to comfortable housing in the hospitals at Alexandria, Washington, Baltimore and New York took very few days.[7] Relieved of their care, the army devoted its full strength to move forward to Petersburg.

Quite early in the war the effective use of railroads in

checking the spread of epidemic disease among soldiers was demonstrated in North Carolina. In the autumn of 1862 an epidemic of malarial fever broke out among troops concentrated at New Bern. It grew so serious that a large hospital was established at Carolina City on the coast, and forty miles of captured Confederate railroad were used to remove the infected patients from the camp to the hospital. Boxcars performed the service well if not too comfortably.[8]

Mention might be made also of how the railroads carried sick and wounded from camps and battlefields to ports for steamer transportation to distant hospitals. After Chancellorsville no less than 9,000 were evacuated from Fredericksburg over the R.,F.&P. to Aquia Creek. There they were placed aboard Potomac River steamers for Washington. During the Peninsular campaign the York River Railroad was much used for the same purpose. When Grant's army was massed about Petersburg, the military railroad he built to connect his widespread positions maintained a regular service to evacuate his disabled. A large base hospital was constructed at City Point on the James River. As the trains, loaded with provisions and supplies, came up from the transports, the disabled were placed aboard the empties for the return trip to City Point. Division field hospitals were evacuated with speed and regularity, and the army left free to concentrate on the enemy.

To evaluate accurately this whole railroad service is quite impossible; but the soldiers released by it from field-hospital details to active duty could be counted by brigades. Field transportation and maintenance were in large measure freed to the fighting forces. The huge demand for medical officers in the field was much reduced, and the necessity for carrying enormous quantities of medical supplies and field-hospital equipment with the moving troops was obviated. The problem of feeding in the field thousands on thousands of men unfit for duty was reduced. Because of better surgery and medical attention in base hospitals far from the combat areas, thousands of wounded were rehabilitated and returned as able soldiers to their commands. Sick men unable to survive the rigors of camp-hospital life recovered in the distant hospitals and went

back to fight again.[9] All this contributed mightily to soldier
and civilian morale.   Who shall say how the war-weary people
of the North would have reacted to Chancellorsville, Chickamauga, Spottsylvania or Cold Harbor had there been no railroads to carry their wounded sons from these bloody fields?

2

Unfortunately the records of the Confederate Surgeon
General's Office were destroyed by fire many years ago, and
insufficient material remains from which to develop a coherent
or authoritative story of Confederate railroad operation in the
dispersal of disabled men from combat areas. The fragmentary
accounts available and known facts concerning the railroads
in general make it abundantly clear that nothing comparable
to the service rendered by the railroads of the North was ever
developed by the roads of the Confederacy.

That for the armies of the West there was no organized
service of evacuation by rail seems the only conclusion to be
drawn from the long and comprehensive journal of Kate
Cumming of Mobile, Alabama.[10] Miss Cumming was a nurse
who entered the Corinth hospitals at the time the wounded
were being brought in from the Battle of Shiloh. She continued to serve in the field until the end of the war. Day by
day and often in much detail she set down the humor and the
horror, the tenderness and the travail she observed in her long
ministration to sick and mangled men, some of whom survived
in clean hospitals and many of whom died in unavoidable
filth. Frequently she wrote of scenes aboard trains or at railroad stations, and always these were scenes of misery. She
saw wounded men laid in windrows on station platforms, exposed to beating rain or broiling sun, hopelessly waiting to be
carried away by trains which never came. She rode on creeping cars packed in stench with sick and wounded who never
reached the end of their journey. Is it thinkable that if there
had been an organized service she would not have known
about it and have mentioned it?

Augustus Dickert recalled that after the First Battle of

Manassas, cars of the supply trains on the O.&A. were used to carry wounded back to Warrenton, Orange, Culpeper and Richmond.[11] In August 1864, during the fighting for Atlanta, Hood's chief of staff made a pitiful plea to Isaac Scott, president of the Macon & Western Railroad, for help in removing the wounded. Great suffering and loss of life were resulting from the delay of trains in transporting wounded men to the rear, and sometimes it took seventy hours to cover the 100 miles from Atlanta to Macon. Was there not some way in which this evil situation could be improved? Could not the road be so cleared as to give priority to trains bearing wounded?[12]

Again on September 5, from Lovejoy's Station, Hood wired Governor Brown stressing the need of cars to transport sick and wounded and asking the use of cars assigned to other duties.[13]

From such widely scattered instances one must conclude that while the railroads in some measure moved the disabled from the front, the service was slow, unorganized, haphazard and inadequate. The service of evacuation could have been no better than the service of supply. The dearth of engines and cars which plagued their supply service from the beginning must have been even more of a handicap to any service of dispersal. For lack of building facilities there could have been but few if any specially built or converted hospital cars. Only the common box and passenger cars could have been used and most of them were in a deplorable condition. The shortness of the lines, the lack of connecting track through cities and towns, the variations in gauge and the necessity to change cars frequently could not have failed to work great hardship in the handling of the severely wounded. The extreme roughness of the run-down and worn-out tracks must have added much to the miseries and mortality rate of recumbents subjected to the torture of crawling boxcar transportation. It will be remembered how in the first recorded instance when a Confederate railroad carried wounded, the men from Fort Donelson were laid on the bare floors of unheated boxcars and rode unattended in the dead of winter from Nashville to Chattanooga.

The lack of co-ordinated operation resulting from the government's policy of noninterference would have made impossible the regular running of hospital trains like those from Sherman's front to Nashville and Louisville during the Atlanta campaign. Awful as was the misery, filth and mortality of the front hospitals which Kate Cumming described, perhaps the suffering would have been as great, 'the death rate as high, if the wounded had lain long in the tangle of trains.

The record, though obscure, goes to show that the Confederate armies suffered far more than their adversaries from inadequate dispersal of disabled personnel. This grave trouble illustrates again how long and how deep was the shadow which the superiority of the Northern railroads cast across the hopes of the Confederacy.

CHAPTER XXIII

Disaster Overtakes Southern Policy

I

By the close of 1863 the North had disclosed not only the celerity with which it could move an entire army and its equipment from one theater of war to another, but also its steady ability to supply all its armies from distant bases. Its well-operated railroad system permitted the North to maintain its civil economy in reasonable health, despite the drain of war, and to sustain its production of goods for civil as well as military use.

Perhaps the situation of Chicago best illustrates how the railroads were serving the Union outside the combat zones. In 1863 Chicago was the world's largest primary market for horses, beef, pork and grain. Day after day trainloads of foodstuffs from the rich farmlands of the West were unloaded into the elevators and stockyards to be processed and loaded out again, much of it consigned to military depots for consumption by the Union armies. During 1863, the government bought 15,000 horses in Chicago and shipped them out by rail. From the mines along the Mississippi River great quantities of army lead came into Chicago for use in making munitions or for reshipment to Eastern manufacturers. By thousands of carloads, manufactured goods in wide variety rolled from the city destined for both military and civilian purposes. To handle this volume of business no less than ninety trains entered and left the city each day.[1]

Far from the battle areas, Chicago at the height of the war

was a growing city whose railroads made her a mighty factor in gathering, fabricating and distributing the equipment and subsistence which sustained the Union soldier in fighting trim. At the same time they made the city a ready market for the grain and livestock producers of the whole Northwest.

In the same way, the railroads carried raw materials to the manufacturing centers of the East, furnished them with coal, and hauled away their finished products to military depot and civilian store. Almost all railroads in the North were prosperous and enjoyed a rapidly increasing business. Engine and car shops were kept busy turning out new rolling stock, for which there was a constant demand. Serving Chicago, the Illinois Central ended 1863 with more than 3,000 freight cars, 500 of which had been acquired within the year. Other roads were as well or better supplied and amply able to meet the requests of the government for rolling stock to be transferred to the U. S. Military Railroads within the combat zones. There was plenty of money for maintenance and repairs. On the whole the railroads of the North were better off and far more effective in December 1863 than when called on to transport the first 75,000 troops to Washington in April 1861.

It nowhere appears that the Confederate Government in Richmond was prepared to evaluate this intelligence even though it was readily available to them through the Northern newspapers.

In its maintenance and operation of military railroads, the North had met with a great misfortune in the summer of 1863. Shortly after the Battle of Gettysburg, General Herman Haupt resigned his commission and quit the Army of the Potomac to return to Massachusetts and attend to his own large personal affairs. Governor Andrew seems solely to blame for this. For political reasons he had long wanted to keep Haupt out of Massachusetts. Badly misjudging his man, he thought he had found a way to stop his recurring visits by forcing the application of certain army regulations which had been waived in Haupt's case in order to procure his voluntary service. To Andrew's chagrin his scheme back-

fired. Haupt returned to Boston to devote his full time and
his prodigious energy to the enterprise the governor sought
to defeat.[2]

Luckily, most of the work for which he was most needed
had been done. His Construction Corps was a well-organized,
permanent and recognized unit prepared to carry on in his
absence under the able direction of Daniel McCallum. The
army had learned how tracks and bridges could be built and
trains operated under most adverse conditions. The emergencies of Aquia Creek, Second Manassas, Antietam and
Gettysburg were in the past. As a military railroad school-
master, he had graduated a goodly class of students who remembered their lessons to the end of the war.

To them he left a legacy of devices he and the members
of the Corps had invented between campaigns. There were
new types of interchangeable bridge trusses stock-piled and
prepared for transportation on flatcars; a simple ark on which
eight loaded freight cars could be transported by water from
one railroad to another without breaking bulk. Many times he
had seen attempts to burn railroad bridges fail for lack of time
or because the timbers were wet. To facilitate bridge wrecking he invented a special torpedo with which a single cavalryman could throw down a wooden bridge in less time than it
took to kindle an effective fire. He taught his men various
methods of straightening and returning to service rails which
the enemy had bent by the crude process of laying them
across piles of burning ties. He devised readily portable equipment with which a squad could speedily put a cold, corkscrew
twist into enemy rails and render them useless for anything
but scrap iron. In destruction he was no less an artist than in
construction.[3] All these devices and many more were developed and thoroughly tested without once interfering with
his job of providing transportation for the Army of the
Potomac. Some of them were never needed and saw no
practical use, but it was characteristic of Haupt that he was
always ready for any emergency. What might such a man
with like authority have done for the Confederacy?

2

Even more rapidly than the railroad strength of the North increased, that of the South declined. In the face of accumulating evidence that rail transportation was about to break down, the Davis administration made no change in policy. Whether his dogged persistence in leaving the railroads to their own resources was due to a curious blindness to their importance, baseless fear of invading state rights, or senseless resentment of advice from railroad executives, is not clear. From some of the correspondence one is led to suspect the last cause. It could not have been due to ignorance, for the record is filled with warnings. In any event, there was no modification of the attitude toward railroad labor, procurement of supplies, control of equipment or co-operation with management.

In February 1863 Captain John M. Robinson was sent to England on a purchasing expedition for the government. Learning of his mission, a small group of railroad executives persuaded the War Department to let him purchase for them certain desperately needed supplies and equipment, but Seddon's instructions to Robinson disclose with what meticulous care he was to avoid any semblance of relation between his mission for the government and his work for the railroads.[4] So helpful was his service to the railroads that when he was ordered home and assigned to line duty, P. V. Daniel of the R.,F.&P. protested and urged that he be sent back to England and kept there to purchase rails and supplies for all the roads in the Confederacy.[5] Promptly and curtly Seddon replied that such matters were the private affairs of the railroads; he would not officially intervene in things relating to their own business.[6] Daniel took him to task and again attempted to make clear that the interests of the government and of the railroads were identical, but nothing came of it and Robinson remained on duty in the field.[7]

No crisis seemed sufficient to move the government to

attempt more than temporary relief. As early as January 1863 the War Department adopted the expedient of taking unlaid rails from one road and sending them to another. For illustration, the chief engineer of the new Piedmont Railroad then under construction[8] was authorized to impress for his own use one half the unlaid iron belonging to the Western North Carolina, the Raleigh & Gaston, the Atlantic & North Carolina and the Virginia Central.[9] Roads which had been able through one means or another to procure some surplus of rails to make repairs and replacements were rewarded for their foresight and ingenuity by having it confiscated. How a policy could have been devised that would more certainly discourage initiative is difficult to imagine.

Soon this policy developed to the extent of taking up the tracks of roads which the Engineer Bureau regarded as of lesser importance and using the rails to repair those lines that seemed more essential. The government considered aid to the railroads beyond its power and province, but evidently claimed the power to ruin roads of its own selection.

Specific evidence of the futility of its policy, continually pointed out, seemed to have no effect. It had taken a full week to move 5,000 men by rail from Charleston to Wilmington, a distance of only 200 miles.[10] General G. W. Smith wrote to Seddon about the movement of two of his brigades by rail. Seddon said, "Railroads are an uncertain reliance; they will worry me out of my life yet I think." He gave President Whitford of the Atlantic & North Carolina credit for rendering all possible aid but said the trouble arose from the condition of the roads and their equipment.

A letter to Seddon in March from President L. E. Harvie of the Richmond & Danville and the Secretary's reply sharply point up the emergency and the failure of the government to foresee the inevitable consequences of its position. No road was more important to the maintenance of the Confederacy than the R.&D. Harvie explained that four or five miles of the road near Amelia Court House were unsafe and could not be repaired except by re-laying with new rails which he could not obtain. If run with great care and caution, the rest of the road might continue to operate though troubled with frequent accidents. They were trying hard to meet the government demands, but if the road was to survive, help was absolutely essential. The iron in use consisted of old flat bars which he would trade to the government yard for yard for T or H rails and pay the difference in weight if new rails could be supplied. He continued: "The constant increase of prices paid in the government shops for mechanics makes it impossible for us to procure and keep machinists enough to keep our rolling stock in repairs. That and deterioration of the track for want of materials presents a gloomy condition."[11] A short answer from the Chief of the Engineer Bureau gave Harvie the meager comfort that the removal of rails from the York River Railroad was then in progress and it was hoped some would soon be available from the Norfolk & Petersburg.[12] Under such a policy nothing could be done except tear up one railroad and use the iron to repair another. Perhaps Longstreet put his finger on the main source of collapse when he wrote General Hill: "Our people have been so accustomed to have all kinds of labor at their hands that they seem at a loss for resources when emergencies arise."[13]

Shortly after Lee returned from the Gettysburg campaign, he complained to Seddon that for all the animals attached to his army he was receiving only 1,000 bushels of grain per day, far from enough to bring his jaded artillery and cavalry horses up to condition. Could something be done? When the letter was referred to Northrop, he had nothing better to suggest than that passenger trains be temporarily stopped.[14]

In July Secretary Seddon appointed D. H. Kenny, an agent of the Engineer Bureau, to purchase or impress the rails and rolling stock belonging to the Alabama & Florida, the Gainesville Branch of the M.&O., the Cahaba, Marion & Greensboro and the Union Town & New Berne.[15] Gradually the short lines outside the combat zones were being put out of service, the operating mileage was shortened and the area from which supplies could be drawn steadily reduced. Later in the year a commission was created to collect and distribute railroad iron and metal scrap from all parts of the Confederacy. Another of its duties was to hold itself in readiness, when called on, to repair bridges and tracks injured or destroyed by the enemy. Recognizing the futility of this, General Gilmer of the Engineer Bureau explained to the War Department that the thing needed was a construction corps such as served the Federal Army.[16] As usual, nothing came of the suggestion.

When in May the Confederate Senate refused to approve the appointment of Wadley as supervisor of transportation, the job was given to Captain F. W. Sims. He was an able man and he tried hard to improve things, but with the limited authority given him he had little more success than his predecessor. In his efforts to persuade the government to detail mechanics for service in the railroad shops and to provide necessary railroad labor generally, he got nowhere. His vigorous exposé of vital faults in government policy fell on deaf ears.

Sims knew where the trouble lay and what would have to be done if rail transportation was not to go to smash. He set forth a reasoned analysis in a letter to Secretary Lawton in late October. All such measures as shifting rails and equipment from one road or area to another amounted to nothing more than temporary relief, did nothing toward solving the rail problem, and only postponed the end. He estimated there were at that time no less than fifty locomotives in the Confederacy standing useless for want of tires. These, he said, could be repaired either in Atlanta or Richmond except for the fact the government kept the shops fully occupied with other business and would not permit them to work on the engines. "The Government controls everything the railroads need but will not share it with them. So long as that policy continues, railroad service will continue to decline. There are no more patriotic people than railroad officials generally but if they are to serve they must have iron ore, permission for the foundries and rolling mills to do work for them and there must be a liberal system of detaching mechanics from the army."[17]

Of course the government was not wholly to blame for the sorry plight of the Confederate railroads at the end of 1863. No policy it might have adopted could have made the roads so efficient as those of the North. It was handicapped by the Union blockade, lack of manufacturing facilities, shortage of materials and man power. But intelligent and farsighted co-operation with the roads would have resulted in vastly improved rail transportation, when for the lack of it total defeat was in sight. The government could have aided the purchase of supplies and equipment abroad. Without perceptibly weakening its fighting strength in the field, it could have detached the necessary mechanics to work in the shops. At all times there were thousands of men, subject to conscription, whom it could have released at intervals to overcome the shortage of workmen. It could have listened to Lee and seen his logic when he asked that a hundred Negroes working on fortifications be sent for sixty days to cut engine wood for the Virginia Central.[18] Of what value are fortifications, asked Lee, if we have not the transportation to support the armies which man them?[19] Before long that question was to be answered at Petersburg and Richmond.

The government could have modified the monopoly it forced on the output of the foundries and metal-working plants and permitted them to help keep rolling stock at work. It could have set up a construction corps. It could have taken control of train operation for military purposes and saved wear, tear and waste while expediting the transportation of supplies to hungry men and animals. All these things it refused to do, although Secretary Seddon admitted "our railroads are daily growing less efficient and serviceable."

What influence moved the Confederate government to let its railroads die of starvation while demanding that they feed its armies? Was Jefferson Davis resentful and vindictive? Would he rather lose the war than be told what had to be done to win it? Did the coming of the war suddenly involve the government in a strange mechanical problem beyond its comprehension? Perhaps it would have been too much to expect of the lords of a cotton kingdom that they suddenly become masters of mechanized transportation.

In any event the wheels were turning ever more slowly on Confederate rails, and weeds were growing where miles of track had been. For the ragged men in gray there was food in plenty, but the withering arm of transportation daily grew less able to reach it and carry it to their hungry mouths. Meanwhile, the blue hurricane of 1864 was gathering along the Rapidan and the Te? nessee.

CHAPTER XXIV

Supplying Sherman in the Atlanta Campaign

I

It was the middle of March 1864. Hidden away in a secluded room of the Burnet Hotel in Cincinnati, two distinguished officers of the Union studied their maps and talked long and earnestly. They were alone. Through three years of war each of them had risen from comparative insignificance to such military prestige that to hold their conference unmolested they had to hide themselves from the crowd of their admirers. One was U. S. Grant, the new Lieutenant General in command of all the Federal armies, successor to George Washington and Winfield Scott, the only men ever to have held that position before him. The other was W. T. Sherman, the newly appointed head of the Military Division of the Mississippi and, save for the small Department of the Gulf, commander of all forces west of the Allegheny Mountains.

The people of the North were weary of the seemingly endless war and were threatening to oust the Lincoln administration at the election in November. Shiloh, Antietam, Vicksburg, Gettysburg and Chattanooga—all these victories were well enough, but the Confederacy was still alive and fighting viciously. When the people looked to Virginia they saw Lee's fearsome army resting snugly behind the Rapidan with Meade's Army of the Potomac halted in their front at about the same point from which Pope had been driven to terrible defeat. In fact, the two armies were within a day's march of the positions they occupied when Burnside failed at

Fredericksburg and Hooker was beaten at Chancellorsville.

When they looked to the West they were pleased to see their boats running on the Mississippi from St. Louis to the Gulf, but at Dalton, Georgia, only thirty-eight miles south of Chattanooga, the fierce army that had won the field at Chickamauga, though later defeated at Missionary Ridge, was confidently resting behind elaborate fortifications in mountainous country which lent itself admirably to defense. Northerners did not understand that the railroads of the South were almost worn out, that the money of the Confederacy was practically worthless and her economy at the point of collapse. They knew only that they were heartily tired of the war and wanted an end put to it. Perhaps it would be better to make peace.

Lincoln understood the threat and knew the danger. He knew also that victory or convincing progress toward it during the summer of 1864 was essential. He needed a fighting general who would take responsibility, could concentrate the power of Union arms, and press the many advantages of the North relentlessly. He had been much impressed by a plan lately submitted by Grant for a spring campaign designed to clear the middle South through the combined impact of his three armies of the Tennessee, the Ohio and the Cumberland. In Lincoln's opinion that was the sort of leadership needed not only in the West but for all the armies. He had sent for Grant to come to Washington. Shortly after he had arrived, the Federal armies had been put under a single commander, and immediately Sherman had been made Grant's successor in the West. So the two were now closeted in the Burnet House.

Twice in the early days of the war Grant had urged the speedy follow-up of great victories to smash the enemy's war potential in the West and force him to confine his operations to the territory east of the mountains; and twice he had been overridden by Halleck. In the winter of 1863 he had decided to try again. This time he proposed to concentrate his forces, strike straight south from Chattanooga, drive off or destroy the Confederate Army of Tennessee, push on to Atlanta and

Pontoon Bridge Being Constructed at Bridgeport, Tennessee to Replace the Railroad Bridge Well Wrecked by the Confederates

SOUTHSIDE RAILROAD AT APPOMATTOX STATION IN APRIL 1865
Note the worn track.

A RAPID REPAIR OF THE HIGH BRIDGE AT APPOMATTOX

open the way to Mobile. Because of the length of his supply line it would be a tough and risky campaign, but if successful would practically end the war in the West and put a Union army in the heart of the Confederacy. He had meant to start as soon as the roads were dry.

Grant had long deplored the lack of concerted action, the failure to exploit victories, the shifting of pressure from one front to another, and the consequent freedom of the enemy to apply his policy of the dispersed defensive.[1] As Grant conceived the struggle it was not one war in Virginia, another in Tennessee, another in Mississippi, and still another in the Carolinas. It was all one fight. He believed that with the North holding vast superiority in man power, arms and all the sinews of war, the road to victory lay through coordination of that strength against the vital organs of the Rebellion.[2]

When he found himself raised suddenly to supreme command he was at no loss for an over-all plan to bring the whole bloody business to an end. Basically the grand strategy was simple. Already he was preparing to throw the maximum Union weight in the West against Joe Johnston and Atlanta. In like manner, he would concentrate the power of Federal arms in the East against Lee and Richmond, and at the proper time both grand armies would strike simultaneously. Each would press the enemy so relentlessly he could not shift his strength from one arena to the other. To his friend Sherman he would turn over responsibility for the conduct of the campaign against Johnston and Atlanta, while he went to Virginia to devote his personal attention to Lee. How best to prepare for and co-ordinate their respective parts in this prodigious undertaking was what Grant and Sherman were talking over in the secluded hotel room. When they left it they were not to meet again until after Appomattox.

For the most part the campaign in Virginia would be a matter of outfighting and outmaneuvering Lee within a comparatively small area. But for Sherman to campaign successfully in Georgia would involve far more than generalship and a preponderance of men and guns. From the outset he confronted a staggering problem in logistics. The center of his concentration was 300 miles from his main base; with the first move his supply line would start growing longer and more tenuous. Whether a railroad could be relied on to supply a huge army so deep within hostile country was highly speculative. Never before had such a thing been attempted. The success of the grand strategy to end the war with victory depended on it.

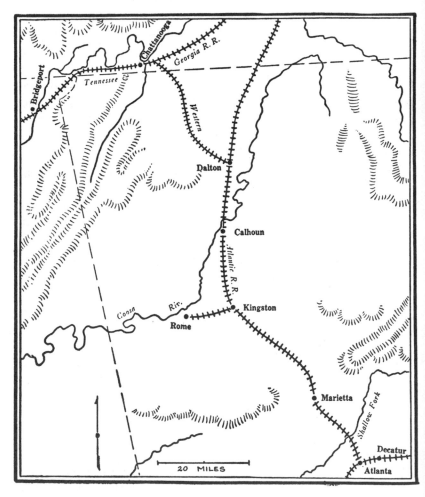

LINES FROM CHATTANOOGA TO ATLANTA

Obviously, Sherman's first responsibility was to see that everything was done that could be done to guarantee the maintenance and continuous operation of the "end-to-end railroads" which comprised the single-track line over which his supplies must come. Before being called to Washington, Grant had accomplished a great deal in that direction. Contemplating the tremendous task the Georgia campaign would impose upon the rail line, he had been disturbed by accumulating evidence that as general manager of railways within the Departments of the Cumberland, the Ohio and the Tennessee, J. B. Anderson lacked the initiative and the ability to measure up under pressure. As assistant to Tom Scott he had done well in earlier campaigns, but as general manager his work had drawn much criticism.

McCallum was brought out from Washington in January to inspect the roads under Anderson's management. To Stanton he reported the Nashville & Chattanooga in such bad condition that though trains were run at a speed of only eight miles an hour, accidents were frequent. It would be economy to lay the entire line with new rails. The supply of rolling stock on all the roads was pitifully short, and Anderson was doing nothing to build it up. In the area between Nashville and Knoxville there were more than 400 miles of track,[3] and McCallum could find only 70 locomotives and 600 freight cars. This supply, he said, was insufficient to permit the army to make any advance. He thought no less than 200 engines and 3,000 cars should be on hand "in this department," with more to be added as the army moved forward. For proof he cited the fact that on the 70 miles of track between Washington and Culpeper they had, in emergency, used 60 engines and 800 cars.

According to McCallum, Anderson's organization was decidedly defective and inefficient. There should be a construction corps of at least 1,000 men with a full supply of tools and materials at hand working under a competent director. There were no spare parts for engines or cars and nothing had been done to improve or expand the shops the enemy had left at Chattanooga.[4]

Important changes promptly followed his report. On February 4 Anderson was relieved and ordered by Stanton to turn over all records and equipment to McCallum.[5] This was the first step toward applying to the military railroads of the West the same methods of construction and operation employed for the Army of the Potomac. McCallum was placed in complete charge, with full authority to take any measures he deemed necessary to put the railroads in good running order.[6]

Between the nature and methods of McCallum and Haupt there was a very great difference—the difference between pride in a sharp pencil and disregard of muddy boots; between a fancy uniform and a sweaty shirt; between paper work at a table under a roof and toting a lantern through the dark of a rainy night. McCallum had lost his job as superintendent of the Erie Railroad because of his autocratic methods in dealing with employees. On the other hand Haupt's great success in managing men derived from his ability and willingness to "make a hand" alongside them on the toughest jobs he called on them to do. One wrote clear and adequate instructions. The other said "Follow me."

McCallum seemed to lack Haupt's astounding facility for anticipating requirements and grasping all angles of a railroad problem instantly. He planned soundly and well but was at his best when there were others on the scene to supervise performance. When he first took over at Nashville, he prepared a detailed analysis of a railroad organization for that area. Complete and admirable though it was, it smacked of the academic, of formality and strict administration. He had yet to learn the distinction between railroaders of the East and those of the West; between the disciplined, paper-collared soldiers of the Army of the Potomac and the grizzled, tobacco-chewing veterans who followed Sherman in long, slouchy strides and talked back when they felt like it.

But McCallum was not hungry for personal credit and knew how to select men able to execute his orders. By good luck some of Haupt's most trusted lieutenants were available,

heirs to his tremendous push and dogged determination. Mc-
Callum sent at once for Adna Anderson and W. W. Wright.
Both had rendered distinguished service in connection with
Haupt's work in Virginia, Maryland and Pennsylvania.
Anderson was appointed general superintendent of transporta-
tion and maintenance, and Wright was made chief engineer of
construction in the military division of the Mississippi. With
Wright's appointment went complete control of the Con-
struction Corps.[7]

Under McCallum's administration, improvements came
rapidly. Rolling stock began to accumulate; rails, tools and
machinery were procured; blockhouses and stockades were
built for defense of tunnels and important bridges, and strong
guards were stationed at intervals beside the long, long line.
This much Grant had accomplished in preparation for the
Georgia campaign before turning his attention to Lee in
Virginia.

All of Sherman's former lack of self-confidence, his
aversion to high independent command and his fear lest
political interference lose the war promptly disappeared.
Now there was a chance to end it in the only way it could
be won. Into his part of the grand plan he plunged with the
enthusiasm of a youth, the wisdom of a sage, the cunning of
an Indian and the foresight of a prophet. To do the fighting
he had Thomas, Schofield and McPherson. To feed, munition
and clothe their men, he had McCallum, Anderson and
Wright, who would first apply themselves to filling his
advance depots. Sherman would permit no interference with
this task. An order required that all trains must be devoted
exclusively to moving military personnel and supplies. Strict
enforcement set off an explosion of protest from sutlers,
newspapers, merchants and civil dignitaries who wished to
shuttle back and forth to the army camps. Especially violent
protests came from the loyal residents of east Tennessee who
had been living on what the railroads brought them. When
the reverberations from this explosion reached Washington,
President Lincoln suggested a modification or revocation of

the order. But Sherman replied that the roads couldn't take
care of both army and civilians, and if either must be slighted
it should not be the army.

Then he told the people of east Tennessee to bring home
supplies from Kentucky by wagon train and drive in their
beef cattle on the hoof. He was ordering all military posts
within thirty miles of Nashville to supply themselves in this
way, and they could do the same voluntarily. This advice
made the complaints of the disgruntled all the louder, but they
were dealing with a man of red hair and whiskers who meant
to go to Atlanta and knew the size of the order he had taken.
Neither grade, politics nor civil authority was going to
interfere with the operation of that single-track line on which
he must rely. There were two short supplemental lines that
might lighten the load if necessary or serve for a time as
detours if the main line should be broken, but they could be
considered only as auxiliaries. One was the road lately completed by General Dodge between Nashville and Decatur to
connect with the M.&C. east of Stevenson. The other was a
newly built military road running westward from Nashville
to wharves on the Tennessee River at Johnsonville. Though
they could help as far as Stevenson, from Stevenson to Chattanooga there was only the single-track line, with no supplementary route.

Before the end of April, Quartermaster General Meigs reported enough food accumulated at Nashville to take care
of 200,000 men for four months, and sufficient grain to feed
50,000 animals through the rest of the year. The next job
was to fill the forward depots out of this store.[8] On the
average, one new engine and fifteen new cars were coming in
every day to help move these supplies.[9]

The railroad guard was heavily reinforced and its personnel
told to defend their sections at all hazards.[10] A string of
blockhouses was built to protect the new line between Nashville and Decatur. That part of the Western & Atlantic which
Johnston had destroyed in his retreat to Dalton was repaired
as far as Ringgold. Spring had come and the roads were dry.
Men were in good health, horses were fat and locomotive

whistles were screaming "Get on-n-n with it." It would not be long now. Sherman was ready.

After the fashion of modern synchronized offensive, a telegram from Grant ordered the "jump-off" on May 4. This was the sort of military precision, orderly conduct, considered purpose and determined aggressiveness to rouse Sherman to the full height of his military stature. No more politicians! No more sacrifice of victory to petty jealousies in military rank and civilian scheming for commercial gain!

With quick step and bristling whiskers Sherman stepped out on May 4 to challenge Joseph E. Johnston's grip on the middle South. With him were 98,797 men and 254 guns.[11] So far as he was concerned, the "Johnnies" were through calling the tune. Johnston expected Sherman to attack his well-fortified positions on Rocky Face Ridge and in front of Dalton. Sherman had no intention of doing any such thing. Dalton was tenable only as long as Johnston held the railroad in his rear. Why fight him there? Thomas would demonstrate in front while McPherson, screened by Rocky Face Ridge, hurried southward to strike the railroad at Resaca, eighteen miles behind the fortified position. When he was discovered there, Johnston let go Dalton and raced back to defend Resaca and his life line of rail. In ten days Sherman had taken a first long step toward Atlanta.

After three days of hard fighting, Johnston, finding himself unable to hold Resaca, fell back successively to Calhoun, Adairsville and Cassville, destroying the railroad as he went. In the valley between the Oostenaula and Etowah rivers, forty miles south of Dalton, he had been joined by Polk's corps. His total force now was near 65,000. At Cassville he paused to throw up earthworks. By pontoon, ferry and ford, Sherman crossed the Oostenaula at Resaca, and sent McPherson hurrying on toward Kingston on the Etowah, where the Rome branch of the railroad joined the main stem. When Sherman heard that McPherson had reached Kingston, he called a halt to allow Wright time to repair the railroad so that supplies could keep up with the advance.

The bridge across the Oostenaula at Resaca had been

burned but in Wright's Construction Corps, now composed of 2,000 men, was Haupt's master bridge builder and good right hand, E. C. Smeed. Smeed had been at Ackakeek, Potomac Creek, Bull Run, and Rappahannock and many another stream over which temporary railroad bridges had been flung wtih incredible speed. He, too, was an inventive genius, tireless and with a passion for getting things done no matter what. In three days he bridged the Oostenaula, and on May 24 loaded trains were running to Kingston.[12]

Sherman was now ready to move on. When he came to Cassville, Johnston was gone. He had crossed the Etowah and taken position behind Allatoona Mountain. Again, as at Dalton, Sherman refused to fight on a field selected by the Confederates and started another flanking movement to reach the railroad in Johnston's rear. Moving by the right flank he set out in the direction of Dallas. Johnston had to come out of his natural fortress at Allatoona to meet him or risk a Federal lodgment on the railroad somewhere above Marietta. Again Sherman's stratagem was successful. Swinging out from Allatoona to their left, the Confederates threw themselves across his path at New Hope Church, but, as at Resaca, were unable to hold. After a week of fierce struggle among the rugged hills and over the densely wooded terrain between Dallas and Acworth, Johnston again moved back, this time to prearranged fortifications on three steep hills known as Kenesaw, Pine and Lost mountains, some eight miles north of Marietta.

Astride the railroad, Sherman pushed up to Big Shanty where he had a good view of the enemy works on Kenesaw Mountain.[13] Again it was time to halt and let Wright bring up McCallum's locomotives, whose screaming whistles were the Yanks' defiant reply to the Rebel yell. Smeed got the Etowah River bridge at Kingston replaced by June 11. The track was repaired to the very foot of Kenesaw, and a train loaded with rations rolled up to Big Shanty, the station at which the Andrews raiders had stolen the General. Just ahead and within range of enemy guns stood an undamaged water tank. As though in payment of his respect to Andrews' memory, the engineer uncoupled his engine and started forward toward the tank. When guns high up on the slope opened fire on him, the contemptuous engineer answered each shot with a blast of his whistle, drove on, helped himself to a supply of Confederate water and returned to his train unharmed. As he coupled up to return to Kingston for another load of provisions, the shriek of his whistle was blanketed by the soldiers' cheers.[14]

Sherman was satisfied that it would take a hostile army behind him to stop his supplies for long; the burning of bridges and breaking of track by minor cavalry and guerrilla raids could cause only short delays in train operation.[15] He knew raids inevitable. He told Anderson to be prepared to lose "a half-dozen or more trains every month" because of them.[16] All the same, he ordered various minor expeditions and diversions to keep enemy cavalry as far as possible from the line of communications.[17]

So far, the grand strategy was working out precisely. Sherman must maintain the pressure on Johnston as relentlessly as Grant was exerting it on Lee. One thing gave him grave concern. He was now almost 100 miles from Chattanooga, 252 miles from Nashville, and 435 miles from Louisville. The long single track was a slender stem on which to hang success until he could reach Atlanta. Except for one man he had no fear of making it stand up. Forrest! Twice strong detachments had gone into Mississippi to hunt him down and twice this pestiferous cavalry genius had sent them scurrying back to Memphis.[18] If Forrest got to his supply line, especially if he should strike it below the great depots in Nashville, the campaign against Johnston might well come to an abrupt, inglorious end.

The hard marching and almost continuous fighting throughout May had consumed subsistence at a terrific rate. Sherman's reserves at Chattanooga were near exhaustion. From Nashville to the front it took the full capacity of the railroad to meet the daily requirements of his 100,000 men and 35,000 animals. There was little chance to accumulate a surplus nearer than Nashville.[19] Sherman had good reason to worry about Forrest.

Since Sherman's first move, Forrest had been saying in effect, "Give me 2,000 picked men and a battery and I'll stop him as I did Grant before Vicksburg and Buell before Chattanooga."[20] Now that the tide was running strongly against Johnston, Forrest's proposal gained advocates from the military and civilians. Confederate Senator Gustavus A. Henry of Tennessee spoke the mind of many a strong Confederate when he asked Secretary Seddon why Forrest's whole force was not sent to camp on Sherman's supply line.[21]

Unknown to Sherman, he had an ally in the Confederate President. Jefferson Davis was having his last fling with his pet policy of the "dispersed defensive" and, encouraged by Bragg, steadily refused to let Forrest leave Mississippi. So, while Sherman worried and Forrest lunged against the leash which held him off Sherman's extended line, Davis and Bragg huddled over the corpse of the long-dead Mississippi defense and let Sherman press on toward Atlanta.

A blazing fight failed to dislodge Johnston from Kenesaw Mountain. But before it ended, Sherman had another flanking movement under way, and Schofield's army with Stoneman's cavalry was swinging around the right flank again, opposite Marietta, and headed toward the Chattahoochee River. Once more Johnston's railroad was threatened. He could come off Kenesaw and assault Thomas in his front, or he could let Kenesaw go entirely and fall back to keep Schofield off the railroad. Sherman was all excitement. Time after time the wily "Old Gray Fox" had slipped out of his grasp, but now he was trapped. Sherman figured it this way. Back of Johnston lay the broad and deep Chattahoochee, and a retreat across it would be slow and difficult. If he came out to assault the strongly entrenched center, Thomas and Mc-Pherson would defeat him. Schofield would be on the railroad in his rear, and between them they would surely crush him. If he fell back through Marietta, they would press him to the river and cut him to pieces in the crossing.

It proved less simple than that. Sherman did not know his opponent had prepared for precisely this contingency.[22] By his orders strong earthworks had been dug on both sides of the river, and Johnston went behind them. He had lost another stretch of railroad, but he was undefeated and little worse off from the fighting.

Still unaware of the Confederate defense works at the river, Sherman was stamping with anger because the pursuit had not been pressed with the vigor he had ordered.[23] That was July 3, and at nightfall he was at Smyrna, six miles below Marietta. Then, as he later described the event, "we celebrated our Fourth of July by a noisy but not a desperate battle designed chiefly to hold the enemy there till General McPherson and Schofield could get well into position below him near the Chattahoochee crossings."[24] Next morning the enemy was gone and the pursuit had to be taken up again.

Hearing gunfire in the neighborhood of the long railroad bridge, Sherman assumed that Thomas had engaged the enemy rear guard fighting to cover Johnston's crossing. In a personal reconnaissance from high ground he found himself looking down on "one of the strongest pieces of field fortification I ever saw."[25] Within the bridgehead and abatis and strong redoubts was the gray army he had thought to grind up in confusion on the riverbanks.

From the hill Sherman could see the buildings in Atlanta, nine miles away.[26] Exactly two months out from Dalton, he was at last in sight of his secondary objective; but the primary one, the destruction of Johnston's army, was by no means accomplished. He reasoned that both purposes might be served in one final, decisive action. Instead of attacking Johnston in his new position, he would flank him out of it and force him to retire to the outer defenses of the city. His defeat there would result in the fall of Atlanta, and with Atlanta in possession of the Federals, Johnston's strength would be gone.

His plan began to take shape. With his superior numbers he could threaten from a much longer line along the riverbank than Johnston could defend. His orders went out. Thomas was set to keep up a show of force at the center without bringing on a battle. Schofield and McPherson stretched their divisions thinly six miles below and six miles above the railroad bridge, seeking out preferred spots at which to cross the river. A cavalry force of 2,000 at Decatur, Alabama, was to ride for Opelika, smash the West Point Railroad and so shut off Atlanta's communication with Mississippi and Alabama.

On July 9 Sherman's flanking troops crossed the Chattahoochee. The same night Johnston evacuated the riverbanks, burned the railroad bridge and started his retreat to Peach Tree Creek where he meant to make his fight in defense of Atlanta. Davis, ever critical of Johnston and exasperated by his Fabian tactics, was convinced the trouble lay with the commander. The President wanted a battle fought to a finish. He replaced Johnston with General John B. Hood, who had been a corps commander throughout the campaign and who was given to that sort of fighting.

Sherman was much encouraged by news of the change. He had always considered Johnston one of America's great soldiers, and this opinion had been fortified in a two-month campaign. He had fought and maneuvered against Johnston with vastly superior numbers and equipment, yet had not been able to come to grips with him. Johnston's army was still intact—a constant threat if Sherman slipped for an instant. The young and impetuous Hood would come out to fight, and that was precisely what Sherman wanted.

He had not long to wait. On July 20 Hood took the gamble Johnston had refused. He lost and was driven into the defense works which encircled Atlanta. One sally after another brought him nothing except a preponderance of losses. He was trapped and besieged.

The Georgia Railroad came into Atlanta from the east. McPherson's men had ripped out thirty miles of it toward Augusta,[27] so it was not a factor. The Macon & Western Central, commonly known as the "Macon Line," came up from the southeast, and to the southwest the Atlanta & West Point provided a connection at Opelika with the east-west line through Montgomery. From East Point, six miles south of Atlanta, both of the last two roads came into the city over the same track. Sherman did not overlook that Hood's army as well as the population of the city was now dependent on them. No use wasting lives assaulting enemy defenses when by cutting the railroads Sherman would force Hood to choose between capitulation, as Pemberton had done at Vicksburg, and seeking an avenue of escape.

Wright was instructed to push the supply line forward from the Chattahoochee to the Federal front at the very outskirts of Atlanta. He had to solve at once the most formidable engineering problem with which the Construction Corps had yet been confronted. Replacing railroad bridges across creeks and gullies had become routine business, but building a bridge over the Chattahoochee was far from routine. Smeed made his calculations: the structure must be 780 feet long and 90 feet high, almost twice as long as the Potomac Creek bridge he had helped Haupt build in 1862. But differences in circumstances should offset the greater magnitude of the job. He had learned much from experience in improvising methods. He had abundant tools and rigging, and whereas Haupt had had to rely on unskilled soldiers, Smeed had a large number of corps members trained in this sort of work.

Endowed with many of the characteristics that had enabled his mentor to perform miracles, Smeed tackled the big task with confidence and courage. Using timber cut from the stump in the near-by woods and the remnants of stone piers which the Rebs had neglected to demolish, he completed the bridge in four and a half days.[28] Haupt called the building of the Chattahoochee bridge "the greatest feat of the kind that the world has ever seen."[29] In any event, it was another feat of railroad construction such as the South was never able to match. So fabulous were the reports on these bridges considered by European military engineers that, in 1868, the British Association for the Advancement of Science invited Haupt to attend its meeting and tell the facts about them.[30]

The Western & Atlantic, which had served since 1862 as the heart line of the gray armies around Chattanooga, was in

Federal hands at the close of July, and heavily loaded trains
from Nashville were arriving daily at Sherman's camps.[31] To
make his siege more effective he sent two strong cavalry detachments around Atlanta to cut the two active railroads.
General Stoneman commanded one column, General McCook
the other. Both lost sight of the main objective, got into
trouble and, although doing much damage to enemy transportation, failed to accomplish what Sherman wanted done.

The western cavalryman would ride "hell for leather" on
any mysterious raid that promised excitement or adventure.
If he found railroad property that could be burned or shot
to pieces he could be depended on, but when it came to dis-
mounting for the dull, backbreaking work of tearing up track
he was noted for his skill in avoidance.

McCook crossed the West Point, doing little harm, and
rode on to Lovejoy's Station on the Macon, where he expected
to join Stoneman. Not finding Stoneman there, he tore up
two miles of track, burned two trains of cars, cut down five
miles of telegraph wire, and then turned his attention to
shooting up an enemy wagon train. Suddenly he found himself surrounded. He had to fight his way out of the trap and
scoot for the Federal lines.[32]

Stoneman had ridden down the Ocmulgee River to where
it crossed the railroad leading from Macon to Savannah.
There he wrecked seventeen locomotives and more than a
hundred cars before moving on to burn the bridge across the
Oconee.[33] He, too, encountered enemy troops, and he wound
up his expedition as a prisoner. To be sure, the Confederates
could ill afford to lose so many engines and cars, but except
for a few hours' repair work, the line had not suffered.
Atlanta and Hood were no worse off for the raids.

Satisfied he could not accomplish his purpose with cavalry
alone, Sherman attacked his problem from a different angle.
He sent Slocum's corps back to occupy the abandoned Confederate works at the Chattahoochee and defend his communications. Then he "cut loose with the balance to make a
circle of desolation around Atlanta."[34] When he reached the
West Point Railroad he ripped up great lengths of track,

burned the ties and heated the rails and twisted them beyond hope of restoration. Deep cuts were filled with trees, brush and earth. Live shells were scattered through the fill, to explode on any attempt to remove the debris.[35]

Swinging to the left, he struck the Macon road in a long line extending from Rough and Ready to Jonesboro and treated it after the same fashion. It was the last day of August. Atlanta was isolated. In the night Sherman listened to the boom of heavy explosions coming from the direction of the city, twenty miles to the north. Hood was destroying his magazines. The jig was up.

Next morning Hardee's Confederate corps crashed into the Federal lines and in a violent and bloody battle escaped toward Macon. Hood left the city with the remainder of his forces, and on September 2 Sherman occupied Atlanta. The campaign was over at last. The long railroad had stood the test and had helped to win the victory so desperately needed to insure the re-election of Lincoln. The railroads had sustained the victor, and the loss of them had ended the resistance of the vanquished.

How was Grant doing against Lee?

Soon after Sherman captured Atlanta, the railroads in the Confederate states west of the mountains lost importance to the Federals. Since they were no longer needed as Union supply lines, why go to great pains to keep them in operating condition? Worn out and broken in many places, they were in miserable shape during the final months of the war. Where they were in Southern hands they were no better. The Confederates lacked the money, man power and material to restore them to dependable service. In the last frantic effort to keep the rebellion alive in Alabama, Mississippi and Tennessee, they resorted to all manner of devices by which scraps of track and rolling stock might be turned to advantage. Stretches of track were torn up at one place and rails used to mend a gap at another. Wherever an engine or a car could be found it was put to work on some section of track that remained intact. Sometimes, where no engine was available, mule teams hauled single cars from one break to another. Of these heroic efforts endless stories might be told, but after all they failed to influence the course of the war.

Through three years of fighting in Kentucky, Tennessee, Mississippi, Alabama and Georgia, the courses of campaigns had followed the lines of the railroad. For possession of important junctions the fiercest battles had been fought. Now, as the war drew to its close, no such thing as an operating rail system remained in the Western theater of operations. Only one more major battle was to be fought there. It, too, was the culmination of a campaign against a railroad.

CHAPTER XXV

THE ROADS IN LEE'S DEFENSE OF RICHMOND

I

Grant was asking himself what maneuver would put him between Lee and Richmond, shut off Lee's supplies and reinforcements, and bring him to battle on the exhausted terrain of northern Virginia. This question was much on his mind when he returned from his conference with Sherman in Cincinnati.

He had two possibilities from which to choose. Should he move by his right, attempt to pass between Lee's left and the Blue Ridge Mountains, then turn east to get in his rear? Or should he go toward the left and try to cross the enemy right by passing through the densely wooded country just west of Fredericksburg? Each route offered its advantages, and each presented its difficulties. The major problem was how to provide a supply line. This factor ultimately determined the route to be followed, and it stamped on American history the names of gory battlefields never to be forgotten—the Wilderness, Spottsylvania and Cold Harbor.

As long as the Army of the Potomac remained in its camps about Culpeper, there was no supply problem. In addition to a large reserve already on hand, the Northern railroad system maintained an adequate and uninterrupted flow to the eastern seaboard. The depots about Washington and Alexandria were full, and the Orange & Alexandria Railroad carried them to Culpeper. But the Confederates controlled all of the railroads south of Culpeper. If Grant moved by the right he would have to rely solely on such munitions, rations and forage as the army could carry with it. The prospect was not inviting. By using the alternative route to the left he could establish bases on the navigable rivers which reached deep into Virginia on Lee's right and rear. Through the use of wagon trains he could assure himself of adequate water-borne supplies. He could forget the Orange & Alexandria and rid himself of the danger of having his big artery cut by the enemy. This was the course he decided to take.[1]

So, while Sherman was collecting locomotives and cars, making extensive improvements of tracks, building block-houses and posting railway guards, Grant was gathering horses, mules and wagons by the thousands and setting up the greatest wagon-train service of the war. His plan involved crossing the Rapidan at two fords, six miles apart, and this might well provoke a stiff fight if Lee chose to contest it. During the period of preparation Burnside's corps was left in the Warrenton neighborhood to guard the Orange & Alexandria over which the army was drawing its subsistence. As a matter of precaution he was to remain there until the river crossings had been accomplished.

Exactly on schedule as arranged with Sherman, Grant marched out from his Culpeper camps on May 4 and suc-ceeded in getting over the Rapidan unopposed. Once safely across, he ordered Burnside to follow and join the main body of the army as quickly as possible.[2] In railroad parlance this was like calling in the flagman; never again was the Army of the Potomac to depend on a railroad supply line. On both fronts the grand strategy was under way.

By narrow and crooked roads Grant's route led through that tangled country west of Fredericksburg known as the Wilderness. It crossed three much better roads, which led directly to Lee's camps in the vicinity of Orange Court House. As they marched through the gloomy and foreboding woods and brush, many a soldier of the Army of the Potomac must have been stirred by bitter memories. Those shot-torn trees, that shell-scarred earth, those crumbling earthworks marked spots where thousands of their comrades had fallen in the Battle of Chancellorsville last May.

Rebel lead began to snip twigs from the bushes and thud into blue-clad bodies. Lee had hurried by the better roads to attack the Federal columns while they were engulfed in the forest's green maze. For two days and much of the corresponding nights the battle raged through the thickets and among the trees. For the first time Grant and Lee were facing each other in a desperate duel. Back and forth the lines bellied and swayed, broke and reformed. The slaughter was appalling. The forest was on fire and wounded men shrieked for succor from the flames. This was the Battle of the Wilderness.

Grant knew by nightfall of May 7 that this was not the place to destroy Lee's army. Already he had lost 17,000 men in killed, wounded and missing.[3] He decided to break off the battle and make another effort to get between Lee and Richmond before renewing the fight. A few miles to the south at Spottsylvania Court House two roads crossed. One of them would be Lee's most likely route if he should decide to head for the Confederate capital. Grant reasoned that he could stealthily sideslip the enemy lines under cover of darkness and reach Spottsylvania by daybreak.[4]

Although he had more than 100,000 men to feed and was using up ammunition at a terrific rate, there was no problem of supply. South of the Rapidan he had more than 4,000 wagons[5]—a train capable of maintaining a nose-to-tail-gate line between his front and Fredericksburg, with no team obliged to work more than one day in three.

The movement from the Wilderness was skillfully executed, and except for one thing might have been a complete success. Lee, master diagnostician, had divined Grant's purpose and was at Spottsylvania to receive him. Once more the two armies were locked in ghastly battle. Back and forth in indecisive struggle they charged and countercharged while thousands fell. Trench positions were blasted by artillery. Guns were taken, turned upon the enemy, recaptured and turned again. Flanks were circled and positions changed. Day after day the fight went on, with an occasional respite on the right and now and then a lull on the left. Protruding into the Union line, the enemy held a narrow salient which came to be known historically as the "Bloody Angle." At the tip of the salient the fighting blazed continuously through night and day. So fierce was the fire that a tree eighteen inches in diameter which stood a few feet outside the works had its trunk cut away by bullets and it fell across the parapet.

This was the memorable battle of Spottsylvania Court House. Starting in the morning of May 8, it lasted until the evening of the eighteenth and when it ended there was victory for neither Blue nor Gray. What next?

From the time he left the Rapidan, Grant had been annoyed by Jeb Stuart's cavalry constantly jabbing at his flanks. To rid himself of this nuisance, and to harass Lee's rail line he sent Sheridan's cavalry to raid in the enemy rear.[6] Sheridan started May 9 on a course directly toward Richmond and at first met little opposition. He reached the Virginia Central Railroad at Beaver Dam Station the following afternoon.[7] It was lucky timing. At Beaver Dam he intercepted two trains. After wrecking the engines and cars, he took time to burn the depot, containing large quantities of rations and medicines for the Rebel army, tear up the track and cut the telegraph wires for a considerable distance in both directions.[8] Soon he was across the South Anna a few miles southwest of Hanover Junction. He sent a detachment to break the R.,F.&P. and tear down the telegraph wires paralleling the track.[9]

Save by courier, Richmond for the moment was completely cut off from Lee. The menace of Sheridan's large force loose below the river aroused Confederate fears and achieved the main object of the raid. Jeb Stuart's cavalry pulled away from Grant's flank and followed Sheridan, trying to divine his intention. Finally Stuart decided he must be headed off, and made a long, exhausting ride to get around him and in his path. Stuart made his stand at Yellow Tavern, six miles out from Richmond. In a furious conflict "the eyes of Lee's army" went out. With a pistol bullet through his abdomen the gallant thirty-one-year-old Jeb Stuart toppled from his horse and soon was dead.[10]

Sheridan rode on. He was at the door of the Rebel capital and might have gone in; but there was no point in that. If he had entered the city he could not have stayed.[11] He had performed his mission. Turning east, he rode across Mc-Clellan's old battlefields on the Peninsula, and after an absence of sixteen days came safely to rejoin Grant for further assignment. Lee could and did repair the damage done to his railroads and telegraph, but for Stuart he had no replacement.

In the meantime Grant, too, had taken some hard knocks. After the firing had ceased at Spottsylvania, Grant waited two days for the enemy to come out of his trenches and renew the fight. When he refused, the stubborn Federal commander who had notified Lincoln he would "fight it out on this line if it takes all summer," decided to try another maneuver—another sideslip to the left in a third attempt to get between Lee and Richmond. It failed. When he got to the North Anna he found Lee there ahead of him, formidably set behind the river.

Two miles south of the river and roughly following its course ran the Virginia Central Railroad, Lee's communication with the Shenandoah Valley. While unable to dislodge Lee from his new position, Grant did get one thing of consequence done. He sent a strong force up the river to Jericho Mills Ford where it crossed to the south bank and attacked Lee's left flank. In a day of fierce fighting it reached and crossed the railroad.[12] Though it did not succeed in turning the Confederate flank, on May 25 this column set about a thorough and systematic destruction of the railway. Miles of the road so important to Lee were completely ripped out, and once more he was cut off from subsistence out of the Shenandoah.[13] Some five miles down the North Anna, near Hanover Junction, Grant had thrown another force across. He was now in the difficult position of having both his right and left south of the river with his center unable to cross. He says in his *Memoirs:* "But we could do nothing where we were unless Lee would assume the offensive. I determined, therefore, to draw out of our present position and make one more effort to get between him and Richmond."[14]

He crossed the R.,F.&P. above Hanover Junction and started the fourth of his sideslipping movements by the left flank. It was unnecessary to maintain the R.,F.&P. as a supply line. His combination water-borne and wagon-train supply system was working perfectly. He directed the War Department to transfer his base to White House on the Pamunkey River toward which he would be moving.[15] Not much space was left within which to maneuver. In two days Lee could, if he chose, be within the defenses of Richmond. It followed, therefore, if Grant was to intercept him he must proceed by the most direct route available. By marching southeastward down the Pamunkey to Hanover Town he would be within fifteen miles of Richmond, could cross the river and utilize a number of roads leading westward toward the Confederate rear. This seemed to offer the best prospect and soon he was on the move. But there was no turning west at Hanover Town. Again he found Lee first on the ground. Taking advantage of the shorter interior line, Lee had cut across to head the Federals off.

At Cold Harbor he brought Grant to battle. From May 31 to June 3 the two armies were locked in such deadly conflict as to overshadow in ferocity and slaughter anything that had gone before. Into the sickening abattoir Grant threw division after division in desperate attempts to finish off Lee's Army of Northern Virginia. Against his best the Confederate veterans returned blow for blow, determined that the Yankees should not pass. In the end, as at the Wilderness, Spottsylvania and the North Anna, neither emerged as victors. Though to gain a drawn battle Lee had suffered casualties he was less able than Grant to afford, Grant had lost his last chance to get between Lee and Richmond. And in another way Lee gained a very substantial advantage. Besides thwarting the Federal effort, he had preserved the all-important railroad loop formed by the R.,F.&P. and the Virginia Central between Richmond and Hanover Junction. Grant was now well to the east of that section of the Virginia Central which he had wrecked and which Lee could repair to re-establish communications with the Shenandoah. Had Grant succeeded in turning west from Hanover Town, both railroads would have been ruined, and Richmond as well as the Confederate army cut off altogether from western Virginia. Perhaps the stalling off of such a disaster was enough to justify a Confederate claim of victory at Cold Harbor.

Precisely as Sherman made steady progress toward Atlanta but was balked in his primary objective of intercepting and destroying Johnston, Grant was making steady progress toward Richmond but could not defeat or destroy Lee. Just as Sherman had to resort to the siege of Atlanta, Grant had to turn to his secondary objective of taking Richmond. The first phase of the campaign was over.

2

Back in the spring on the Confederate side, Lee had waited through April for the Federal offensive which he expected from across the Rapidan. Since the previous autumn he had been disturbed by the condition into which his men and animals were falling.[16] As at Fredericksburg in the winter of 1862-1863, he wondered whether they could maintain the vigor to meet the thrust of the great Army of the Potomac. A day of full rations was a rarity. For weeks at a time they had barely enough food to maintain strength for scanty foraging in a country almost bare.[17] Horses of the artillery and wagon trains were scattered wherever enough fodder could be found to keep them alive, but hundreds were dying of starvation and disease. To forage their mounts, the cavalry was sent as much as six miles away from their proper positions.[18]

Lee had been able to do little to improve things before the blow fell. As far as the railroads were concerned, he was in a preferred position. He had easy access to the Virginia Central, which tapped the fertile Shenandoah Valley on the one hand and reached Richmond on the other. Still he could not get the necessary subsistence to keep men and beasts in condition. In southern Georgia, western Virginia and the Carolinas an abundance of pork, grain and fodder was available, but the railroads were totally unable to carry it to him. The rolling stock and tracks of the Virginia Central had become so dilapidated that under no possible improvement in management could it supply the army's bare needs.[19] However, the Rebel soldier, as he had done time after time, tightened his belt and stoically got along on next to nothing. When the time came to strike Grant in the Wilderness, he was ready.

Feeble as it had become, the Virginia Central had remained an artery of sorts. The damage done it at Beaver Dam Station by Sheridan and his raiders and the devastation wrought by Grant's right wing at the North Anna fell like heavy blows on the hungry Confederates. Fortunately, more food and grain were within reach of the foragers when they got to the North Anna—enough to fortify Lee's army for the fighting at Cold Harbor and beyond.

When he saw that Grant's next move would be over the old battlefields of the Peninsula and across to the south side of the James River, Lee moved quickly within the defenses of Richmond. With or without military justification the government, the citizenry and the soldiers alike long had held the preservation of Richmond essential to the life of the Confederacy. Now on both sides of the James more than 125,000 well-fed and well-equipped Federal soldiers were drawing near.[20] Lee had less than half that number. What chance had he? Evidently that portion of Grant's army south of the James was aiming at the capture of Petersburg twenty miles below Richmond. It was the southern gateway to the capital. Including the Richmond & Petersburg, four lines met there. The Petersburg line ran south to Weldon, the Carolinas and Wilmington. The South Side Railroad ran westward to Lynchburg and southwestern Virginia. A fourth line, which had run eastward to Norfolk, was no longer of any importance. The South Side crossed the Richmond & Danville at Burkeville, about forty miles out of Petersburg.

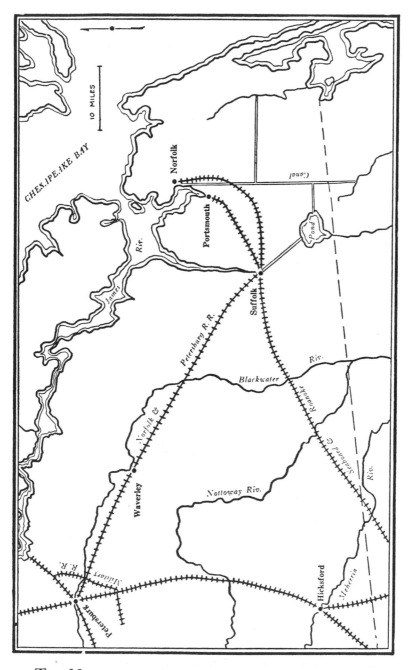

THE NETWORK OF RAILROADS AROUND PETERSBURG

In Lee's view the successful defense of Richmond depended on his ability to keep the Federals out of Petersburg. If Petersburg should fall, nothing would prevent the enemy from moving on to destroy the Richmond & Danville as well as the South Side. With these roads in Grant's control, there would be no way to feed the Confederate army or the people of Richmond.

Lee sent large numbers of his troops across the James to reinforce Beauregard, who then commanded at Petersburg. All hands were set to work strengthening the fortifications east and southeast of the city. Once again Grant found his objective blocked by strong enemy fortifications. Vicious and frequent though his early assaults were, Beauregard repulsed them all.

It was past the middle of June. On his frequent visits to the Petersburg sector Lee saw enemy earthworks rising rapidly directly in front of his own. Day by day it grew clearer that the problem of defending Richmond was first of all a problem of feeding his men. They had beaten off the attacks of the Blue time after time, and given food and ammunition, they could keep it up.

But to fight men must eat. No matter how much food there was in the Shenandoah, in Georgia and the Carolinas, it would be useless unless the railroads could deliver it. Since coming within wagon-haul distance of Richmond, the men had fared comparatively well, but the depots must be constantly replenished. The burden on the feeble Virginia Central had been greatly reduced. The damage done at the North Anna had been repaired, and if the road could be kept running it could be depended on to bring necessities from the Shenandoah. So important was its maintenance that early in June Lee had dispatched Wade Hampton's much-needed cavalry to Trevilian Station to beat off an attack by Sheridan.[21] The Union estimate of the importance of the Virginia Central to the Confederate defense was expressed by General Meade when he wrote: "Until that road is destroyed we can not compel the evacuation of Richmond, even if we succeed in seizing or breaking the Southside and the Danville Roads."[22]

Hampton succeeded but this did not entirely solve the problem of protecting the Virginia Central. Throughout the campaign a sizable Union army had been operating under Grant's direction in the Shenandoah Valley. To stop it from laying waste to the crops and stored supplies, Lee sent large detachments from the Army of Northern Virginia. On June 16 they had been forced back to Lynchburg. Though every unit of his army was needed to defend Petersburg and Richmond, Lee was obliged to send Early's corps to retrieve the situation at Lynchburg and drive the Federals back down the Valley.[23]

Most of July was a comparatively quiet period on the siege lines. On both sides of the narrow no man's land new forts were built and trenches were extended. Anticipating an effort by Grant to wreck the railroads entering Petersburg, Lee was especially busy improving and extending his fortifications south and southwest of the city. Already there had been sharp fighting on the Weldon Railroad near Globe Tavern.[24] The danger of losing the line was apparent. Short breaks had been made in the track, but the Federals had been repulsed and the road was by no means beyond repair.

On July 30 the famous Petersburg mine was exploded underneath the Confederate trenches, but this came as no surprise. Lee had known for some time that it was imminent, and again Grant found him ready for the emergency. The mine was a complete failure. It did more damage to the miners than to the mined. After that the fighting for Petersburg and Richmond started in double earnest.

All through the autumn it continued. First Grant would strike directly at Richmond on the north side of the James, then thrust at Petersburg on the south. So skillfully did Lee shuffle his forces back and forth that the Federals accomplished little of importance until August 20. It was then that Lee suffered his first great loss in the game of strike and go. On that date a detachment of Union soldiers seized the Weldon Railroad at Reams's Station.[25] All attempts to recover it failed with heavy losses. The Weldon was finally lost to Lee. In October the Confederates suffered a still more disastrous loss. Sheridan, who had been sent to command in the Shenandoah, so decisively defeated Early at Winchester that any further effort to defend the Valley was futile. Sheridan mopped up by laying waste everything of military value from Winchester to Staunton. The Virginia Central was no longer of any use to Lee.

Grant's base of supply was now at City Point on the James. This was the eastern terminus of the South Side Railroad, which Grant operated to the point where it reached his army. Connecting with the South Side there, a new military railroad had been constructed which extended from one end of the long Union line to the other. Supplies were always at hand. Late in October a Federal expedition tried to cut the South Side Railroad west of Petersburg.[26] When it was frustrated, and the troops were returned to their former position in the trenches, active operations about Richmond and Petersburg ended for the winter.

So it was that the Army of Northern Virginia spent its last Christmas in comparative quiet, but well aware that supplies were running painfully low.[27]

CHAPTER XXVI

WHEELS STOP TURNING IN TENNESSEE
AND GEORGIA

I

Until the middle of September, Hood rested with his army at Lovejoy's Station on the Macon Railroad twenty-seven miles south of Atlanta. Meanwhile Sherman's men were comfortably situated in their camps about Atlanta with an abundance of supplies coming to them over the railroad from Nashville and Chattanooga.

In no position to risk another pitched battle with Sherman's superior forces, Hood set about devising a plan to meet Sherman's threat to lay waste the whole of Georgia.[1] Perhaps he recalled how persistently Johnston and Forrest had contended that Sherman's operations in Georgia could be brought to an end by destroying the railroad supply lines in his rear.[2] At any rate he decided not to wait for the development of further plans by the enemy but to launch a bold offensive of his own against Federal communications north of Atlanta.

By such a campaign Sherman might be forced for want of supplies to abandon Atlanta and retreat. He might even be drawn back into the mountains about Dalton, be forced to divide his army in order to protect Tennessee and so be defeated. In that event Nashville could be recovered along with the lost prestige of the Confederacy in the West. If Sherman should refuse to retreat and attempt to live off the country, the way would be open to cut across country behind him and help Lee dispose of Grant. Of such fabric were woven the dreams of the impetuous John B. Hood into whose hands Jefferson Davis had delivered the army of cautious Joe Johnston.[3] In theory the plan was worthy of a soldier of his courage, but it failed to allow for two important considerations: the large number of troops under Sherman's command and the intrepidity of the man he must lead to disaster.

On September 18, Hood moved out by his left in an attempt to get behind Sherman and operate on the Western & Atlantic Railroad, reversing the process by which Sherman had attempted to seize that road between Johnston and Atlanta. But before the last of his units left Lovejoy's, Federal spies reported to their commander that the Confederates were moving out in a northwesterly direction.[4] To discover the purpose and general plan of Hood's campaign, Sherman had only three days to wait, and for the information he was indebted to none other than Jefferson Davis.

At about the time Hood was preparing to cross the Chattahoochee River, Davis came to visit him and delivered a bombastic and boastful speech to the army. Many of the men to whom he spoke were from Kentucky and Tennessee. In an effort to inspire them and revive their hopes, Davis told them they were at last on their way to recover possession of their home soil. Sherman's railroad supply line was to be destroyed, the Yankee army forced to retreat or starve and he promised this retreat would be more disastrous than Napoleon's from Moscow.[5] Moreover, he said, Forrest was at that very moment marching toward Sherman's railroads through middle Tennessee and would join them in their great enterprise of recovering their lost possessions.[6]

By this rash speech Davis had done Hood no favor, for Federal spies listened to every word and hurried the news to headquarters. It was to be a fight for the railroad. Forewarned, Sherman had every advantage. Thomas had already been sent to Chattanooga to command in middle Tennessee and Schofield was well on his way to join him. Strong railroad guards sufficient to beat off cavalry attacks had been left at a dozen strategic spots on the line and every important bridge had its guarding blockhouse and garrison. Only Hood's infantry threatened damage to the railroad beyond quick repair. To meet that threat Sherman acted quickly. Cavalry units north of the Tennessee River were alerted and ordered to move immediately to meet Forrest's raid. Leaving a corps to protect Atlanta and the Chattahoochee River bridge, Sherman moved up the railroad toward Marietta. The Confederates had gained a slight lead and on October 4 and 5, units of Hood's command struck the railroad at Acworth and Big Shanty, where they destroyed some fifteen miles of track.[7] Their attack at Allatoona, however, met stiff resistance and failed. By the time that battle ended, Sherman's men were approaching the break in the track at Big Shanty. Learning of this, Hood pulled his detachments off the railroad to join the main column and headed for a crossing of the Etowah River near Rome.

Bringing iron and ties from Chattanooga, Wright had the railroad back in operation in just seven days. Meantime, Hood marched rapidly toward Resaca and thence to Dalton. On the afternoon of October 13, the Federal garrison at Dalton surrendered and the railroad was destroyed from Resaca north to Tunnel Hill where it passed through Rocky Face Ridge.[8] That was the end of his campaign against the Western & Atlantic. Sherman had followed in such force that Hood was no better prepared to fight him in North Georgia than he had been at Lovejoy's. He abandoned the plan to bring on a battle there and moved off toward the Alabama line to rest a few days and plan his next move. The campaign was not working out as he had anticipated and the horrible disaster Jefferson Davis had predicted for Sherman had come to be nothing but another sample of the Confederate President's wishful thinking. Very shortly Hood learned the damage done the Western & Atlantic had been repaired and Sherman was in force near Resaca. In fact the promised Federal "retreat from Moscow" had become instead, a very real and pressing pursuit of the Confederates.[9]

Despite the inconsequential results in Georgia, Hood could do nothing except continue his offensive and hope for better results in Tennessee, although the capture of Nashville would be more difficult with the Western & Atlantic Railroad below Chattanooga repaired and still in possession of the Federals. Reinforcements for Thomas and Schofield would be moving up by rail to interpose between him and his objective. He doubted, however, that Sherman would bring his whole army to follow him into Tennessee. If Hood could not force Sherman, perhaps he could tease him into dividing his forces and offering an opportunity which would enable the Confederates to win in Tennessee the battle they had vainly hoped to win in north Georgia. Once more the ambitious Hood indulged in wishful dreams of a history-making campaign which would recover Tennessee and establish the Confederate line in Kentucky, from which he could threaten Cincinnati and perhaps accomplish what Bragg and Kirby Smith had failed to do in 1862.[10]

As a first step he decided to march swiftly, cross the Tennessee at or near Guntersville, destroy Federal rail communications at Bridgeport and Stevenson, Alabama, then pursue Thomas and Schofield in an attempt to rout or capture their scattered armies before they could combine at Nashville.[11] Before reaching the river, however, he learned that Forrest's cavalry was still far away and not yet ready to join him. Without it, he dared not risk the river crossing and pursuit of the Federal forces.

It was now October 22. As early as the ninth Hood had asked to have the Memphis & Charleston repaired between Corinth and Decatur, but on the twenty-second nothing had been done. Hood needed supplies before he turned north for Nashville. Since the railroad could not bring them, he would have to march to meet them—safely south of the river. Tuscumbia had been designated as his chief supply base for the campaign in Tennessee.[12] Although he had not intended to go so far west, he determined to go there. On arrival, he was disappointed to find the railroad still out of commission, repair crews still to the west and the town almost without supplies. In spite of his impatient effort to hurry along the work, he was obliged to wait until mid-November.

When at last he crossed the river to Florence, Alabama,

Forrest was there to join him. Unfortunately for Hood, the timing of Confederate operations had not permitted him to take full advantage of Forrest's skillful work south of Nashville. The co-ordination promised by Davis in his speech to the soldiers had failed to come off. Before that speech was made, Forrest had been given his long-sought chance to go to work on Sherman's railroad supply lines in Tennessee. At the time the President spoke he was well on his way from Mississippi toward the fulfillment of his cherished task.

At daybreak of September 21 he had crossed the Tennessee River and headed directly east for Athens, Alabama, on the Tennessee & Alabama. This would put him on the railroad between Nashville and Decatur, thirteen miles north of Decatur, a well-garrisoned town.[13] Three days later, with 4,500 veterans trained in the Forrest manner, he set about the business of showing the surprised and frustrated Union guards how to wreck railroads so they would stay wrecked. Bluffing when he could and fighting when he must, he moved north along the line toward Nashville, destroying one blockhouse after another, gobbling up their garrisons, burning bridges and destroying track. He ripped up miles of rails and at Sulphur Branch reduced to ashes a trestle 72 feet high and 300 feet long.[14] In the end, this road was so badly damaged it could not be restored to full service until late in November.[15]

Having put this railroad out of business to a point above Pulaski, he turned his attention to another and rode east to Tullahoma on the Nashville & Chattanooga, bent on similar operations against the line which had been so vital to Sherman's operations in north Georgia. He had come too late. Before much damage was done his ever-present swarm of elusive scouts reported that every vulnerable point on the road was guarded by strong detachments of Federal troops, prepared and waiting for his approach. They reported columns of infantry and cavalry closing in on him from all directions. He had stirred up a hornets' nest in middle Tennessee and now it was time for him to make another of the remarkable escapes for which he had become famous. Eluding all pursuers, he reached Florence about October 5, and within two days was safely across the swollen river.[16]

So while Hood still jabbed at the Western & Atlantic below the Etowah River, Forrest had made his thrust into middle Tennessee and returned. His opportunity came much too late. Brilliant though it was, his expedition brought no result of major importance. However, his accomplishments were such as to raise the question of what the result might have been if he had been permitted to make it before Sherman took Atlanta and could hurry reinforcements back to Tennessee. There were times during Sherman's campaign when interruption of traffic over the Nashville & Chattanooga for as much as a week would have been a catastrophe. While by no means a certainty, there remains room for strong argument that if Forrest had been permitted to make a similar raid before Atlanta fell, the whole course of the war in 1864 would have been changed. As it came about, he could do no more than was done. He had time for a damaging raid into west Tennessee before joining Hood, who was at last ready to march.

Once across the river at Florence, Hood moved as rapidly as possible and directly toward Nashville. He knew time was working on the side of the Federals and that Thomas at Nashville was being strongly reinforced, that Schofield's army was off to his right and keeping pace with him as they both marched toward Nashville. In spite of all this he clung to the hope he might get between them and defeat both of them. In fact, Jeff Davis had telegraphed him as late as November 7, setting the Ohio River as the objective to be striven for.[17] From all these dreams there came a sudden and gruesome awakening. At Spring Hill, Hood missed a good chance; the next afternoon he took a bad one. At Franklin, only eighteen miles from Nashville, in the last daylight hour of November, he collided with Schofield and 4,500 of Hood's men were killed or wounded.[18] There are those who say this was the bloodiest single hour of the war.

When the fighting ended, Schofield went on to Nashville

with Hood following part of the way. It was a vain pursuit. Behind unassailable fortifications, Thomas now outnumbered him two to one. Attack would have been suicidal and to by-pass the city and leave Thomas in his rear would have been equally so. He lacked both strength and supplies to conduct a siege and he knew retreat would result in the certain disintegration of his army. Hood was caught in a desperate plight. Going into camp on a line of hills four miles south of Nashville, he settled down to ponder the situation and await developments.

Two weeks later Thomas moved out to attack him there and the ensuing battle resulted in a complete rout of the Confederates. Closely pursued, Hood made for the Tennessee River which he succeeded in crossing on December 26 and 27.[19] The Confederate Army of Tennessee was broken and as they marched in retreat, cold, hungry and barefoot, the indefatigable veterans expressed their opinion of the futile campaign through newly written words for an old song. To the tune of "The Yellow Rose of Texas" they sang:

> And now I'm going southward,
> For my heart is full of woe,
> I'm going back to Georgia
> To find my "Uncle Joe."
> You may sing about your dearest maid,
> And sing of Rosalie,
> But the gallant Hood of Texas
> Played hell in Tennessee.

2

Throughout the summer Sherman had spent many anxious weeks contemplating the possible fate of his army if the Confederates should launch a determined campaign against his railroad communications with Nashville. He was conscious of the fact that such a campaign might very well put an end to the grand plan to force an early close of the war. With the capture of Atlanta, most of his worries on this score came to an end, and by the time Hood started north he was seriously concerned with keeping the roads in operation only long enough to get the troops of Thomas and Schofield back into Tennessee. For the remainder of his army he had other plans which would make the further maintenance of the long supply line entirely unnecessary.

Hood was still far too strong to be neglected but he could not be permitted to disrupt the larger Federal strategy by turning the war in the West back toward north Georgia and Tennessee. That was why it was so very important that Thomas and Schofield be hurried to Chattanooga before the railroad was destroyed. With a sizable force under Thomas in Tennessee, Sherman needed to keep Hood engaged only long enough for the "Rock" to get established and concentrate his troops. Then Sherman could return to Atlanta and give his attention to the Georgia campaign on which his heart was set.

His opportunity to break off the pursuit came when Hood left the line of the Western & Atlantic and turned west into Alabama. Quickly the railroad was repaired. Thomas went on to Nashville, Schofield moved forward and occupied the towns along the Nashville & Chattanooga below Murfreesborough, while reinforcements poured in from both north and south. Sherman knew that northern Alabama was bare of provisions and that for rations, ammunition and stores, Hood would be obliged to rely on shipments from Mobile, Montgomery and Selma routed by way of Meridian and Corinth. He knew also that the railroads over which such shipments must be made had been effectually disabled early in the year and could not have been fully restored.[20] Hood would be handicapped and delayed in making any further advance. Thomas could take care of him now.

Since the fall of Atlanta it had been Sherman's opinion that the best way to exploit that great victory was for him to turn east, march through Georgia to the seacoast at Savannah or thereabouts, then turn north through the Carolinas and join

Grant in the reduction of Richmond and the defeat of Lee. While Hood's operations had delayed the opening of his campaign and caused a vast amount of inconvenience, they had not weakened Sherman's determination to proceed as he had planned. With Hood marching west toward Tuscumbia, the time for the audacious undertaking was at hand. He would turn his back to Hood and abandon the railroad from Chattanooga to Atlanta. His army, living off the country, would cut a desolate swath from Atlanta through the heart of Georgia to the eastern seaboard.[21]

In preparation for the unprecedented move, he ordered that all supplies and equipment accumulated at Atlanta and at depots along the railroad be shipped back to Chattanooga as quickly as possible. He said: "On the first of November I want nothing in front of Chattanooga except what we can use as food and clothing and haul in our wagons."[22] All troops selected for the campaign were then ordered to march for Atlanta. As they moved along the railroad they met the trains speeding their supplies back toward Chattanooga. When the last of these trains had passed, the work of destroying the railroad and telegraph began. While Sherman paused to rest a bit at Cartersville, his personal telegraph operator pulled down the wire from a pole and with a small pocket instrument held on his knee, sent Sherman's last telegram to Thomas. It was in reply to Thomas' message of assurance that he was prepared to handle Hood and said only this: "Dispatch received—all right."[23]

November 16, 1864, was a day of brilliant autumn sunshine. From a hilltop just outside the old Confederate works, Sherman looked back on Atlanta "smoldering and in ruins, black smoke rising in air and hanging like a pall over the ruined city." Sherman's famous march through Georgia was under way. Formed in an army of two wings, 60,000 Yanks headed for strange fields and new adventures, and as they swung along the roads at a lively step they cheered and sang lustily. Of the route they were to follow they knew nothing, but as to their ultimate destination they had little doubt. As Sherman rode along the lines they called out to him, "Uncle Billy, I guess Grant is waiting for us at Richmond!"

With them they had 2,500 wagons, 65 guns and 600 ambulances. Each wagon was drawn by 6 mules. There were 4 horses to each gun and a single team of 2 horses pulled each ambulance. In addition to the cavalry mounts, no less than 17,000 animals made up the long trains. The spectacle, the singing and the exuberant spirit exhibited by officers and men made a deep impression on Sherman. Writing of it in after years, he said the beginning of the march "made me feel the full load of responsibility, for success would be accepted as a matter of course, whereas, should we fail, this march would be adjudged the wild adventure of a crazy fool."[24]

Before leaving Atlanta he had ordered destroyed all property of possible military use to the Confederates. Accordingly, the railroad depots, roundhouses, machine shops and a large quantity of rolling stock were burned.[25] It was the smoke from these fires on which the departing soldiers looked back. Contrary to Southern opinion, remnants of which persist to this day, this destruction was prompted by no spirit of revenge or vindictiveness. Sherman believed the war was nearing its end and the merciful thing to do was to destroy all the facilities which would enable the South to prolong it. In pursuit of this policy he was particularly insistent on getting rid of all railroad equipment. Throughout the war Georgia had been the source of great quantities of subsistence for the Confederate armies and still her granaries and storehouses were full. To destroy the means of transporting these supplies to the soldiers in the field was an important feature in Sherman's plan.

With the Western & Atlantic under his control, two important lines remained in Confederate service. One was the Georgia Railroad running directly east from Atlanta to Augusta on the Savannah River. From Augusta, Confederate supplies could be transferred to barges and shipped down the river or carried by rail over the South Carolina Railroad through Kingsville and Florence to Wilmington, North

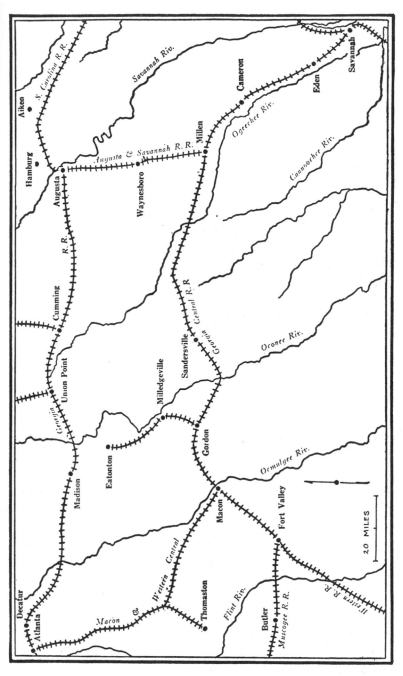

ATLANTA TO THE SEA

Carolina. The other was the Macon line running southward from Atlanta to Macon and thence east to Savannah. Roughly paralleling each other, these railroads were approximately sixty miles apart. It was by virtue of this fact that the swath Sherman cut through Georgia is commonly said to have been sixty miles in width.

When they marched out of Atlanta, the right wing was commanded by General O. O. Howard, and the left wing by General H. W. Slocum. Howard took the road toward Macon and Slocum moved out along the railroad toward Augusta. Distant about 100 miles southeast of Atlanta lay Milledgeville, then the capital of the state. Sherman's orders called for a meeting of the two columns at that point and he allowed each commander seven days in which to arrive there.[26]

During these seven days the two railroads were systematically reduced to scrap iron and ashes. Two methods of destroying track were generally employed. Sherman preferred that of taking up the rails, heating them over burning piles of ties and bending them around trees. Others preferred the single operation of putting a cold twist in the rails as they were torn from the ties through use of the hook and lever device invented by Haupt's Construction Corps in 1862. Since Sherman was with Slocum's column, the heating and bending process was most frequently employed by Slocum's men. On the other hand, Howard carried with him a large number of the twisting tools and made good use of them. Whichever method was used, the iron on the two railroads was left valueless except for scrap.

At Madison, Slocum left the railroad and turned right toward Milledgeville. He had met no opposition and was moving according to schedule.[27] His men were now in a land not previously visited by a hostile army, in which they found an abundance of corn, molasses, meal, bacon and sweet potatoes. They had to deal, however, with one serious problem. Negroes by the hundreds insisted on attaching themselves to the column and moving with it. The Negroes, young and old, had heard that "Massa Sherman" was coming to deliver them from bondage, and they believed the way to freedom was to follow the marching soldiers. They came on foot, riding aged and worthless mules and in all manner of dilapidated vehicles. Not only able-bodied men and women but mothers with children, the feeble and the decrepit sought to join in what they expected to be the journey to the Promised Land.[28]

The growing aggregation presented a serious threat to the success of the campaign. Fortunately there were leaders among the Negroes to whom the others were willing to listen. Patiently Sherman explained to these men that to win their freedom the army must first win the war, that to win the war they must march rapidly, and his thousands of soldiers must gather their food from farms along the way. He told them that their people, by following the army, were only eating up the food which should go to the soldiers, slowing down their progress and delaying the real day of deliverance. Would they please spread this word far and wide among the Negroes in the country and ask them to remain at home and not attempt to follow the soldiers? There is no doubt that this policy and these talks accomplished great good. While the handicap of the Negro following was never entirely eliminated, it ceased to grow in the proportion threatened in the early days of the campaign.[29]

On November 22 and 23, Slocum's left wing reached Milledgeville. There Sherman received a report from General Howard. From Atlanta the right wing had ripped up the Macon railroad as far as Barnesville. From there the main body veered to the left of the railroad and passed through Monticello. Cavalry and a brigade of infantry made a feint at Macon, having an easy skirmish with Georgia militia units, but Howard made no real attack on the city. He continued to Gordon, once more on the railroad at a point where a branch line ran north to Milledgeville. He was reporting from Gordon, twelve miles south of Milledgeville, the rendezvous point.[30]

Of the situation found at Milledgeville, Sherman wrote: "The people remained at home, except the Governor

(Brown), the State officers, and Legislature, who had ignominiously fled, in the utmost disorder and confusion; standing not on the order of their going, but going at once— some by rail, some by carriages, and many on foot."[31] Sherman had the arsenal with its contents and such public buildings as could be converted to military use promptly destroyed but carefully avoided unnecessary damage to private property. The first leg of the journey to the sea had been successfully completed.

Since there was no trouble at Milledgeville there was no need for Howard to march the twelve miles from Gordon. Instead, he was ordered to continue eastward along the main line of the railroad. On November 24 Sherman with Slocum's left wing renewed the march. Instead of returning to the line of the Augusta railroad they marched directly east, paralleling Howard's route which lay a few miles to the south. Two days later the columns were abreast each other in the neighborhood of Sandersville.[32] Never before had foraging been done on such a scale or with such skill. The whole business was thoroughly organized and supervised by officers who had control of an abundance of men and wagons and who had authority to take food and forage from wherever it might be found. The cribs were full of corn, smoke houses were filled with hams and bacon. Honey was in the beehives and the barnyards supplied poultry of all descriptions. Army fare was forgotten; the soldiers feasted on the fat of the land. Horses and mules were fat and sleek.

Largely from the operations of the foraging details, Sherman derived his reputation among Southerners as a ruthless and barbaric fiend. Under the rules of war, living off a hostile country was legitimate, and his orders against needless waste and mistreatment of the population were specific. Because of the magnitude of this operation, it was of course impossible to prevent some violations of his orders or to punish all offenders. The army moved by many roads and foragers operated far out on the flanks. Cases of needless and un- justified waste and destruction, of theft or carrying off of cherished personal and household items were unavoidable.[33]

Moreover, a horde of irresponsibles, mainly civilians and deserters from both Union and Confederate armies, hung on the flanks. Naturally the stories of marauding were exaggerated in the telling and Sherman was charged with responsibility for the conduct of all such hoodlums.

By wild speeches and through the columns of Southern newspapers, Confederate leaders were telling the people still in front of Sherman's army that the Federals were in desperate straits, cut off from all communications and starving. They exhorted the people to rise against the marauders in the defense of Georgia, burn all subsistence, obstruct the roads over which they were traveling and burn the bridges across the streams.[34] To these appeals there was not much response. Too many people had seen Sherman's army and knew there was no basis for the claims that it was in a desperate condition. At the outset Sherman had told his officers that in any case where there was an attempt made to sabotage their equipment or destroy their subsistence, they should lay waste the offending neighborhood. Occasionally the Georgians undertook to follow the exhortations of their leaders, and it was only in such cases that Sherman ordered or condoned the destruction of private property.[35]

About December 1, when Sherman's columns were approaching Millen, fifty-four miles south of Augusta, they met their first opposition of consequence. Although the Confederates were easily pushed back and caused little delay, they continued to skirmish with the advance troops of the Federals all the way to Savannah.[36] On the roads below Millen, Slocum's men had their first experience with booby traps and land mines, then referred to as torpedoes. As the Johnnies retreated they buried live artillery shells in the roads and rigged them with contact fuses. Sherman solved that problem in a hurry. He had captured a number of prisoners and, arming them with picks and shovels, he forced them to move in close formations along the roads ahead of his own columns to explode or dig up the torpedoes. A little of that procedure satisfied the enemy that such practice was not profitable.[37]

By the middle of December Sherman was in the vicinity

of Savannah. Finding the place thoroughly fortified, he made his plans to reduce it. Already he had established communications with the blockading fleet and was assured of supplies. The story of how he captured the city is one of great interest but the railroads were not involved. He had finished the railroad job he had started out to do. The line from Savannah to Macon was destroyed throughout its length, and the road to Augusta was in ruins over many miles.[38] As an important source of food for the Confederate armies, Georgia had been eliminated. For these pages it is sufficient in this connection to add that while Grant and Lee spent Christmas of 1864 facing each other in fortifications about Petersburg, Sherman lay safely in Savannah, ready and waiting to carry his work of devastation on to the railroads of the Carolinas.

CHAPTER XXVII

RAILHEAD AT LAST

With the loss of the Weldon Railroad, the devastation of the Shenandoah Valley and the breaking up of the Virginia Central, Lee's besieged army of Northern Virginia came to the early weeks of 1865 wholly dependent on two feeble and extremely vulnerable railroads for subsistence. One of these was the Richmond & Danville running southwest from Richmond and the other was the South Side Railroad running west from Petersburg to Lynchburg. At Burkeville, fifty-five miles west of Petersburg, the two roads crossed.

It will be recalled that very early in the war Lee had recognized the importance of a supplemental rail connection between Richmond and the Carolinas and had urged the government to build such a connection with the Danville line. He had pointed out that a situation might arise which would make this essential to the safety of his army.[1] The loss of the Weldon line had produced that precise condition. How the Confederate Congress authorized the President to survey and build such a connection and how Jefferson Davis frittered away valuable time in starting its construction are told in a previous chapter. Before the road could be opened for use in 1864, Grant's campaign which was to make it so vital to the defense of Richmond was well under way. Completed under pressure, the Piedmont Railroad was poorly constructed and equipped with worn-out and broken-down rolling stock. Frequent wrecks and long delays in operation were inevitable. However, it was a railroad of sorts and it contributed in some measure to transporting supplies from North Carolina to Richmond and Petersburg.[2] Had it been well built and

365

equipped at an earlier date, Lee's position in January 1865 well might have been less hazardous.

The war which was to have ended in ninety days was now almost four years old. Great battles had been won or lost by virtue of rail transportation or the lack of it. The order of many campaigns had been determined by the courses followed by the railroads. Time and again major strategy had hinged on the question of available rail transportation. Now, in the last desperate days of the struggle, the further defense of Richmond and, indeed, the survival of Lee's army, hung on the ability of the Confederates to protect and maintain the two roads which crossed at Burkeville. At the opening of the war they had been among the better railroads of the South, but by the close of 1864 depreciation of track and rolling stock had worked a great reduction in their carrying capacity.

As in the two previous winters, Lee's troops were suffering from lack of food.[3] His horses were starving and too weak to draw guns and wagons over the muddy roads. Subsistence within foraging range was exhausted. Once more he had been obliged to remove many of his horses to a distance where forage for them might be found. With all his might he sought to impress on the President, the Congress and the people how desperate things were.[4] He pointed out the danger of weakening his main defense lines by withdrawing men to protect the railroads. All through the winter he had begged President Davis and the Congress for a stricter application of the conscription law in order to provide him with additional troops to guard these vital supply lines.[5] He asked that Negroes be brought in to build roads and work on fortifications in order that all able-bodied soldiers might be employed in the defenses.[6] His efforts resulted in abundant promises but little performance. Under pressure, Jefferson Davis was forced at last to relieve his long-favored Commissary General Northrop[7] and for a short time after there was more food available. But he had waited too long to remove this bullheaded and petulant officer and the improvement was short-lived.

Gradually Grant's long investment line was being extended

around to the south and southwest of Petersburg, and with each extension the defenders in the Confederate trenches had to be spread thinner and thinner. Many of Lee's officers were in despair. Above the incessant roar of Federal artillery they could hear the death rattle in the throat of the Confederacy. Although scrupulously avoiding any disclosure of his feelings in the presence of his troops, Lee, too, knew that little less than a miracle could save Richmond.

By late winter despair was by no means confined to officers. Hungry, cold and ragged, large numbers of enlisted men were giving up the fight, deserting to go home or stealing across to the Federal lines in individual surrender. Vastly outnumbered and heavily outgunned, they might for a time be able to hold the Petersburg entrenchments against all Federal assaults, but they could see no hope of preventing the ever-growing, blue-clad horde from continuing the movement across their front until it reached the South Side Railroad. When that was accomplished there would be no defending the Danville line and ultimate surrender would be inevitable. In such circumstances, thousands of them could see no reason for prolonging the struggle. The Confederate soldier in the ranks had come to understand that while the Army of Northern Virginia had been able through four years of war to win its share of battles against the Yankees, its final surrender now could be forced by the Federal destruction of a single railroad track.

Steadily the strength of Lee's defensive power was being sapped by desertion, casualties and loss of spirit. Sherman had left Savannah and was marching northward through the Carolinas, undoubtedly bent on joining Grant before Richmond. Was it more important to continue the defense of Richmond and risk the loss of his army, or would it be better to abandon Petersburg and attempt to save the army? This was the question which Lee pondered throughout sleepless hours of the long winter nights.

By force of circumstances rather than because of any lessening of his dislike for Joseph E. Johnston, Jefferson Davis had been obliged to approve Lee's assignment of him to command in the Carolinas.⁸ By consolidating the various units operating in that area, Johnston had formed them into a respectable army to stop or delay Sherman's advance toward Richmond. In the few quiet hours allowed him, Lee studied the possibility of abandoning his position and slipping away to the southwest in the hope of joining his troops with Johnston's somewhere in the Carolinas. If the two armies could be combined he thought they might be able to dispose of Sherman, draw Grant out of his fortified position and thus revive the Confederacy.⁹

Just such a move was the thing Grant most feared. The Union commander had no doubt as to the ultimate success of his siege, provided the enemy remained in his fortifications about Petersburg long enough for the Federal army to complete its investment by cutting the South Side and the Richmond & Danville. Feeling that this situation must be equally clear to Lee, he wondered why the Confederate commander had not moved out while the corridor of escape was still open. Grant fully expected to wake some morning and find himself confronted by nothing more than a picket line, the strong Confederate fortifications abandoned, and Lee's army well on its way toward the North Carolina border. He reasoned that if Lee escaped him at Petersburg, hope of ending the war in the early spring was gone and the conflict would likely drag on for another year.¹⁰

The thought of such a possibility distressed him. To extend his line enough to close the corridor was a matter of first concern. But as long as the water in the streams was high and the roads were deep in mud from the late winter rains, a further move to his far left would entail too much hardship and too much danger. Impatiently he waited for the weather and the roads to improve.¹¹

Unknown to Grant, there were two good reasons why Lee had not tried to join Johnston. In the first place, Jefferson Davis and the Confederate Congress would not consent to his abandoning Richmond. Either unable or unwilling to comprehend the military situation, Davis clung persistently to the theory that Petersburg and Richmond still could be defended. In the second place, Lee had a much more practical reason for remaining within his fortified lines. He did not believe the horses he had available were strong enough to move the necessary wagons and guns over the heavy roads. To bring back more of the pitiable animals to the neighborhood of Petersburg would only increase his difficulty. Carrying sufficient food to keep the soldiers from starving was a burden the two remaining railroads were barely able to sustain. To add to that load the transport of forage for more horses was an utter impossibility. There was nothing to do except to fight and hope and wait for the roads to dry.[12]

With great quantities of food, grain and forage remaining elsewhere in the Confederacy while Lee's army starved and waited immobile for want of transportation for it, the government wrote the final ironic chapter in the story of its railroad policy. When the war was all but lost and the entire South littered with the wreck of its railroads, Congress passed an act authorizing the President to take control of the properties and operations of the lines.[13] In all respects the law was similar to that under which the Federal roads had been operating so successfully since early 1862. Coming at least three years too late, the action amounted to nothing more than a tragic and futile gesture. By the February day on which the law was enacted only the feeble Piedmont line, the South Side and the Richmond & Danville remained subject to its application, and all three were beyond hope of restoration. Through the late days of February, Lee studied the possibilities and found little to encourage him. The strength of Grant's army was steadily increasing and Sherman was approaching the North Carolina line.[14] The swamps and difficult river crossings of South Carolina were behind him and he had destroyed the South Carolina railroads even more thoroughly than he had wrecked those in Georgia. Johnston's small opposing army was being plagued by mass desertion; it was doubtful he could muster more than 15,000 effectives.[15] Lee had no more than 50,000, and of these only about 35,000 were fit for duty. Whatever was to be done had to be done quickly.

On March 4 Lee rode from his headquarters into Richmond and told President Davis that there was no alternative to certain defeat other than to abandon Richmond and make the attempt to unite with Johnston. At last Davis was convinced and plans for evacuation of the capital were started.[16] To execute the evacuation successfully, Lee held it essential that some extra supplies and subsistence be brought to the men before the start was made.[17] Also, some depots of supplies must be established along the route they were to follow. Despite the condition of the railroads, the commissary officers promised that if they could be protected a short time longer these supplies could be accumulated. Through extraordinary efforts they did contrive to improve the rations in the Richmond-Petersburg area and to fill some depots at Lynchburg, Danville and Greensboro.[18]

While this was in process, Grant ordered the long-anticipated move to extend the Federal left and reach the South Side Railroad. Sheridan, to whom the job was assigned, moved out on March 29 and started his march around Petersburg with the dual objective of cutting Lee's last supply line and closing the lane through which he might escape.[19] Lee simply had to stop Sheridan before he got to the South Side Railroad. All of his available cavalry and every scrap of infantry support he dared spare from the fortifications he hurried south of the Appomattox River to the neighborhood of Five Forks and Dinwiddie Court House.[20]

Federal artillery was playing heavily on the Confederate trenches all along the line back to the James River. Immediately in front of Petersburg Grant carried on extensive demonstrations throughout the night of the twenty-ninth.[21] Apparently it was his purpose to prevent Lee from transferring troops to his right in defense against Sheridan. Had the Federals known how thin that line in front of them had become they might have saved their ammunition. Lee dared not move another man from that sector.

To save his railroads, Lee decided to take the offensive in a desperate attempt to flank Sheridan's column.[22] The effort failed and Sheridan moved on. Instead of being flanked he

became the flanker and was riding hard toward the Confederate right. In the afternoon of April 1, he struck the
Confederates at Five Forks and in two hours of vicious fighting routed the mobile force Lee had attempted to set up in
protection of his right flank. Grant's infantry lost no time in
taking advantage of Sheridan's victory at Five Forks. During
the rest of the afternoon and all through the night they
pounded the main defense line southwest of Petersburg and
drove the Confederates from their positions. Late in the
evening, Lee hurried a dispatch to Longstreet on the north
side of the James to bring all available troops at top speed.
Lee's headquarters were now about a half mile south of the
Appomattox River and two or three miles west of Petersburg. Longstreet arrived before daylight and reported that
4,600 men were following as speedily as the decrepit railroad
could carry them.[23]

At dawn Lee and Longstreet stepped out of the house
where Lee was quartered to face an appalling development.
Across the fields they saw a blue line approaching from the
southwest. The Sixth Corps under General Wright had
broken the outer defense line.[24] Meanwhile, Sheridan, on the
loose again, had cut the South Side Railroad close in and
was racing to get astride the last escape route near the
Appomattox. Lee saw at once what must be done if his army
was to escape the rapidly closing jaws of the trap. First of all,
Grant must be held off during the day in order that the men
in the Petersburg trenches might pull out under cover of
darkness. Secondly, all his troops from both sides of the
James must be brought into a new concentration as quickly as
possible, and this concentration must be made somewhere on
the line of the Richmond & Danville. Hard pressed for time,
he paused long enough to send a telegram to the War Department warning the government to be ready to leave Richmond
that night.[25] With amazing clarity and precision in the midst
of disaster, he dictated the necessary orders for the withdrawal of all his troops and their reconcentration at Amelia
Court House, a little railroad station on the Appomattox forty
miles southwest of Petersburg. Because of the weakened con-

dition of his men and horses, the heavy rain, the high water in
the streams and the deep mud of the roads, he knew that
some of his units would find it a terribly difficult if not impossible march; but it must be undertaken.

Grant must have been overconfident that his line of en-
velopment was sufficiently completed, for he permitted the
thin line of Confederates to hold throughout the second day
of April and thereby enable Lee to accomplish the first
essential in his plan to escape. When darkness fell on the
two cities in the defense of which so much blood had been
spilled, the gallant defenders of Richmond and Petersburg
filed out of their works and took to the road.[26] Now everything depended on timing. Fortunately for Lee, he was not
closely pursued. By marching throughout the night and the
daylight of April 3 he gained a full day on Meade's pursuing
infantry in the final race for position. If he succeeded in
reaching Amelia, he planned then to bear off to the southwest
along the line of the railroad to where it crossed the South
Side at Burkeville.

With a day's start on his pursuers, Lee's hopes for escape
and ultimately reaching Johnston's army were somewhat
revived, but he was distressed by the condition of his men and
horses. Their suffering was acute. How long could these
hungry men keep up the pace? How far could the few
famished horses he had been able to collect drag the guns and
wagons over the muddy roads? It was the sort of retreat
Jefferson Davis had pictured for Sherman's army when Hood
should destroy its railroad supply line north of Atlanta.

To bolster the strength and spirits of his men, Lee was
relying on a shipment of rations supposedly coming up the
railroad from Danville to Amelia Courthouse. During the
morning of April 4, the van of the struggling and hopeful
army reached that station only to suffer bitter disappointment.
They found nothing there to eat. The train had not arrived.
By whose fault this terrible hardship was visited upon the
fleeing army remains to this day a controversial question.[27]
Whoever was to blame, the important fact remains that the
absence of the expected food for Lee's men at Amelia cost

him the lead he had on the pursuing Federals. He was obliged to halt his march while foraging parties scoured the neighboring farms for such scant subsistence as remained in the surrounding country.

In desperation he sent off a telegram to Danville ordering a train of rations to be sent up the railroad immediately. Thinking that some time might be gained by taking up the march along the railroad to meet the train, he sent the advance units forward. They had not gone far when they met small detachments of Union cavalry in their front and on their left flank. This opposition was readily dispersed and the advance column moved on toward Jetersville, the first station on the railroad below Amelia. Then they came on Federal troops so firmly entrenched across their way as to prevent any supply train from reaching them from Danville and to deny them any further advance along the railroad.[28]

Lee's foraging parties were returning almost empty-handed. So little food remained in the country that foraging was not worth the effort. Soon Federal cavalrymen were dashing in like hornets to sting the various units of Lee's retreating column. Above Amelia they cut the Richmond & Danville and shut off any possibility of food reaching the retreating troops from the scant stores yet remaining in Richmond. With the South Side line east of Burkeville in Union hands[29] and the Danville line severed on both sides of him,[30] Lee was cut off from all supplies except such as might reach him over the South Side line from Lynchburg.

Hunger rather than Federal arms seemed likely to defeat the Army of Northern Virginia in the end. At the height of this crisis the new commissary general, I. M. St. John, arrived unexpectedly at Lee's headquarters to bring a measure of new hope. By the Federal capture of the junction at Burkeville, trains from Lynchburg bearing 80,000 rations had been unable to reach the army. These trains, however, had been backed out of danger and now stood on the South Side track near Farmville. The news gave Lee an alternative to massing all his strength in a final desperate effort to fight his way through the Federal lines which confronted him at Jetersville. If, by turning west from Amelia he could cut across the angle between the two railroads and reach Farmville, he might be able to pass the left flank of the new Federal position without a fight. In that event he could pick up the 80,000 rations, then turn south and move on toward Danville.

Farmville was approximately twenty miles away. The intervening country was interspersed with woodland, and crossed by substantial ridges between which a number of streams flowed northward to the near-by Appomattox River. Only by a forced march under cover of darkness was there any hope of reaching Farmville before the Federal cavalry could destroy the trains. Despite the misery and danger the march would entail, Lee undertook it on the night of April 5.[31] It seemed to offer the better of the two last chances to escape.

In the darkness the march became a tangled and futile scramble over strange and difficult roads. At dawn of April 6, little more than half the necessary distance had been covered. From utter exhaustion hundreds of men were falling out of line while others were hobbling along with the assistance of their stronger comrades. Staggering horses had to be cut from their traces and left by the roadside to die. A dispatch intercepted during the night informed Lee that the main Federal army was on his heels and that Grant himself was at Jetersville.[32] Word came that Sheridan's forces were driving swiftly along the railroad toward Farmville. There was no use continuing the march in that direction for the enemy would be there ahead of him. Fortunately, General St. John had reached Farmville on the previous day, hurriedly loaded all available wagons with rations from the cars and sent them out to meet the oncoming troops.

With his men thus somewhat refreshed, Lee decided to cross to the north side of the Appomattox River and march still farther westward in an attempt to get to the railroad at a point where it could bring him supplies from Lynchburg. The story of how the Confederates were intercepted and overwhelmed at Sayler's Creek is not for these pages. Neither need it be recounted here how the remnants of the beaten army crossed the river and came to the neighborhood of Appomattox Court House on April 8, only to find themselves virtually surrounded.

Loaded with rations, four trains from Lynchburg had arrived at Appomattox Station three miles to the south.[33] But as far as the Confederates were concerned, these trains might as well have been 300 miles away. They were in the hands of Sheridan's cavalrymen, who were having fun running them back and forth along the track in noisy celebration of the victory they knew was soon to come.[34] The South Side Railroad had shipped out its last load of Confederate supplies.

Next day, April 9, 1865, the long struggle between Grant and Lee came to an end. In the quiet parlor of Wilmer Mc-Lean's modest home at Appomattox Court House, Virginia, two of America's greatest soldiers met face to face and shook hands. The brief conference which followed was marked by dignity and courteous gentility. Each recognized in the other the worthy leader of men of valor who believed in the cause for which they had fought. When the ceremony of formal surrender was completed, Lee told Grant that his men were hungry and without provisions. He explained that he was expecting some rations down from Lynchburg and asked that on their arrival at Appomattox Station they be given to his men.

Unknown to Lee, these trains had already arrived—those which Sheridan had captured on the previous afternoon. In generous consideration for the feelings of Robert E. Lee in his great extremity, Grant told him nothing of the capture. Instead, he asked how many rations would be required and, when told that 25,000 would suffice, he ordered them delivered to the Confederate commissary at once. So it came about that while the soldiers of Lee's gallant Army of Northern Virginia waited for their paroles, they ate the food brought to them by their own railroad—too late.

Four years had passed since that April day when militia captain John B. Imboden had taken the cars to capture the arsenal at Harper's Ferry; four years since the railroads had carried the first great Union army to Washington. During those years it had been conclusively demonstrated that valor was not enough. The projection of locomotives into warfare disproved the thesis that victory must come to the side with the bravest men. In a battle area which extended from the Atlantic coastline to the Mississippi River, and beyond, the first year of the war made it apparent to some and should have made it obvious to all that, regardless of all other factors involved, mobility was of prime importance. It should have been equally clear to all that mobility of men, munitions and supplies depended in large measure on the railroads. More quickly than the South, the North capitalized on the advantage it held in this particular. Slow to recognize its railroad handicap, the Confederate government quarreled with its railroad men and did nothing to lessen that handicap.

On the fateful day of Appomattox, the railroad system in the North was stronger than when the war began. Except for the lines taken over by the Federal army and rehabilitated for its military use, practically all the railroads of the South were a pitiable mass of wreckage.

Fortunately for all Americans, the war was over and the period of railroad destruction in the South had come to an end. It was time to rebuild. Not only was it time to rebuild in the South, but time to start the construction of the great trunk lines which would connect North with South and both with the great Far West.

Today, as one rides the sleek streamliners over the modern bridge which spans Potomac Creek, past the little white house at Guiney's Station and on through Petersburg and across the Carolinas, one cannot forget that thousands of men died to hold these railroads for the cause they thought right. As one pauses on the battlefields of Stone's River, Chickamauga or Peach Tree Creek, to watch great Diesels hurry by with a hundred freight cars bearing the nation's commerce, one pays silent tribute to their predecessors, the little wood burners with funnel stacks and bullet-splintered cabs, which served so well and so effectively in the long struggle to preserve the Union.

Notes

NOTES

CHAPTER I

The Railroads Draw the Boundaries

1. Later Imboden became a distinguished brigadier general of Confederate cavalry. For his personal account of this early expedition against the Harper's Ferry arsenal see R. U. Johnson and C. C. Buel, editors, *Battles and Leaders of the Civil War* (The Century Company, 1884), I, 111, *et seq.* Hereafter cited as *Battles and Leaders*.

2. Dwight L. Agnew, "Jefferson Davis and the Rock Island Bridge" *(Iowa Journal of History,* Vol. 47, 1949).

3. For an interesting summary of military use and the study of railroads as a military potential in Europe prior to the Civil War in America, see E. A. Pratt, *The Rise of Rail-Power in War and Conquest* (London: P. S. King, 1915) 1-13, inc.

4. Edward Hungerford, *The Story of the Baltimore and Ohio Railroad 1827-1897* (New York: G. P. Putnam's Sons, 1928), I, 264.

5. Sixth Annual Report of the Pennsylvania Railroad (1852).

6. Minutes of a special meeting of the Board of Directors of the Erie Railroad, held December 24, 1851. Minute Book 452.

CHAPTER II

Roads North and South

1. For a detailed account of the financing and construction and early operation of the Charleston & Hamburg Railroad, see U. B. Phillips, *A History of Transportation in the Eastern Cotton Belt to 1860* (Columbia University Press, 1908), Chap. III, 132-167, inc.

2. For the most part the individual railroads of the South were short. In most cases where continuous track extended for any great distance or crossed state lines, two or more railroads were connected to form a single line. In traveling between Memphis and Lynchburg, over what we group as the Memphis & Charleston, four separate roads were traversed from end to end. When in 1862 the Confederate government was struggling to have a second trunk connection completed through Montgomery to the Mississippi, the link between West Point and Montgomery was the

Montgomery & West Point; from Montgomery to Selma there was only a river connection; from Selma to Reagan was the Alabama & Mississippi never quite completed; from Reagan to Meridian, the Northeast & Southwest Railroad Company owned the track; from Meridian to Vicksburg it was the Southern of Mississippi. To avoid the repetitious tedium of using all these names, the longer routes are herein identified by termini or the name of the major railroad involved, as, for instance, the Memphis & Charleston to identify the northernmost east-west trunk line.

3. Poor's *Manual of Railroads*, XXIII, vi of Introduction.
4. "Railway Statistics Before 1890" (Bureau of Statistics of the Interstate Commerce Commission), 2.

CHAPTER III

Rolling Stock

1. The rough usage to which engines were subjected during the war discouraged the highly decorative vogue in locomotive trimming. The practice was soon abandoned.
2. The vexatious problem of devising a valve gear for the regulation of all locomotive speeds forward and in reverse had been solved sometime prior to 1861 and link motion had become almost universal.
3. Hungerford, *op. cit.*, I, 231.
4. Among the many Northern builders of various types and sizes of locomotives, the following were leaders in the field:
    Baldwin and Company, Philadelphia, Pa.
    Baltimore & Ohio Railroad Shops, Baltimore, Md.
    William Mason, Taunton, Mass.
    New Jersey Locomotive Works, Paterson, N. J.
    Norris & Son, Philadelphia, Pa.
    Rogers Locomotive Works, Paterson, N. J.
    Taunton Locomotive Co., Taunton, Mass.
5. Robert M. Sutton, *The Illinois Central Railroad in Peace and War*, 1858-1868 (unpublished doctoral dissertation, University of Illinois, 1948), 103-105. Hereafter cited as Sutton.

CHAPTER IV

The Itching Palm of Simon Cameron

1. U. S. War Department, *War of the Rebellion: A Compilation of the Official Records of the Union and Confederate Armies* (Washington, 1899), series 3, I, 71. (This work is hereafter referred to as *O.R.* All such references are to series 1 unless otherwise indicated.)

2. *Ibid.*, 69.
3. *Ibid.*, 86.
4. Samuel Richey Kamm, *The Civil War Career of Thomas A. Scott* (published doctoral dissertation, University of Pennsylvania, 1940), 24.
5. Festus P. Summers, *The Baltimore and Ohio in the Civil War* (G. P. Putnam's Sons, 1939), 48-49. This material, as well as all succeeding passages from *The Baltimore and Ohio in the Civil War*, is reprinted by permission from Festus P. Summers, Copyright, 1939.
6. *O.R.*, LI, pt. 1, 327.
7. Kamm, *op. cit.*, 24.
8. *O.R.*, LI, pt. 1, 327.
9. *O.R.*, II, 577.
10. Summers, *op. cit.*, 53*ff.*
11. *Ibid.*, 54.
12. *O.R.*, II, 11.
13. *Ibid*, 10*ff.*
14. *Ibid.*, 10.
15. For the detailed story of the events transpiring in Baltimore on April 17, 18, 19, 1861, see reports made to the Maryland Assembly by various city officers and observers, *O.R.*, II, 10-20, inc.
16. *Ibid.*, 578.
17. *Ibid.*
18. *Ibid.*, 581.
19. *Ibid.*, 584.
20. *Ibid.*, 582.
21. Kamm, *op. cit.*, 32.
22. *Ibid.*, 34.
23. *Ibid.*, 36.
24. *O.R.*, II, 616.
25. *Ibid.*, 617.
26. Kamm, *op. cit.*, 39.
27. *O.R.*, II, 617.
28. *Ibid.*, 606.
29. On page 41, Kamm *(op. cit.)* attributes this move to the influence of Thomson, Felton and Scott.
30. *O.R.*, LI, pt. 2, 21.
31. *Ibid.*, II, 597.
32. *Battles and Leaders*, I, 123.
33. For detailed accounts of railroad operations in and about Baltimore during April and May 1861, see Kamm, Chap. II. Also Summers, Chap. III.
34. Sutton, *op. cit.*, 178.

CHAPTER V

Concentration in Virginia

1. Robert S. Henry, *The Story of the Confederacy* (Indianapolis: The Bobbs-Merrill Company, 1931, 1936), 43.
2. *O.R.*, II, 793.
3. For a complete and detailed account of Lee's preparations for the defense of Virginia, see Douglas Southall Freeman, *R. E. Lee* (Charles Scribner's Sons, 1934), I, Chap. XXVII-XXX, inc.
4. *O.R.*, II, 778.
5. *Ibid.*, 776-777.
6. *Ibid.*, 849.
7. *Ibid.*, 858.
8. *Ibid.*, 872.
9. *Ibid.*, 795.
10. *Ibid.*, 806.
11. *Ibid.*, 807.
12. Charles W. Ramsdell, "The Confederate Government and the Railroads" *(American Historical Review*, XXII, 1917), 797. Hereafter cited as Ramsdell.
13. *Ibid.*, 798.
14. *O.R.*, II, 937.
15. *Ibid.*, 830.
16. *O.R.*, series 4, I, 405-406.
17. *Ibid.*, 240-241.
18. *Ibid.*, 120, 224, 236, 238.
19. *Ibid.*, 269.

CHAPTER VI

Railroads in the Western Virginia Campaign

1. Summers, *op. cit.*, 66-67.
2. For a full and dramatic account of Jackson's operations in relation to B.&O. property about Harper's Ferry and Martinsburg see Hungerford, *op. cit.*, II, 6-14, inc.
3. *Ibid.*, 9.
4. *National Intelligencer* (Washington, D.C.), July 12, 1861.
5. *O.R.*, II, 788.
6. *Ibid.*, 790-791.
7. *Ibid.*, 802-803.
8. *Ibid.*, 51-52.
9. *Ibid.*, 46.
10. *Ibid.*, 47.

11. *Ibid.*, 49-50.
12. It is unlikely that McClellan knew of J. M. Mason's letter to Lee urging him to get to this structure with adequate guards in advance of the invaders and prepare for its demolition in the event Virginia was unable to hold control of the road.
13. Summers, *op. cit.*, 84.
14. Whitelaw Reid, *Ohio in the War: Her Statesmen, Her Generals, and Soldiers* (New York, 1868), I, 811.
15. *O.R.*, II, 236-238.
16. *Ibid.*, 239.
17. *Ibid.*, 242.
18. *Ibid.*, 201-202.
19. *Ibid.*, 224.
20. For the detailed story of the abortive attempt to intercept the Confederate retreat, see the comprehensive report of the affair made by General Hill to General McClellan. Also reports of Hill's subordinate officers. *O.R.*, II, 224-235, inc.
21. *O.R.*, V, 7.
22. *Ibid.*

CHAPTER VII

First Bull Run

1. While in the North the battle was known as the Battle of Bull Run, the Confederates always referred to the struggle as the Battle of Manassas.
2. McDowell's report of August 14, 1861. *O.R.*, II, 320.
3. *Battles and Leaders*, I, 175.
4. In justice to McDowell it must be pointed out that in planning his battle he had not completely overlooked the Manassas Gap Railroad. J. B. Fry, his assistant adjutant general at the time, quotes his commander as saying, ". . . if possible destroy the railroad leading from Manassas to the valley of Virginia where the enemy has a large force." *Battles and Leaders*, I, 183. Although this was part of the general plan for the major engagement, it nowhere appears that any effort was made to cut this road before battle was joined. It is unlikely that later in the war any commander would have undertaken such an operation as the Bull Run attack without first subjecting the railroad to cavalry raiding.
5. Hungerford, *op. cit.*, II, 114.
6. Summers, *op. cit.*, 100.
7. Hungerford, *op. cit.*, II, 10-12.
8. *Ibid.*, 13.

9. *Ibid.*, 14.
10. Summers, *op. cit.*, 100.
11. Quoted by *Baltimore Sun*, October 4, 1861.
12. Summers, *op. cit.*, 101.
13. *Baltimore Evening Patriot*, October 15, 1861.
14. Quoted by *Wheeling Intelligencer*, October 9, 1861.
15. Summers, *op. cit.*, 101-104.
16. *Ibid.*, 104.
17. *Ibid.*, 109.

CHAPTER VIII

No Compromise in Missouri

1. For details of the early attempt to take Missouri out of the Union and seize the arsenal at St. Louis, see *Battles and Leaders*, I, 262, *et seq.* Snead was the custodian of the private and official papers of General Price.
2. *Battles and Leaders*, I, 289.
3. For a full account of the battle of Wilson's Creek and the death of Lyon, see *Ibid.*, 289, *et seq.*
4. *Ibid.*, 307, *et seq.*
5. *Ibid.*, 283.
6. William Preston Johnston, *The Life of Gen. Albert Sydney Johnston* (D. Appleton, 1878), 355. Hereafter cited as Johnston.
7. *Ibid.*, 310.
8. *Ibid.*, 411.
9. *Ibid.*, 350.
10. Lloyd Lewis, *Sherman, Fighting Prophet* (Harcourt, Brace and Company, 1932), 190.
11. Johnston, *op. cit.*, 316.
12. Lewis, *op. cit.*, 192.
13. Sherman's letters and dispatches of the period are filled with expressions of fear as to the fate of his army.
14. Johnston, *op. cit.*, 356.
15. *Ibid.*, 317.

CHAPTER IX

At the End of '61

1. *O.R.*, series 4, I, 613.
2. *Ibid.*, 945.
3. *Ibid.*, 1049.
4. Charles W. Turner, "The Virginia Central Railroad at War,

1861-1865" (*Journal of Southern History*, XII, No. 4, November 1946), 521.

5. Charles W. Turner, "The Richmond, Fredericksburg and Potomac at War, 1861-1865" (*The Historian*, Spring 1946), 112.

6. Figures from the annual report of the company for the year 1859. It is unlikely the rolling stock was increased before the war opened. No reports were filed during the war years.

7. *O.R.*, series 4, I, 617.

8. *Ibid.*, 634. It will be recalled this was the vital link of the east-west trunk line which Thomas of the Union Army had wanted to attack.

9. *O.R., op. cit.*, 646.

10. Johnston, *op. cit.*, 530.

11. *O.R., op. cit.*, 417-418.

12. *Ibid.*, 484.

13. *Ibid.*, 724.

14. Charles S. Anderson, "Train-running with the Confederacy" (*Locomotive Engineering*, Vol. VI, 1893), 177. Throughout the war, Anderson was a train conductor in the service of the Virginia Central.

15. *O.R.*, series 3, I, 699.

16. Kamm, *op. cit.*, 65.

17. *Ibid.*, 69.

18. *O.R.*, series 3, I, 749.

19. *Ibid.*, 751.

20. *Ibid.*, 325.

21. Kamm, *op. cit.*, 51.

22. For the full text of the Morley report to Cameron see *O.R.*, series 3, I, 673-674.

CHAPTER X

The Roads in the Tennessee Fighting, Spring '62

1. *Personal Memoirs of U. S. Grant* (Charles L. Webster & Co., 1886), I, 293. Hereafter cited as Grant.

2. Robert S. Henry "*First with the Most*" *Forrest* (The Bobbs-Merrill Company, 1944), 49.

3. *Ibid.*, 64.

4. Probably these were the first war refugee trains in history.

5. Henry, "*First with the Most*" *Forrest*, 69.

6. Johnston, *op. cit.*, 503.

7. Henry, "*First with the Most*" *Forrest*, 72.

8. Johnston, *op. cit.*, 507.

9. Grant, *op. cit.*, I, 330.

10. *Ibid.*
11. General Pope had joined him with 30,000 men " . . . fresh from the capture of Island No. 10 in the Mississippi River." Grant, *op. cit.*, I, 371.
12. For the detailed story of Halleck's move from Pittsburg Landing to Corinth, see Grant, *op. cit.*, I, Chap. XXVI. Although Grant had been all but ignored by Halleck and had good cause to resent the treatment accorded him, his reporting of the move is entirely consistent with well-known facts concerning Halleck's stubborn procrastinations, his calling back Buell on the right and Pope on the left after they had approached to within a short distance of Corinth and found the way open, and concerning the success of the enemy in escaping with little or no loss of men or matériel.
13. Johnston, *op. cit.*, 485.

CHAPTER XI

Stonewall Jackson Knows How to Use a Railroad

1. Later, General Johnston claimed this plant was erected without his consent or approval. See Joseph E. Johnston, *Narrative of Military Operations* (Appleton, 1874), 98. Hereafter cited as Joseph E. Johnston.
2. *Ibid.*, 99.
3. *Ibid.*, 98.
4. Jefferson Davis, *Rise and Fall of the Confederate Government* (Appleton, 1881), I, 460-465. Also *Jefferson Davis, Constitutionalist: His Letters and Speeches*, edited by Dunbar Rowland (Mississippi State Department of Archives), VII, 493-495.
5. *Ibid.*, 493. Later Johnston disputed the charge he had selected no line to which to retreat, and says he had scouted the roads to be used in the move to the Rappahannock. See Joseph E. Johnston, *op. cit.*, 101.
6. *Ibid.*, 97.
7. It has been estimated that on the entire line between Alexandria and Lynchburg there were no more than four miles of sidetrack.
8. *O.R.*, V, 1083.
9. *Ibid.*
10. *Ibid.*, 1093.
11. Douglas Southall Freeman, *Lee's Lieutenants* (Charles Scribner's Sons, 1942), I, 139, footnote 11.
12. *Battles and Leaders*, I, 261. Also *O.R.*, series 4, I, 1038.
13. *O.R.*, V, 1100. Also *O.R.*, LI, 497.
14. *O.R.*, V, 1096.
15. *Battles and Leaders*, II, 202.

16. Freeman, *R. E. Lee*, II, 61.
17. Anderson, *op. cit.*, 245.
18. Unpublished diary of Lucy R. Buck of Front Royal, May 24, 1862. Markham was about thirteen miles east of Front Royal.
19. *O.R.*, II, pt. 3, 594.
20. Anderson, *op. cit.*, 245, *et seq.*
21. *Battles and Leaders*, II, 296-297.
22. The territory through which the railroad ran from Louisa to Beaver Dam was at that time unoccupied by the Confederates and therefore open to raids by the Federals. Doubtless Mr. Fontaine had reason to fear the crowded trains might be attacked or wrecked and felt he could not assume the responsibility for moving the troops through unguarded country.
23. The recital of details in connection with train operations in the transportation of Jackson's army via the Virginia Central Railroad from Staunton to Beaver Dam Station is taken, for the most part, from a series of articles written by Charles S. Anderson for the magazine *Locomotive Engineering.* There is no verification for his stories as they relate to personal experiences and his memory may have been faulty as to the exact timing of some of the happenings described. However, he discloses an accurate knowledge of the basic events. A trusted employee of the Virginia Central before and throughout the war, a train conductor with full opportunity to observe the scenes he describes, he says nothing about rolling stock or train running that is inconsistent with the known facts. We have, therefore, chosen to rely on his narrative as the best firsthand description of troop-train operation in the Confederacy of the time. For his complete stories, see *Locomotive Engineering*, V, 245, 287, 369, 405; VI, 177, 267, 341, 421, 531.
24. The surprise Jackson had worked so hard to accomplish was by no means complete. When the troops left Gordonsville a deserter from the ranks correctly guessed the destination of the army and slipped away to warn McClellan that Jackson had left the Valley and was headed east. Perhaps Jackson had overdone his mysterious train shuffling. *O.R.*, XI, pt. 1, 49.

CHAPTER XII

The North Finds an Engineering Genius

1. *Battles and Leaders*, II, 163.
2. Haupt had no military ambitions and accepted this appointment to rank only because it would facilitate his handling of the work to be done. Although graduated from West Point when only

eighteen years of age, he served less than a year and resigned his commission to become an engineer in private employment. His first job was in connection with the construction of a new railroad and before another year ended he was tapped by his native state of Pennsylvania to serve as principal assistant in its extensive system of railroad and canal development. From that start he rose with incredible swiftness to the top of his profession.

3. The automatic compressed air drill.

4. The three companies were from the Sixth and Seventh Wisconsin and Nineteenth Indiana regiments.

5. For his own account of the reconstruction of the railroad and the building of the Potomac Creek bridge, together with copies of his correspondence and orders relating thereto, see *Reminiscences of General Herman Haupt* (Published by the author, 1901), 43-54. Hereafter cited as Haupt.

6. *Ibid.*, 50.

7. *Ibid.*

8. *O.R.*, series 3, I, 879.

9. *O.R.*, series 3, V, 974.

10. Haupt, *op. cit.*, 53.

11. *Ibid.*

12. *Ibid.*

13. *Ibid.*, 54.

14. *Ibid.*, 55.

15. *Ibid.*, 56.

16. *Ibid.*

17. *Ibid.*, 59.

18. *Ibid.*, 60.

19. When conditions on the road improved and sufficient supplies were accumulated, telegraph dispatching was resumed, most likely, it seems, because the War Department for some reason insisted on it.

20. Haupt, *op. cit.*, 69.

21. *O.R.*, series 3, V, 974.

22. *Ibid.*

23. Freeman, *R. E. Lee*, II, 159.

24. *Ibid.*, 160.

25. *O.R.*, XI, pt. 2, 200.

26. The accounts of this episode are many and varied. Some make no reference to explosions while others say the ammunition-laden cars were set on fire when started for the river and while on their way to the broken bridge supplied an awesome spectacle of speeding fire and explosion. One such description is found in the diary of the Rev. James J. Marks, a Union Chaplain. Contemplating such a scene, one regrets having no opportunity to ask

the diarist how it happened that the exploding shells did not derail or destroy the train before it reached the river.

27. Freeman, *R. E. Lee*, II, 173. Also *Battles and Leaders*, II, 373. At various times railroad batteries were used by both sides but usually proved much more terrifying in contemplation than effective in actual use.

28. All of the rolling stock McCallum sent to the Peninsula was destroyed or disabled to prevent its falling into the hands of the enemy. McCallum reported this was done when the army retired to Harrison's Landing. Either he was mistaken as to the time or careless of his language, for the entire railroad was in possession of the enemy before the army went to Harrison's Landing. This destruction must have taken place at the time White House was abandoned. *O.R.*, series 3, V, 975.

CHAPTER XIII

The Saga of the "General"

1. *Battles and Leaders*, II, 701.
2. *Ibid.*, 716.
3. *Ibid.*, 702-703.
4. Now Kenesaw.
5. The General is now on permanent display in the depot of the Nashville, Chattanooga and St. Louis Railroad at Chattanooga. The Texas may be seen in the Confederate Museum in Atlanta.
6. Immediately following the event and for many years thereafter, the Andrews raid was a favorite subject for the tellers of wartime stories. As told by those of the raiders who survived, by those who participated in the capture, by those who witnessed some small part of the wild race and endlessly elaborated on it, by those who only heard the telling of it, the story developed weird exaggerations and inconsistencies which persist. However, one of the raiders and an exchanged prisoner was William Pittenger, a young soldier from Ohio who later became a minister and wrote a detailed account of the affair in which he participated from beginning to end. Except for what happened at Kingston while he was inside the closed boxcar, he had an opportunity to observe all that occurred in connection with the theft and flight of the General. Furthermore, it seems he must have heard the testimony of Fuller, for his story of those portions of the pursuit he could not have observed is entirely consistent with what he saw and with the known facts. No one had a better opportunity to know the story from both sides. Because of Pittenger's quali-

fications and his reputation for integrity, the author has drawn heavily on his account for the material in this chapter. *Battles and Leaders*, II, 709, *et seq.* O.R., X, pt. 1, 630-639.

Among others of the raiders who lived to tell the story was William Reddick of Locust Grove, Ohio. Living in the same village at the time was a little girl who later became Mrs. Elizabeth Dunlap. She distinctly remembers Reddick and his story of the adventure. In the summer of 1950, Mrs. Dunlap told this author of being present at a banquet given Reddick by the people of Locust Grove, celebrating his return from prison.

CHAPTER XIV

The Railroads and Bragg's Invasion

1. Grant, *op. cit.*, I, 383.
2. *Ibid.*, 381.
3. *Ibid.*, 383.
4. O.R., XVI, pt. 2, 145-151.
5. Henry, *"First with the Most" Forrest*, 93.
6. O.R., XVI, 198.
7. *Ibid.*, pt. 2, 729.
8. *Ibid.*, 731.
9. Of this move, Robert S. Henry says it was " . . . the first time an army had been shifted from one theater to another by rail." *"First with the Most" Forrest*, 91.
10. *Ibid.*, 96.
11. Grant, *op. cit.*, I, 384.
12. O.R., XVI, pt. 2, 266.
13. Grant, *op. cit.*, I, 393.
14. *Ibid.*, 394.
15. *Ibid.*, 395.
16. *Ibid.*, 404-405.
17. O.R., XVI, pt. 2, 329.
18. *Battles and Leaders*, III, 37. It appears that throughout the war, most soldiers intensely disliked being detailed to the duty of guarding railroad bridges. As a rule it was a lonely task with the threat of surprise attack ever present and the hope for support almost futile.
19. *Ibid.*, 41.
20. Henry, *"First with the Most" Forrest*, 100.
21. *Battles and Leaders*, III, 13.

CHAPTER XV

Jackson, Haupt and Second Bull Run

1. It will be remembered that at Louisa Court House the railroad officials had refused to assume the responsibility for the movement of the trains beyond that point and the military had taken charge of them. The army having made no arrangement for the return of the trains, the crews were left stranded at Beaver Dam.
2. Anderson, *op. cit.*, 367.
3. *Ibid.*, 405
4. *O.R.*, XII, pt. 3, 915.
5. *O.R.*, XIV, 594.
6. Also known as Slaughter Mountain.
7. Freeman, *Lee's Lieutenants*, II, 52.
8. Anderson, *op. cit.*, VI, 177.
9. Freeman, *R. E. Lee*, II, 260.
10. Haupt, *op. cit.*, 70.
11. *O.R.*, XII, pt. 3, 598.
12. *Ibid.*, 602.
13. Haupt, *op. cit.*, 73.
14. Freeman, *R. E. Lee*, II, 279-303. Also Freeman, *Lee's Lieutenants*, II, 67-82. In these works the story will be found well told.
15. Haupt, *op. cit.*, 75.
16. *Ibid.*
17. *Ibid.*, 83.
18. *Ibid.*, 94-100.
19. *O.R.*, XII, pt. 2, 554, 642-643.
20. Freeman, *Lee's Lieutenants*, II, 95.
21. *O.R.*, XII, pt. 2, 670.
22. For a graphic description of the plundering of Federal stores at Manassas see Freeman, *Lee's Lieutenants*, II, 96-101.
23. Haupt, *op. cit.*, 98.
24. *Ibid.*, 104.
25. *Ibid.*
26. *Ibid.*, 119.
27. *Ibid.*, 124.
28. W. T. Sherman, Memoirs of W. T. Sherman (Webster, 1892), II, 151.
29. *Ibid.*, 151-152.

CHAPTER XVI

The Rails in the Antietam Campaign and After

1. Freeman, *Lee's Lieutenants*, II, 144, and cases cited.
2. For a complete study of the controlling reasons why Lee undertook the invasion, see Freeman, *R. E. Lee*, II, 350, *et seq.; Lee's Lieutenants*, II, 144, *et seq.*
3. *O.R.*, XIX, pt. 2, 593.
4. *O.R.*, XIX, pt. 1, 966. Also *O.R.*, XXV, pt. 2, 711.
5. Special Order No. 248. *O.R.*, XIX, pt. 2, 326.
6. Haupt, *op. cit.*, 139.
7. *Ibid.*, 138.
8. *Ibid.*, 136-144.
9. *O.R.*, XIX, pt. 2, 494.
10. He was referring to the destruction of the road by Federal soldiers at the time of Pope's retreat.
11. Haupt, *op. cit.*, 146.
12. *Ibid.*, 147.
13. *Ibid.*, 155.
14. *Ibid.*, 158.

CHAPTER XVII

Forrest Finds Grant's Achilles' Heel

1. *Battles and Leaders*, III, 28.
2. Grant, *op. cit.*, I, 407-408.
3. *Ibid.*
4. *Ibid.*, 419-420.
5. *Ibid.*, 415.
6. *Ibid.*, 420.
7. *Ibid.*, 423.
8. *Ibid.* Within his jurisdiction also lay the Memphis & Ohio between Memphis and Humboldt which, for some reason, he does not mention in his catalogue of railroads he controlled.
9. *O.R.*, XVII, pt. 1, 528, 530.
10. Grant, *op. cit.*, I, 246.
11. It was at this stage of the campaign that a supplementary line of approach to Vicksburg was developed. Sherman was sent back to Memphis to co-operate with Admiral Porter in an expedition down the river and from that time until the capitulation, the navy played an ever-increasing part in the undertaking; but since the

railroads were only indirectly involved, that part of the Vicksburg campaign finds no proper place in these pages.
12. Grant, *op. cit.*, I, 431.

CHAPTER XVIII

Government Railroad Policy, South and North

1. *O.R.*, series 4, I, 912.
2. *Ibid.*, 941.
3. *Ibid.*, 1073.
4. *Ibid.*, II, 200.
5. Ramsdell, *op. cit.*, 802.
6. *O.R.*, series 4, I, 1026.
7. *Ibid.*, 1022.
8. *Ibid.*, 1086.
9. *Ibid.*, 1085.
10. *Ibid.*, 1025.
11. *Ibid.*, 1107.
12. *Ibid.*, III, 392.
13. *Ibid.*, I, 1049.
14. *Ibid.*, 1053.
15. *Ibid.*, 1145.
16. Turner, "The Virginia Central Railroad at War," 521.
17. *O.R.*, series 4, I, 839.
18. *Ibid.*, 880.
19. James Ford Rhodes, *History of the Civil War* (The Macmillan
    Company, 1917), 375.
20. *O.R.*, series 4, I, 843.
21. *Ibid.*, 868, 882.
22. Turner, "The Richmond, Fredericksburg and Potomac Railroad
    at War," 115.
23. *O.R.*, series 4, I, 842.
24. Turner, "The Virginia Central Railroad at War," 523.
25. *Ibid.*, 511.
26. Ramsdell, *op. cit.*, 799.
27. *O.R.*, series 4, II, 225.
28. *Ibid.*, 373.
29. Ramsdell, *op. cit.*, 800.
30. R. S. Cotterill, "The Louisville and Nashville Railroad"
    (*American Historical Review*, XXIX), 701.
31. *Ibid.*
32. Summers, *op. cit.*, 116.
33. *Ibid.*

34. *Journal of the House of Delegates of the State of Virginia for Called Session of 1862*, appended Document No. 1, x.
35. O.R., LI, pt. 2, 635-636.
36. Thirty-seventh Annual Report of President Garrett to Stockholders of the B.&O., 42.
37. Kamm, *op. cit.*, 77, *et seq.* Here Kamm discusses this report at length.
38. O.R., series 3, II, 794-795.
39. *Ibid.*

CHAPTER XIX

The Railroads in the Vicksburg Campaign

1. *Battles and Leaders*, III, 611-612.
2. Henry, *"First with the Most" Forrest*, 139.
3. For a full and detailed account of the Streight raid, see *Ibid.*, 139-159.
4. Grant, *op. cit.*, I, 442.
5. *Ibid.*, 441.
6. *Ibid.*, 488.
7. *Ibid.*, 489.
8. *Ibid.*
9. *Ibid.*
10. *Ibid.*
11. Henry, *The Story of the Confederacy*, 257.
12. Grant, *op. cit.*, I, 501.
13. *Ibid.*, 506.
14. *Ibid.*, 507.
15. Henry, *The Story of the Confederacy*, 262.
16. Grant, *op. cit.*, I, 578.
17. *Ibid.*, 579.

CHAPTER XX

Gettysburg—and Haupt Again

1. O.R., XVIII, 813.
2. *Ibid.*, XXI, 1110.
3. *Ibid.*, XVIII, 784.
4. *Ibid.*, 873.
5. O.R., XXI, 1110.
6. *Ibid.*, 1077, 1110. Also *Ibid.*, XXV, pt. 2, 618, 632, 599, 681, 727, 749.
7. Freeman, *R. E. Lee*, II, 477.

8. *O.R.*, XXV, pt. 2, 730.
9. *Ibid.*, 610-611.
10. *Ibid.*, XXI, pt. 2, 612.
11. *Ibid.*, XXV, pt. 2, 693.
12. *Ibid.*, 612.
13. For an analysis of Northrop and his attitude toward Lee, see Freeman, *R. E. Lee*, II, 494-495.
14. *O.R.*, XXV, pt. 2, 652, 653, 711.
15. *Ibid.*, 730.
16. E. P. Alexander, *Memoirs of a Confederate* (Charles Scribner's Sons, 1907), 318.
17. Freeman, *R. E. Lee*, III, 19.
18. *Ibid.*, 29, *et seq.*
19. *Battles and Leaders*, III, 271.
20. At that time, Stuart was in the last place Lee would have expected to find him. He was east of the mountains, as he was supposed to be, but he was also east of Meade's army where he was not supposed to be. With the Federal army between him and the troops who were depending on him for information, he was in no position to discharge his duty. When he had ridden off to feel the dispositions of Hooker before crossing the Potomac, he found himself in the midst of intriguing adventure. In pursuit of it, he rode far afield and after much delay, crossed the river at Rowser's Ford within twenty miles of Washington. That was when he decided to ride around Hooker's entire army as he had ridden around McClellan on the Peninsula.

Shortly after crossing into Maryland he came on a long Federal wagon train which presented such a temptation as neither he nor his troopers ever was able to resist. The capture of it entailed the loss of valuable time and thereafter he was obliged to move more slowly in order to carry the booty. along with him. True, there were 125 beautiful, brand-new wagons such as never were seen in the South. The mules were sleek and fat, the harness new and gay and the cargo consisted of things much needed by the Confederates; but while he chuckled over his slowly moving prize, his ever so important assignment in the intricate but otherwise smoothly running plans of Lee was being neglected. As a result Lee went into the battle of Gettysburg wholly uninformed as to the approach of his adversary. For a full account of Stuart's fateful diversion, see Freeman, *Lee's Lieutenants*, III, Chap. IV, appropriately entitled "The Price of 125 Wagons."
21. Haupt, *op. cit.*, 204.
22. *Ibid.*, 208.
23. *Ibid.*, 211.

24. *Ibid.*
25. *Ibid.*, 236.
26. *Ibid.* Haupt was famous for his uncanny foresight in anticipating requirements and for never overlooking minute details.
27. *O.R.*, XXVII, pt. 3, 523.
28. Haupt, *op. cit.*, 220-221.
29. *Ibid.*, 236.
30. In attempted justification of his failure to follow up his victory, Meade contended that at the close of the battle his troops were too short of supplies to permit an immediate move to cut off Lee's retreat at the Potomac. However, the weight of evidence was against him. Both Quartermaster General Meigs and General Haupt, the two men who had the opportunity to know most about the situation, declared that Meade's men had more supplies than they could have carried with them, that the railroad was open on and after July 5 and surplus supplies were brought back to the hospitals. It is possible that because of faulty distribution within the army organization, some units may have been short of supplies, but that the shortage applied to the army as a whole is quite improbable.
31. Haupt, *op. cit.*, 224.

CHAPTER XXI

Transportation Feats in the Chattanooga Campaign

1. Alexander, *op. cit.*, 447.
2. G. Moxley Sorrel, *Recollections of a Confederate Staff Officer* (Neale Publishing Company, 1905), 189.
3. Augustus Dickert, *History of Kershaw's Brigade* (E. H. Ault Company, 1899), 70.
4. *Battles and Leaders*, III, 640-641.
5. Sorrel, *op. cit.*, 192.
6. *Ibid.*, 193.
7. Alexander, *op. cit.*, 449. Beginning at Petersburg the detailed schedule of the artillery as Alexander recorded it was as follows:
   Left Petersburg at 4 p.m., September 17.
   Arrived at Wilmington 2 a.m., September 20. 225 miles in 58 hours.
   Ferried the Cape Fear River and left for Kingsville, South Carolina at 2 p.m.
   Covered the 192 miles to Kingsville in 28 hours.
   Changed trains for Augusta and arrived there 2 p.m., September 22.
   Left Augusta 7 p.m. for Atlanta 171 miles away.

Arrived at Atlanta 2 p.m., September 23.

Left Atlanta 4 a.m., September 24.

Arrived at Ringgold 2 a.m., September 25.

Total distance traveled 843 miles.

Total elapsed time seven days and ten hours.

8. Grant, *op. cit.*, II, 45.
9. Collected papers of Edward M. Stanton (Library of Congress), Sept., 1863.
10. Summers, *op. cit.*, 165.
11. The collected papers of Salmon P. Chase (Library of Congress), Sept. 24, 1863.
12. *O.R.*, XXIX, 151.
13. *Ibid.*, 153.
14. *Ibid.*, 148, 149, 152.
15. *Ibid.*, 158.
16. *Ibid.*, 161.
17. *Ibid.*
18. *Ibid.*, 162.
19. *Ibid.*
20. *Ibid.*, 149.
21. *Ibid.*, 150.
22. The Stanton Papers, September 27, 1863.
23. *O.R.*, XXIX, 172-173.
24. *Ibid.*, 173.
25. *Ibid.*, 176.
26. David H. Bates, *Lincoln in the Telegraph Office* (The Century Company, 1907), 179.
27. Banks's command on the lower Mississippi was excepted.
28. Grant, *op. cit.*, II, 19.
29. *Ibid.*, 26.
30. *Ibid.*, 46.
31. After the war Dodge served as Chief Engineer in the building of the Union Pacific.
32. Grant, *op. cit.*, II, 46.
33. *Ibid.*, 46, 48.

CHAPTER XXII

Wounded and Disabled Ride Away

1. Report of Assistant Surgeon C. K. Winne from Fifth Corps Headquarters.
2. Report of Surgeon F. L. Town, United States Army.
3. Report of Assistant Surgeon Dallas Bache, United States Army.
4. *Medical History of the Civil War*, 963.

5. Dr. Jonathan Letterman, *Recollections of the Army of the Potomac*, 158.

6. *Battles and Leaders*, III, 423, *et seq.*

7. Letterman, *op. cit.*

8. Surgeon George A. Otis, *Report of Transporting Wounded Soldiers by Railway*.

9. Most of the material for this brief study of the contribution of the railroads to the solution of the huge problem of caring for the many thousands of sick and wounded soldiers of the Union armies was derived from the voluminous and highly specialized collection in the Library of the Surgeon General, United States Army, Washington, D.C.

10. Kate Cumming, *Journal of Hospital Life in the Confederate Army of Tennessee*.

11. Dickert, *op. cit.*, 70.

12. *O.R.*, XXXVIII, pt. 5, 938.

13. *Ibid.*, 1022.

CHAPTER XXIII

Disaster Overtakes Southern Policy

1. "Fifteenth Annual Review of Trade and Commerce of Chicago," compiled by the *Chicago Tribune*.

2. When Haupt first was called by Stanton in April 1862, he was deeply involved in a serious controversy with Governor Andrew and other hostile interests in Massachusetts growing out of the construction of the Hoosac Tunnel. During the administration of Governor Banks, Haupt had contracted with the state to build the tunnel and a large part of the work was done. However, politically powerful Chester W. Chapin, President of the Boston & Albany Railroad, violently opposed the building of the tunnel and threw his support to the election of John A. Andrew as governor. Immediately following the election a divided legislature voted to stop payment to Haupt for work already done and turn over the completion of the construction to the state under the supervision of the State Engineer. This officer was then replaced by a man of Andrew's own choosing and reportedly recommended by Chapin.

As a result, Haupt's large personal fortune was tied up in the unfinished bore and Andrew and Chapin were fighting every move of the legislature to reimburse him for the money advanced. Despite the powerful force arrayed against him, Haupt's cause was popular with the public and his fight was gaining such support as to threaten the political power and prestige of the governor. That was why Haupt's recurring appearances before the legislature were so irksome to Andrew.

In August 1863 he delivered an ultimatum to Stanton. Either Haupt must be subjected to rigid observance of army regulations or Massachusetts would discontinue its support of the war. Since Andrew was in a position to work irreparable harm to the military operations, Stanton could do nothing except to demand of Haupt the strict observance of regulations which would have kept him out of Massachusetts. But since Haupt had no interest in army rank or pay and knew that under such conditions the things he had come to do could not be accomplished, he promptly resigned.

Thus, by his political chicanery, Andrew accomplished nothing for himself while depriving the army of the services of a railroad genius it could ill afford to lose. Haupt was, of course, charged with placing his own personal interests above those of his country but in his behalf let it be said that with his resignation he submitted an offer to serve as a civilian at any time the War Department considered his services essential to the cause of the Union. For a full account of the Hoosac Tunnel affair, see Haupt, *op. cit.*

3. Haupt, *op. cit.*, 197, *et seq.*
4. O.R., series 4, II, 409.
5. *Ibid.*, 841.
6. *Ibid.*, 852.
7. *Ibid.*, 886.
8. This was the extension being built by the government from Danville, Virginia, to connect with the Carolina roads at Greensboro, North Carolina.
9. *O.R.*, XVIII, 825.
10. *Ibid.*, XXXIII, 1177.
11. *Ibid.*, XVI, 951.
12. *Ibid.*, 952.
13. *Ibid.*, XVIII, 903.
14. *Ibid.*, XXIX, pt. 2, 628.
15. *Ibid.*, series 4, II, 655.
16. *Ibid.*, 1085.
17. *Ibid.*, 881-882.
18. *Ibid.*, XXV, pt. 2, 683.
19. *Ibid.*

CHAPTER XXIV

Supplying Sherman in the Atlanta Campaign

1. Grant, *op. cit.*, II, 127.
2. *Ibid.*, 556.

3. Table of Mileage; Nashville & Northwestern RR from Nashville to Johnsonville, 72 miles; Nashville to Chattanooga, via N.&C., 151 miles; Nashville to Stevenson via Decatur, 185 miles; Chattanooga to Knoxville, 111 miles.

4. *O.R.*, XXXII, pt. 2, 143.

5. *Ibid.*, 329.

6. *Ibid.*, 73.

7. *Ibid.*, 365, 372.

8. See Sherman *Memoirs*, II, 27, 29. Note letters to Grant dated April 10 and April 24.

9. *O.R.*, XXXII, pt. 3, 434.

10. *Ibid.*, 434.

11. *Ibid*, XXXVIII, pt. 4, 9.

12. *Battles and Leaders*, III, 252.

13. Sherman, *op. cit.*, II, 42.

14. *Ibid.*, 51.

15. *Ibid.*

16. *O.R.*, XXXVIII, pt. 4, 56.

17. *Ibid.*, pt. 5, 4.

18. *Ibid.*, pt. 4, 648.

19. Forrest had stopped William Sooy Smith at Okolona, Mississippi, and soundly whipped Sturgis at Brice's Cross Roads.

20. *Home Letters of General Sherman* (Charles S. Scribner's Sons, 1909), 296.

21. *O.R.*, LII, pt. 2, 672.

22. *Ibid.*, XXXIX, pt. 2, 628. Also, *Ibid.*, XXXVIII, pt. 4, 747.

23. Sherman, *Memoirs*, II, 65.

24. *Ibid.*

25. *Ibid.*, 66.

26. *Ibid.*

27. *Ibid.*, 67.

28. *Ibid.*, 85.

29. Haupt, *op. cit.*, 51. As between Haupt and Sherman, there is a discrepancy of one and one-half days in the time required to complete the bridge. Sherman in his *Memoirs*, II, 92, says it took six days. Sherman also gives credit for the accomplishment to Wright and fails to mention Smeed in connection with it. Since Haupt was especially interested in bridges, knew Smeed intimately and wrote in glowing terms of his ability as a bridge builder, while praising Wright as an administrator, it seems that Haupt would have known what went on. Though Sherman was near by, it may reasonably be assumed he saw nothing of the operation and gave credit to Wright solely because he was in command of the entire Construction Corps. In later years both McCallum and Wright were credited with having built the bridge.

30. Haupt, *op. cit.*, 317.
31. *Ibid.*, 296.
32. Sherman, *Memoirs*, II, 92.
33. *Ibid.*, 97.
34. *Ibid.*, 98.
35. *Ibid.*, 102. Sherman's own words.

CHAPTER XXV

The Roads in Lee's Defense of Richmond

1. For a comparative study of the factors which led Grant to move by his left and abandon his direct railroad supply line, see his own analysis of the situation. Grant, *op. cit.*, II, 134, *et seq.*
2. O.R., XXXVI, pt. 2, 337. Also Grant, *op. cit.*, II, 183-184, 192.
3. O.R., XXXVI, pt. 1, 133.
4. Grant, *op. cit.*, II, 208.
5. *Ibid.*, 188-189. For the assembly, organization and operating efficiency of this remarkable field transportation system, Grant gave full credit to Quartermaster General Rufus Ingalls.
6. *Battles and Leaders*, IV, 116, 148.
7. P. H. Sheridan, *Personal Memoirs of P. H. Sheridan* (Webster, 1888), I, 374.
8. *Ibid.*
9. *Ibid.*, 376.
10. For General Lee's report of the death of Stuart see *O.R.*, XXXVI, pt. 3, 800.
11. Sheridan, *op. cit.*, I, 386.
12. Grant, *op. cit.*, II, 248.
13. *Ibid.*, 249.
14. *Ibid.* Meantime Grant was destroying rails on the Virginia Central and the R.,F.&P. On May 26 he wrote Halleck: "I want to leave a gap in the roads north of Richmond so big that to get a single track they will have to import rails from elsewhere."
15. *Ibid.*, 254.
16. O.R., XXIX, pt. 2, 830, 835, 837-838, 844, 862.
17. *Ibid.*, 823-824.
18. *Ibid.*, 863-864. Also *O.R.*, XXXIII, 1095, 1100. Also *O.R.*, LI, pt. 2, 859.
19. O.R., XXXIII, 1073.
20. *Battles and Leaders*, IV, 593.
21. O.R., LI, pt. 2, 1012-1013.
22. George Meade, *Life and Letters of George Gordon Meade* (Charles Scribner's Sons, 1913), II, 236.

23. *O.R.*, XXXVII, pt. 1, 346.
24. *Ibid.*, XLII, pt. 1, 428, 940.
25. Grant, *op. cit.*, II, 324-325.
26. *Ibid.*, 341.
27. *O.R.*, XLII, pt. 3, 1156-1157.

CHAPTER XXVI

Wheels Stop Turning in Tennessee and Georgia

1. John B. Hood, *Advance and Retreat* (Copyrighted for the Hood Orphan Memorial Publication Fund of New Orleans, 1879), 245-246. Hereafter cited as Hood.
2. *O.R.*, XXXVIII, pt. 4, 756, 769, 770, 772, 792. Also *O.R.*, XXXVIII, pt. 5, 875, and *O.R.*, LII, pt. 2, 692. Throughout the Atlanta campaign Johnston continued to plead with Davis and Bragg to send cavalry from Mississippi to operate against Sherman's vital rail supply line below Nashville. Likewise, Forrest stoutly maintained that, given the permission to do so, he could destroy Sherman's railroads through Tennessee. See *Ibid.*, 731.
3. Hood, *op. cit.*, 254.
4. Sherman, *Memoirs*, II, 140.
5. *Ibid.*, 141.
6. It was not until September 5 that Forrest was given the long-sought permission to strike in middle Tennessee. *O.R.*, LII, pt. 2, 729.
7. Hood, *op. cit.*, 257. Also *Battles and Leaders*, IV, 425.
8. Hood, *op. cit.*, 262.
9. Railroad repairs had been made so rapidly that the damage done by Hood's men caused Sherman no distress and only slight delay.
10. Hood, *op. cit.*, 267.
11. *Ibid.*
12. *Ibid.*, 271, 272.
13. Henry, *"First with the Most" Forrest*, 352.
14. These are the dimensions of the trestlework as given in Forrest's report. See *O.R.*, XXXIX, pt. 1, 545. However, General McCallum says the structure was 1,100 feet long and about 90 feet high. See *Ibid.*, 507.
15. *Ibid.*, 517, 631.
16. Henry, *"First with the Most" Forrest*, 362.
17. *O.R.*, XXXIX, pt. 3, 896.
18. *O.R.*, XLV, pt. 1, 654. These are the casualties reported by Hood but there are those who think his figures much too conservative. See Stanley F. Horn, *The Army of Tennessee* (The Bobbs-Merrill Company, 1941), 403. In no single battle of the war did

any Confederate army lose so many general officers. Five were killed outright, six wounded (one fatally) and one was captured.

19. Hood, *op. cit.*, 307.
20. Sherman, *Memoirs*, II, 163. These railroads were within the area of Sherman's command and it will be remembered he was campaigning there at the time Grant called him in March to prepare for the drive against Johnston and Atlanta.
21. Sherman, *Memoirs*, II, 153-154.
22. *Ibid.*, 159.
23. *Ibid.*, 169.
24. *Ibid.*, 179.
25. *O.R.*, XXXIX, pt. 3, 680, 741, 746. Also *O.R.*, XLIV, 56.
26. Sherman, *Memoirs*, II, 177.
27. *O.R.*, XLIV, 157.
28. *Ibid.*, 159. Slocum estimated the number of Negroes following his column at no less than 14,000.
29. Sherman, *Memoirs*, II, 181.
30. *O.R.*, XLIV, 66.
31. Sherman, *Memoirs*, II, 188.
32. *O.R.*, XLIV, 68, 157.
33. *Ibid.*, 67.
34. Sherman, *Memoirs*, II, 189.
35. *Ibid.*, 175.
36. *O.R.*, XLIV, 69.
37. Sherman, *Memoirs*, II, 194.
38. For detailed accounts of the manner and extent of this destruction of railroad tracks, bridges and equipment, see the report of General Howard in *O.R.*, XLIV, 65-71. Also the report of General Slocum, *O.R.*, XLIV, 156-160. Slocum says: " . . . 119 miles of railroad were thoroughly and effectually destroyed, scarcely a tie or rail, a bridge or culvert on the entire line being left in condition to be of use again." Machine shops, turntables, depots and water tanks also were destroyed. This was the work of Slocum's men on the road between Atlanta and Augusta. Howard's column had done an equally thorough job on the line to Savannah via Macon.

CHAPTER XXVII

Railhead at Last

1. *O.R.*, II, 830.
2. Ramsdell, *op. cit.*, 802.
3. *O.R.*, XLII, pt. 3, 1156. Also *O.R.*, LI, pt. 2, 1054. Also *Ibid.*,

series 4, III, 930. For a detailed description of conditions see Freeman, *R. E. Lee*, II, 535-536, 538-539.

4. *O.R.*, XLVI, pt. 2, 1035, 1040-1041, 1075.

5. *Ibid.*, XLII, pt. 3, 1144, 1176.

6. *Ibid.*, series 4, pt. 3, 838.

7. *Ibid.*, XLVI, pt. 2, 1210.

8. *Ibid.*, XLVII, pt. 2, 1303-1304.

9. *Ibid.*, pt. 1, 1044. Also *Ibid.*, XLVI, pt. 2, 1247, 1250.

10. Grant, *op. cit.*, II, 424-425.

11. *Ibid.*, 427. Sheridan, *op. cit.*, II, 144.

12. Davis, II, 648. Also *O.R.*, XLVI, pt. 3, 1328.

13. *Journal of the Confederate States Congress*, VII, 584-586.

14. Sherman's advance units reached Cheraw, South Carolina, about March 1. Sherman, *op. cit.*, II, 290.

15. *O.R.*, XLVII, pt. 1, 1053, 1055, 1058.

16. Davis, *op. cit.*, II, 648.

17. *Ibid.*, 648.

18. *Ibid.*, 669-670.

19. Grant, *op. cit.*, II, 430.

20. Sheridan, *op. cit.*, II, 148-149.

21. Grant, *op. cit.*, II, 447.

22. *O.R.*, XLVI, pt. 1, 1263.

23. Freeman, *R. E. Lee*, IV, 44.

24. James Longstreet, *From Manassas to Appomattox* (Philadelphia, 1896), 605.

25. *O.R.*, XLVI, pt. 3, 1378.

26. *Ibid.*, 1379.

27. For a full and detailed discussion of this question see Freeman, *R. E. Lee*, Appendix IV-2.

28. *O.R.*, XLVI, pt. 3, 560-561. Also Sheridan, *op. cit.*, 174.

29. *O.R.*, XLVI, pt. 3, 562, 1382.

30. *Ibid.*, 1385.

31. Sheridan, *op. cit.*, II, 179.

32. *O.R.*, XLVI, pt. 3, 1387. Also Sheridan, *op. cit.*, II, 178.

33. *Ibid.*, II, 190.

34. *Ibid.*, 196.

Index

INDEX

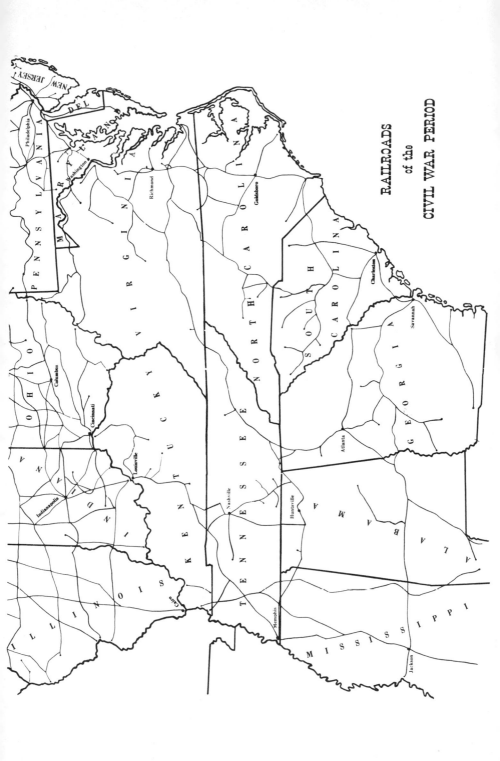

RAILROADS
of the
CIVIL WAR PERIOD